VERMONT WRITERS

# VERMONT WRITERS:

Yvonne Daley

# A STATE OF MIND

A VERMONT STATE COLLEGE

PUBLISHED BY UNIVERSITY PRESS OF NEW ENGLAND

HANOVER AND LONDON

CASTLETON STATE COLLEGE

Published by University Press of New England
One Court Street, Lebanon, NH 03766
www.upne.com

© 2005 by Yvonne Daley
Printed in the United States of America
5 4 3 2 1

LIBRARY OF CONGRESS CATALOGING-IN-PUBLICATION DATA
Daley, Yvonne.
Vermont writers : a state of mind / Yvonne Daley.
    p.    cm.
ISBN-13: 978-1-58465-400-1 (alk. paper)
ISBN-10: 1-58465-400-7 (alk. paper)
ISBN-13: 978-1-58465-401-8 (pbk. : alk. paper)
ISBN-10: 1-58465-401-5 (pbk. : alk. paper)
    1. American literature—Vermont—History and criticism. 2. Authors, American—Homes and haunts—Vermont. 3. Authors, American—20th century—Interviews. 4. Vermont—Literary collections. 5. American literature—Vermont. 6. Vermont—Intellectual life. 7. Vermont—In literature. I. Title.
PS253.V4D35 2005
810.9'9743'0904—dc22                                    2005011115

for CHUCK CLARINO
munificent patience and support

and for Philip, Haley, MacKenzie, Zachary, and Brendan,
the grandchildren, the future

# CONTENTS

# PREFACE

Vermont is a state of mind—a place that breeds rugged individuals, quirky politicians, hard workers, stubborn idealists, unconventional economists, and gifted artists, including many of the most popular and important writers of our time. Indeed, as novelist, poet, and essayist Jay Parini of Middlebury says, "Vermont is the main place for writers of all sorts. We have the mother lode."

Why is this so when Vermont is relatively distant, both geographically and metaphysically, from the centers of publishing as well as from the issues that confront contemporary Americans (overcrowding, pollution, rampant crime, to name a few) issues that are often at the heart of current literature? It's not that Vermont and Vermonters are immune to societal, economic, and moral dilemmas. Unfortunately, like residents of most rural states that have experienced declines in both agricultural income and factory jobs, many Vermonters, including several of the writers profiled in this book, struggle to make a living or do so by working several jobs at once. The recent influx of hard drugs into our towns and cities has brought home the harsh realities of contemporary life. And the friction between development and environmental protection makes front-page news on an almost daily basis. In some areas, such as gay rights and environmental protection, Vermont seems to be on the forefront of change and our writers have proclaimed that position to the nation. But our dark side has also been widely publicized. We've made the news too often with vicious slayings among our own and the threat that terrorists could invade our border. Nonetheless, because Vermont is a small state where it's possible to know your neighbors with just a bit of effort, the scope of human travail seems more manageable here. Maybe that is why Vermont is viewed as a safe haven for writers: we can manage the commerce of daily life more easily here. Or escape from it.

Despite its small population—612,000 in the 2001 census—Vermont has always drawn a disproportionate number of writers (and artists in general) to live within its borders. Charles Edward Crane wrote in his collection of Vermont stories, data, and history, *Let Me Show You Vermont*, first published in 1942, "The risk Vermont parents run of having a poet or other would-be writer born into the family appears to be about one in a thousand, which is considerably higher than the risk of having twins."[1] (Actually, twins occur naturally once in every eighty-six births.)

Some years ago, Ellen Lovell, executive director of the Vermont Arts Council from 1975 to 1983, estimated there were more artists per capita in Vermont than in New York City. *Vermont Life* editor Thomas Slayton responded more grandly, suggesting that Vermont may have more writers per capita than any other state in America. While all that may be true, most of the talented writers you shall meet within the pages of this book were not born here. In fact, the only two who were born here are Joseph Citro and Jeffrey Lent. The other profiled writers have chosen Vermont as their adopted home. Their reasons have much to do with elusive concepts that set Vermont apart from other places. This book explores these concepts, which resonate not just for contemporary writers but throughout the state's history.

Recognition of place is at the heart of this inquiry. "Whenever I go to Vermont I feel that I am traveling toward my own place," writer and teacher Bernard DeVoto, a faculty member at the Bread Loaf Writers Conference in its early years, wrote in the December 1951 *Harper's Magazine*. "You do not have to be a Vermonter to experience this sense of returning home. The home that Vermont represents may be a dream of rural life. It may be a picture of a white church presiding over the elms on a village green. It may be the smell of wood smoke in a farmhouse kitchen or the patches of bluets like mirages of recent snows on rocky pastures in May. But there are few of us, no matter where we were born, who haven't felt this tingle of recognition, and the Vermonter away from Vermont is an exile indeed."[2]

That sentiment is both his and ours; there is something about the place that speaks to today's residents as deeply as it did to our predecessors. That something is in part the natural world, of course: the cycle of the seasons, the rich and varied environments that compose Vermont, weather that both soothes and challenges us, and a natural beauty to which our native soul responds. And, perhaps because artists are apt to pay more attention to these inner responses than people who must attend to more measured urgings, for them the attraction to beautiful places remains most vital. Thus, quite simply, some writers are drawn to live and work in Vermont by the innate beauty of the land and Vermont's pastoral environment.

The allure also lies in the strength of Vermont's small communities, which offer a support system often absent in more urban centers, a way of dealing together with the overwhelming problems of our lives and time. Beyond that, Vermont is attractive to writers, particularly beginning ones or those whose work has not yet provided economic stability; one can live simply here, without the pressures to overachieve and overconsume. While self-sufficiency is a hard and arduous lifestyle choice, some writers ( poet and playwright David Budbill comes to mind, as does essayist Noel Perrin of Thetford) have achieved a modicum of financial independence by cutting their own wood, growing their own vegetables, and otherwise reducing expenses. Of course, these activities take time from writing. Nonetheless, it's a great deal easier to raise a few beets or lambs in a Vermont garden or meadow than on the rooftop of a Manhattan apartment building. As novelist Jeffrey Lent, a Vermont native who returned here to live after his first novel was accepted for publication, can attest, few activities provide a better balance to the sedentary work of a writer than those of the barn and the pasture.

Yet there is something more about Vermont's magnetism that appeals to those with a sensitivity for place. Fifty years ago, essayist Marguerite Hurrey Wolf wrote an article for the Green Mountain Folklore Society in which she gathered quotes about Vermont, including Hiram Fay's observation in 1801 that, as he traveled back to Vermont, passing valleys hemmed in by mountains and an occasional group of children or cows meandering through the fields, he was filled by a "melancholy yet pleasing joy in my bosom which surpasses all the pleasure that it is in the power of riches or splendor to bestow."[3] Few have captured better that sense of belonging that attracts Vermont writers and is often celebrated in their work.

For some of our resident writers, the path here has been long and circuitous; for others, it was swift. Still others found themselves here as a matter of happenstance—and stayed. Each writer portrayed in this book tells the story of how he or she came to live in Vermont, by design or chance, and each reflects upon the state's impact on his or her life and work.


Perhaps more than any other profession, writing is a full-time job. Writers are working when they shop at the grocery store, canoe a river, sleep in bed, pay their bills, and take a shower. Ideas, characters, settings, lines of poetry, and complex plots can come to us at any time; indeed, it's often when we're *not* trying to write that the best material presents itself. The hard part, of course, is getting the image, the idea, the character, the environment, the story or poem itself from the brain to the page in a manner that will engage the reader. In this book, twenty-one authors share their writing approaches and techniques; they open their toolboxes and show us their instruments, their tricks of the trade. And, because the first rule of good writing is "Show, don't tell," the book includes excerpts from the featured writer's body of written work, chosen to demonstrate the author's skill and subject matter.

Thus, the reader can expect to learn much about each of the writers profiled in this book and his or her relationship to Vermont while also gleaning from each a little insight into that marvelous process we call writing—both the craft of it and the magic. Writing is not easy. It requires diligence and attention to all sorts of detail. But it is one of life's most rewarding pursuits. In my travels as a writer and teacher, I hear from people every day who express a desire to tell a story. I hope this book will inspire writers at all stages of development to put pen to paper or fingers to keyboard, to find their own words and express their own stories in poem and story, in memoir, profile, and essay. To that end, each chapter ends with suggestions for reflection and writing exercises. Students of writing will discover that these "assignments" often result in pleasantly surprising outcomes. I urge those of you who are experienced workers in a particular genre (poetry, for example, or short story) as well as those of you who are exploring the craft of writing for the first time to try as many of the exercises as you can. Experiment. Try something unfamiliar. You're likely to be happy with the results. Most of the exercises in this book can be completed in twenty minutes or so, but they may also be used for lifelong projects.

Most important, I hope this book will add to the understanding and appreciation of Vermont's rich literary tradition. It's a resource too many of us take for granted, and one we should not.

This book is the result of many years of research that began when I was a journalist writing for the *Rutland Daily Herald* and the *Boston Globe*, from about 1979 to 1997. During that time, I wrote many articles about Vermont writers and their work and began to gain an appreciation of the amazing storehouse of literary talent living within Vermont's borders.

In the early 1990s, I began studying for a Master of Fine Arts degree at Vermont College. One day, faculty member Seta Jeter Naslund complained that *place* had all but disappeared from contemporary fiction: far too many short stories and novels were located in generic apartments, malls, and cities, places that had little individuality and were populated with nearly interchangeable characters. The result, she opined, was that these stories were immediately forgettable. I thought about the work of the Vermont writers I had met over the years; their works were rich with environmental detail and unforgettable characters. This seemed to be true not just for Vermont authors whose stories took place in Vermont but also for those who lived here but wrote about far-flung places such as the Dominican Republic, the former Soviet Union, or New York City.

For my thesis, I revisited some of these writers and asked them what had brought them to Vermont and kept them here. I wanted to know what about the state sustained them and how Vermont affected their writing. To a one, these writers told me that living in Vermont filled them with an awareness of place—not just in terms of geography, but also weather and mood and that elusive element we call atmosphere.

Beyond that, I came to see that their characters—whether fictional or real, Vermont resident or not—were not only richly drawn from life but also had a relationship with their environment, with the place where they lived, that gave their works a profundity often lacking in contemporary writing. Many of the writers I interviewed observed that their deep relationship with Vermont's natural world and the communities in which they lived had informed their understanding of human life and drama, an understanding that quite naturally was reflected in their work. All this, then, became the subject of my thesis.

It also was apparent that another element attracted artists to Vermont, one many embraced in their private lives and in the lives of their characters: the idea that Vermonters are just naturally ornery, independent-minded, contrary, and willful. After all, Vermont initially chose to be an independent republic after the American Revolution. Although the Green Mountain Boys had played an important role in the war, one of their mottos, "Don't Tread on Me," shouted their desire for independence. Enough other residents of the region shared that desire for independence and resented attempts by neighboring states to grab Vermont for themselves that Vermont remained an independent republic until 1791. When Vermont finally did become the fourteenth state, it was the first to outlaw slavery. The state constitution clearly defends autonomy and the rights of its citizenry to control their land and their destinies. The state motto, "Freedom and Unity," expresses in three words the desire of the populace to live without undue restrictions while also living in harmony with one another.

Contrariness has been evident socially and politically throughout Vermont history. Per capita, Vermonters lost more soldiers than any other state during the Civil War. Yet their most beloved statesman, the late Senator George Aiken, a rock-ribbed Republican, was among the first U.S. senators to question the Vietnam War. Vermonters in more recent years have voted to keep their towns nuclear-free, and to tell Congress to keep the military out of Central America. And they have repeatedly elected a socialist, Independent Bernard Sanders, as their lone congressman. Just when you think you've got them figured out, they surprise you.

Vermont authors have long celebrated this desire of the citizenry to make up their own minds about local matters. Burgess Johnson expressed this orneriness rather bluntly in a 1953 article in *Saturday Review*. Johnson wrote that Vermont is "just a lot of lovable but pig-headed individuals divided up into townships widely scattered in valleys who will not let even their chosen officials command them or their chosen leaders lead them." [4]

Ah, what better place for an artist to feel at home.

I was, of course, not the first to ponder the attraction of writers to Vermont. Arthur W. Biddle and Paul A. Eschholz wrote in their notable anthology *The Literature of Vermont: A Sampler* (published by the University Press of New England in 1973) that there has always been an interest in Vermont. They note that fascination has grown as the rest of America became more and more alike: "As American society in the twentieth century has become increasingly homogenous, more and more Americans have begun to seek their identity in that which is distinctive and local, an impulse that has been nourished by the nostalgic yearnings for a simpler past." [5]

Those yearnings, coupled with a desire to put what is written and said about Vermont today in historical perspective led nine scholars to contribute papers exploring Vermont's literary tradition at a conference held at Trinity College in 1986. Those papers were gathered together in a small volume entitled *Literature: Vermont as a Setting*, published by the Vermont Academy of Arts and Sciences in 1989.

This entertaining collection explores subjects as diverse as "The Cat in the Oven and Other Quaint Fables," (which explores old Vermont stories) to a rambling talk by Noel Perrin that, in part, critiques the television program *Newhart* and its depiction of contemporary Vermont. Tony Magistrale, an associate professor at the University of Vermont, wrote in the volume's introduction, "There are changes in the landscape going on all around us, and as these changes continue to occur, the state will need its artists and writers more than ever before. We will need them to describe the new Vermont with an unsentimental eye, at the same time as they will be called upon to remember the past and to use its examples as a guide to the future. For what is the literature of a place and people if it does not reflect an accurate vision of a particular time in history?"[6]

As a professor of writing and journalism at San Francisco State University in faraway California, I came to appreciate these observations on an entirely different level. In Vermont, when we talk about environment, we're not just talking about country villages and deep woods; we include the characters who live in those towns and hide out in the woods. We're talking about a way of life that is vanishing even here: the family farm, the independent logger, the subsistence hunter, the hermit, the volunteer fireman, the operator of the country store. These things seemed so much more precious to me from afar. I spend about twenty weeks in Vermont each year and continue to write about the state because it continues to fascinate and sustain me. But, even more precious to me now is the relationship we in Vermont have with one another and the openness of our society. You may notice I wrote "we." Even though I am currently living and working away for two-thirds of the year, I still consider Vermont home.

As a journalist, I did not fully appreciate the openness with which the writers I interviewed over the years welcomed me into their homes. Nor did I adequately value their willingness to discuss their work and their relationship to Vermont. I knew that people who have received a good deal of media attention often treat journalists with understandable distrust. But Vermonters as a whole had been so astonishingly generous with their time and information during my years as a reporter that I had come to expect it. As a journalist, it had long been my conclusion that, if you treated people with respect, if you took your time and let them see that your main purpose was to give voice to their ideas, most people would share what they knew with you. But my reckoning was based on limited experience. You see, I had lived in Vermont so long that I had almost forgotten how the rest of the world operated. I didn't fully appreciate how unusual this generosity (and trust) was until I lived elsewhere long enough to experience firsthand the cloak of self-protection most people have fashioned for themselves. When you are used to greeting your neighbors by name or making eye contact on the street or at the market, you fail to fully comprehend that, in many places on the planet, people are more guarded. Self-protection is wise but it also closes people down emotionally. Vermonters are not closed down in this way, including most of our writers—even the most successful ones. It took my going far away, to write of far-distant places, for me to realize how generous the subjects of this book were. And how lucky I have been. I got to sit in Grace Paley and Robert Nichols' humble cabin in Thetford, eat their homemade soup and talk of peace while their grand-child crawled among the books piled on the floor; I crawled on my hands and knees with Jamaica Kincaid as we tried to find all the holes a pesky woodchuck had made in her voluptuous garden; David Budbill made tea and entertained me with an array of Asian instruments while summer birds sang outside his window; and Howard Frank Mosher took me on a tour of places in the Northeast King-dom that had made their way into his fiction. For each writer in this book, I have a memory of precious time (perhaps our least-valued but most priceless gift on this planet) in which Vermont writers welcomed me into their homes and offices, setting aside the demands of life and work so I could share some of their expert-ise with you, the reader.

No book, of course, can include all that has been written here in Vermont nor profile all the writers currently living here. Some important contemporary writ-ers did their best work here but have moved away in recent years. These include the poets Louise Gluck, Robert Pack, and Hayden Carruth, and the novelist E. Annie Proulx. I have chosen to include Aleksandr Solzhenitsyn in this volume, even though he has returned to his native Russia, because his time here was so productive. His experience with his Vermont neighbors stands as a tribute to their respect for the individual.

The authors included in this volume were chosen because of their diversity in terms of genre, geography, age, and experience as well as their willingness to take part in this project. Because books of this sort are limited by space, I also chose writers whose work speaks particularly eloquently to Vermont values, values pro-moted by the earliest of the state's authors. I also wanted to provide adequate room for each writer's story to unfold. Other Vermont writers will be included in subsequent editions.

I am aware that there are dangers in looking at Vermont (or any place) through the rose-colored glasses of simplicity, self-protection, or idealism. Poverty, incest, domestic violence, ignorance, and loneliness—Vermont is immune to none of these. Yet, while these social ills are not unique to Vermont, there exists a uniquely Vermont take on all of them. Several of the authors were chosen for this text in part because they boldly address these issues head-on, simultaneously celebrating the best of Vermont while also shedding light on the negative aspects of rural society and the inherent problems that shadow our history. They believe writers have a responsibility to be honest.

I cannot express how fortunate I feel to have spent time with such a group of talented people or thank them enough for taking time to talk about the writing life. I hope my words do justice to their gifts and that this book will continue a dialogue about the importance of place and of writing and reading in our lives. To these Vermont writers, therefore, my most profound thanks.

Rutland, Vermont, August 2004

*Yvonne Daley with Grace Paley at the Green Mountain*
*Writers Conference*

*With Special Appreciation for Grace Paley and Ruth Stone*

They have shown us how to live
as women
as humans
as peacemakers
as writers

They have given us beautiful words

*Ruth Stone and Yvonne Daley, also at the Green Moun-*
*tain Writers Conference*

# ACKNOWLEDGMENTS

I thank Richard Abel, director of the University Press of New England, for his faith in this project. I'm grateful to David Wolk, president of Castleton State College, for his kind support over the years and his belief in Vermont teachers. To Joe Mark, dean of students at Castleton, deep appreciation for his thoughtful insights on teaching and writing. Special thanks to my friend Janet Wells for her careful reading of the text, her diligent edits, and intelligent suggestions. Janet saved me from many embarrassing errors. Merci, merci. I also sing the praises of Elizabeth A. Brash at UPNE who patiently guided me through the editing process. To the Vermont teachers who gave feedback on drafts of this book—Frank Barnes, Jeff Bender, Paul Cillo, Scott Holliman, Linnie Laws, Susan Lihner, Linda Lunna, Donna Masterson, Mary McCallum, Colin McKaig, Mary Perkins, Karon Perron, Joan Poepoe, Judy Pond, Ellen Saltonstall, Alison Dominick Sauter, and Peter Thomas—thanks again for your perceptive comments and helpful suggestions. I'm grateful to Susan Simon at the Vermont Center for the School at Castleton State College for her delightful nature. Gratitude is also owed to the members of my writing group at San Francisco State University—Jo Keroes, Ellen Peel, Judith Pruchner Breen, Elise Earthman, and Beverly Veloshin—who read several chapters in draft and helped me see the book's potential. Warmest regards as well for the Rutland, Vermont, writing group that I've long been associated with: Sharon Nimtz, Margie Wood, Jeff Bender, Liz Sojourner, Walter O'Brien, Burnham Holmes, Eileen Blackman, and Susan Farrow. Bookseller Kathy Roberts of Burlington sent several relevant texts; I am proud to claim her as a dear friend and good reader. To John Burks, chair of the journalism department at San Francisco

State University, my gratitude for your encouragement for my work, and to Robert Corrigan, president of San Francisco State University, my sincere thanks for leave time to complete this project. Special appreciation to Vyto Starinskas, Ann Day, and Rob Woolmington for the generous use of photographs. Lastly, thanks to Chuck Clarino, again and again. He read every word.

I gratefully acknowledge the following authors and publishers.

From *A True Account* by Howard Frank Mosher. Copyright © 2003 by Howard Frank Mosher. Reprinted by permission of Houghton Mifflin Company. All rights reserved.

"So Says Wang Wei," "What Issa Heard," and "What It Is Like to Read the Ancients" from *Moment to Moment: Poems of a Mountain Recluse*, copyright © 1999 by David Budbill. "Litany for the Emperor," "Easy as Pie," "A Little Story About an Ancient Chinese Emperor," and "No Escape" from *While We've Still Got Feet*, copyright © 2005 by David Budbill. All reprinted with the permission of the author and Copper Canyon Press, P. O. Box 271, Port Townsend, WA 98368–0271. "Talk/Poem Delivered at the Peace Rally/War Protest in Montpelier, Vt., 18 January 2003." Copyright © 2003 by David Budbill. Reprinted by permission of the author.

From *Midwives* by Chris Bohjalian. Copyright © 1997 by Chris Bohjalian. Used by permission of Harmony Books, a division of Random House, Inc.

From "Chittenden's Ghost Shop," *Ghosts, Ghouls and Unsolved Mysteries* by Joseph A. Citro, copyright © 1994 by Joseph A. Citro. Reprinted with permission of the author.

From *In the Fall*, copyright © 2000 by Jeffrey Lent, reprinted with permission by Grove Atlantic, Inc., 841 Broadway, New York, NY, 10003, and the author; From *Lost Nation*, copyright ©2002 by Jeffrey Lent, reprinted with permission by Grove Atlantic, Inc. and the author.

"A Charitable View," "A Conscientious Start," "A Courageous Step," from the *Rutland Herald*. Copyright © 2000 by The Rutland Herald, Inc. Reprinted by permission of the Rutland Herald, 27 Wales St., Rutland, Vt., 05701.

From *To the Bone*. Copyright ©1996 by Sydney Lea. Reprinted with permission from University of Illinois Press and the poet.

"The Poet's Occasional Alternative," *Begin Again: Collected Poems* by Grace Paley, copyright © 2000 by Grace Paley; "Traveling" from *Just As I Thought*, copyright ©1998 by Grace Paley. All reprinted by permission of Farrar, Straus and Giroux, LLC, 19 Union Square West, New York, NY 10003.

"Prologue," "[All ears, nose, tongue and gut]," "[Dear Mattie, You're sweet to write me every day]," "[This is the double bed where she'd been born]," "[Dear Mattie, Pug says even a year of camp]" from *Kyrie* by Ellen Bryant Voigt, copyright © 1995 by Ellen Bryant Voigt, used by permission of W. W. Norton & Company, Inc.; "Largesse" and "Dooryard Flower," *Shadow of Heaven* by Ellen Bryant Voigt, copyright © 2002 by Ellen Bryant Voigt, used by permission of W. W. Norton & Company, Inc.

*(acknowledgments continued p. 330)*

# AUTHOR'S NOTE

Unless otherwise noted, the direct quotes from Vermont writers profiled in this book come from interviews conducted by the author, almost entirely in person, usually at the writers' homes. Some of these conversations were conducted over the course of the last two decades, but the majority took place between 2000 and 2004. The one exception is Aleksandr Solzhenitsyn. The author had only a brief interview with Solzhenitsyn in 1994; most of the material for the Solzhenitsyn chapter was garnered from interviews conducted by the author with Solzhenitsyn's publisher, Roger Straus, president of Farrar, Straus & Giroux in New York City; with residents of Solzhenitsyn's adopted town of Cavendish, where he lived from 1976 to 1994; and with others close to the Solzhenitsyn family.

# Vermont Writers

Mosher
*Irasburg*

Kinnell
*Sheffield*

Budbill
*Wolcott*

Citro & Huddle
*Burlington*

Voigt
*Cabot*

Bohjalian
*Lincoln*

Lea
*Newbury*

A. Stone
*Middlebury*

R. Stone
*Goshen*

Lent
*Tunbridge*

Alvarez & Parini
*Weybridge*

Moats
*Salisbury*

Paley
*Thetford*

P. Stone
*Whiting*

Daley
*Rutland*

Smith
*Castleton*

Connor
*Belmont*

Solzhenitsyn
*Cavendish*

Kincaid
*Bennington*

Porche
*Guilford*

# Introduction
## Celebrating "Freedom and Unity"

## A SHORT HISTORY OF WRITING IN VERMONT

VERMONT'S ATTRACTION for those who write has long been established. Indeed, "the road less traveled" has seen more than its measure of literary traffic both before and since Robert Frost first ambled here from Franconia, New Hampshire, in 1919.

From the earliest days of its habitation by Westerners, Vermont established a tradition of respect for learning and writing almost equal to its reputation for rebelliousness and independence. As Arthur W. Biddle and Paul A. Eschholz wrote in their notable anthology *The Literature of Vermont: A Sampler*, "Literature has always played a role in Vermont. The early settlers were learned men, not in terms of formal education but in being widely read and experienced. They valued books, no small expense in colonial times, and supported the cause of public education. Many of these settlers kept diaries or journals in which they recorded their reactions to the pioneer experience. . . . Although it is difficult to measure literary activity in a rural state like Vermont, some indication of the remarkable output is afforded by Abby Maria Hemenway's anthology *Poets and Poetry of Vermont*, published in 1858; the volume contains the work of 111 Vermont poets. By 1900, according to G. G. Benedict, there were "no less than 3,489 distinctively Vermont imprints—that is titles of books and pamphlets printed and published in Vermont—while the titles of books and pamphlets by Vermont authors, printed and published outside of Vermont . . . swell the total to upwards of seven thousand titles."[1]

Throughout the state's history, writers have used their talents to promote social causes and protect a way of life they considered more valuable than that lived elsewhere. In novels, plays, poems, political treatises, newspaper editorials, short stories, and essays, Vermont writers seem to have an innate appreciation of the state motto "Freedom and Unity."

Vermont's storytelling tradition begins, of course, with the Abenaki people, Vermont's first inhabitants who settled the long, rich valleys along Lake Champlain and the Missisquoi River and lived in harmony with the land. The Abenaki have left us their names for places—Lake Memphramagog, Bomoseen, and the Winooski River, to mention a few—and their stories of how these places were formed. Today, their stories are kept alive by writers like Michael J. Caduto of Chester and members of the Abenaki Nation, who have retold the oral stories of their ancestors in print.[2]

Ethan and Ira Allen, the most famous of the Green Mountain Boys, were among the state's first published writers, recording (sometimes with a bit of exaggeration) the details of their history-making exploits while promoting their political views. Ethan Allen's *Reason, the Only Oracle of Man*, was philosophical, while Ira Allen's pamphlet *Some Reasons Why the District of the New Hampshire Grants had Best Become a State* outlined the political reasons why the people who would become Vermonters thought they were different (and better) than their neighbors to the south, east, and west. The Allens, along with Thomas Rowley, another Green Mountain Boy, believed in Vermont's motto and used the written word to sing the praises of a free Vermont. The broadside, a one-page pamphlet or "newspaper" that could be easily distributed by hand or pasted to a wall or building, was also a popular means used by the Green Mountain Boys to publish and distribute their messages. Rowley was their official bard, capable of extemporizing a rhyming poem on a minute's notice.[3] "[H]e composed songs for their campfires and fired the settlers with enthusiasm by the wit and pungency of his rude ditties against the Yorkers. His influence on formative Vermont was tremendous, his lyrics being recited and sung among the remotest mountain hamlets during the War for Independence."[4]

Early Vermonters also benefited from the existence of one of the nation's oldest daily newspapers; the precursor of today's *Rutland Herald* was first published in 1793; today, the *Herald* is considered the oldest continually published and family-owned newspaper in the United States. The ever-popular *Vermont Life* magazine, known for the quality of both its art and writing, had its origins in *The Vermonter*, a magazine first published in 1885 as one of the nation's first state promotional publications.

Just as today's Vermonters are protective of their history and traditions, many early writers sought to preserve Vermont's vanishing and precious past. For example, as Eschholz and Biddle describe, the prolific Rowland E. Robinson (1833–1900), was so concerned about the erosion of Vermont's "odd similes and figures of speech" that he wrote *Danvis Folks* in 1894 as a means of recording the customs and vernacular speech of Vermonters living a half century earlier.[5] Robinson brought tales of Vermont, both from its past and his lifetime, to readers nationwide, publishing articles, fictional stories, and illustrations in such magazines as *Forest and Stream*, the *Atlantic Monthly*, and *Youth's Companion*.[6]

One of his more famous characters, Sam Lovel, often sang the praises of the rustic life, as in this excerpt from *Danvis Tales*: "It comes nat'ral fer me tu run in the woods. 'F I du git more tu show for it 'n some does, I get suthin besides 't I can't show. The air o' the woods tastes good tu me, fer't hain't ben breathed by nuthin but wild creeturs. I lufffter breathe it 'fore common folks has. The smell o' the woods smells good to me, dead leaves 'n spruce boughs 'n' rotten wood, 'n' it don't hurt none if it's spiced up a leetle bit wi' skunk an' mink an' weasel an' fox p'fum'ry."[7]

Robinson, a Quaker from Ferrisburgh, had worked as an artist for magazines for many years but he was forced to give up drawing after he lost his eyesight. He took up writing and compensated for his vision problem by creating a "thin board with slots cut in it to guide his hand, and his stories of early Vermont are more vivid than those anyone blessed with sight has written since," according to Charles Edward Crane, whose entertaining *Let Me Show You Vermont* (1942) contains a wealth of trivia about early Vermont writers.[8] Crane describes how Robinson's homemade device allowed him to write in a straight line without writing over previously recorded lines.

Robinson continued the Vermont tradition of using literature as a vehicle for promoting social views, especially progressive ones that are based on a deep respect for civil rights. His collection *Out of Bondage and Other Stories* told of Vermonters who protected runaway slaves as their way of opposing slavery.[9] The stories were based upon the experiences of his own family, which had hidden runaway slaves in their home; today, you can visit the Rokeby Museum, formerly the Robinson home in Ferrisburgh, and view the secret chamber used for hiding slaves.

Today the name of Royall Tyler is just about forgotten everywhere except the University of Vermont's Royall Tyler Theatre. Yet Crane considered Tyler more responsible for the birth of American literature than New York's Washington Irving, who usually gets the honor.[10] Tyler (1757–1826) was a literary pioneer; he created some of the first "genuine American folk character[s]," generally hayseeds who struggled and succeeded against city slickers.[11] In his play *The Contrast*, for example, Tyler "urged his countrymen to be true to themselves, and pointed the way to a new and native American literature for the generation of writers that followed."[12] A Boston native, the Harvard-educated Tyler moved to Guilford in southern Vermont when he was thirty-seven. His theme became a popular motif in Vermont writing: that the simple rural man can be easily taken advantage of, especially if he lets himself be swayed by greed or impatience. But, Tyler suggested, if he practices fortitude and relies on his innate intelligence, the countryman could outwit even the most sophisticated opponent. It's a version of the city mouse and country mouse theme. Beyond that, according to Biddle and Eschholz, Tyler created "the first American comedy and . . . the prototype of the stage Yankee."[13] His character "Brother Jonathan" is said to be the model for Uncle Sam.[14]

Vermonters have always been interested in their own history. Many of our writers have over the ages articulated the lives and challenges of the populace with a particularly earnest brand of pride and self-assuredness. Biddle and Eschholz note that Ira Allen, Samuel Williams (an early editor of the *Rutland Herald*), and Zadock Thompson, filled the role of "Vermont's first generation of historians, [and] established a foundation upon which future historians and writers could build."[15] Thompson's work, in particular, provides an interesting view into the mind-set of the early settlers and their predilection toward independence and defiance. He created his own almanac, called *Thompson's Gazetteer*, in which he described "in amazing detail . . . [Vermont's] animals, birds, fishes, plants, trees and flowers."[16]

Daniel Pierce Thompson (1795–1868), who was no relation to Zadock Thompson, was once Vermont's best-known author, if not one of its best-selling. His fictionalized history *The Green Mountain Boys*, written in 1839, and other lesser-known books, were standard school reading in Vermont and elsewhere. He was born in Boston but grew up on a farm in Berlin, Vermont, and had such a love for his adopted home state that he petitioned the Vermont General Assembly to establish the Vermont Historical Society in 1838.[17] He ardently opposed slavery and used a paper he founded, the *Vermont Freeman,* to promote the cause of freedom.[18]

Another theme introduced early into Vermont writing was a respect for and defense of the environment. Woodstock native George Perkins Marsh (1801–1882) is considered the father of American conservation, in part because of his 1864 book *Man and Nature*, revised ten years later and published as *The Earth as Modified by Human Action: Man and Nature*. Marsh may have been the first American to write that humans are responsible for the earth.[19]

Marsh observed as a young boy that large-scale timber harvesting led to erosion and destroyed the habitats of many creatures. He was often quoted as saying few of us "could make as good a claim to personality as a respectable oak tree."[20]

His observations about the impacts of change on entire ecological systems were revolutionary. They also sometimes pitted him against his fellow Vermont farmers and timbermen. Yet he remained steadfast in his beliefs. Later in life, he was appointed America's ambassador to the Kingdom of Italy and traveled throughout Europe and the Middle East. According to Clark University's website, "Foresters throughout Europe found his work valuable and one English forester even carried the tome (*Man and Nature*) with him to Kashmir and Tibet."[21]

Writer Walter Hard's public service was closer to home. Hard (1882–

1967) was one of those remarkable Vermonters who managed to juggle many interests and avocations. A Manchester native, he ran the family's drugstore—an undertaking he considered a temporary move—for thirty-one years. Simultaneously, he wrote a weekly column in the *Rutland Herald,* served five terms in the Vermont legislature and wrote prolific verse. *Holiday Magazine* called him "a 120-pound, leather-bound compendium of Vermontiana, a genuine, ear-to-the-ground listener who has recorded the rural wit, homespun wisdom, and often enough the stoic melancholy of his people"[22]

Like several of his literary predecessors, Hard wanted to preserve a part of Vermont that he saw changing. In the foreword to *Some Vermonters,* he wrote, "Many of these local stories I have heard my Father tell time and time again. To him I am indebted for a slight understanding of and a deep appreciation for the people of a day that has passed."[23] Hard's poems, written in a style reminiscent of today's narrative poetry, tell the stories of local people, often with a message about the value of personal integrity—as in his story about the "pious" family who puts on a big show at church then steals from their neighbors, or the general-store owner who shorts his customers.

Not great poetry by most standards, Hard's work was, however, appreciated by the great American poet Carl Sandburg, who said about Hard's poetry, "I treasure and reread his volumes."[24] What's significant about Hard's work in relation to contemporary writers is the furthering of a theme of respect for the simple, honest man and a disdain for hypocrites who put on airs or think dishonest behavior goes unnoticed.

Vermont writers across the genres have rarely been afraid to use their writing as a vehicle for promoting political and social opinions and agendas. Frances Frost (1905–1959), a St. Albans native and graduate of Middlebury College who worked as a newspaper reporter and teacher, wrote poems and novels, often speaking quite eloquently against war and sport hunting. Her loveliest work establishes a premise followed over the decades by many Vermont writers, especially poets Robert Frost (no relative), and, in our time, Galway Kinnell and Ruth Stone: the use of the smaller, more ordinary moments of life as vehicles to explore and illuminate larger themes, such as the relationships between men and women and the planet.

Frances Frost's poem, "Footnote," is worth reading simply because it sounds so contemporary:

> What can I say of the death of the russet vixen,
> her young in her belly, of the beautiful and shy
> and breaking heart of the young buck brought to his knees?
> What can I say when the lean bell-throated hound
> Closes upon the spent hare's throat?
>
>                           I seize
> The meaning of the poet's suicide

And the refugee's. I annotate the breath
Turned fire in the airman's lungs, or torn from what
Was once a soldier's mouth.

But there is neither

Proportion nor equality in death:
What can I say of the dying of the vixen,
What can I say of the fawn on the spattered ground?[25]

Activist Dorothy Canfield Fisher (1879–1958) was one of Vermont's most prolific and important writers. Well educated and traveled, she chose to live and work at her family's ancestral property in Arlington, Vermont; yet her impact extended far and wide. Like that of earlier Vermont writers, her work was grounded in a deep respect for learning and the conviction that most social problems stemmed from poverty, inequality, and mechanization. She believed the solution to social ills came from improving education and health services, and in living close to the land.

During World War I, she and her husband John Fisher were leading proponents of American intervention in the fight against the Germans. By intervention, she did not necessarily mean military might. Fisher was a strong pacifist and a promoter of the role of volunteerism. She believed in the responsibility of all humans to act against human rights violations rather than sit on the sidelines. She believed equality, education, and opportunity for healthy self-expression were the keys to world peace. Fisher followed her convictions and risked personal safety by traveling overseas to France during the war. There she was a guiding force in relief work for the war blind and spearheaded the publication of books in Braille.

Subsequently, Eleanor Roosevelt named Fisher as one of the ten most influential women in the United States, undoubtedly because of her work in promoting education and reading. Fisher presided over the nation's first adult-education program and, as a member of the influential Book of the Month Club selection committee from 1926 to 1951, she helped shape America's literary tastes and promoted the work of many new writers.

In the field of education, she brought the Montessori method of child rearing to the states from Europe and worked tirelessly for educational reform. Meanwhile, she produced twenty-two works of fiction and eighteen nonfiction books on a broad range of subjects.

Her work with the Vermont's Eugenics Project has remained controversial because of its inherent association with social and biological engineering. Even here, however, Fisher is credited with a desire to improve the lot of the average person through social reform and education as much as through sterilization and other unsavory ideas promulgated under the general rubric of the eugenics movement.

Throughout her life, Fisher wrote and spoke out against the "dehumanizing aspects of industrialization, as well as war and those ideologies which threaten basic human rights."[26] According to Biddle and Eschholz, she found the kind of society she cherished in Vermont, one in which village life had not been too much supplanted by the materialistic and alienating affects of industrialization and one where individual rights were still cherished. Like Tyler's, Fisher's work often revolves around the theme of village-versus-city living. In her novel *The Brimming Cup*, for example, an outsider tries unsuccessfully to lure a young woman from Vermont to the big city.

In an article in *The Nation* entitled "Vermont: Our Rich Little Poor State," Fisher promoted the idea that Vermonters were better-off than residents of other states because they had never experienced prosperity. Residents of other places, she wrote, were driven by fear "of poverty or social inferiority, or change, or politics" while Vermonters did not know that kind of fear. "It seems incredible, in our modern world, so tormented with fears about safety, that a whole stateful [*sic*] of people have no ground for apprehension, but it is true." She believed the lack of prosperity was amply rewarded by a richness in inner resources, a condition she attributed to Vermonters' independence of character.[27]

Fisher's *Vermont Tradition: The Biography of an Outlook on Life* richly catalogues Vermont lore, history, and people, celebrating that which is distinctly Vermont while also glorifying Vermont virtues as models for all Americans.[28] In writing about Ethan Allen, for example, Fisher promotes him as an archetype whom people all over the world can emulate, a person for whom values were more important than money or power: "When Ethan Allen spoke as the voice of the Green Mountain men, he was trying to find words to express the feeling binding them together in the face of danger. In time this feeling brought into being not an old civilization reborn, not a mighty new nation—only a plain, small rural American state, never rich, never powerful."[29]

Allen, Fisher wrote, "was, as few men are, wildly passionate. Not passionate about women, not about power over others, not about getting money. He was passionate about an idea—the ancient idea that men and women live best and most fruitfully in as much freedom and equality as is possible. He was the voice of Vermont. He still is."[30]

Manchester resident Sarah Norcliffe Cleghorn was a collaborator of Fisher's and a successful writer in her own right, as well as a nationally acknowledged pacifist, socialist, and anti-vivisectionist.[31] Cleghorn (1874–1947) wrote of the working conditions of the poor and satirized the disparity between the rich and the poor. In "The Golf Links Lie So Near the Mill," Cleghorn wrote four powerful lines that deftly identify a social wrong:

> The golf links lie so near the mill
>     That almost every day
> The laboring children can look out
>     And see the men at play.[32]

Over the decades, many writers of note have come to Vermont to live, not so much to write about the state and its residents but rather because they too cherished the concept so aptly described by Fisher: "the ancient idea that men and women live best and most fruitfully in as much freedom and equality as is possible."

For some, freedom came simply from the ability to live in relative privacy. The name Rudyard Kipling, for example, does not readily suggest Vermont, but it was here that this apologist for colonial England wrote some of his most important books, including *The Jungle Book*, *Day's Work*, *The Seven Seas*, and *Captains Courageous*. Kipling (1865–1936) bought a house in Brattleboro shortly after he married a Vermonter named Caroline Balestier. Balestier was the sister of one of Kipling's closest friends; the two had married just a few weeks after the friend's death. In this emotionally charged atmosphere, Kipling grew to love the quiet and harmony he found at his Vermont home (which he called Naulakha) and the Vermont landscape, describing a Vermont winter as "white velvet." Kipling wrote that he would have been happy living here forever. Stuart Murray, Kipling's biographer, describes him as a man who felt like an outsider everywhere, a man haunted by international fame who sought privacy for himself and his family and who found it, only briefly, in Vermont. Family matters, however, took Kipling elsewhere and he wrote little about his Vermont experience.[33]

One of Kipling's rare Vermont pieces is the delightful if difficult poem entitled "Pan in Vermont" (1893). Inspired by the arrival of the annual spring seed catalogues, Kipling writes of Pan coming through town flinging the painted pages of perfect flowers like a traveling salesman with the promise of winter's end up his sleeve:

> He's off along the drifted pent to catch the Windsor train,
> And swindle every citizen from Keene to Lake Champlain;
> But where his goat's-hoof cuts the crust—beloved, look below—
> He's left us (I'll forgive him all) the may-flower 'neath her snow!

Pearl Buck also came to Vermont seeking a bit of privacy after a life of achievement and acclaim. Buck (1892–1973) was an unusual woman. Perhaps more than any other person of her time she worked ceaselessly through her writing and other efforts to bridge the gap between East and West. She had been born Pearl Comfort Sydenstricke in Hillsboro, West Virginia, but spent her youth in China, to which she returned after graduating from college in 1914. Her best-selling novel *The Good Earth* was made into a movie and earned for Buck in 1931 the Pulitzer Prize for Literature. In 1938 Buck was granted the Nobel Prize for Literature, the first American woman to have received such an honor. Indeed, Buck is the only person ever to have received both a Nobel Prize and a Pulitzer. Buck's books often illustrate the fundamental prejudices that can lead to war between neighbors and nations.

Buck had first come to Vermont in 1953. In subsequent years, she had several camps in the Manchester area. She moved to the hardscrabble town of Danby, Vermont, in the early 1960s. There, she bought many of the buildings in the village, painting each with her signature red and white paint. She sometimes shocked the locals with her behavior and the odd collection of people who came and went through a town that, until then, had been content to entertain itself with stories of its long-dead and eccentric millionaire, Silas Griffith. Like Kipling, Buck did not come to Vermont to seek literary material but rather to maintain a low profile. Of course, that's hard to do in a small Vermont town (especially if, as she did, one keeps company with a male dance instructor who was forty years her junior). Buck was quoted in the local press as feeling that her Vermont neighbors gave her more privacy than she might have received almost anywhere else in the country. She wrote little about Vermont with the exception of one of the novels she penned under the pseudonym of John Sedges.[34] Part of a triptych, *Voices in the House* tells the story of a Vermont servant girl.

Scott Nearing (1883–1983) was credited with introducing Buck to the idea of self-sufficiency and to Vermont. Nearing is best known for the book he and his wife Helen wrote in 1954 entitled *Living the Good Life: How to Live Sanely and Simply in a Troubled World*.[35] The book and the Nearings themselves—engaging, enthusiastic, creative and healthy—stimulated a back-to-the-land movement that they personally embodied for fifty years until Scott Nearing's death in 1983 at the age of one hundred. The book was much revered by many of the back-to-the-earthers who migrated to Vermont in the late 1960s and 1970s.

In one of his first published pieces, a thirty-two-page pamphlet entitled *The Great Madness*, Nearing reflected on the commercial causes of war, expressing the opinion that countries waged war to make money for the rich and powerful rather than to rid the world of tyrants. Written at the start of World War I, his message is relevant—and controversial—to this day.[36] At the time, Nearing was working as a University of Pennsylvania economics professor but he was fired for expressing antiwar views. These views were expressed in several pamphlets, such as *The Menace of Militarism* and *Oil and the Germs of War*, in which he connected the petroleum industry and other big business interests to the machinery of government and war.[37]

Disgusted with city life and responding to a long-held desire for self-sufficiency, Nearing and his wife moved to Vermont inn 1932 and established their Forest Farm in Jamaica, where they lived until 1952, when they moved to Maine. There, they continued as much as possible to live self-sufficiently and in harmony with the seasons. In their classic, *The Maple Sugar Book*, Helen and Scott Nearing write, "What we have been developing here in the Green Mountains is a source of livelihood that leaves us time and room to live life simply and surely and worthily."[38]

Other writers who came here to practice a bit of self-sufficiency or at least to pretend they were doing so include award-winning journalist Dorothy Thompson (1894–1961) and her husband, (Harry) Sinclair Lewis

(1885–1951), the first American to receive the Nobel Prize for Literature. In 1928, Thompson and Lewis bought a 235-acre estate in Barnard, which they called Twin Farms. Both writers loved Vermont from the moment they first saw it.

"I have traveled through thirty-six states and have lived in eight or ten," Lewis told the Rutland Rotary Club in a speech in 1929. "But Vermont is the first place I have seen where I really wanted to have my home. There was nothing to prevent me from making any other state my home, but I have found in Vermont precisely the opposite to that peculiar thing pointed out and boasted of as 'very American': the desire for terrific speed and the desire to make things grow. I like Vermont because it is quiet, because you have a population that is solid and not driven mad by the American mania—that mania which considers a town of four thousand as twice as good as a town of two thousand, or a city of one hundred thousand, fifty times as good as a town of two thousand.

"It is hard in this day, in which the American tempo is so speeded up, to sit back and be satisfied with what you have. It requires education and culture to appreciate a quiet place, but any fool can appreciate noise. Florida was ruined by that mania. It must not happen in Vermont. You have priceless heritages—old houses that must not be torn down, beauty that must not be defiled, roads that must not be cluttered with billboards and hot dog stands. You are to be guardians of this priceless heritage and you are fortunate to have the honor of that task instead of being horn-blowers."[39]

Thompson, the world traveler and career journalist (whom Hitler kicked out of Germany after her unsympathetic early profile of him), said of Vermont, "It's the only place that reconciles me to being in America." On another occasion, she explained why people feel at home here: "Englishmen say it is like Cumberland; Germans like Thuringia; Austrians like Upper Austria; Frenchmen like parts of Savoie. Indeed, its verdured hills are very ancient; and its contours, its clouds, its gusty rains, its winter stillness, its soft air, there is a sweet and nostalgic melancholy."[40]

She particularly liked Vermont's live-and-let-live conservatism, which mirrored her own philosophy "based in a long tradition, in toleration, in common sense, in 'the divine right of every citizen to be left in peace.'"[41]

In 1935, Lewis published *It Can't Happen Here*, a novel whose hero, Vermont newspaper editor Doremus Jessup, battles against a dictator named Buzz Windrip (Windrip was modeled after Huey Long, the notorious senator from Louisiana who was planning to challenge Roosevelt for the Democratic nomination for president in 1936. Long was assassinated while Lewis was writing the book.) The title of the book refers to its central question, can a politician with dictatorial goals like Hitler hoodwink the American public into electing him simply on the basis of quick, gimmicky solutions to economic and social problems? In the novel, Jessup struggles for a year against the government's efforts to censor his newspaper. He is eventually sentenced to a concentration camp, but escapes to Canada, from which he makes forays back into the states to lead an underground attack against the dictator.[42i]

Lewis was a ribald drinker; he and his wife threw many parties at their Barnard farm; their famous guests often treated the locals to more than a bit of outlandish behavior. But, although she enjoyed a good time herself, Thompson grew tired of Lewis's alcoholism. They divorced in 1942.

Thompson continued to live at Twin Farms off and on throughout the years, routinely spending the entire summer on her farm until the year of her death. A champion of world causes that included relief to farmers and an end to nuclear proliferation, Thompson's literary output was formidable. She took to farming with equal vengeance. Her biographer Peter Kurth of Burlington describes how Thompson, with help from various farmhands, "built up a thriving eggs-and-poultry business, some fine herds of sheep and dairy cows, a working fruit orchard, and a vegetable garden that in summer could feed half the neighborhood."[43]

Thompson gave refuge to many Jewish people and others escaping the Holocaust, some of whom moved to Vermont. They included Carl Zuckmayer, the novelist and playwright, and Princess Annie Schwarzenberg of Austria, who set up a home-knitting enterprise in Bethel.

Lewis and Thompson's literary love-ins were rivaled only by those of literary critic Alexander Woollcott (1887–1943). On weekends, particularly when the weather allowed, Woollcott entertained members of New York's elite literary set—the famous Algonquin Circle, so named for their weekly meetings at Manhattan's Algonquin Hotel—at his retreat on Neshobe Island, a spit of land in Lake Bomoseen in Castleton near Vermont's western border. From the mid-1920s to the early 1940s, actors including the Marx Brothers, Laurence Olivier, Vivien Leigh, and Ethel Barrymore, playwrights Thornton Wilder and Noel Coward, composer Irving Berlin, and many other notable performers, visited the seven-acre island, often creating an avalanche of gossip and speculation. A favorite local tale about the shenanigans at the island holds that Harpo Marx once stripped naked and painted himself blue to scare off some picnickers who were trespassing on the island. Apparently, it worked. Although Woollcott paid homage to Vermont on the air and the printed page, not much lasting literary material, alas, came out of these adventures.

In contrast, however, the nation's first poet laureate, Robert Penn Warren (1905–1989), was so admiring of the Green Mountain State that its landscape, weather, wild creatures and people often inhabited his later poems, even though he was really only a part-time resident at his summer home in West Wardsboro. He had been born in Kentucky and attended Vanderbilt University where he was the youngest member of a group of Southern poets called The Fugitives, advocates of agrarian life and classical aesthetic ideals. Later, his novels brought him widespread acclaim, especially *All the King's Men*, for which he won the Pulitzer Prize for Fiction in 1947.

In later years, Warren exchanged his southern roots and sensibilities for more liberal attitudes; simultaneously, as New England had its way with him, Warren's poetry became less formal and more expansive. It's understandable that he would love Vermont with his lifelong appreciation of nature. Lines like "We live in time so little time / And we learn all so painfully, / That we may spare this hour's term / To practice for eternity" (from "Bearded Oaks") show his rich awareness of man's place in the wider universe.[44] The poem's recognition of man's smallness in the face of eternity is a sentiment that many a Vermonter, whether poet or priest, bus driver or laborer, can appreciate when February dumps a four-foot snowstorm.

This rich awareness of self, balanced by a humbling awareness of the immensity of the universe, dominates much of Vermont's literary history. You can see it in the work of Robert Frost, of course. Frost (1874–1963) attended both Dartmouth and Harvard, but graduated from neither. He had bought a farm in South Shaftsbury, Vermont, in 1919, but spent many years traveling, teaching, and writing in England, New Hampshire, Massachusetts, New York, Connecticut, and Michigan before moving to his Ripton farm. In 1926, he convinced the president of Middlebury College to establish a literary retreat on its Bread Loaf campus in Ripton and, although he sometimes lived elsewhere, Frost remained a presence at Bread Loaf almost until his death. Many states claim Frost but when he writes of birch trees and roads not taken, most of us picture a place like Vermont.[45]

While Bread Loaf has attracted serious writers who often find themselves falling in love with Vermont and spreading its lore far and wide, writers with more humorous and offbeat tales to tell have long had success in the mass market far from the state's borders. Indeed, outsiders have simultaneously been intrigued and humorously entertained by Vermonters' tolerance for (and celebration of) the eccentric oddballs in our midst—not to mention the challenges of our weather. Throughout the decades, Vermont writers have provided the material that has allowed armchair visitors and wannabes to wonder, sometimes with grudging admiration, why we live here at all.

Some of the more successful writers of this sort include Marguerite Hurrey Wolf (1914–) and Elsie Masterton (1914–1966). Wolf and Masterton wrote in memoir fashion, telling everyday stories about the life around them, from farming in Vermont's fickle weather to playing midwife to the family sow or cat. Their books are chock-full of whimsy as they greet the first frost by making apple butter or wax poetic about the annual fall color show. But their books also include plenty of frustrating comedies as they battle overflowing septic systems and marauding minks in the chicken coop.

Wolf's books include best-sellers like *Anything Can Happen in Vermont*, *Vermont is Always with You*, and *The Sheep's In the Meadow, Raccoons in the Corn*. Still active, Wolf published *A Window on Vermont* (New England Press) in 1998, comtemplating life as an octogenarian in modern society. Elsie Masterton, the grande dame of the first Blueberry Hill Inn in Goshen and author of *Off My Toes, Nothing Whatever To Do,* and *The Blueberry Hill Cookbook*, delivers a sometimes unsettling blend of candid observation and ill-disguised ridicule of the locals in her humerous books. Both authors knew what was best about Vermont: its blend of the unpredictable and the likely, the way in which the most mundane of tasks (emptying the scrapings in the compost, for example) can turn into a moment of reverie with the simple entry of a bluebird or the western sky turning crimson at sunset.

## WRITING IN VERMONT TODAY

### Finding One's Material

Today's writers have embraced the themes laid down by their predecessors: advocacy for human rights and peace; appreciation of native intelligence; respect for the individual; curiosity and tolerance toward the eccentric; love of nature; desire for community; a sense of awe toward man's relationship with the universe; self-pride and pride in being a Vermonter; and an often self-deprecating sense of humor.

That sense of self-irony is a thread that runs through Vermont's literary history. You can see it today in books like Frank Bryan and Bill Mares's *Real Vermonters Don't Milk Goats, The Vermont Owner's Manual, Out! The Vermont Secession Book, Out of Order!* and *The Vermont Quiz Book*. These spoofs on Vermont life poke fun at the very institutions that define Vermont— independence, maple syrup and town meeting—but always lovingly. The list of contemporary books in this genre is shockingly long and funny in and of itself. It includes Michael Tougias's *There's a Porcupine in My Outhouse: Misadventures of a Mountain Man* and the late Keith Jennison's affectionate collections, which include *Yup, Nope and Other Vermont Dialogues* and *Green Mountains and Rock Ribs*.

But it is more serious themes that distinguish Vermont writing. A survey of contemporary writing by Vermonters, whether they are writing about life in the Green Mountains or far away in places like Antigua or the former Soviet Union, demonstrates a respect for the land and for those who work close to it; a desire for autonomy and privacy balanced with restrained interaction with one's neighbor; recognition of the right to be different; concern about the impact of mechanization and technology on the human spirit; protectiveness toward democracy and human rights, and always an awe-inspiring insight into man's place in the universe—all themes laid down by earlier Vermont writers.

Many contemporary Vermont writers (Chris Bohjalian, Howard Frank Mosher, Sydney Lea, David Budbill, Joseph Citro, and Noel Perrin come immediately to mind) have found their material here in the Green Mountains. Their stories, poems, essays, and plays are inspired not just by nature and geography but by the farmers and hunters, politicians and housewives, eccentrics and rebels, newcomers and old-timers who live around them.

These writers are following the tradition established by their predecessors who sought to record the stories and speech of a Vermont they felt was endangered. When Mosher says, "I'm recording the stories of a vanishing breed, the men and women who lived from the land and struggled with it, who were often defeated by it but loved it all the same, the way I do," he is echoing the sentiment of writers like Robinson and Tyler, writers who recognized something special here that needed to be captured before it disappeared.

Today's writers, however, often present a more rounded and less idealized view of life in the Green Mountains than their predecessors. While celebrating all that is wonderful here, they're also apt to explore the underbelly of rural life and the disparities between the few wealthy and the many poor. They're not afraid to find disharmony in the Green Mountains. Here, by way of example, is how David Budbill summarizes the plot of one of his best-known plays, *Judevine*: "Twenty-four characters in a town called Judevine, a poor, rural mountain town in northern Vermont, which is a kind of Third World country within the boundaries of the United States where, like so many Third World countries, there is incredible physical beauty, great suffering and hardship and a tenacious and indomitable will to survive."[46]

In the years since coming to Vermont, Budbill's work has evolved from the telling of the tales around him in Wolcott to broader themes. While continuing to celebrate nature and record both the hardships and rewards of life in rural northeastern Vermont, his more recent work centers on threats to the environment, to world peace, and to the independence of the individual in the face of governmental intervention—themes laid down by Vermont writers since the time of the Green Mountain Boys. Budbill says that the two compulsions are really one: the drive that leads people to live in a challenging yet inspirational environment like Vermont is the same impetus that makes one care about the future of the planet. He believes that Vermont has long attracted people with strong political urgings because of their love for their fellow human beings and their concern about the future of the world.

Understanding that will to survive in the face of forces beyond our control is at the heart of what continues to attract writers here; Vermont provides them with their best material. As it was with writers living in Vermont before us, at the heart of so many contemporary Vermont poems and stories are these questions: Why do we do it? Why put up with winters that can be seven months long or more, where frosts aren't uncommon in June or August, where torrential rains often cause unpredictable floods, where fuel bills run high and you need snow tires for more than half the year, where gnats and mosquitoes are as plentiful as dandelions in spring and, as likely as not, the snow will disappear the night before a long-planned cross-country ski outing? Why? Because these challenges define who we are; they provide us with daily opportunities to show our true grit, to pit ourselves against something bigger than ourselves but that, with determination and patience and creativity, we can often overcome—or at least withstand.

Vermont and its inhabitants intrigued Chris Bohjalian from the moment he arrived here from Manhattan in 1986. Life can be tough anywhere you live, he knew, but the man-against-man story coupled with the man-against-nature story had a simple reality to it here that he had not experienced in New York City. He was equally curious about something he recognized early on: a tolerance among Vermonters for the people living on the fringes of society. That tolerance provides good material for writers—and, adds Bohjalian, it's good in itself for writers, who tend to be an idiosyncratic lot. "Vermont is a place where people can live life as honestly as possible, I believe. It gives us permission to be who we are. It's not just the people on the fringes who are free to be themselves here; their acceptance frees everyone. Tolerance provides a wonderful environment for writers—freeing in a completely different way. It allows us to explore what-ifs in our work, a theme I've been experimenting with in much of my fiction."

While Bohjalian thinks that Vermonters tolerate odd behavior more than residents of many other places, he also realizes there are limitations to Vermonters' tolerance, especially when people mess up or go too far. He has explored that theme, over and over, with greater and greater risk, writing about dowsers, midwives, transsexuals, foster African American children and animal rights advocates, each one presented as part of the landscape of easily recognizable if fictionalized Vermont towns.

Sydney Lea explores another rich Vermont theme: man's relationship to the natural world. He does so not as an outside observer but as a participant, as a hunter, fisher, hiker, and lover of the outdoors. Lea's world, like that of those early Vermont writers, however, is not simply the world of the woods and streams and the animals that populate them, but also the world of the people who live in the Connecticut River Valley (where Lea has made his home for several decades). Along with his intimate understanding of the region, he brings a deep knowledge of classic literature and an uncanny ear for language to the subjects that interest him most: his dogs, the hunt, the dispossessed, and the unlucky. For Lea, Vermont is subject matter at its most essential and elemental level; like the ancient poets and Robert Frost before him, his struggle to understand the fragility of life is made more poignant by his concern that a world he cherishes is at risk. It's Vermont, of course, that he worries about. But beyond that, it is our first world, the world outside our doors, the natural world, that he feels compelled to celebrate and protect in his writing.

Joseph Citro has mined the state's history for a different sort of material, for tales and myths, some quite spooky, that are rooted in the physical place where he grew up. A native Vermonter, Citro began collecting stories of hermits and eccentrics as a child, a habit he's put to good use as the premier recorder of Vermont's lesser known history, the tales of the dark side, the incomprehensible and the bizarre. Citro says Vermonters' relationship with the land and the cycles of nature provide them with a ready appreciation of the unknown and unpredictable. And, in a climate with an abundance of cold winter nights, it's not surprising that he has found a treasure of spooky old tales to explore and retell. "I'm a lucky guy. From the moment I was born, people started telling me stories," Citro says. "Vermont is rich that way; we love a good tale."

Another Vermont native, Jeffrey Lent, has also plumbed the region's past for material. His first novel, *In the Fall*, explores the impact of war, in this case the Civil War, on a Vermont farm boy who brings back from the South an understanding of the horrors of battle along with a young runaway slave whom he has "married." The plot allows Lent to explore the impact of slavery and discrimination across several generations, along with Vermont's role as the first state to outlaw slavery in its constitution while remaining among the whitest states in the union.

Lent's second novel takes place in neighboring New Hampshire. Located in the Connecticut Lakes region parallel with far-northern Vermont, *Lost Nation* explores the often ruthless and even more frequently desperate lives of the early residents of the northeastern wilderness. Says Lent: "Vermont is interesting as a subject because its people are interesting. Historically, we have much to say about what it is to be an American while also retaining an individual identity. Vermonters are not natural joiners. They appreciate their orneriness. They've struggled with good and evil, like people all over the planet. But, just as the state's size and population make it something knowable or at least a place you can try to know, it also makes it a manageable place to tell a big human tale."

### Community and Nature

Perhaps no institution has introduced more writers to Vermont than the Bread Loaf Writers Conference and, as a result, induced so many to live here (at least part-time). Among them are William Lederer, coauthor of *The Ugly American* and a host of other books about Navy life, failures of the American democratic system, and health and fitness. Lederer lived for twenty years in Peacham on a farm he often bragged was the most photographed property in Vermont. During his tenure here, he not only wrote his "life novel," *I Giorgio*, but also designed sawed-off skis for bushwhacking in hilly, rocky terrain. "My time in Vermont was one of my most productive. It's the serenity, the fresh air, the sense of being one with nature, the ability to step outside and clear one's mind of all the paraphernalia of phone calls and deadlines, all the stuff that keeps you from being able to see your story, to be in touch with your material without thinking about it. That's what I miss most about Vermont," Lederer said in a 2002 interview at his Florida home. "Bread Loaf got me to Vermont and, for that, I am eternally grateful. I immediately recognized a place that was *good* for the writer, a place where you could be of a community but on your own terms. If you needed three months of seclusion to finish your novel, people let you take it. They treated it as routinely as the sugarer who needed three weeks in March to get in the sap and boil it up. In the end, I came to think, it was all pretty much the same."

According to Howard Bain, author of *Whose Woods These Are: A History of the Bread Loaf Writers' Conference, 1926–1992*, the writer Wallace Stegner said of his first visit to the campus in 1938, "Bread Loaf was, in a curious way, my Paris and my Rome. It was there that I met Frost, DeVoto, and many other writers who later became important in my life."[47] Bread Loaf played that role for many contemporary writers as well—Jay Parini, Julia Alvarez, and Ron Powers among them.

Parini, known internationally as a Frost scholar, writes eloquently of place, whether it's the coal mines of Scranton, Pennsylvania, near where he grew up; the Italy he came to know during his twenties; or the Vermont that he fell in love with as a child of ten visiting for the first time. Parini believes that he and other writers share a similar relationship to Vermont, one that has been at the heart of writing in Vermont throughout state history. He explains it this way: "Vermont is the main place for literature. Why? Its beauty, its peacefulness. The landscape speaks to you in a kind of spiritual way. I've never taken it for granted." For writers like Parini, Vermont has provided a place from which to live a writers' life. Although his poetry is often inspired by both the natural world and village life, Parini's novels, scholarly works, and political essays draw on more diverse themes. He lives here for community, for sanity, for a pace of life that allows room for thinking and writing.

Those attributes also attracted former state poet Galway Kinnell. Like Robert Penn Warren before him, Kinnell is ever aware of the mystical pull of Vermont and its value to his writing and sense of self. Kinnell's house in Sheffield feels back behind and gone some more, there in its high meadows and surrounding hills in Vermont's Northeast Kingdom. Although he also keeps an apartment in New York City, Kinnell returns to his Vermont property quite consciously to be reminded of his place in the universe, to be made to feel small and powerless, to put himself in perspective, to reflect upon the miracle of man and the world he inhabits, both in his backyard and light-years away. Kinnell's ability to capture these big, amorphous emotions is one of the elements that make his poetry so successful—and important—and contributed to his winning the Pulitzer Prize in Poetry and being named Vermont State Poet from 1989 to 1993.

Another state poet, Ellen Bryan Voigt of Cabot says she chose Vermont as her place to write simply because Vermonters let you be a writer. For her, creativity is more possible in a place where people tend not to make a big deal about one's work as a writer, where independence is honored, and where the mind isn't constantly assaulted by sensory material. "There's a much greater tolerance for solitude and idiosyncrasy in Vermont than most anywhere else," she says. "That's essential to me and my writing. I find myself depleted and exhausted by all that comes at me; living in a city would eventually overwhelm me. Instead, I am renewed by Vermont—both the nature and the community of it."

These elements also give State Poet Grace Paley a reason to live in Vermont. Paley is perhaps America's best-known and most admired short story author; her fans are often surprised to learn that she lives in Vermont. That's because her stories are populated by the people and places she knows from her native Bronx and Greenwich Village, where she raised her children. Nonetheless, she says, "I can live without New York City these days but not without Vermont." For her, there is something special about the relationship you can have with people who share a geography, who endure the vagaries of weather together. She likens the recycling center and the village store to the playgrounds, community centers, and political action headquarters where mothers like her traded stories and strategies during her many years living in New York City. As in New York City, she says, likely as not, the complaints go beyond griping about politics and policies to include forces even further from one's control. Here, however, the choice of complaints is apt to have a particularly Vermont twist—the weather, for example, or the disappearance of migratory birds from our fields and woods. Because their environment is forever imposing itself upon them, Vermonters are ever mindful of its importance, says Paley. And, in that, she says, comes its growing presence in her own work, especially her poems and essays.

In some important ways, Paley can be seen as continuing the progressive political work of other women writers who called Vermont home, especially Sarah Cleghorn, Dorothy Canfield Fisher, Dorothy Thompson, and Pearl Buck. Although her work certainly differs from theirs in many important ways, Paley is part of a rich Vermont tradition of social radicalism that has at its center humanitarian goals, peace, equality for minorities, and a recognition of the importance of the environment as both a physical and spiritual source of nourishment.[48]

Poet, fiction writer, and essayist David Huddle would have been a writer wherever he chose to hang his hat, but his subject matter might have been different without Vermont, at least in his earliest years. Vermont provided him a place from which he could explore the material of his youth. He observes that it's fairly difficult to write objectively about home with Mom or Dad or your old high school teacher or your in-laws or anyone else who knows you or feels they do peering over your shoulder. Huddle believes the distance from home, geographically as well as politically and philosophically, allowed him to write of Virginia, his first topic. And it wasn't just distance that provided that permission, but also the anonymity of his early life in Vermont. Burlington was large enough when Huddle arrived in 1971 that he has not had to cope with star status, something he might have experienced either in a smaller Vermont town or where he grew up. Star status, he believes, is deadly for the developing writer. "I might have been respected and given too much attention as a writer in my old environment," he explains. "Instead, I found myself surrounded by a group of other young writers, all struggling to find their voice. I stepped into an instant community and have loved it ever since."

In its purest form, newspapers are the journal of a community. Perhaps more than any other writers, journalists record the history of a state. Journalism is public writing: words designed to inform first and entertain second. One of the reasons that the job of the journalist is so important and the need for accuracy so strong is that, once something appears in a respected newspaper, it takes on the mantle of history. One could spend pages lamenting about declines in the profession and the move to short and shallow reporting rather than deep and long articles. Here in Vermont, we have one of the nation's journalistic treasures, David Moats, the editorial page writer for the *Rutland Herald*. Moats moved here in the 1970s after serving three years in the Peace Corps. Shortly after his arrival, he began working in small papers, recording first the day-to-day history of small-town Vermont, then helping to shape it through his editorials. When he won the Pulitzer Prize in editorial writing in 2000 for his writing about Vermont's civil union law, he noted that such writing was possible in part because of Vermont's innate tolerance. He views Vermont as a place where reasoned debate and invigorating inquiry have long been admired. Like his predecessors who broadcasted their political opinions on broadsides and in pamphlets that were distributed, often by hand, to fellow Vermonters, Moats sees himself as part of the literary landscape of Vermont, part of a tradition that remains independent while much of the world (not to mention the world's media) has become amalgamated into an ever bigger and bigger machinery.

*Sanctuary*

While many of the writers who moved to Vermont found a refuge here from middle-class America, the doldrums of academia, or the relentlessness of the city, others—Jamaica Kincaid, Julia Alvarez and, for eighteen years, the reclusive and prolific Russian exile Aleksandr Solzhenitsyn among them—have chosen to live in Vermont because it provided a safe haven. Here, they could write about issues and events that occurred far away, and about events and people who frightened, harmed, or disturbed them. Alvarez writes about the political misery that the dictator Raphael Trujillo subjected the people of her native Dominican Republic to during his thirty-one-year reign of terror. She exemplifies a theme that has also been evident in Vermont literature: that it can be easier to write about disturbing issues and frightening events from a safe distance.

Alvarez first came to Vermont as a student at Middlebury College and was hired to teach at Middlebury College in 1988. She explains Vermont's pull this way: "I . . . simply fell in love with the community of writers and with the Vermont landscape. It was the place where I could fully be." It really is that simple. Alvarez's notion of fully being rises not just from the landscape but from the relationship of people to that landscape. And, because her formative years as a writer occurred here in Vermont—years in which she was able to relive and investigate the events that had sent her family into exile—that landscape continues to offer her a sense of security.

Jamaica Kincaid grew up on the warm Caribbean island of Antigua but chooses to live in North Bennington. She considers Vermont a safe haven for many reasons; first and foremost, it is not Antigua. If she were there, she would feel the constraints of the life she was supposed to choose. There, a woman's role is ordained—or it was when she was a girl growing up. Had she stayed, it might have been very difficult for her to find her voice and write her stories. Yet it is the island and its people that she writes most fervently about. Even when Kincaid writes of her Vermont garden and her passion for growing things, her Antiguan past often weaves its way into the narrative. The solace of Vermont's abundant green in summer and the security of winter's snowy blanket provide comfort and distance that allow Kincaid permission to delve ever more deeply into her past and the events that formed her.

The idea of Vermont as refuge is especially relevant to the life and work of Aleksandr Solzhenitsyn. Vermont represented refuge in the most literal meaning of the word. It provided him a safe and calming environment, a sanctuary where he was able to write many of his most important works. Here, he completed the second and third volumes of *The Gulag Archipelago*, which described the horrendous life of political prisoners in the Soviet Union; *The Oak and the Calf*, which portrayed literary life in the Soviet Union; *The Mortal Danger*, which warned of American misconceptions about Russia, and several other important books. As described later in this book, Solzhenitsyn's neighbors in his adopted town of Cavendish went out of their way to protect his privacy, aiding in a quiet way the great writer's desire to devote the rest of his life to his work.

Vermont and Vermonters offered Castleton poet Tom Smith a different kind of sanctuary. Smith knew from the time he was a young boy that he was gay. This consciousness did not make life any easier growing up in a working-class family in upstate New York. After college and a helter-skelter career in acting, writing, and teaching, Smith found himself teaching in what he considered a backwater town. But Castleton and Castleton State College proved to be exactly what he needed. And, as it turned out, marriage and raising a family also turned out to be exactly what he wanted. While still acknowledging himself as a gay man, Smith has lived a happy and productive life as husband, father, writer and college professor. Over nearly five decades, he has pursued his interests in community arts and drama and has been an active community member at Castleton State College and in Castleton.

Smith says, "Vermont was a place I could be without pretensions, a place where I found community and acceptance. People here respect that you are different, that your path is not theirs, that your lifestyle may be somewhat different than theirs, but that, in the end, whether poet or farmer, we have the same needs: to love and be loved, to express ourselves, to feel safe, to be part of something larger than oneself. I feel so lucky that I ended up here, rather than simply ending up."

Vermont was also a haven for poet Ruth Stone, the recent winner of the Wallace Stevens Award—considered the top prize in poetry—given annually by the Academy of American Poets. She retreated to the small mountain town of Goshen to heal after her husband, the novelist and poet Walter Stone, committed suicide in 1959, leaving her a single mother of three daughters. She explains, "First, there was the beauty of the place and the calming effect it had on me. Nature is healing and it healed me; it continues to heal that which will not heal.

"Beyond that, life was manageable here," she says. "The house was cheap. So too was the wood. We didn't mind the extra work and, without TV or the other distractions of fast-paced life, the children were able to develop their own artistic understandings. They were free to be creative in an environment that constantly inspired and surprised them."

The result of all this is a tremendous outpouring of inventiveness: Stone's daughter Phoebe Stone is a flourishing fine artist, children's book illustrator, and author; daughter Abigail Stone is a successful novelist, singer, and songwriter; and daughter Marcia Croll helps other children who have experienced trauma through her work as a school counselor. The Stone grandchildren, raised with the same appreciation of art and nature, have launched careers in writing, filmmaking and photography. Ruth Stone says of her family's creative output, "Vermont is at the heart of it. It's a place that nourishes the soul."

Another group who came to Vermont seeking refuge were a collection of young people from New York and Boston who had written for the underground newspaper, the *Liberation News Service*, a clearinghouse of alternative articles and information during the Vietnam War. At some point in their activism, they traded protests against the war for local action and headed north to Guilford, Vermont, where they founded a commune they called Packers Corner. They wanted to "start over," to create a sane world within what they viewed as an insane system. Poet Verandah Porche, a writer of uncommon generosity, came to Vermont in 1968 as part of that migration north. Like other Packers Corner refugees, she sought to create community in the true meaning of the word: common unity. While other members of the commune have come and gone, Porche has continued to live on the property and has eked out a living for herself and her two daughters through teaching, publishing, and working to help others record their lives.

Fiction writer Joan Connor also considers Vermont her sanctuary. Connor, a professor of creative writing at Ohio University, comes back to Vermont as often as possible to get grounded and renewed. As soon as her winter or summer break from the university arrives, she jumps in her car and drives, sometimes all night, to get to Vermont as quickly as possible. "I hate giving up a day of the place," she says. Even though her family didn't live in the state when she was a girl, Vermont always represented home. Her father was in the military, then university, then a young teacher when Connor was growing up; despite the frequent moves, however, Vermont was a constant in their lives, the place they would travel to for important holidays and every summer vacation. Here, Connor learned to hike and ski, to name the flowers and the birds, and to wonder about the odd characters, the lonely walkers, the mumblers at town meeting, and the sweet old ladies at the Grange functions. She also came to cherish all the tasks and avocations still practiced in Vermont—spinning and dowsing, fiddling and tatting, volunteering and storytelling.

When in Vermont, Connor lives on her family property in a barn that she refurbished herself by hand over the past decade. "I do my best writing here. I'm not sure why it is but I think it has to do with the closeness of nature, there waiting right outside the door, and the odd and wonderful characters that one can meet on any ordinary day, ordinary people whose lives are extraordinary simply because they have endured the hardships of a seven-month winter, or because they have a dedication to their communities that becomes rarer and rarer every year."

Connor adds: "And, also, there is the awareness of being part of a continuum, a heritage of respect for the land, for the individual and for the written word. I never lose sight of the fact that I am blessed, that writing here in Vermont is a gift."

# I · Finding One's Material

Photo by Phillis Mosher

# 1    Howard Frank Mosher

*Finding One's Material in Vermont*

Born 2 June 1942, Chichester, New York

Education: B.A.: Syracuse University; M.A.: University of Vermont

Lives in Irasburg

First published work: A short story, "Alabama Jones," in *Cimarron Review*
[University of Oklahoma Press] 16 (July 1971): 35–45

Novels: *Disappearances* (1977); *Where the Rivers Flow North* (1978); *Marie Blythe* (1983); *A Stranger in the Kingdom* (1989); *Northern Borders* (1994); *The Fall of the Year* (1999); *The True Account* (2003); *Waiting for Teddy Williams* (2004)

Memoir: *North Country: A Personal Journey through the Borderland* (1997)

Books made into movies: *Where the Rivers Flow North* (1994); *A Stranger in the Kingdom* (1998); *Disappearances* (2002)

Awards: American Academy of Arts and Letters Literature Award (1981); New England Book Award for Fiction (1991)

HOWARD FRANK MOSHER and his wife Phillis fell in love with the Northeast Kingdom on 1 May 1964, the day they drove into Vermont's remotest corner to be interviewed for teaching positions at Orleans High School. In truth, the couple was looking for more than work. They were seeking a community where they might settle and raise a family, a community reminiscent of Chichester, New York, the Catskill Mountain town where Mosher had grown up. Chichester was one of those old, rural towns that had literally been run by a single family—in this case the Chichesters—who owned most of the woods, the lumber mills, and the furniture factory where nearly everyone in town was employed. The Chichesters had been kind overseers; work and therefore town life had been secure and fairly stress-free. In 1939, however, three years before Mosher was born, the Chichesters went bankrupt. Much of the town was sold at auction, including the woodworking mill, all in one day. Mosher grew up hearing stories of the good old days in Chichester and fell in love with the legend of the place. He romanticized its past and longed to live in a close, tight-knit town like it. His father and uncles, fabulous storytellers who didn't mind infusing a tale with a bit of hyperbole, had filled his young head with stories of how life used to be in this mountain town.[1] They were also great outdoorsmen and throughout his youth Mosher went on fishing expeditions with them—the wilder, the better. Somehow the stories and the expeditions into the wilderness became entwined into a dream of living in a wild and wonderful place where everyone knew one another and nature and man worked in consort with each other.

All that was what Mosher hoped to find as he traveled north toward Orleans, a small, close, working-class community located near wilderness that offered opportunities for hiking and fishing. Phillis was also drawn to life in a rural village far from the demands and quick pace of contemporary society.

The couple had already been charmed by Vermont as they wound their slow way across scenic rolling hills into the Northeast Kingdom. Some people might have looked at the dense woods that hugged the rural roads, the scraggy farms, the empty acres upon acres of land, and seen depression and boredom. Mosher saw trailers with abandoned cars in the front yards and town centers that invariably contained a mix of handsome, well-preserved relics of eras past and examples of bad architectural modernization, and felt enchanted and curious. He wanted to know the people who inhabited these trailers and colonial mansions; he wanted to hear their stories.

Just across the Orleans border, Mosher and his wife saw two local men who happened to be standing at the side of the road surveying an old beat-up truck. Mosher stopped to ask for directions to the local high school, where he and his wife were to be interviewed. Howard and Phillis didn't notice until they'd pulled up next to the men that they were sipping Budweisers. The fellows were parked by the Orleans furniture factory store, a warren of buildings that was at that time the Kingdom's largest employer. It all began to remind Mosher of Chichester.

"We can take you to the christly high school," one of the beer drinkers said as he opened the back door of the couple's car and quickly slipped inside. At first, Mosher and his wife were perplexed by the interjection of the word "christly" into almost every one of the men's sentences. It was used as an adjective, as in "Move your christly arse over," spoken by one of the locals to the other, or "Look at that christly wood pile," as they passed a mound of fresh-cut hardwood. Neither man was apologetic or even aware that the word christly might offend anyone else. It also took a moment for Howard and Phillis to get used to the onslaught of direct questions the two men directed their way, questions that were made up perhaps of two or three words but sounded as if they were one word. To the Moshers' ears, "Where are you from?" sounded more like "Whereyafroim?" "What are you doing here?" came out sounding like, "Whatchadoonghere?" Howard was delighted with the accent. In the back of his mind he kept trying to take it apart, to figure out its roots, whether it was a mix of French Canadian and Old English or some other hybrid.

After the preliminaries, the men got down to the essential question: "You fish?" The next thing Howard and Phillis Mosher knew, they were not driving to the high school for their appointments, but rather were being directed to the Orleans Falls to watch the christly fish jump the christly falls. The men in the back seat had had no trouble convincing the couple that their interviews could wait a few minutes; all the men had to point out was that it was spring and the fish were spawning.

The scene of the trout literally launching themselves against gravity, thrashing and gashing themselves across the rocks of the falls made a powerful impression on Mosher. When he and his wife finally arrived at the high school a good half-hour late for their interviews, they didn't tell the superintendent and the principal that they'd been watching the fish jump the falls. They didn't use the word "christly." They blamed their tardiness on the roads and poor directions. But the interviews went well enough and both Phillis and Howard were offered teaching jobs. Later that night in their hotel room, Phillis broached the subject of whether to accept work here. Her husband's response had little to do with the jobs they'd been offered. Still daydreaming of the scene at the falls, what he said was, "I'd really like to live here and fish." And that's exactly what happened.

Soon enough, the word "christly" made its way into Mosher's vernacular. Soon, too, he learned to appreciate both the climate and the personality of the Northeast Kingdom, the northeastern corner of Vermont comprising Caledonia, Essex, and Orleans counties. The sparsely populated (roughly 34,000 people) area is rich in natural resources, including 35,575 acres of public lakes and ponds and nearly 4,000 miles of public rivers and streams. The winters are long; the summers are lovely but mosquitoes and black flies can dampen one's enjoyment of them. The late Governor George Aiken is credited with naming the area the Northeast Kingdom, expressing both admiration for the region's deep beauty and recognition of the sheer independence (some might say orneriness) of its residents.

You won't hear Mosher complain about either aspect of the Kingdom. It's hard to say which he enjoys most: the wilderness or his Kingdom neighbors, especially the remnants of self-ruling, self-reliant hill people who still entertain a disdain for official law, politicians, and flatlanders. He laments that the Kingdom is a bit tamer today than when he arrived—and a *lot* tamer than it was one hundred years ago—but he is most thankful that he got to hear the old-timers' stories of life fifty or more years ago, and that he got to record them.

Mosher has written about other locations but even these tend to be places off the beaten path, places that haven't caught up with contemporary life. During the summer of his fiftieth year, for instance, Mosher explored the entire length of the border between the United States and Canada. In his memoir, *North Country: A Personal Journey Through the Borderland*, he encountered smugglers, cowboys, farmers, and miners.[2] In an interview with Katie Bacon for the *Atlantic Monthly*'s online magazine, Mosher describes the people he met along the border in the same kind of language that he'd use to describe his Vermont neighbors: "independent-minded people, most of whom are still intimately in touch with the land they live on. . . . The North Country certainly has its own share of outlaws and survivalists, but most of the people I met on my trip were very hardworking, serious, intelligent people who were trying somehow to make a living from the land, even though that's getting more difficult every day. Many of them were still doing traditional kinds of work that their ancestors had done, like farming, lumbering, ranching, and mining. It was this contact, this interdependence between the people of the North Country and the land, that seemed to me to set them apart."[3]

Mosher lives just on the edge of Irasburg's pretty village in a twelve-room, once-white clapboard house. The building has a worn, weathered look, little surprise given the drama of the weather up here. Material success has never been Mosher's goal and his house, with its peeling paint, reflects the realities of life way up north. But Mosher never seems downhearted. He's sprightly by nature, small in stature with thinning fair hair and bright blue eyes. Even on the coldest day, Mosher is often bareheaded and coatless when he's outdoors, as if he's immune to the cold. His inner energy keeps him warm.

As you drive toward his house, you first notice his garage, a building pock-marked with holes. Those holes were made by shotgun pellets, fired by Mosher in moments of creative frustration or upon receipt of a rejection notice or bad review. He likes to tell the story of the first time he shot up a negative review—in this case, a *New York Times* reviewer had skewered his novel *Disappearances*. "Phillis heard this racket outside and came out to see what was going on. Here's this newspaper riddled with birdshot tacked to the garage and me standing there with my shotgun. She takes one look at it all and says, 'Good job but you aimed a little low. Next time, get the reviewer's name.' I knew right there and then I'd married the right woman."

Mosher's office is tucked into an upstairs eave, a room with good light and little distraction. There, day after day, from very early in the morning until evening, with just a quick break for lunch and an occasional walk in the woods, he spends his days turning the tales he has collected during four decades of living in the Kingdom into fictional accounts that have delighted loyal fans and have been adapted into movies that have brought national attention to Mosher's little world. Despite his popularity, however, Mosher refuses almost all offers (even for pay) to give public readings, to teach, or to otherwise take part in literary events. He doesn't have time to talk about writing; he's too busy actually doing it. Nonetheless, few writers anywhere are more generous with their time and support for other writers. Dozens of authors around the country tell stories about sending drafts of books to Mosher and receiving long, useful comments in return. He's generous in writing reviews and blurbs for book covers, as well, and in promoting the work of promising writers to agents and publishers alike.

Mosher arrived in Vermont with several short stories and a novel completed but he hadn't yet sold much, or, as he puts it, "settled on a subject matter." But once he arrived in the Northeast Kingdom, "I knew immediately that I'd discovered a last New England frontier," populated by "the most independent-minded and self-sufficient people left on the face of the Earth and—best of all, so far as I was concerned—hundreds of wonderful stories just waiting to be written. Every hill farmer and horse logger and old-time hunter and trapper seemed to have dozens of spellbinding tales to tell. As an apprentice storyteller myself, I felt as though I'd struck a bonanza."

Subject matter was handed to him in the form of idle conversation and chats about the good old days overheard or instigated at the local store, the gas station, the dump, and the post office. His first landlady told him this story: During Prohibition, after her husband got sick, the woman resorted to making moonshine to make ends meet. One day, a government revenuer showed up, pursuing a rumor that she was operating an illegal still. "There's a sick man in there," she told the revenuer. "If you investigate what we do here or arrest me, you will kill him." The government man looked her over, thought for a moment, then turned around and left the property without a word. Later, after the woman's husband had died, the government man returned. "You come to arrest me now?" Mosher's landlady asked. "No," he said, "I've come to marry you." He took her to the ocean and Fenway Park on their honeymoon.

Mosher loves the tale. He laughs every time he tells it, enjoying the ending as much as when he first heard the story forty years ago. When Mosher laughs, his whole body gets into the laughter. If he's sitting, he puts his head down low between his knees and just sort of rocks into it. If he's standing, he might throw his head back and give a hearty chuckle. It's clear that what he likes about this particular story is what he enjoys so much about living in the Northeast Kingdom. The story of the government revenuer who gets seduced by the landlady's indomitable spirit and gives up any hope of conventional life to marry her is a metaphor for Mosher's own love affair with the Northeast Kingdom. Like the government man, Mosher gave up conventional life and financial security to live and write here. And, he has never regretted it.

The landlady's tale made its way into "Burl," one of the stories in *Where the Rivers Flow North*. Mosher has fictionalized the tale but the core of the original story is there.[4] Most of Mosher's stories start this way, from something heard or pieced together from several tales. His stories are, for the most part, grounded in the Kingdom, in its villages and people, and in events that actually took place here—or could have. It's the wonderful things Mosher does with these bits of real story that make them so fascinating.

For example, the spawning fish that Mosher and his wife watched that first day at the Orleans falls made their way into the opening chapter of *Disappearances,* Mosher's first novel. The book introduces one of Mosher's most engaging characters, the ever-optimistic Quebec Bill Bonhomme and his son Wild Bill. It opens with Quebec Bill and Wild Bill surveying the river on the first day of spring just as the ice has gone out of the river. Half the town has turned out to watch the trout run the rapids. Warden R. W. Kinneson (a member of a family that reappears throughout Mosher's fiction) is there as well, making sure that the spawning fish are left alone. (It's against Vermont law to touch a spawning fish.) The trout are having a hard time fighting against the torrent. They thrash against the current and many will not make it.

"One fish in particular," writes Mosher in *Disappearances*, "smashed against the granite shelf as it tried to ascend the near side of the falls. It tail-walked frantically, as though trying to portage around the falls. Cutting across the broad band of vivid red along its side was a raw gray gash.

"Quebec Bill can't stand to see the trout struggle.

"Quick as an otter he pounced on the flailing trout. In a single motion he caught it behind the gills and heaved it high over the falls. For a second it churned on top of the water; then it was gone up river. All along the ledge men were laughing and cheering."

Well, as you can imagine, Mosher's fictional warden was not impressed with Quebec Bill's interference with nature, not to mention his blatant abuse of the law. Warden Kinneson informs Quebec Bill that he now faces a $100 fine for "molesting a spawning fish." For someone with Quebec Bill's disdain for the law, the fine is bad enough but then Kinneson does the unforgivable; he insults Quebec Bill's French Canadian heritage. With not a minute's thought, Quebec Bill jumps in the air and, in an almost graceful movement, kicks his feet into the warden's uniformed chest, sending Kinneson into the swirling rapids. As the crowd roars, Quebec Bill quips, "See him flounder."[5]

It's an unbelievable action. Would someone actually kick a warden into dangerous falls with a whole crowd of townspeople watching? Would the townspeople approve of such a move, even if the warden was a real jerk? Would he get away with it? Quebec Bill does get away with it and many other outrageous deeds—well, nearly; you'll have to read the book to see what happens.

But although the plot of *Disappearances* is utterly improbable, readers go along for the delightful ride even though they doubt that the characters could pull off half the daring deeds that unfold on the book's pages. "It's a young writer's book. I couldn't write it that way now," Mosher says of the book's implausible plot. "I couldn't pull it off. You have to be young and not have been told the rules of story-writing to write like that."

When Mosher says "the rules of story-writing," he means that, when he wrote the book in 1970, he had not heard writing teachers say that characters must be believable, that plot must seem likely, that you can't ask too much of your readers in terms of suspending their common sense. On one level, *Disappearances* is so unbelievable that it's completely preposterous; yet among Mosher's legion of fans it remains a favorite. It's really Mosher's own optimistic nature, his pure energy of spirit, and the full-hearted glee with which he writes that allow him to pull it off.

Some writers pen plot-driven books; others are character-driven. Mosher's novels fall into the latter category. That means that, although the plot or the drama of his story is important, it is the characters and their responses to one another and the events of the book that move the plot forward. Essentially, the characters determine the plot.

### Tips and Techniques

The narrator in a written work is the person telling the story to the reader. To determine who is telling the story, the reader can simply ask: Through whose eyes is the story seen? Stories are traditionally narrated from one of three points of view: first-, second-, or third-person. When a story is told from the *first-person* point of view, the narrator tells the story from the "I" point of view. Sometimes the "I" is the central character in the story or novel and, thus, is referred to as the central narrator. Sometimes the first-person narrator is telling someone else's story; in that case, we refer to the storyteller as the *peripheral first-person* narrator. When a story is told from the first-person point of view (often abbreviated as pov), you should not assume that the narrator (the "I") is the author. Except in an autobiography or memoir in which the author has made it clear that he or she is telling his or her own story, the "I" of a story should be viewed as a fictional person. This point becomes especially important in workshops and writing classes. In all fictional works, assume that the "I" in a story is a creation of the author and not the author himself.

In *second-person* point of view, the actor in the story is referred to as "you," as in "You walk into a room." or "Dear reader, do you want to know more?" In the first instance, the "you" can refer to a specific person who is being addressed directly by the author. The reader may feel as if the author is speaking directly to her. In the second example, however, it's clear that the "you" is plural, all readers. Second-person narration is very quirky and very interesting. It's also very difficult to pull off and can become quite confusing if not adeptly handled.

*Third-person* narration occurs when a story is told from a particular character's point of view: he, she, or a named individual. When a story is told from one character's point of view, as in "Max Whelton strolled into the room," we refer to the narrator as *limited third-person*. The bulk of the action (and feelings and thoughts) will be told from that one character's point of view. When the narrator has access to the thoughts of all the characters, we call that an *omniscient narrator*. It's as if the narrator is a god who has access to the thoughts and feelings of many characters and can go in and out of their minds and follow them through the story effortlessly. Many of the classic epic novels are told from the omniscient point of view.

Mosher's approach to finding out what the characters want to do in a book is quite arduous but the beginning writer can learn much from his process. Mosher begins with some loose thoughts about a novel he wants to write or one scene from a story he's been told and sets out to write it, simply beginning with what he knows and answering a series of "what if" questions. For example: What if the warden is there when Quebec Bill shows up at the falls? What is the warden likely to say or do? How might Quebec Bill react? And then, what might happen? Mosher gives the characters free rein, simply recording their conversations and actions, writing in longhand on yellow legal pads, letting the story unfold as he goes along.

Mosher doesn't go back and revise as he writes his first draft. Rather, each morning, he reads the last page of what he's written the day before and picks up his story where he left off, writing again toward some often ambiguous ending. When he thinks he has finished with the first draft of a novel, he starts the process over again, writing the book straight through again from beginning to end on his yellow pad, sometimes coming up with an entirely different plot and new characters. Sooner or later, he says, his characters come alive; they tell him what the story is really about. This process of discovery may involve as many as sixty revisions. "My life consists of getting up early in the morning, working on whatever book I'm working on all day long, and then going to bed," Mosher says. "It is long, tedious, wonderful work. I wouldn't recommend it to anyone, but I don't know how to do anything else, at least not well."

Indeed, one of Mosher's more recent novels, *The True Account: A Novel of the Lewis & Clark & Kinneson Expeditions* took Mosher five years to write.[6] It began as a straightforward biographical novel about Merriwether Lewis, half of the pioneering duo who set off to be the first persons to chart a course across the American continent to the Pacific in 1804. But, "that approach didn't work out at all," Mosher says of his first draft of *The True Account*. "I wrote a whole book and just never found a story there that hadn't already been told, that engaged me. I came up with a better character, Thomas Jefferson's illegitimate son conceived with his slave Sally Hemmings, and figured I would write a book about him as if he had accompanied Lewis and Clark on their expedition. Thirty drafts and over a thousand pages later, it still hadn't worked out and I'd put three years of work into it. I didn't feel like I had found the heart of the book.

"Then Phillis and I went on the road. We retraced the Lewis and Clark expedition, gathering as much historical and physical details of the country that Lewis and Clark had traversed as we could, really seeing the country and trying to envision it in the days of Lewis and Clark. One day, Pvt. True Teague Kinneson, a Vermont schoolmaster, veteran of Ethan Allen's Green Mountain Boys, playwright, inventor, and explorer, appeared to me, fully dressed in his chain mail, galoshes, an Elizabethan codpiece and a belled nightcap (made to cover the copper plate screwed into his skull, a prosthetic device he acquired after a life-altering blow sustained while drinking rum with Ethan Allen). Eventually, Pvt. Kinneson became the main character of my novel and I got rid of the president's son," Mosher says.

The result is an extremely amusing fiction about Pvt. True Kinneson—another member of one of Mosher's favorite fictional families—and his nephew Ti (short for Ticonderoga), their adventures and misadventures as they cross the country competing against the great explorers. Along their path to the Pacific, True and Ti encounter highwaymen, hostile and not-so-hostile Indians, lusty women, a circus of freaks, cannibals, and some of the great real-life people of the time, such as Thomas Jefferson, Daniel Boone (and his frisky daughter Flame) and Sacagawea, the Native American who actually befriended Lewis and Clark. Even though Mosher says that *Disappearances* is a young person's book with too fantastic a story to pull off today, he's managed another one in *The True Account*. The tale is fantastic but, as with *Disappearances* and so many of his books, Mosher keeps us engaged because we so enjoy the wacky character of Pvt. Kinneson and his oddball antics. The reader is willing to suspend credibility out of his affection for the characters.

But the question remains how Mosher keeps himself going after so many pages and so many drafts. Here, again, it's Mosher's own indomitable spirit—his hope that he will find the story—that keeps him writing, draft after draft. He explains, "As I wrote all those drafts, I just had a gut sense that I hadn't found the right characters yet. When True showed up, of his own volition, I felt I finally had something totally original and the book wrote itself fairly quickly after that, which was a relief after so many attempts and failures. Initially, True had a very minor role. He was a small character who I introduced to put a few Vermont elements into the book. But my editor Harry Foster kept urging me to move this guy up, to give him more space, more time on the page. As it turned out he was right; the secret to making this book come alive for me—and it's got to come alive for me or it doesn't happen—was coming up with this Vermont character and finding out what he would do on the great expedition across America.

"One thing I realized in writing this book—and it's something I keep rediscovering—is that I have to personalize the narrative somehow. Private True is probably my alter ego; he says and does what I'd really like to do. Because he's funny and doesn't take himself or anyone else too seriously, the reader goes along with the gag. He's crazy but not as crazy as he pretends to be and, because we know that, we take him seriously when we need to. He's kind of like me in that," Mosher says. "It takes a long time for me to get a book right. You have to be patient. For me, writing is simply something I want to do badly enough so I keep at it."

Early on in his writing career, Mosher almost left the Northeast Kingdom—and his material—behind. After moving to Irasburg, he had begun to have some success publishing his short stories of the Northeast Kingdom but his teaching (he taught at Orleans High School and Lake Region High School and at the University of Vermont while earning a master's degree) took so much time from his writing that he began to resent the time away from what he considered his real work. He was thrilled when he was offered a fellowship to study writing at the University of California at Irvine in 1969. The fellowship would provide money to live on and required little in return in terms of actual work. Mosher had to teach a couple of courses a year but would have plenty of time to write. The couple packed up everything they owned and headed west. They expected to spend two years in sunny southern California. They spent three days, hating every moment. "I felt desperately cut off from my material and my home. No trees. No place to fish or hunt. It was inimical to everything we cared about or were interested in," Mosher recalls. "Of course, we should have known how miserable we would be."

Broke, with no job or prospects for one, and no home, the couple turned tail and headed back to the Northeast Kingdom. Phillis returned to teaching; Mosher took a job with a local logger named Jake Blodgett. The year before he'd left for California, Mosher's office at the University of Vermont overlooked the west side of Mount Mansfield. Now, here he was, one year later, culling timber from a lot that overlooked the other side of Mount Mansfield. The irony of his situation didn't escape him. The year before, he'd had professional prospects, the chance of becoming a tenure-track college professor and, with it, practically guaranteed financial security. Now, here he was in work boots and heavy, outdoor clothing, muddy and sweaty as he tramped through the woods, earning a minimal wage with about as much job security as any day laborer. Mosher loved every second. Jake Blodgett, his boss, was a hard-driving man of few words, a local fiddler, rum-runner and outlaw. He never referred to Mosher by name, but called him "School Teacher," always saying the words disdainfully. Mosher was so enthralled with Blodgett that he named his first child Jake. Blodgett also became the prototype for many of his characters. Among these are Noel Lord of *Where the Rivers Flow North* and Quebec Bill Bonhomme of *Disappearances*. Both are improbable, larger-than-life characters. Like Blodgett, Lord and Quebec Bill live by a code hewn from hardship and austerity, from doing without rather than making concessions to modern life, men who like to mingle with more urbane humans as little as possible and on their own terms.

"Jake figures into all my books in one way or another; there was my material. He introduced me to dozens of other reprobates. He was good material because he had done everything a person could do around here to make a living," Mosher recalls. "He had farmed, logged, run a cedar still and smuggled whiskey over the border. And, he was a great storyteller. Any one of his stories could become a whole novel in my imagination. What a treasure."

Two of Mosher's books have found their way to the movie screen. *Where the Rivers Flow North,* a novella and collection of short stories that deftly explore the lengths that men will go to gain the object of their desire or to protect something they value, was made into a film in 1994 by Jay Craven, founding director of Caledonia Pictures in Barnet. Set in the late 1920s, logger Noel Lord, the Jake Blodgett–inspired character, was played by Rip Torn while his Native American mate Bangor was played by Tantoo Cardinal. The movie focuses on the collection's central issue: the possible extinction of the couple's way of life when a proposed hydroelectric dam threatens to flood them off their land. Lord and Bangor battle emotional and physical challenges as they struggle not only with the power company but also with unforgiving terrain and weather and their own quirky and sometimes competing commitment to independence.

Craven also made Mosher's most ambitious project, the novel *A Stranger in the Kingdom*, into a movie.[7] Both the novel, written in 1989, and the subsequent movie, which starred Ernie Hudson and Martin Sheen, were daring projects that focused on one of the ugliest episodes in recent Vermont history. In 1968, the peace of Irasburg, Mosher's adopted hometown, was shattered when a black minister new to the town reported that his home had been shot at. The minister was a former Air Force chaplain who had been hired sight unseen as the new pastor of the local church. Although parishioners were stunned to find they had hired a black man, they initially welcomed the minister into their town—until people began to hear the details of his living arrangements. Along with his wife and children, the pastor's household included a white woman and her children. Vermonters were already feeling the threat of change from the outside as the counterculture and the back-to-the-earth movement brought young people with new ideas into the Green Mountain State. A black minister with an extended family that included a single white mother was definitely something new for this town. Out of curiosity, people occasionally drove by the parson's house to gawk. Sometimes, they yelled nasty remarks and, as the days went by, the minister and his family became increasingly anxious about how they were being treated.

Then one night, a group of young men who had been partying all day at the local county fair took a drive by; one of the men in the car shot at the minister's house. The minister was understandably concerned about his and his family's safety and filed a complaint with the police. But, rather than pursue the shooters, the state police began an aggressive investigation of the minister. They went so far as to hire a local family who lived near the parsonage to watch the pastor and his house and report their activities back to police. The incident came to a head when a police officer alleged that he had seen the pastor and his white housemate in an "intimate exchange." The exchange was never publicly described but the pastor was subsequently charged with adultery, an accusation that hadn't been brought to a Vermont criminal court in many years. Eventually, the adultery charge was dropped. Later, police charged the local man who had fired the rifle with disturbing the peace. The minister left town soon after that. But the entire incident remains a dark spot in Vermont history. The Vermont State Police's image suffered because of its handling of the event and several newspapers can hardly be proud of the inflammatory stories and editorials, some of which were downright racist, that they published.

On a broader, more philosophical level, the incident troubled many Vermonters who took pride in their heritage as the first state to outlaw slavery in the state constitution. At the same time, the incident proved to Kingdom residents that their geographical isolation could not insulate them from the changes that were sweeping Vermont and the nation. Phil Hoff had just been elected the first Democratic governor of Vermont in 108 years and hippies had established the first Earth People's Park, "free land" open to anyone who wanted to build or squat within its borders, in the Northeast Kingdom town of Norton. In the midst of all these social and political changes, the African American minister who moved into Irasburg proved to be the stranger that the town could not handle.

As he contemplated the Irasburg Affair, as the incident came to be called, Mosher knew that the idea of Vermont's great racial tolerance had rarely been tested, simply because the state's population had changed so little in comparison to almost everywhere else. It wasn't just that few African Americans had moved here. The word "diversity" could barely be applied to a place whose ethnic makeup was composed primarily of British, Irish, Polish, French Canadian, and Italian residents. Vermont was ranked the whitest state in the union until recently; diversity has improved in recent years, although not enough. Back in the 1960s when the incident with the minister occurred, the state had very few nonwhite residents. As a newcomer himself, Mosher had a small sense of how difficult it was to make oneself fit into a community where families had known one another for generations; he could only begin to imagine how difficult it might be for someone with dark skin.

Like so many others living in Vermont, Mosher had initially given little conscious thought to the state's lack of diversity. But the longer he lived in the town, the more the Irasburg Affair both fascinated and bothered him. He abhorred the blatant racism of the event but he was forced to acknowledge it also made him confront his own fears, particularly fear of the unknown.

Mosher came to believe that suspicion had dogged the minister from the moment he had arrived in Irasburg: in part, of course, because he was black but also—and maybe primarily—because he was a stranger, someone from the outside, someone who had lived in California, who not only traveled with a white woman but lived in an integrated home in a nontraditional family. Considered on that level, Mosher viewed the Irasburg Affair as a story as ancient as that of tribesmen killing a stranger who wanders into their cave, merely because he is an unknown, an outsider. In olden days, those tribesmen killed the stranger because they feared he might be carrying a virus, or might challenge one of them over a woman, or might have a more powerful weapon, or might bring news of a foreign god or religion. In our modern era, the motivations behind social behavior are not always so obvious as the caveman's but, Mosher believes, they are often as primitive and instinctive—and powerful.

These were terribly ambitious themes to take on, far more demanding for a writer than the fantastic adventures of Quebec Bill Bonhomme. In Mosher's fictional account, the black minister who comes to Kingdom County gets caught up in a murder mystery with many twists and turns that have nothing to do with the actual Irasburg Affair. Yet, in an oddly intuitive way, Mosher's fiction confronts the same issues that the people of Irasburg did in 1968: the tendency to distrust the stranger while overlooking disturbing behaviors within oneself; the corrupting influence of stereotypes and ignorance; and the lasting damage that comes of racial incidents, even when insults are not intentional. The book won the New England Book Award and has been favorably compared to *To Kill A Mockingbird*.

The cover of *A Stranger in the Kingdom* depicts a fictionalized view of Mosher's hometown but there is no question that it's Irasburg. There's the church and the green and Mosher's house tucked into a corner. One can't help wondering how the locals had felt about this outsider who came into their town to tell their most embarrassing story, even if in a fictionalized form. Just how *did* the locals feel having their dirty laundry hung out again on the public clothesline? "They seemed more perturbed with my license-taking with the local geography than they did with the retelling of the story," says Mosher, who was nervous at first about his neighbors' reaction, then perplexed, then relieved. Fictionalizing the account apparently made the retelling more palatable to his neighbors. He says no one has ever chastised him for writing the book. He thinks enough time had gone by for the town to heal from the initial attention.

Mosher's alteration of the actual plot may have also allowed people to look at themselves and their town with some degree of objectivity. But it cannot be said that he skirted the issue of racism or the failure of neighbors to treat others as they would want to be treated themselves. Mosher addressed these issue in very direct language in a letter that ends the book. Entitled "A Conspiracy of Silence," the letter is written by Charles Kinneson, the editor of the local paper of Mosher's fictional town (and a relative, of course, to Warden Kinneson in *Disappearances* and Pvt. True Teague Kinneson of *The True Account*.) Writes editor Kinneson: "Years hence, we may have to say that a stranger came to our village, and we failed him, and by doing so failed ourselves and what it truly means to live in 'God's Kingdom.'"

Mosher wrote *Waiting for Teddy Williams* in 2003 out of his frustration with the Red Sox. Rather than wait yet another year for his Boston team to win the World Series, he creates an opportunity for a Kingdom County kid to save the day and reverse the Babe Ruth curse.[8] The charming story has Mosher's usual cast of over-the-top oddballs who behave outrageously. While this is a baseball lover's book, at its heart, like so many of Mosher's tales, this is a story of hope, of overcoming adversity, of the strength of the human spirit.

---

◄§ FROM CHAPTER I OF *The True Account: A Novel of the Lewis & Clark & Kinneson Expeditions*

We had set a very close watch over my uncle, Private True Teague Kinneson, since his triumphal return from the Pacific and the Columbia River. I say "we," but in fact, keeping track of the comings and goings of the renowned expeditionary, schoolmaster, inventor, and playwright had, since my early boyhood, devolved mainly to me. My father had his newspaper to print, the Kingdom County Monitor, in which he kept track of the events in our remote little Vermont village. My mother kept track of our family farm, a job that required her entire attention from before dawn until after dark each day. And ours being a very small, if very affectionate, family, this left me to keep track of my uncle, who, as my father often said, clapping the heels of his hands to his temples and pressing as hard as he was able, as if to keep his brain from exploding, bore much watching.

From the time I was six or seven I was the private's constant companion, pupil, fishing partner, apprentice, and confidant, not to mention his co-expeditionary. Nor is it surprising that we were inseparable, when one stops to think that it was he who christened me Ticonderoga—Ti for short—after the principal matter of his play and the signal event of his life—the fall of the fortress of that name on the narrows of Lake Champlain to Ethan Allen and a handful of Vermont woodsmen and farmers in 1775.

Unfortunately, it was that same milestone in the history of our Republic that resulted in Private True Teague Kinneson's own fall and subsequent affliction—or, as my kindhearted mother called his strange disorder of the imagination, his "little ways and stays." As he was drinking rum flip with Ethan and celebrating their victory by singing a ballad, most of which has now been lost to posterity but whose refrain was "Tooleree, toolera, tooleroo," my uncle lost his footing and struck his head so sharp a blow on the gate of the fort that he never, I am grieved to report, quite regained his correct wits.

It is an important point of information in the history of the Kinneson family that from the moment of his mishap at Fort Ti, my uncle supposed himself to be constantly engaged in the prosecution of many heroic enterprises. These adventures often involved travel to far-flung places, great raging battles, and encounters with all manner of plenipotentiaries and unusual personages. The hillock behind my mother's cow barn he called the Heights of Quebec; and many a summer afternoon we stormed it together, taking the Citadel on the Plains of Abraham a large granite boulder atop the hill—as he believed he had done with General Wolfe in '59. In the winter, when a thick sheet of ice and snow covered the hill, he stationed me on this boulder in the role of the French commander, Montcalm, and had me repel his assaults by pushing him whirling back down the frozen slope on the seat of his woolen pantaloons—a terrifying spectacle to me and to my parents, calling up in our recollections his fateful accident of years before. There was no doubt, from my uncle's easy talk of embrasures, fortifications, enfilades, scaling-ladders, and cannonadings, that he fully imagined himself to have been present at the fall of Quebec. But when I drew my father aside and asked him privately whether True had been involved in that battle, his hands shot up to his head and he said that, while he ruled out no improbability when it came to his older brother, if he had been, he was the youngest foot-soldier in the history of the world—being, according to my father's calculations, but seven years of age at the time.

Sometimes my uncle and I journeyed to the rapids on the St. Lawrence just west of Montreal to reenact a historic meeting between the explorer Jacques Cartier and my great-great-great-great-great-grandfather, Chief Tumkin Tumkin of the Abenaki tribe. Hearing that Cartier was searching for China and the Great Khan, and learning something of the dress and customs of that distinguished emperor, Tumkin Tumkin had stationed himself just up-river from the rapids in a robe of muskrat pelts dyed bright vermilion, with an absurd little round yellow hat on his head; his design was to impersonate the Celestial Personage and receive whatever gifts the French explorer had laid aside for him. In the event, Cartier instantly saw through our ancestor's ruse, but was so amused that he gave Tumkin Tumkin his second-best chain-mail vest and named the region of the rapids Lachine—or China, as it is called to this day.

The cedar bog to the north of our farm my uncle designated variously as the Great Dismal Swamp, or Saratoga, or Yorktown. From it we routed many a vile Redcoat, every last one of whom we put to the sword. For Private True Teague Kinneson was a ruthless soldier and showed no mercy to his captives. In his capacity as an inventor, he attached a sail made from an old flannel sheet to my little fishing raft on the Kingdom River, where we played by the hour at Captain Cook and the South Sea Cannibals. And when the ice began to form on my mother's stock pond, we recreated the scene of Washington crossing the Delaware.

During the long Vermont winters, when the wind came howling down out of Canada and the drifts lay six feet deep between the house and the barn, my uncle taught me Latin and Greek and astronomy and mathematics and the physical sciences. He read to me by the hour from both the ancients and moderns, and in the evenings we frequently cleared away my mother's kitchen table and chairs and performed scenes from Homer or Virgil.

"Arma virumque cano," he would roar out in his booming stage voice. And it was off to the races with the brave hero of the Aeneid, while my mother, baking the next day's bread or peeling apples or doing the farm accounts in her black daybook, smiled, and my father's ink-stained hands shot headward. When we undertook the Iliad, my mother sometimes agreed to play the part of Helen, and my uncle and I carried her in her rocker from the window by the door to the chimney corner we called Troy; and indeed, with her tall slender form and long golden hair and eyes as blue as the sky over the Green Mountains on the fairest day of summer, she fit the role of Helen as well as any woman could. But on another occasion my uncle mistook my father for a Cyclops and chased him round and round the kitchen with the fire poker.

"None of this is your fault, Ti," my terrified sire cried from the other side of the barricaded woodshed door. "Above all, remember that none of this is your fault."

Well. I had never supposed that my uncle's little ways and stays were my fault, or anyone else's, including his. Nor did I for a single moment believe that he meant the least harm to my father or any other creature in the universe. Though as my uncle's own history amply illustrated, accidents would happen; and perhaps it was as well for my father that he had the presence of mind to retreat until our version of the Odyssey had ended with the hero's return to Ithaca and his loving Penelope. Penelope was my mother's cat.

My uncle's favorite play, however, was his own. I shall come to that drama very soon. But first, a few words about the appearance of the playwright himself. Private True Teague Kinneson—I refer to him by his full title because my uncle set great store by his military rank—was very tall and very lanky, with sloping, rugged shoulders, a trim, soldierly mustache, and keen yellow eyes that appeared to be as pitiless as a hawk's, though in fact he was the most sympathetic man I have ever known. He wore, over his scout's buckskins, Jacques Cartier's chain-mail vest, which had been handed down in our family from Tumkin Tumkin and which he believed had saved his life in battle a dozen times over; a copper dome, which had been screwed to the crown of his head by the regimental surgeon who operated on him after his fall at Fort Ti; a loose-fitting pair of galoshes, whose tops he rolled up to his bony knees for winter and down around his ankles for summer; a red sash about his middle somewhat resembling an Elizabethan codpiece; and, to cover the shining metal crown of his head, a red woolen night-stocking with a harness bell on the end, like the bell of a fool's cap, to remind himself where he was at all times, and also that "compared to the Almighty Jehovah, all men are fools."

My uncle was somewhat hard of hearing from being so much subjected to cannon fire over the course of his military expeditions, so he carried at all times a tin ear trumpet as long as my mother's yard measure. On those expeditions he went armed with a home-made wooden sword; an arquebus with a great bell-like mouth, of such incredible antiquity that even he was uncertain of its origin, though family tradition had it that this ancient firelock had been used by his Kinneson grandfather on the field of battle at Culloden just before the clan moved from Scotland to Vermont; and a large black umbrella to keep off the sun and rain, embellished on top with the family coat of arms—a crossed pen and sword, signifying that from time immemorial Kinnesons had "lived by the one and died by the other."

When not off adventuring, my uncle divided his time between his playwriting, his angling, his books, my education, his garden, and his inventions. To begin with the play. He had been working on his Tragical History of Ethan Allen, or The Fall of Fort Ticonderoga for twenty years and more. He styled it a tragedy because he believed Colonel Allen to have been much undervalued, and indeed thought that the old Vermonter should have been our first president. It was a long play, running well over three hours. And on the occasions when he had arranged for it to be performed, it had not met with a very kindly reception, even in our own state. From certain hints my uncle himself had let drop, I feared that it had been roundly hissed off the stage. But he had the greatest faith in the world in his Tragical History, and pegged away at it year after year, firmly believing it to be nothing short of a masterpiece-in-progress. What pleased him most about the play was that it violated none of Aristotle's dramatic unities. Aristotle the Greek philosopher, pupil of Plato, and chronicler of all branches of human knowledge known to his time? No, sir. Scholia Scholasticus Aristotle—my uncle's great tutor during his time at Oxford University—of whom you will soon hear more.

When it came to angling, my uncle loved to cast flies, like our Scottish ancestors. In fact, he and my father were both avid flycasters and had taught me this noble art when I was very young. We three enjoyed many a fine May morning on our little river, enticing native brook trout to the lovely feathered creations that my uncle tied during winter evenings. He fashioned long, limber rods from elm and ash poles, wove fine horsehair leaders, and was the neatest hand in all Kingdom County at laying his high-floating colored artifices deftly over rising fish. There was just one difficulty. Private True Teague Kinneson was so tenderhearted that he could not bear to kill his catch, and so released every last trout he caught unharmed to the cold waters from which it had come. Yet no man ever enjoyed the art of fly-fishing more or took more pains to match his flies to the natural insects emerging on the water; and the sight of my copper-crowned uncle, rod held high and bent, playing a fine splashing trout, and crying, for all the world to hear, "Hi, hi, fish on!" was a most splendid spectacle.

My uncle's books, of which he had many hundreds in several languages, he kept in his snug little schoolhouse-dwelling behind our farmhouse, which dwelling he called the Library at Alexandria. He spared no expense when it came to purchasing these volumes, and he supported his scholarly avocation with the proceeds from his garden in my mother's loamy water meadow near the river. There he tended half an acre of the tall, forest-green plants known as cannabis, whose fragrant leaves and flower buds he ground into a mildly euphoric smoking tobacco very popular in Vermont and of which he himself faithfully smoked half a pipeful each evening after supper.

Of all his books, my uncle loved best a hefty old tome bound in red buckram called The Ingenious Gentleman Don Quixote de La Mancha—of which he believed every last syllable to be the revealed gospel truth. In fact, it was partly in honor of this same ingenious gentleman that my uncle wore his chain mail and polished his copper crown until it shone like the top of a cathedral. For ever since his accident, he had fancied himself something of a modern-day knight-errant. Yet it was not giants disguised as windmills that he sought to fight but the Devil himself—until he cast that horned fellow out of the Green Mountains in a tow sack, in consequence of which expulsion he feared that "the Gentleman from Vermont," as he termed Old Scratch, might be doing great mischief elsewhere. Being a kind of perpetual boy himself, though a big one, my uncle was a great favorite with all the boys and girls in the village, for whom he invented huge kites, spinning whirligigs, velocipedes with sails, magic lanterns, catapults, wheeled siege-towers, fireships, rockets, and I don't know what else—none of which ever, to the best of my knowledge, had the slightest practical application. Besides his vast fund of classical stories and poems, he knew a thousand tales of witches, ghouls, and ghosties, in the telling of which he terrified no one so much as himself. He was deathly afraid of large dogs, small serpents, lightning—he had been struck eight times since the installation of his copper crown, and it was said in the village that, like a tall ash tree in a Vermont hedgerow, he "drew electricity"—and of nearly all women, though he had the greatest respect for and confidence in my mother, as did my father and I.

One of my uncle's most curious inventions was a wooden, Dutch-style shelf clock, about a foot and a half tall, without any works or innards but with a very passable painting he had done on it of his hero Quixote, that Knight of the Woeful Countenance, doing combat with a windmill. The painted hands of this clock were set forever at twenty minutes past twelve, which hour had a triple significance to my uncle. First, he was utterly certain that this was perpetually the correct time at Greenwich, England, so that by knowing the hour where he was, and the altitude of the sun, he could always calculate his correct longitude and divine where he was in the universe. And it distressed him not in the least that no matter how many times he made these calculations, his position never came out the same twice but varied wildly, from the longitude of Calcutta to that of Venice.

The second point of significance concerned a saying in our family, which was that whenever a lull fell over the conversation, it must be twenty after the hour. Admittedly, between my uncle the ex-schoolmaster and my father the editor, one or both of whom seemed always to be discoursing from dawn straight through until midnight, there were not many such lapses of silence in our household. But when by chance no one happened to be talking, my uncle would leap up and dash out to his Library at Alexandria to check the time on the Dutch clock and confirm that it was indeed twenty past the hour, which was a great relief to him. And though the clock was less reliable as a timepiece than was entirely convenient to one wishing to know the actual hour, it was so reliable as a conversation piece that it never failed to set the talk in motion again.

Third, and finally, it was inside the hollow case of this remarkable clock that my uncle stored his hemp tobacco. From what I have retailed to you thus far, you might well suppose that mine was a very odd and somber boyhood. Odd, I will grant you. But

somber? Never in this world. For my uncle was ever a second father to me. In fact, it might be said that between my true father
and my uncle True, the pair of brothers made one complete and
perfect father. Or so I thought, at least. And no boy could ever
have had a more complete education than I. When my interest first
in sketching, then painting, birds and wildlife began to emerge, my
uncle even took me on a tour of the great museums of England,
France, Italy, and the Lowlands. By which I mean that we canoed
across the "Atlantic Ocean"—our pond, that is—and on the far side
he described the great paintings of the world so exactly that I all
but saw them. Say what the village might, then, it was a splendid
way to grow up. And to anyone who thought differently, Private
True Teague Kinneson doffed his belled cap, bowed low, and said,
"Why, bless you, too, sir. With a tooleree and a toolera and a
tooleroo!"

Of all my uncle's many schemes and projections, the one nearest his heart was no more and no less than to discover the North-
west Passage. From my earliest visits to the Library at Alexandria,
I remember him poring over the old histories of his mostly ill-fated
fellow expeditionaries and visionaries who for more than three
centuries had sailed in quest of that elusive route to the riches of
Cathay. On a wall map of North America behind his writing desk,
the blank territory to the north and west of the Missouri River was
labeled terra incognita; and when my uncle's saffron-colored eyes
grew weary during our school lessons or his interminable revisions
of his play, he liked to pause and gaze at those intriguing words
and muse about the great foray that he and I would someday make
into that unknown land.

## Questions and Exercises for Reflection and Inspiration

One of the most important things beginning writers need to learn is the
dictum "show, don't tell." That means that writers should avoid abstracts
like "he felt angry" or "she was proud," but rather show the character's emotional response in a scene. Thus, for example, in the scene of Quebec Bill's
response to Warden Kinneson in *Disappearances*, we learn that Quebec Bill
is at once compassionate and angry, proud and impetuous. Mosher doesn't
tell us this; he shows us in the scene in which Quebec Bill, without stopping to think, kicks the warden into the water.

In Mosher's writing, as in all good writing, whether real or fictional,
people come alive on the page much the same as they do in real life. In real
life, we come to know people by observing and experiencing essential aspects of their personalities. These invariably include what a person looks
like, how he speaks and what he says, how and what he does, what he
thinks; how he reacts to those around him and how others react to him.

These aspects can be expressed in five words commonly used in literary discussion: description, dialogue, action, thought and reaction. Writers combine these five aspects of showing character—think of them as tools—to create character.

When it comes to description, remember that vague adjectives, such as large, small, or quiet, impetuous, or rebellious don't help the reader very much to picture a character. What's large to one person may be quite normal to another. Descriptions need to be specific and detailed; they usually work best when they are combined with dialogue, action, thought, and reaction. In the example given at the Orleans falls, for example, we learn the following about Quebec Bill:

> **Physical description:** he's "quick as an otter"; he's agile; he's strong enough to kick Kinneson into the water with one swift punt.
>
> **Dialogue:** He says, "See him flounder," a short, witty sentence in which Quebec Bill cleverly compares the warden to a fish (a flounder).
>
> **Action:** Quebec Bill pounces on a flailing trout; he catches it behind the gills and heaves it over the falls; he responds to the warden's insult by kicking him into the falls; he shows off for the crowd.
>
> **Thought:** Quebec Bill can't stand to see the trout struggle.
>
> **Reaction:** He responds to the warden's insult by kicking him into the falls; he shows off for the crowd and the crowd applauds him.

These details work together to create a picture of a person who is sympathetic to the spawning fish, but also rebellious and impulsive, comical and arrogant. Mosher doesn't use any of these adjectives. Rather, he illustrates Quebec Bill's character through a combination of description, dialogue, action, thought, and reaction. He *shows* us Quebec Bill. And, because he so concretely paints the scene at the falls through the use of strong verbs (smashed, tailwalked, pounced, heaved) combined with effective character development, the reader can see the scene in his own mind. This scene from *Disappearances* is a great example of the "Show, don't tell" mantra.

Does Mosher do the same thing with the characters in *A True Account*? Read the excerpt above again and make a list of attributes that you glean about each character, including the narrator, and how you learned it. For example, we begin to learn early on about the various ways in which each family member copes with Private True Teague's odd behavior. What do each of these coping mechanisms tell us about each of the characters? For each character, list descriptions, dialogue, actions, thoughts, and reactions that show their personalities and temperament.

> **Exercise 1:** Make a list of attributes for a real or imagined character that you want to write about. Using the five tools commonly employed to create character—description, dialogue, action, thought, and reaction—write a short scene in which you show some aspect of your character's personality or temperament. Be as specific as possible. Re-

member that words like large or angry, pretty or sad are relative, ambiguous words. Use concrete comparisons and action to make your character come alive on the page. Show, don't tell.

**Exercise 2:** If you are having trouble coming up with your own character, begin by trying to describe in a scene one of the following clichéd personality types without using any of the adjectives or verbs normally attributed to the type: A tyrannical teacher, a domineering bully, a rock band groupie, a timid computer programmer, an aging film star, a frisky cat, a mean dog, a spoiled brat.

**Exercise 3:** Write a character sketch based upon someone you know but change something essential, such as the person's sex, age, occupation, or time when he or she is living. As you revise your character sketch, change some other important element. Keep doing this until you have radically altered the real person into a fictional character.

Environment is an essential part of scene-setting. Where a person lives or works tells us much about his or her personality and sets a mood for a piece. A character living in a tree house overlooking the Pacific Ocean is necessarily different from someone living in a basement apartment in Manhattan. Similarly, if we read that a character has paved over the lawn in front of his suburban home, we begin to imagine something about his need for efficiency and disdain for manual labor. A person who surrounds herself with potted plants is different than one who keeps the tops of every surface in her house, from dressers to countertops, free of personal items.

**Exercise 4:** Take a story you are already working on or one you'd like to write and describe the setting carefully, paying close attention to how the items you describe in your scene can help show the personality, interests and dislikes of your character. What calendar is on the wall? Are the curtains drawn tight or absent? Does the view from the window show telephone lines or maple trees and how does your character feel about that view?

Photo by Ann Day

# 2 David Budbill

## *The Ornery Hermit Activist Poet*

Born 13 June 1940, Cleveland, Ohio

Education: B.A., Muskingum College; M.A. in Divinity, Union Theological
   Seminary

Lives in Wolcott

First publication: *Mannequin's Demise* (1966)

Poetry: *Barking Dog* (1968); *The Chain Saw Dance* (1977); *From Down to the Vil-
   lage* (1981); *The Pulp Cutters' Nativity* (1981); *Why I Came to Judevine* (1987);
   *Judevine: The Complete Poems* (1989); *Moment to Moment: Poems of a
   Mountain Recluse* (1999); *Judevine: the Complete Poems (revised)* (1999);
   *While We've Still Got Feet* (2005)

A libretto for an opera: *A Fleeting Animal: an Opera from Judevine* (2000)

Short story collection: *Snowshoe Trek to Otter River* (1976)

Novel: *Bones on Black Spruce Mountain* (1978)

Plays: *Mannequin's Demise* (1966); *Knucklehead Rides Again* (1967); *A Pulp Cutters' Nativity* (1981/1991); *Thingy World!* (1991); *Part of It* (1993); *Little Acts of
   Kindness* (1995); *Judevine* (1992, 1996, 2000)

Children's Book: *The Christmas Tree Farm* (1974)

Music: *Zen Mountains-Zen Streets: A Duet for Poet and Improvised Bass* (1999);
   *Songs for a Suffering World: A Prayer for Peace, a Protest Against War* (2003)

Edited volume: *Danvis Tales: Selected Short Stories of Rowland Robinson* (1995)

Awards: *Moment to Moment* was listed on Booklist's top ten books of poetry
   published in 1999; Vermont Arts Council Walter Cerf Award for Lifetime
   Achievement in the Arts (2002)

THE SOUND OF DEER COUGHING in the nearby woods punctuates the black air studded with stars that surrounds David Budbill's small circle of domesticity. The deer's guttural noises announce the start of the rutting season, but also signal that winter is not far away from Wolcott, the Northeast Kingdom hamlet where Budbill and his wife, painter Lois Eby, built their home more than three decades ago. From the deck, you can look out onto a large garden and apple orchard, harvested now and readied for the long winter, and up to Judevine Mountain, a place Budbill has written much about and the name of the imaginary hermit poet whose haiku-like poems Budbill is conduit for.

The house is weathered wood, a story-and-a-half high. It cost the couple less than ten thousand dollars to build back in the late 1960s and early 1970s. Downstairs, there is a pleasant living space, a big old woodstove, a wall of books, a snug, practical kitchen, and plants on the windowsills. The walls hold Eby's dramatic artwork. Upstairs, in Budbill's tidy studio, a small Buddhist altar is tucked into one corner; in another, a music stand tells of his passion, first for the saxophone, and more recently for Asian musical instruments, such as the shakuhachi, a vertical Japanese flute whose sound Budbill describes as "intrinsically melancholic," a sound he finds inexplicably soothing.

Budbill is the author of nine collections of poetry, six plays, a novel, a collection of short stories, a picture book for children, and dozens of essays, introductions, speeches, book reviews, and the libretto for an opera. He publishes an online magazine, has been an occasional commentator on National Public Radio and his poetry is frequently heard on Garrison Keillor's *Writer's Almanac* and the *Prairie Home Companion*. Along with all that, he's recorded several spoken word CDs, accompanied by jazz musicians. How does he do it all?

Budbill begins each workday early, writing by 7:00 A.M., and often working for six or more hours without a break. His schedule is somewhat dictated by the seasons. Winter is his most productive time for writing. "I love winters here; they're so pulled in and isolated," he says. In summer and early fall, the demands and pleasures of the garden and the woodlot consume much of his time. Regardless of the season, on almost any day, Budbill gets out for several hours on foot or bicycle, hiking Judevine Mountain or biking the long, circuitous dirt roads surrounding his house. "I have to have this concrete point for my imagination or my imagination doesn't work," he says of his relationship to the natural world and its relationship to his writing. "There's this deep connection for me between what I am and what I do and where I do it. I'm lucky to have been able to do it in such a remarkable place. I do not take it for granted."

To talk of Budbill and his work almost requires two essays. First, there would be the one that speaks of his early work, which was almost entirely rooted in the streams and mountains and people he came to know here in northern Vermont. His earliest poems and plays told the stories of fictional characters living in Judevine, a fictional setting quite similar to Wolcott but re-created in Budbill's mind. While he loves the Northeast Kingdom and its residents, Budbill's poems and stories are not about idyllic characters living in bucolic reverie. Rather, Budbill writes the stories of the rural poor and disenfranchised, stories that you are unlikely to read in *Vermont Life* or other promotional publications, stories of a Vermont that he feels has gone too long unnoticed and unredeemed.

His imagination has also created a second, more contemporary, body of work. While his imagery and inspiration still comes from the natural and manmade world around him, Budbill's newer works often take him far from Wolcott. The new work is sparser, more direct, written with an ever-increasing sense of urgency. His subject matter is now apt to be the larger world, war and its consequences, the continued threat of nuclear proliferation, disparity between the haves and have-nots, and world hunger.

These are hard subjects but hard subjects are nothing new for Budbill who, regardless of subject matter or format, has consistently used his gifts to write of the down-and-out and the overlooked, the unsung, and the unprotected, both here in Vermont and around the world.

Budbill was born in Cleveland, Ohio, in 1940. His father was a streetcar driver who never made it past seventh grade; his mother was a minister's daughter. Budbill's first hero was Larry Doby, the second black man to play major league baseball. Doby joined the American League Cleveland Indians only eleven weeks after Jackie Robinson became the first black athlete in the National League, playing for the Brooklyn Dodgers. In 1948, when he was eight years old, Budbill was obsessed with Doby, identifying with him as "an underdog . . . like me, a painfully shy, skinny, good-at-nothing, ignored-by-everyone little kid from the streets of a working-class neighborhood."[1]

From that moment on (and maybe even before; his father always urged him to stick up for the little guy) Budbill was a champion of the downtrodden. After Budbill earned his master's degree in divinity from Union Seminary, he and his wife traveled to New York City to work as teachers in an inner-city school for a couple of years. In 1967, at the height of the civil rights movement, they took jobs as teachers at Lincoln University, an all-black college in Pennsylvania.

Two years later, Budbill wanted to take a year off from teaching to concentrate on his writing. He had attended the Bread Loaf Writers Conference as a student in 1964. He hated Bread Loaf, considering it an elitist institution. But he had developed a deep affection for Vermont and dreamed of returning here to write. Even then, he was aware of Vermont's strong literary tradition and wanted to experience it, to see what would happen if he could put himself in a place where he could be free to write without economic pressures or the distractions of urban life. "I had fallen in love with the mountains because I'm a flatlander. I said to my wife, 'Jezum, let's go to Vermont.' Well, I didn't say Jezum yet," he says, laughing at his use of the most famous Vermontism, Jezum as in Jezum Crow, the fictitious state bird.

As luck would have it, while Budbill was dreaming of taking a year off and contemplating how he might do so, he learned that a friend of a friend of a friend of a friend (it was the 1960s) had a cabin (actually, an old school house) in South Albany, Vermont, and that the place was available. Budbill and his wife had saved up five thousand dollars so they could live here for a year. The plan was that Budbill would write and Eby would paint. "First and foremost for me was that Vermont was a cheap place to live. Our goal was to build a house to store our books, live for a year or so and be able to take off when we wanted to. We wanted to be able to live on as little as possible so there would be as much time as possible to do our art and travel. Also, I was looking for that kind of isolation, to 'drink a cup of loneliness,' to live somewhere where you're not surrounded by the crush of the world," he explains. What he didn't figure into his formula was that, even though Vermont is a relatively inexpensive place to live, you still have to earn enough money to make ends meet. And, if the goal is also to save enough for a humble piece of property and home, you'll need to make more than what you need to live on. As with so many others who moved here in those years, the money ran out sooner than Budbill and Eby had planned.

Budbill recalls, "We got here and couldn't leave. We'd fallen in love with the place, of course. But we couldn't make a living. It's that perpetual problem in Vermont, how to survive if you don't have a big nest egg." Budbill got a job working for a Christmas tree farmer and, in 1974, published a children's book called *Christmas Tree Farm* based on his experience. That project didn't bring in much revenue. At various times in his life, besides working as a high school and college teacher, Budbill has worked as a carpenter's apprentice, short-order cook, manager of a coffeehouse, street gang worker, forester, gardener, and pastor of a church to supplement his writing income.

The couple could have returned to Lincoln, but they had other reasons for staying in Vermont, besides their love for the place. They had tired of academia but, more important, had come to think that teaching at Lincoln as part of a predominantly white faculty was an insult to the black students. Over the preceding few years, Budbill had watched and worried, expressed outrage, and protested as black and white leaders were assassinated, as riots had spread to American cities, and black and white kids had been killed in the South. "One Christmas vacation," he wrote in *Seven Days*, a Burlington, Vermont, weekly newspaper, "one of our students was shot to death by the police in Trenton, New Jersey, for nothing more than standing on the street."[2]

At Lincoln and other black institutions, African Americans were telling the white folks to move over and let them take care of their own. Budbill heard their demand and applauded it. Ironically, he landed in Vermont, then the whitest state in the nation. Over the years, he has revisited the issue of Vermont's lack of diversity and applauded the small steps made by minorities who have moved here. In the 1999 *Seven Days* article, he wrote, "As Vermont becomes more and more non-white, we will have the chance to admit that the way we have lived here in the past is not only odd, but seriously at odds with the rest of the world."[3] Budbill might have loved Vermont but he wasn't blind to its limitations.

Budbill intended his first published book of poems in Vermont, entitled *The Chain Saw Dance,* as a kind of love poem to his neighbors, a tribute to their inventiveness, their backwoods ingenuity.[4] His tales about Anson, Arnie, Old Man Pike, and the other inhabitants of his imaginary town of Judevine quickly got the attention of Wolcott residents, who perused the book at the town's unofficial library—a shelf beneath the counter of the local garage.

The neighbors he meant to praise thought *Chainsaw* vulgar and felt it insulted their intelligence and morality. They weren't enthralled with Antoine, whose life was characterized by labor and loneliness; or Hermie, who lived in a bread truck near Bear Swamp; or Anson, who lost his father's home because he couldn't pay the taxes; or of slovenly Arnie, who wiped his nose on his sleeve. Beauty is in the eye of the beholder, Budbill tried to say, insisting he saw more beauty in the petunias growing from the rubber tire planter in front of a rusty trailer home than he did in the meticulous gardens found behind white-painted picket fences in more upscale Vermont towns. And he might have told them that the place he called Judevine in his writing "is not Wolcott. It's as if the place in my imagination, an acetate map of Judevine, is superimposed upon Wolcott." The neighbors were having none of it. They demanded that he quit the school board. Someone threatened to burn his house down. At the same time, Eby was pregnant with the couple's daughter; both she and the baby were sick with toxemia. Finances were slim and the demands of Vermont's weather had taken their toll on Budbill's spirit.

He thought about moving, but didn't. His neighbors might not have loved him back— at least not then. But the mountains did. Not only did the mountains give him a context for the ideas in his head but his isolated home gave him "the absolute emptiness I need as a writer. There are so many events, so many characters in my head calling to me. My problem is making them get in line. I need a kind of emptiness in which to hear all this stuff in my imagination and to write it down," Budbill says. He hears the irony in his words: "I live in an incredibly remote spot, as far away from humanity as you can get, almost, and all I write about is people."

His next published work, a play called *Judevine: A Play in Five Acts*, was equally controversial but the hullabaloo spread far beyond Wolcott.[5] The Woodstock High School principal canceled a performance of the play because it "contained strong language"—that is, words people often use when they're frustrated, poor, down-trodden, or just plain angry. Vermont legislators also rejected a suggestion by the Vermont Arts Council that excerpts of *Judevine* be enacted during Farmer's Night, an annual event of entertainment at the State House. The lawmakers had learned the play contained rude language, something they surely were unused to hearing.

The play's intertwining vignettes are taken from three of Budbill's books of poems, *The Chain Saw Dance, From Down to the Village*,[6] and *The Pulp Cutters Nativity*.[7] Six actors play several roles each and also serve as an ad hoc chorus of commentary and sound effects. There is Antoine, the play's exuberant, fun-loving French Canadian lumberjack; Raymond and his wife Anne, rock-ribbed in their devotion to each other and the land; Conrad, the alcoholic who works at Gerry's garage and drinks beer every night; Grace, a single mother of two who takes to child abuse when the odds get too high to conquer; and Tommy, the Vietnam vet who returns to find himself changed while Judevine has not. *Judevine* may have been a bit controversial in Vermont but it garnered rave reviews as it was acted on stages from New York City to San Francisco. Critics, directors, actors, and audiences alike saw the universal themes in Budbill's portrayal of rural people bypassed by the twentieth century, and the play brought him national acclaim.

Budbill's name was thereafter much mentioned for Vermont poet laureate. In writing as an advocate for the oppressed and downtrodden, he seemed to be following the tradition laid down by some of Vermont's most cherished writers, people like Alice Mary Kimball,[8] Dorothy Canfield Fisher, and Sarah Cleghorn, especially in terms of seeing art as a tool for social reform.

But such was not to be—at least, as yet. Although Budbill's approach to exposing the injustices of contemporary life in Vermont—poverty and unemployment, alcoholism, domestic abuse—has consistently had the ear (and enthusiastic appreciation) of ordinary people, it has also sometimes proved embarrassing to the literary establishment and to those who wanted to sell Vermont as a way of life, a picture-perfect postcard existence of rural tranquillity. Thus, along with "brilliant" and "insightful," the other words used to describe his work—gutsy, gritty, troubling, rough-edged and unsoothing—have kept him thus far from the honor of being chosen state poet. Budbill's sense of being estranged from the establishment (*all* establishments, especially the literary establishments) has its advantages, however. It enables him to speak in the voice of the paranoid, the neglected, the frustrated, and the angry. That's why he has remained popular with ordinary folk. At least that's what he believes, noting that people come up to him constantly to say that they hate poetry but they really like his stuff.

Still, those early years were frustrating. In typical Budbill fashion, he wrote out his anger. In his play *Part of It/Little Acts of Kindness*, for instance, Budbill's character, the mad poet, raves on like this: "The reason my stuff never gets anywhere is because it isn't like anybody else's. It's original, unique, one of a kind. That's where I went wrong! I mean, I been stupid enough to think that being original counts. That's exactly what doesn't count. Write like everybody else, Sucker, if you want to get ahead!"[9] He's not simply complaining about his own treatment. Budbill has also earned a reputation as a frank spokesperson for the struggling artist, criticizing politicians publicly about the lack of state and national support for artists, speaking out against censorship and against the marketing of Vermont. He upset some members of the Vermont Arts Council in 1987 with a speech in which he addressed the difficulties of the artist in rural society. His comments speak to advantages and disadvantages that artists encounter here in Vermont.[10]

In the speech, he said artists like himself came to Vermont because "we believed, some of us at least, and naively I am afraid, that given a fresh start, free of the urban assumptions and constraints, that we would be able to make our art in an atmosphere and for an audience that would measure our vision of the critical importance of art as a meaningful and necessary part of ordinary human life. Unfortunately in too many instances, the attitudes and assumptions we were fleeing from, we ran directly into. The narrow artistic and economic pressures of the city were replaced by the narrow economic and artistic attitudes of the country."

Budbill spoke of the shabby treatment he had received from the legislature., saying "because my play contains some harsh language, and also, I believe, because it is a deeply political play, and most importantly because *Judevine* gets too close to the truth about the lives of many of the people in Vermont, people the lawmakers would rather not have confronting them in the sacrosanct chambers of the State House, it was deemed inappropriate for those who make the laws that govern that society to be exposed to this play." He also used the speech as an opportunity to espouse his philosophy about the true role of the artist in society: "To pretend that all is right with the world when it is not, to use art as a pair of rose-colored glasses to distort the reality of the world, to paint over the agonies of our time, is to misuse art," he said. "Any light and life, joy and ecstasy we can derive from art in our time must be paid for with the admission that this joy and goodness comes to us out of the barbarous darkness all around us."

As it turned out, Budbill long ago made it without the approval of the literati. Today, he's more popular than ever. Along with essays and poetry readings on National Public Radio and his extensive publications, he's asked to give readings and performances nationwide and is written about extensively in literary, political, and even Buddhist publications. And, in 2002, the Vermont Arts Council presented him with its Walter Cerf Award for Lifetime Achievement in the Arts.

Orneriness just comes naturally to Budbill. As a young reader and then a young poet, he had admired the poetry of Robert Frost. By the time Frost died in 1962, Budbill had read everything Frost had written and just about everything that had been written about him; "I was devoted to him," he told Sebastian Matthews in an interview for *Rivendell* magazine. "This was while I was still living in Ohio, long before I ever came to Vermont. I think coming to Vermont requires of writers a kind of divorce from Frost, if you're going to be yourself. I have a poem called "Killing the Ghost of Rip-ton" about getting rid of this guy, getting him out of my life."[11]

All that is not to say that Budbill is unaware how lucky he is to live and write in Vermont. It's precisely because it is so precious to him that Bud-bill is so outspoken in his outrage and protectiveness. He is worried about Vermont. He doesn't want it to become a gated white community. He wants to share it: "This privilege—to be alive on a day like today, to have this view, to be a writer, to be part of this great literary tradition—carries an important responsibility. I'm not interested in analyzing Vermont's ef-fect on me. I just know what it does. This connection to the natural world, the four seasons, it's the fecund ground in which my imagination grows. Could I write anywhere? Sure. But this is what I have chosen."

Ever since his days in seminary school, Budbill has been interested in world religions and drawn to Confucius's teachings, to the Tao and Bud-dhism, and to Chinese and Japanese poetry. As he's aged and matured, that interest has grown deeper. As he explains it, "The interest in a mystical con-templative approach to the world has always been there but it didn't bur-geon forth for me until *Moment to Moment: Poems of a Mountain Recluse*," a collection of Budbill's poems published by Copper Canyon Press in 1999.[12]

The book, which was listed on Booklist's top ten books of poetry pub-lished in 1999, reflects not only Budbill's reclusive nature and his habitation in the remote mountains of Vermont but also his thirty years of studying the ancient Chinese poets and Taoist texts. The book is both self-mocking and humorous. While decidedly Budbill's own intelligent, wry voice, the poems have been compared to those of ancient Asian poets. These include Wang Wei, Li Po, Tu Fu, and, especially, the irascible T'ang dynasty poet Han Shan, who referred to himself as Cold Mountain, much as Budbill refers to himself as the conduit for the poet named Judevine Mountain.

In Budbill's mythology, he relates this story of how he discovered the poet Judevine Mountain: one afternoon, several years ago, while hiking in the woods behind his house, he came upon a cabin on the eastern side of Judevine Mountain inhabited by a hermit poet. This hermit poet was liv-ing "in the ancient Chinese style. He, like his progenitor, had named him-self for the place where he lived." The poet Judevine Mountain became one of the voices in Budbill's head, along with a host of others, poets who offer him lovely, sparse poems like this one:

### So Says Wang Wei

When the Emperor is a sage
There are no hermits,
so says Wang Wei

which is why I've spent
the past thirty years
hiding in these mountains.

—from *Moment to Moment*[13]

By using the device of writing the poems of Judevine Mountain, Budbill not only allows himself to step outside of himself and the everyday demands of life; he also brings to his work the rich contextual authority of the ancients who wrote aesthetic poetry that celebrated a world of simplicity, oneness with nature, and freedom from material want. In reading these poems, therefore, the reader is presented with unfamiliar challenges. The reader of any poem is interested in who the speaker is and who he is addressing. These questions have new depth and meaning in Budbill's poetry. Our natural inclination as readers is to assume that the speaker is the author. But, when confronted by a poem like this, we are forced to pay more attention. We discover that the poem may seem quite simple on the surface but, upon reflection, it presents complex questions. Who is this Wang Wei? And what is an ancient Asian poet doing in a contemporary poem written by a Vermont author?

### Tips and Techniques

When talking or writing about poetry or analyzing your own, we often ask the following questions:

1. **Who speaks?** In some poems, the speaker is a specific person or thing. In others, the speaker may be simply a voice contemplating or commenting on a theme. Some poems are told from the first-person point-of-view, the "I." As in fiction, the "I" is not necessarily the author of the poem, although the poem may be autobiographical.

2. **To whom does the speaker address the poem?** Some poems are addressed to a specific person and we, as readers, are simply voyeurs. The addressee may be named or assumed. Sometimes the poem reveals something about the person being addressed. Sometimes the poem is addressed to a specific "you." Most poems, however, address an unidentified audience, the more generic "you," either named or unnamed.

3. **Does the poem have a setting or environment?** In poetry, setting is location as much as atmosphere. Sometimes, the location is quite specific, a place or room; sometimes, a poem does not have a locale but it does have mood or tone. Sometimes, a poem has both setting and environment and they work together to create an intended atmosphere that, in turn, suggests meaning.

4. **Does the poem have a theme? If so, is it stated directly or indirectly?** It's not uncommon for a poet to state the subject of her contemplation rather directly; other times, the theme is less obvious or expressed in metaphoric language that requires the reader to contemplate its meaning and even analyze the language for clues to the poem's theme.

5. **Does the poem contain metaphorical language? What imagery and metaphors are used both to provide information and establish mood?** Remember, a simile compares one thing to another: "The man was like

a god." In a metaphor, the subject *is* that which it is being compared to: "He was god."

6. **What role does sound play in the poem?** Sound can convey meaning and mood as much as words. Hard consonants sound harsh and strong while vowels sound soft and gentle. We read short words faster than long ones but we tend to give more space to the words in short lines. Always read a poem aloud to savor the sounds in your mouth and ear and to hear the rhythm of the language.

As Budbill has aged, his "more contemplative, reclusive, quasi-religious bent has come out." Yet, at the same time, he has found himself drawn back to the city. With increasing frequency, he travels to Manhattan and other locations where he often performs spoken poetry in collaboration with jazz musicians. "There's always been this yin-yang thing going on with me—light/dark; active/passive; city/country. It just seems that, as I get older, the two sides, my two pulls are more pronounced. I love going to New York, hanging out, riding the subway, eating in Chinese restaurants, playing jazz. I need that and I need this too," he says, waving his hand to include his snug cabin and the wilder world outside.

Budbill has been in love with jazz music since he was about twelve years old and in junior high school. While the other kids were listening to Elvis Presley, he was listening to Zoot Sims, Chet Baker, "and the other West Coast Cool players—all white players," he told Matthews in the interview in *Rivendell* magazine . "Then I discovered East Coast Hot, which was, very nearly, all Black players. Why I got obsessed with this music I don't know. But I remember very clearly sitting in my room getting stoned out of my mind listening to Gerry Mulligan's Tentet. Maybe it was the harmonies, the rhythm, the swing; I don't know what it was, but that stuff blew my mind.

"The more I listened, the more I wanted to listen. It took me away from my life. It was like traveling in outer space. I was playing trumpet at that time. My interest in jazz just grew and grew and it's never stopped growing. And even though in *Judevine* there is no obvious connection to Black American classical music, I know that that long, loping kind of prosy line that those narrative poems are written in is directly influenced by my lifetime of listening to jazz."[14]

Budbill met jazz musician William Parker in the mid-1980s after reading about him in a Canadian jazz magazine. He wrote Parker, who wrote back. Parker sent Budbill some of his recordings and Budbill sent Parker some poems. Soon, the two began working together and, in 1999, after *Moment to Moment* was published, Parker and Budbill recorded together, improvising on the poems. Since then, they've produced another CD and give live performances of a show they call *Zen Mountains—Zen Streets*. Boxholder Records brought out a double CD of a live performance of *Zen Mountains* in 1999.[15] More recently, there have been other collaborations, such as Budbill's *The Fire of Compassion: A Found Poem for Black Music*, produced with a quintet that includes Parker on bass, Hamid Drake on drums, Roy Campbell on trumpet, and Kidd Jordan on tenor saxophone.

These performances and recordings are reminiscent of the material produced by the Beat poets who often collaborated with jazz musicians. And they have something in common with the rap music movement and slam poetry of today. Budbill effectively uses repetition much the way the great black poet Langston Hughes did or the way today's black performance poets, like Jayne Cortez, do. Yet this new work also embraces the ancient poems, both Eastern and Western. Says Budbill, "Putting words with music is ancient, it's as old as Chinese poetry. All poetry was originally song. *The Book of Songs*, which is a poetry collection that Confucius put together, was meant to be sung, not recited. The concept of a white guy standing before a lectern, droning on in a monotone, now that's a really new concept."

As with almost everything else about Budbill, his CDs and performances are one of a kind. His combination of spare, rhythmic poetry, political commentary, jazz music, and Eastern instrumentalism is like nothing else, something new and old at the same time. And, while his use of public performance and published works as a way of promoting political views is part of a long tradition, it's particularly evocative of the writing of some of the earliest Vermonters, especially Thomas Rowley, the bard of the Green Mountain Boys. Budbill's online publication, the *Judevine Mountain Emailite: An Online and On-going Journal of Politics and Opinion* that he began publishing in January 1999, is also redolent of those early Vermonters who used the broadside and other quick and immediate tools to promote the values of independence and freedom.[16]

It's a comparison that Budbill welcomes: "Sure, I'm a pamphleteer. My cyberzine is the contemporary version of the broadside, the new form of political subversion. So, too is the CD. These are the new vehicles of the writer. Those Green Mountain Boys would have had great fun with them."

---

◄§ Poems by David Budbill

### What Issa Heard

Two hundred years ago Issa heard the morning birds
singing sutras to this suffering world.

I heard them too, this morning, which must mean
since we will always have a suffering world
we must also always have a song.

—From *Moment to Moment*[17]

### What It Is Like to Read the Ancients

There was a man who left the city, went away into the mountains,
built a cabin and lived in it. He said nothing and saw no one,
    except
an occasional friend who came to visit, eat a meal of stew,
    and leave.
After a while when friends arrived they could not see the man.

But they always found a pot of stew cooking on the stove, and
since they were hungry, they ate, then waited for their friend.
When he did not return, they left saying how sorry they were
that they had missed him and vowed to return to see him again.

Year after year the friends returned. Each time they found
    the stew
but not the man, and always they filled their bowls and ate.
This happened two thousand years ago on a remote
    mountainside
in China. Yet even today the man's cabin remains, not far
    from here.

Clean, well kept, the woodshed full of wood, a pot of stew
cooking on the stove. I was there just yesterday to fill my bowl.

—From *Moment to Moment* [18]

### Easy As Pie

The Emperor divides the world
into two parts:
the Good and the Evil.

If you don't want to accept that,
The Emperor says
you are Evil.

The Emperor declares himself
and his friends:
Good.

The Emperor says as soon as
Good has destroyed Evil,
all will be Good.

Simple as one, two, three.
Clear as night and day.
Different as black and white.

Easy as pie.

—From *While We've Still Got Feet* [19]

## A Little Story About an Ancient Chinese Emperor

Thousands of years ago in ancient China a boy emperor ruled for a while.
The Imperial Court had placed the child on the throne so that he could be
a mouthpiece for the Imperial Court's desires.

Coddled from birth, surrounded by servants and sycophants,
told by The Imperial Court that he was The Son of Heaven,
given to believe he had no obligation to anyone but his Imperial Court,
pampered and protected from any notion of what the real world was like,
from any idea of what The People had to put up with every day,

The Emperor stomped and swaggered through the world
telling The People what to do, taking whatever He wanted,
robbing from the poor and giving to the rich, and sending
his armies out to terrorize whomever He took a notion to despise.

The Emperor ruled for a long time and thousands of The People
died, killed by his armies and because of his abuse and neglect.
But eventually, after great suffering, The People rose up and
crushed the man who called himself The Son of Heaven.
And they crushed his Imperial Court as well.

Then some time passed in which The People lived in relative calm
until another Emperor, like the one in this story, came along.

—From *While We've Still Got Feet* [20]


## LET THE PEOPLE LIVE!
### Talk/Poem Delivered at the Peace Rally/War Protest
### in Montpelier, Vermont, 18 January 2003

Every year the world dies and comes alive again.
It makes a new year.
It renews itself over and over, again and again.

And in that circle around and around we all go and where we stop
we all know. Bending as all breaths bend toward the dead,
our flesh toward soil.

Tomorrow we are bones and ash, the roots of weeds poking
through our skulls. But Today is our life! Today we want to live!

Today we want to go for a walk under the cold sun. We want to go
skiing and snow shoeing, slidin' and tubin', and snowmachinin'.
We want to go ice fishing. We want to stand out here in the snow
and freeze our butts off so we can tell George Bush where to go.

It's not time for war. It's not time for war and killing.

It's time to come inside at the end of the day, take off
your snowy clothes and stand beside the woodstove
and drink tea and port, eat hot stew and warm bread.

It's not time for war and killing.

It's time to sit in the evening in the warm house and look at
seed catalogues and dream about spring, time to draw maps
of where the new apple trees and day lilies will go and think about
how many more blueberry plants you think you'll buy.

It's not time for war and killing.

It's time for life, it's time to make love, time to visit with friends.
It's time to play music and sing, sit down and eat, rise up and dance.
It's time for music and dancing.

It's not time for war and killing.

Presidents and Prime Ministers, Despots and Dictators,
Tyrants and Terrorists, We don't want to fight your wars.
We want to eat and love and dance.
We want to lie down and die in our own good time.

Let us die our own natural deaths, old and wizened,
crippled and suffering, but let us die our natural deaths.
Don't let us die from your bullets and bombs. Don't let us die
from your fire and poison gas. Let us die in the peace
of our own old age. Let us all grow old and die in peace.
Let us die in peace.[21]

### Questions and Exercises for Reflection and Inspiration

Discuss the sacrifices and risks Budbill has accepted in writing about the
less than attractive underbelly of rural life. How do you think you would
feel if you found your community, its residents, or its actions described in
less than glowing terms? Is there a story you would tell about your community that shows its dark side? Could you tell that story fairly or would
you be afraid to do so?

> **Exercise 1.** Try writing a poem, short story, essay, or scene from a play in
> which you explore some aspect of your community's life that people
> find embarrassing. Feel free to change names, blend characters and re-
> arrange facts to make your story a fiction. As you write, think about
> what the response to your piece would be if someone recognized the
> people upon whom you modeled your story—or if someone recog-
> nized himself. Also, as you write, think about Budbill's comments on
> truth-telling and the responsibility of the artist to expose "the agonies

of our time." How do you feel about balancing truth-telling with being kind to one's neighbors?

Another area to explore is the subject of poverty. On the one hand, we often feel sorry for people who don't have enough money to live comfortably, eat, and heat their homes. But in today's hurried life, few people do anything about the poverty all around them. These are rich subjects for any form of writing. One of the questions that's integral to this subject is, who gets to define what is poverty and what is thriftiness? Budbill himself lives on little and celebrates a life lived close to the bone, a life in which material frugalness is a virtue. Many of us have more clothes or books or other possessions than we need; yet we keep buying. Budbill takes his pleasure and happiness from his creative life and the natural world, rather than from material things. Do you share his values or consider them oversimplistic?

> **Exercise 2.** Write a poem, short story, or scene inspired by the tension between frugality and materialism. You might consider having a dialogue between two characters—husband and wife or parent and child, for example—who have different views on the value of either parsimony or materialism. You might use a holiday, such as Christmas, or a birthday or anniversary as a vehicle for exploring the subject of spending. Or, you might consider writing an essay that begins, "All I need is . . . " Your essay would list the items you couldn't live without and why. Are your wants material, spiritual, or emotional?

David Budbill feels strongly about peace and war. Who do you think is the Emperor in his poems? Is it someone living thousands of years ago or someone specific living now? When he writes, "Presidents and Prime Ministers, Despots and Dictators, Tyrants and Terrorists, we don't want to fight your wars," he is referring to leaders who are in power today but, also, because of the plural nouns, to the long line of leaders throughout time, men who have either led their people into war or approved of the fighting. Writers, and in particular Vermont writers, have used their words to oppose not only war but also the conditions that lead to war, such as inequality, poverty, and powerlessness. These writers employ allegory, metaphor, fable, and other traditional literary devices to address these issues.

These themes have consistently been the great themes of literature throughout time: Man against man, man against nature, man against himself; and their opposites, of course: man for man, man for nature, man for possibility.

> **Exercise 3.** Tell your own story that illustrates one of these big themes. It need not be a life- or planet-threatening event but, as so aptly shown by Budbill, something as simple as making a pie or learning how to ride a bicycle can symbolize something more important. In learning to

ride your bike, for example, you probably gained a degree of independence from your parents and conquered a physical skill that would help you in later years. In making a pie, we take simple ingredients, fruit and sugar and flour, and from these make something that expresses love and gives comfort. Use any format for your piece that you like—memoir, poem, short story, anecdote—to write about some simple task or challenge that represents a larger issue or demonstrates on a small level one of the "man against" themes listed above.

In Budbill's *Moment to Moment: Poems of a Mountain Recluse*, the poems' narrator is Judevine Mountain, an ancient Chinese poet who has taken the name of the mountain behind Budbill's home in Wolcott. In naming his poet after a mountain, Budbill provides himself with a "character to hide behind." He's expressing his thoughts and observations through Judevine Mountain. Like Budbill, Judevine Mountain is inscrutable and witty at once. His believability comes not from logic but from the human, innate desire for mystery, from our need to transcend physical barriers. It derives from our frustration with our weaknesses as much as it does from our willingness to do good.

**Exercise 4.** Try creating your own mythical speaker, a person through whom you can express your thoughts and observations, your hopes and fears. Give your fictional character a name and other specifics, modeling these after yourself while also providing characteristics that are not yours, such as the ability to see but not be seen or the power to bestow wishes. Write a short story or poem in which your fictional character grants a wish that you would like to be able to bestow or otherwise acts in a way that surpasses normal human capability—such as walking on water, disappearing, reading minds, turning people into frogs. Remember as you are doing so, that you are following an ancient literary tradition that includes all sorts of writing from fairy tales to science fiction. Have fun with this exercise by sending your sense of logic and possibility on vacation.

Photo by Victoria Blewer

# 3    Chris Bohjalian
*Making Fact of Fiction*

Born 12 August 1960, White Plains, New York

Education: B.A., Amherst College

Lives in Lincoln

First published work: "Sparks," a short story, published in *Cosmopolitan* magazine in 1984

Novels: *Hangman* (1991); *Past the Bleachers* (1992); *A Killing in the Real World* (1994); *Water Witches* (1995); *Midwives* (1997); *The Law of Similars* (1999); *Trans-Sister Radio* (2000); *The Buffalo Soldier* (2002); and *Before You Know Kindness* (2004)

Nonfiction: *Idyll Banter* (2003), a collection of newspaper columns and articles

Movies: *Midwives*; *Past the Bleachers*

Awards: Oprah Winfrey selection for *Midwives*, 1997; New England Book Award, 2002

IN 1986, CHRIS BOHJALIAN and his wife, the photographer Victoria Blewer, were living in Brooklyn. Bohjalian was a successful advertising executive while Blewer was pursuing a career as a trust trader. The couple sometimes talked of escaping New York and moving to New England, but they had made no move in that direction. Then, one Saturday night in March, they were "cab-napped" and taken for a terrifying joy ride. When he'd had enough fun with them, the cabbie deposited the couple in a nearly deserted section of the city populated by crack addicts. Just then, police officers stormed one of the buildings near them, yelling to Bohjalian and his wife to hit the ground. As they cowered on the sidewalk, Blewer turned to Bohjalian and suggested now was the time for their move. Bohjalian had never seen his adopted hometown of Lincoln. In fact, he'd never been to Vermont but Blewer retained fond memories from the month she'd spent at a camp near Lake Champlain. Their idea of Vermont was, as Bohjalian describes in his book *Idyll Banter*, "an image of green hills dotted with black-and-white Holsteins, an ethic of hard work that was symbolized for us by a mythic image of a barn lit before daybreak. We imagined villages in which everyone knew everyone's name and neighbors took care of one another. We imagined a place like Lincoln."[1]

Within a few months of that fateful cab ride, Bohjalian and his wife had sold their co-op, moved into an 1898 Victorian house in the heart of Lincoln, and Bohjalian began chronicling life and events in Vermont for a weekly column in the *Burlington Free Press* and in magazine articles that appeared in the *Boston Globe Sunday Magazine, Cosmopolitan,* and other publications.

But what Bohjalian really wanted to be was a novelist. And thus he began a process that he follows religiously to this day. He gets up at 5:00 A.M. and immediately goes to his office to write. Don't picture a gloomy office stuck in a corner of the house or a garret on a top floor. Bohjalian's office is a tidy, spacious room right off the main hallway. From his desk, he can look up at Mount Abraham and watch the sun rise. Later in the morning, Blewer gets Grace, the couple's young daughter, ready for school or morning activities. Meanwhile, Bohjalian writes uninterrupted, drinking only coffee, until 10:30 or so. He does research for his columns or a book in progress until about 1:00 P.M., then has lunch and goes for a bike ride or to the gym. At 3:15, Grace arrives home from school. Bohjalian generally spends the rest of the day with her while his wife works in the field or in her photography studio.

But even though his actual writing takes place during those five and a half hours of dedicated time every morning, Bohjalian says that his characters are always with him; part of his writer's brain is always at work. As he's riding his bike or working out, taking a shower or driving the car, part of Bohjalian's mind may be wondering about one of his characters: What would she be experiencing? What would he be feeling right now? He falls asleep thinking about the next day and what the characters might be up to, or at least what they'll begin doing. As Bohjalian has learned over the years, plots are best when he lets the characters tell him what they plan to do, when he sets them free to act.

Bohjalian's writing process involves a complex mix of intention and chance. The ideas for plots and characters often come from real-life experiences, quirks of happenstance or snippets of conversation that snake into his mind and, once there, coil about and transform, shedding the skin of their origins in his imagination to become complex plots far removed from the original event or conversation that inspired them. As Bohjalian explained in an interview on Nashville Public Radio a few years ago, his intention as a writer is to explore "happy families we see everyday on the street, who are suddenly thrown into crucibles that are not of their own making. How do these families circle the wagons and try and survive—and keep the bonds between parents and children (and husbands and wives) intact?"[2] Each of his books, therefore, has at its heart a contemporary problem: suspicion of alternative medicine, transsexuality, racism, and foster children. Yet, each book is about people as much as it is about issues. And, except for his first novel, *A Killing in the Real World*,[3] and his most recent book, *Before You Know Kindness*,[4] the books take place in Vermont.

This combination of the ordinary and the extraordinary, coupled with an exploration of contemporary social issues played out in the lives of likable characters, has contributed to Bohjalian's success. Because the impetus for his books comes from a real-life experience, the reader feels a familiarity with the characters and their situation right off. Because something dramatic and disturbing fuels the plot, however, and the decisions the characters make, the reader is also entertained and challenged. And, because in each book there are children who need comfort and security, we find ourselves often pulling for a happy ending despite the odds. Sometimes, we get one.

Vermont also contributes to Bohjalian's success. When Oprah Winfrey chose his novel *Midwives*[5] as one of her book of the month selections—a move that practically made Bohjalian a household name—she spoke of the novel's location as the kind of place where life is still lived on an intimate scale, where people are known to their neighbors and held responsible in a manner that has vanished from most American communities.

*Midwives* had been inspired by a simple conversation at a dinner party soon after Grace was born. Bohjalian found himself seated next to a lay midwife who began teasing Bohjalian that if she had delivered their child, rather than the birth taking place in a hospital, the birth could have occurred in their home and he could have "caught" his daughter. That phrase, "catching a baby," stuck in his head and was reinforced as he learned that this particular midwife had assisted at nearly seven hundred home births. He became fascinated with the tensions inherent in such an old profession, the way midwifery embodied the past and challenged the future. As he began to fashion his story around the pros and cons of home birth, he interviewed more than sixty-five people, including midwives, parents who had used the services of midwives, opponents of home birth, and traditional doctors. He came to see that midwifery is a profession that challenges society's inherent ideas about progress and technology.

The plot of *Midwives* revolves around the death of a mother during childbirth. And, because the book is set in Vermont, it's the weather—a freak ice storm—that sets the tragedy in motion. Early on, we learn that the midwife, Sibyl Danforth, is put on trial for manslaughter. The narrator of this story is Danforth's daughter, Connie Danforth, who was present at the ill-fated birth and tells the story of her mother's trial. The book is a page-turner because we come to care deeply about Sibyl Danforth and the other characters whose lives have been affected by this death. More profoundly, the book reveals the everlasting bond of love between mother/midwife and her child.

Because Connie's knowledge of her mother's thoughts is, quite naturally, limited, Bohjalian interjects excerpts from Sibyl's diaries throughout the text. These excerpts advance the plot while letting the accused Sibyl speak to the reader directly about her profession, her hopes and fears. Thus, the story has two narrators: Connie as the main teller of the story and Sibyl as a commentator through her diaries.

### Tips and Techniques
Chris Bohjalian's Ten Tips to Help Stretch Your Fiction

1. Don't merely write what you know. Write what you don't know. It might be more difficult at first, but—unless you've just scaled Mount Everest or married a transsexual—it will be more interesting to your readers.

2. Do some research. Read the letters John Winthrop wrote to his wife, or the letters a Vermont private sent home to his family from Antietam, or the stories the metalworkers told of their experiences on the girders high in the air when they were building the Empire State Building. Good fiction is rich with minutiae—what people wore, how they cooked, how they filled the mattresses on which they slept—and often the details you discover will help you dramatically with your narrative.

3. Interview someone who knows something about your topic. Fiction may be a solitary business when you're actually writing, but prior to sitting down with computer (or pencil or pen), it often demands getting out into the real world and learning how (for instance) an ob-gyn spends her day, what a lawyer does when he isn't in the courtroom, or exactly what it feels like to a farmer to milk a cow when he's been doing it for thirty-five years. Ask questions and listen.

4. Interview someone else. Anyone else. Ask questions that are absolutely none of your business about their childhood, their marriage, their sex life. They don't have to be interesting (though it helps.) They don't even have to be honest.

5. Read some fiction you wouldn't normally read: A translation of a Czech novel, a mystery, a book you heard someone in authority dismiss as "women's fiction" (a term so offensive that the remark alone offers sufficient justification to buy the book or check it out of the library).

6. Write for a day without quote marks. It will encourage you to see the

conversation differently, and help you to hear in your head more precisely what people are saying and thereby create dialogue that sounds more realistic. You may even decide you don't need quote marks in the finished story.

7. Skim the thesaurus, flip through the dictionary. Find new words and words you use rarely—lurch, churn, disconsolate, effulgent, intimations, sepulchral, percolate, pallid, reproach—and use them in sentences.

8. Lie. Put down on paper the most interesting lies you can imagine—and then make them plausible.

9. Write one terrific sentence. Don't worry about anything else—not where the story is going, not where it should end. Don't pressure yourself to write five hundred or a thousand words this morning. Just write ten or fifteen ones that are very, very sound.

10. Pretend you're a banker, but you write in the night to prove to some writing professor that she was wrong, wrong, wrong. Allow yourself a small dram of righteous anger.

In a later novel, *Trans-Sister Radio*, a middle-aged divorced schoolteacher named Allison Banks falls in love as her daughter Carly is about to leave home for college.[6] Allison's ex-husband Will is unexpectedly jealous about his wife's new life and love, especially after he learns that the new boyfriend, a college professor named Dana, is taking female hormones and is about to undergo a sex-change operation to become her "true self," a lesbian.

The story unfolds in a series of flashbacks told by Allison, Dana, Will, and especially Carly. Bohjalian invents a weeklong series on the National Public Radio program *All Things Considered* that Carly has produced as part of a periodic series entitled "The Nature of Love." The NPR show is the thread that connects the characters and their stories. Bohjalian became interested in the idea of the novel after a friend of his, a divorced woman, fell in love with a man who was planning to have a sex change. The friend didn't believe their love could endure the stresses of such an unusual situation and they broke up. Years later, however, Bohjalian was talking to his friend again and she revealed to him that she had never loved anyone other than her own daughter as much; she thought of her old love, whom she referred to as her "soul mate," every day. "*Trans-Sister Radio* is my answer to that wistful 'What if?' What if my friend had picked up the phone? Could their love have transcended our ingrained notions of sexual preference?" Bohjalian explains. "I'm fascinated by these ideas because sexuality is one of the ways by which we identify ourselves, how we are viewed by the world and how we view the world. What happens when love transcends these preconceived notions?"

This topic allowed Bohjalian to explore another theme that is central to his work: how far will the traditional Vermonter's tolerance for oddity and otherness go? Is there a limit to a community's tolerance when it comes to embracing or at least stomaching the eccentrics in their midst? In this case, the tension turns on the fact that it is a middle-school teacher who is spending time with someone who is undergoing a sex-change procedure. Is this just too much for a Vermont community to accept? Again, with this as a background, Bohjalian explores how the relationships between the central characters—mother and lover and daughter and ex-husband—withstand the pressures of scrutiny.

Bohjalian has been interested in whether Vermont's reputation for tolerance is real or simply untested ever since he moved here: "We talk about it and celebrate it. We have terms for it: rugged individualism, independence, and the like, and we take great pride in such facts as our state being the first to outlaw slavery or our new law granting gays the right to civil unions. What I'm fascinated with is how deep this dedication to tolerance goes and where does it break."

Midwifery, for example, is an unusual career. You don't hear too many young girls saying, "When I grow up, I'll become a midwife." Yet, it's been part of the human culture throughout history. Like anything that goes against the flow of what society ordains as routine or normal, however, midwifery is suspect and those who practice it are objects of curiosity too, simply by association. Yet in a place like Vermont, where calves are still being born on the farm and some people desire to live as close to nature as possible, there's also an inherent respect for the profession of midwifery and for those women who elect to have their babies delivered at home by a midwife. Indeed, recognition of the desire to give birth in as homey an environment as possible has led hospitals across the state (and nationwide) to create birthing rooms that feel more like bedrooms and living rooms than sterile hospital rooms. And it's not uncommon for fathers—and sometimes siblings—to attend a birth. Still, when something goes wrong in a home birth, there's apt to be more blame placed on the midwife and the parents than if the same misfortune had occurred in a hospital setting. That scrutiny can be even harsher when the individuals involved are all well known to one another and to their neighbors.

"Because I live in a small town, I'm well aware of the values of community, that small towns engender in us great comfort and great paranoia. On the one hand, there is the support they offer: Everyone knows everyone's name, and there will always be someone there for you if you're in need. You don't find many homeless people in Vermont," Bohjalian says. "It's not just the weather; I don't think people would tolerate it. They'd do something about it. Vermonters are famous for helping one another out. But, on the other hand, there is no anonymity and little privacy to living in a small town and, whatever you do, don't even think of doing something clandestine! You'll be found out and revealed in no time whatsoever."

The question of Vermonters' tolerance is also at the heart of Bohjalian's book, *The Law of Similars*, in which a rather conservative prosecutor named Leland Fowler is the beneficiary of generous support after the freak death of his wife. Later on, however, he believes his neighbors are scrutinizing his every move when he begins an affair with a liberal homeopath named Carissa Lake. That scrutiny heightens when one of Lake's clients, well known in the town, dies from an asthma attack after eating nuts recommended by Lake.[7] Again, we have a central character who follows a profession that is out of the norm—in this case a practitioner of alternative medicine—and Bohjalian's inquiry into how a small town will react when her unorthodox medical practices result in tragedy.

Bohjalian is certainly prescient in his choice of subject matter. *Trans-Sister Radio* came out just as Vermont was debating its civil union law, which allows same-sex couples to formally acknowledge their relationship and share some of the benefits and responsibilities of married couples. An earlier book, *Water Witches*, explores the collision between a ski resort's plans for expansion and environmentalists who want to save a mountainous wildlife habit and river ecosystem.[8] It was published just as two of Vermont's largest ski areas were in the midst of heated permit hearings over expansion proposals.

Central to the plot of *Water Witches* is a drought that underscores the question of who owns public waters: the ski areas whose lands abut rivers and streams or the people of Vermont. That summer, as the book was hitting the stands, Vermont was simultaneously experiencing one of the worst droughts in state history. Here, as in the other books, Bohjalian explores the themes of tolerance and the affect that change can have on a family. The narrator of *Water Witches*, Scott Winston, is a transplanted New York City lawyer who represents the ski resort. The book deals with traditional themes of literature: progress versus tradition, science versus magic. But these battles are fought out on Vermont's countryside as Winston's wife, his little girl, and his sister-in-law all hope he'll fail in his efforts on behalf of the ski developers. The women are all dowsers or water witches. Dowsers use divining rods or Y-shaped sticks to find underground water; the profession has its roots in our more primitive past. But Winston's sister-in-law's talents go far beyond helping people locate the right spot to drill a well. She can also find lost objects and people, a talent that becomes central to the book's plot. She's the odd person in the mix, the person whose talents lie beyond the ordinary, and are therefore suspect. Bohjalian could not have known about the drought beforehand, any more than he could have predicted that Vermont's Supreme Court would rule that homosexual couples had the right to the same privileges as heterosexual couples. But as a newspaper columnist and an avid news hound, he knew that both subjects—gender identification and ski development—were on many Vermonters' minds.

Because Bohjalian has some journalistic background, his books show the depth of his research. For *Trans-Sister Radio*, for example, he interviewed dozens of people in the transgendered community, including people who had chosen male-to-female sexual reassignment. He also interviewed some of the leading surgeons who conduct sex-change operations in Trinidad,

Colorado, and Pittsburgh, Pennsylvania. He urges developing writers to do research when they are writing about subjects about which others will know more than they. Nothing destroys a book's credibility more than a factual error. Yet, even though he had many notebooks and tapes from his interviews, he wrote the book pretty much without the aid of this material. It allowed him to write about his subject with confidence and authority. Unlike the journalist, he's not transcribing notes or using them to fuel the novel but rather to ensure that he understood the motivations and emotions of his fictional characters.

A freak flood in Bohjalian's hometown of Lincoln provided the impetus for another novel, *The Buffalo Soldier*, in which he explores the topical issues of racism and the care of foster children.[9] *The Buffalo Soldier* tells the story of Terry and Laura Sheldon, parents of twin daughters who die in a Vermont flood when a river overflows its banks and sweeps the girls away. A flood of that magnitude had occurred in Bohjalian's adopted hometown of Lincoln in 1998. The water had crested twice during the night, washing out bridges and making car travel impossible. Fortunately, there were no fatalities.

Bohjalian spent the days after the flood bicycling from one spot in town to another looking at the damage and checking on people. He watched fellow residents rescue the books that had been stored in the town library's basement by forming a human chain to remove the books from the encroaching mud. As he surveyed the damage, he also began formulating the idea for a novel in his mind, again growing out of a series of what-if questions: What would have happened had the water crested at another time, when people were on the bridges? What if children had died in a freak act of nature? How would the parents go on with their lives? And, more crucial to this particular novel, he pondered whether men and women mourn differently.

Again, we have a plot that involves a sudden change and its impact on a family, the central theme of his books. And, again, he invents Vermont characters as vehicles for exploring these questions. For Bohjalian, the question is not how generic people will respond to crises but how will the people he knows and loves respond. Their reactions are important to him because he knows that Vermonters are not so numbed by the harshness of city living or the dulling anonymity of suburban life as their counterparts living elsewhere. He believes Vermonters are engaged in life in a way that characterized life in general around the planet not that long ago, when people still believed they could individually make a difference, help a neighbor, change laws, or be disgraced by their actions.

Bohjalian says the success of a story often relies upon his ability to find the voice of the narrator(s). By this, he means that it is his job as author to find and maintain the voice of a particular character. Voice in literature doesn't mean just the way a person talks—his or her particular language, nuances and metaphors—but also words that reflect the singular history of a character, the subtle and the obvious ways in which life has formed his or her responses, and made the fictional character whole and believable. Some of his novels have a main narrator through whom the story is told while others have what's called *revolving narrators*. In the latter, several characters tell the story from their particular viewpoints and frames of reference; the story revolves through their voices. Finding out who is the right person to tell the story, therefore, is an essential part of the author's job.

In *Midwives*, for example, once Bohjalian realized that it was the midwife's daughter who had to tell the story, the writing came easier and he could see the whole story. The idea of giving Sibyl voice through her diaries satisfied his frustration with needing a way to allow her to tell parts of her own story that her daughter couldn't know or appreciate. With *Trans-Sister Radio*, he wanted each of the main people in the book—Allison Banks, her daughter, her lover, and ex-husband—to tell the story from his or her point of view. That book is therefore told in the voices of the characters using the technique of revolving narration.

Sometimes, Bohjalian struggles through several versions of a story, writing and rewriting it, as he strives to find the right voice for the book. That was particularly true with his novel *The Buffalo Soldier*, the story of the Sheldons and their life after the death of their twin daughters. It wasn't until a young black boy named Alfred, a foster child, showed up on about page eighty that the book came alive. As it turned out, Alfred became central to this story and it is through him that the characters are redeemed. Again, it was Bohjalian's response to a passing event in his personal life that triggered the inclusion of a black child in the novel. Bohjalian was deep into writing the novel but not satisfied with its story line when his daughter Grace arrived home from school one afternoon with a class photo. There among the faces of sixteen children in her class were blonds and brunettes, even a redhead, but no one with brown or black skin. Bohjalian had grown up in New York and Miami, both racially diverse places. Here, his daughter was growing up in racial homogeneity. He asked his daughter if there were any children of color in the school, thinking there might be a black or Asian child in another class. The answer was no. (A year later, however, an African American family moved into town.) Again, Bohjalian began to ask questions: What would happen if this fictional family of his, one that has lost its two daughters, had the opportunity to nurture a child and that child turned out to be black? Would it make a difference? How would that boy fit into his rural Vermont community? Could he find a home with Laura and Terry Sheldon?

Another moment of serendipity brought added depth to *The Buffalo Soldier*. One afternoon while he was writing the book, Bohjalian and his wife took a drive up north and, on their way home, stopped to view permanent artwork erected on Vermont's I-91 highway. While there, Blewer used the restroom. When she returned to the car, she said, "I just saw the saddest thing, a pregnancy test kit in the restroom." "Why's that so sad?" Bohjalian asked. Blewer quickly explained that no one looking forward to a pregnancy would resort to administering a test in an anonymous highway bathroom. "Her remarks became central to the novel," explains Bohjalian. "With that in the back of my mind, Terry's affair, which had already occurred, suddenly resulted in the woman, Phoebe, becoming pregnant. I had no idea that was going to happen or what they would do about it. Just like the reader, I had to wait to find out. That's what makes writing so much fun for me—the discovery of what my characters are going to do."

His most recent book, *Before You Know Kindness*, takes on another hot-button subject: animal rights.[10] In this one, two brothers-in-law are opposites in the philosophical argument over animal rights. One, a Vermonter, has become an avid hunter and longs to shoot his first deer; the other, a Manhattan lawyer, is a vegetarian and zealous advocate for animal rights. Both men have daughters about the same age. The controversy comes home to this family when one of the daughters gets her hand on a gun and uses it. The results threaten to tear this family apart but, at its core, the book, like so many of Bohjalian's tales, remains a celebration of the human instinct for love and inclusion, for forgiveness and redemption.

Bohjalian calls his books "fictional memoirs" in which the characters chronicle their lives before and after the life-changing moment that is central to each tale. *The Buffalo Soldier*, for example, began that way. Bohjalian initially wrote each chapter in the first person to gain insight into how each of the characters would see the events of the novel from his or her particular vantage point. He then rewrote the chapters in the objective, third-person voice. This process required many drafts, each of which allowed him to understand his characters and their interactions more fully. Working diligently through version after version, he was able to discover each character's individual pattern of language, thoughts, and motivations. It's a process he's used, with some variation, in constructing most of his novels.

"I rewrite constantly. My books always take at least a half-dozen drafts. I can fall in love with my characters—Sibyl Danforth was the first character I fell for but I am also very fond of Dana in *Trans-Sister Radio*. Despite this, I can't say I'm ever in love with the finished product. I can't reread my books, never have. I'll pick a few sections to read at a book signing but I don't dare go near other sections. I'm afraid I'll see sentences that will totally appall me, and I'll find dialogue that will ring false when I hear it in my head. Once a book is in print, it's too late for re-writing. That's why I am so fastidious about working on the drafts and trying to get everything right. Still, I must say that I do not find the work agonizing. It's fun. I enjoy writing very much."

Bohjalian is the first to concede that he's a bit of a control freak when it comes to his writing habits. First there are the hours he keeps, religiously. Even when he's on the road and staying in hotel rooms or has been up late, he keeps to his morning schedule of getting up early and writing. He's fastidious also about fact-checking, both going over a novel or article himself to check every date, spellings, and factual descriptions, and also calling on experts to review his work for errors.

That fastidiousness made it hard at first for him to allow his characters lives of their own. To compensate, he devised a couple of techniques that gave him some control over his material while allowing the characters to work out the details of the plot. To help him avoid mistakes of timing, for example, he creates calendars for his characters, charting their actions as the plot evolves, revising the calendars as the characters surprise him or new characters enter the scene, often going back in fictional time to set up the background for an event or to gently introduce a new character into the narrative. And he creates maps of his towns and charts his characters' movements through them so that the characters are in the right place at the right time. For *Water Witches*, he created an intricate map of ski trails at his fictional ski area so he could chart Scott Winston's hikes with his daughter and choreograph geographically the event that changes Winston's views on environmental protection, the turning point in the novel. He has made rough sketches and road maps for his fictional town of Bartlett, which appears in *The Law of Similars* and *Trans-Sister Radio*. Bohjalian says Bartlett is similar to Lincoln with dollops of neighboring towns of Bristol and Plainfield thrown in. He plays with his reality, creating a fiction by alternating what he knows with the made-up, because he doesn't want to be dependent on real geography. For other books, he's actually created architectural renderings of his character's houses so that he can see where they are as they move through the pages.

While Vermont and its residents are central to Bohjalian's novels, he also recognizes the state's place in the wider world. Change and conflict happen more slowly here and in smaller doses, but Bohjalian believes that the state is a microcosm for cultural conflicts occurring everywhere. His books illustrate this—environment versus development, alternative versus traditional medicine, and the conflicting views on gender—yet they do so on a smaller, more manageable scale, a more idealized one.

He's explored similar themes in "Idyll Banter," the *Burlington Free Press* column he has written since moving to Vermont. During that time, he's seen dairy farming plummet, downtowns suffer from the influx of malls, and drugs make their ways into cities and hamlets. Yet, he has also seen the good deeds of neighbors, the generosity of Vermonters, the beauties of undefiled nature, the stubborn independence of people living far off the beaten track, and a continuously strong support system among the state's residents who continue to fight for the ideals upon which Vermont was founded: human rights, education, health, and an appreciation of nature and wildlife. In *Idyll Banter*, a collection of columns, he tries "to find in our hardscrabble soil the stories (comic and poignant and surprising and sad) that bring these changes to life." He writes, "My sense is that Lincoln shares certain universalities with small towns in (for example) Nebraska, New Mexico, and parts of New York: a powerful feeling of kinship; a tolerance for human eccentricity that is often unappreciated; and a glorification of neighborliness for the simple reason that it is easier to be civil than ornery when on any given day you're likely to run into someone at the library, the post office, or while watching the annual outhouse races—faux outhouses on wheels, a single person inside—that precede the local parade on the Fourth of July. Besides, we need each other."[11]

Bohjalian's work has been well received. He won the New England Book Award in 2002. His novel *Midwives* was a number-one *New York Times* best seller, a selection of Oprah Winfrey's Book Club, a *Publishers Weekly* "Best Book," and a New England Booksellers Association "Discovery Pick." As of 2003, his work had been translated into seventeen languages, published in twenty countries, and twice become acclaimed movies (*Midwives* and *Past the Bleachers*). *Trans-Sister Radio* and *The Buffalo Soldier* are in development for movies, as well.

For Bohjalian, Vermont is at the heart of this success. "I'm never leaving. I love the Vermont environment. I love writing about Vermont because it is a state in transition. I find that very, very interesting, because it's in conflict and conflict is essential to any good tale. On one hand, it's a state with tradition, a state that represents independence; yet it's undergoing tremendous change. It used to be two hundred and fifty independent communities and, to some extent, there's still a resistance here to joining, to being part of the pack. I like that. Yet, there are forces at work that threaten that independence. It's interesting to be part of that resistance and to record it. I also like the fact that only about forty-seven percent of Vermont roads are paved. That has contributed to its tremendous independence. People here fend for themselves. And yet, because of the tremendous jump in population in the last half of the twentieth century, people like me and my wife have come to Vermont, bringing with us an urban sensibility that, whether or not we like to admit it, has resulted in change.

"I love Vermonters who have been here all their lives, who have tolerated people like me and taken us under their wings. People who taught me how to stack wood, build a hearth. Yet, there's no question that we are very different from the people who lived here fifty years ago. It's interesting who has moved here—writers, artists in general, people with an appreciation for life lived on a smaller, saner scale, an appreciation of Vermont values and nature. I like to think we're the right people to move to Vermont. And, as I say these things, I amend my words. There's no escaping the fact that we have brought change to the state, change that's created much tension and conflict. Of course, that's precisely why Vermont is such a great subject for fiction and why I find Vermont inordinately fascinating."

His most frequently quoted advice to writers is one you'll read over and over in this book: "Read lots and write often. And, truly, savor the process of writing. I had amassed over two hundred and fifty rejections before I sold my first short story (to *Cosmopolitan*) when I was twenty-four, so it's important to enjoy those moments when you are, literally, crafting sentences."

Throughout the long summer before my mother's trial began, and then during those crisp days in the fall when her life was paraded publicly before the county—her character lynched, her wisdom impugned—I overheard much more than my parents realized, and I understood more than they would have liked.

Through the register in the floor of my bedroom I could listen to the discussions my parents would have with my mother's attorney in the den late at night, after the adults had assumed I'd been sleeping for hours. If the three of them happened to be in the suite off the kitchen my mother used as her office and examining room, perhaps searching for an old document in her records or a patient's prenatal history, I would lie on the bathroom floor above them and listen as their words traveled up to me through the holes that had been cut for the water pipes to the sink. And while I never went so far as to lift the receiver of an upstairs telephone when I heard my mother speaking on the kitchen extension, often I stepped silently down the stairs until I could hear every word that she said. I must have listened to dozens of phone conversations this way—standing completely still on the bottom step, invisible from the kitchen because the phone cord stretched barely six feet—and by the time the trial began, I believe I could have reconstructed almost exactly what the lawyer, friend, or midwife was saying at the other end of the line.

I was always an avid parent watcher, but in those months surrounding the trial I became especially fanatic. I monitored their fights, and noted how the arguments grew nasty fast under pressure; I listened to them apologize, one of them often sobbing, and then I'd wait for the more muffled (but still decipherable) sounds they would make when they would climb into bed and make love. I caught the gist of their debates with doctors and lawyers, I understood why some witnesses would be more damning than others, I learned to hate people I'd never met and whose faces I'd never seen. The state's medical examiner. The state's attorney. An apparently expert midwife from Washington, D.C.

The morning the judge gave the jury its instructions and sent them away to decide my mother's fate, I overheard her attorney explain to my parents what he said was one of the great myths in litigation: You can tell what a jury has decided the moment they reenter the courtroom after their deliberations, by the way they look at the defendant. Or refuse to look at him. But don't believe it, he told them. It's just a myth.

I was fourteen years old that fall, however, and it sounded like more than a myth to me. It had that ring of truth to it that I heard in many wives'—and midwives'—tales, a core of common sense hardened firm by centuries of observation. Babies come when the moon is full. If the boiled potatoes burn, it'll rain before dark. A bushy caterpillar's a sign of a cold winter. Don't ever sugar till the river runs free.

My mother's attorney may not have believed the myth that he shared with my parents, but I sure did. It made sense to me. I had heard much over the past six months. I'd learned well which myths to take to my heart and which ones to discard.

And so when the jury filed into the courtroom, an apostolic procession of twelve, I studied their eyes. I watched to see whether they would look at my mother or whether they would look away. Sitting beside my father in the first row, sitting directly behind my mother and her attorney as I had every day for two weeks, I began to pray to myself, *Please don't look at your shoes, please don't look at the judge. Don't look down or up or out the window. Please, please, look at me, look at my mother. Look at us, look here, look here, look here.*

I'd watched the jurors for days, I'd seen them watch me. I'd counted beards, I'd noted wrinkles, I'd stared beyond reason and courtesy at the way the fellow who would become the foreman had sat with his arms folded across his chest, hiding the hand disfigured years earlier by a chain saw. He had a thumb but no fingers.

They walked in from the room adjacent to their twelve chairs and found their seats. Some of the women crossed their legs at their knees, one of the men rubbed his eyes and rocked his chair back for a brief second on its rear legs. Some scanned the far wall of the courtroom, some looked toward the exit sign above the front door as if they realized their ordeal was almost over and emancipation was at hand.

One, the elderly woman with white hair and a closet full of absolutely beautiful red flowered dresses, the woman who I was sure was a Lipponcott from Craftsbury, looked toward the table behind which the state's attorney and his deputy were sitting.

And that's when I broke down. I tried not to, but I could feel my eyes fill with tears, I could feel my shoulders beginning to quiver. I blinked, but a fourteen-year-old girl's eyelids are no match for the lament I had welling inside me. My cries were quiet at first, the sound of a mournful whisper, but they gathered fury fast. I have been told that I howled.

And while I am not proud of whatever hysteria I succumbed to that day in the courtroom, I am not ashamed of it either. If anyone should feel shame for whatever occurred that moment in a small courthouse in northeastern Vermont, in my mind it is the jury: Amidst my sobs and wails, people have said that I pleaded aloud, "Look at us! Oh, God, please, please look at us!" and still not one of the jurors would even glance in my mother's or my direction.

## Questions and Exercises for Reflection and Inspiration

After Charlotte Bedford dies during a long and arduous labor, midwife Sibyl Danforth is brought to trial for her death. *Midwives* is told in the voice of Connie Danforth, Sibyl's daughter who was fourteen at the time of the tragedy. As you've just read, the first chapter opens with Connie, now an adult, reflecting back on the months leading up to the trial and quickly summarizing the last moments of the trial.

Bohjalian says he often constructs his novels from fictional memoirs in which he allows a character to tell the story in the first person. A memoir is not a biography or autobiography, which is the complete story of a person's life from birth to adulthood, usually told when a person is dead or quite elderly. In contrast, a memoir is a narrative of any length that tells the story of a person (or fictional character) during a specific period of time, usually a time when something momentous has happened. In this case, the fictional memoir centers on the events leading up to and immediately following Charlotte Bedforth's labor and death.

One of the challenges of memoir writing—whether it's a fictional character's memoir or a real person's—is that the narrator is relating events as she recalls them rather than as they happen. Yet, despite these inherent limitations with the form, we learn a tremendous amount about the characters in this short excerpt. Remembering what we learned about creating character from the Howard Frank Mosher chapter—that character is created through a combination of description, dialogue, action, thought, and reaction—consider what you know about Connie by the end of the chapter. How would you characterize Connie's personality, moral fiber, and disposition? Is she intelligent, curious, passive, realistic? What tools does Bohjalian use to create her character? Did you learn anything about her parents and their personalities and values? What do you know about some of the jurors from this brief excerpt?

> **Exercise 1:** Write a fictional memoir of a character—either a stand-alone piece or the first chapter or section of a longer piece—that centers around an event that is life-changing. Life-changing events are often the death of a loved one, a disease or illness, a move, a change of jobs, financial problems, and events outside one's personal realm that affect one's life such as war, natural disasters, and manmade disasters. But life-changing events can also be small things: a decision to take a class or change majors, a decision to walk a different way home or to work, a chance meeting, receipt of a letter, discovering a family secret. Write a fictional or real memoir centering on one

of these events told in the first person. The voice may be your own or that of another person, fictional or real. Remember the lessons on creating character and strive to include description, dialogue, action, thought, and reaction in your memoir.

**Exercise 2:** Bohjalian uses various techniques to give him control over and provide internal accuracy in his writing. Draw a picture of a real setting (your childhood house, bedroom, or secret hiding place, for example) or fictional setting (a town, building, or forest). Be as specific as you can be in your drawing, including physical details, such as furniture, photos, or artwork on the walls and books on the shelves, or street names, architectural particulars, specific plants and animals you might encounter, and other fine points. Write a real or fictional scene that benefits from the specifics you have detailed, remembering, of course, that your memoir needs action—an important, life-changing event—if it is to be interesting. Use your physical details to help the reader see and feel the environment where this event takes place.

**Exercise 3:** Another tool Bohjalian uses is to create a calendar in which he charts his character's or characters' actions. Using a calendar for one month, write an action for one or more of your fictional characters on each of several dates. Then use these to construct a plot or part of a plot. This exercise works with both real and fictional stories.

Photo by Dianne Foulds

# 4  Joseph A. Citro
## *Vermont's Bard of the Bizarre*

Born in Rutland, 5 January 1948; grew up in Chester

Lives in Burlington

First publication: *Vermont Lifer*, a parody of *Vermont Life* magazine (1986)

Novels: *Shadow Child* (1987); *Guardian Angels* (1988); *The Gore* (1990);
  *Lake Monsters* (2001), originally published as *Dark Twilight*, (1991);
  *Deus-X: The Reality Conspiracy* (2003).

Collections of lore: *Green Mountain Ghosts, Ghouls, and Unsolved Myster-
  ies* (1994); *Passing Strange* (1996); *Green Mountains, Dark Tales* (1999);
  *The Vermont Ghost Guide* (2000); *Curious New England* (2003);
  *Cursed in New England: Stories of Damned Yankees* (2004)

"Living in Vermont is like living in a storybook filled with hundreds and
  hundreds of wonderful stories ... I'm a conservationist; some of
  these stories will vanish if we don't record them."

VERMONT'S OWN KING OF THE Gothic genre, Joseph Citro,
loves his home state not just because of its deep woods and pictur-
esque pastures but also because of its great store of myth and legend.
Whether writing about the Lake Champlain monster that Vermonters affectionately call Champ or exploring the ancient stone chambers found
around Vermont whose origins still confound scientists, Citro considers
Vermont a storehouse of untold stories. And he's taken on the job of
recording the state's more mysterious history.

"I can't tie it to any one thing, but maybe it's not essential to understand
why I was drawn to this sort of thing," he says of his interest in the obscure,

the inexplicable and macabre, and his lifelong hobby of collecting weird and unusual stories about Vermont. Those collected tales have been translated into twelve books, which include five novels of suspense, three volumes of historical oddities, a collection of regional humor, two travel guides, and a coedited book of essays about Vermont and New England. Of these, perhaps the most popular has been his best-selling book, *Green Mountain Ghosts, Ghouls, and Unsolved Mysteries*, the most comprehensive collection of offbeat Vermont lore ever assembled. Its popularity can be judged by the fact that it has gone through ten printings.[1]

Citro's novels—three of which have been optioned for motion pictures—present a dark and mystical side of the Vermont experience. They include *Shadow Child, Guardian Angels, The Gore, Lake Monsters,* and *Deus-X*. He's also a popular lecturer; his commentaries have been heard on Vermont Public Radio and he's appeared frequently on television, in Vermont and nationally. He says he's lucky to have been born in Vermont, where there's a rich heritage of storytelling and of unsolved mysteries. Few people, he notes, have been able to pursue as a career the subjects that fascinated them as a child. But Citro has. He says, "Vermont is full of stories—ghosts and monsters and things that go bump in the night—I've been lucky enough to have plumbed this resource for decades now."

Like many writers, Citro mines his childhood memories for stories and characters that resonate with readers, simply because they call up our own experiences as children—our own fears and questions, along with the human's love of a good scare. An early novel grew out of an experience Citro had as a boy, growing up in Chester. The town had a resident hermit who lived in the deep woods and occasionally walked into town for supplies; no one knew much about the man. When the hermit died, Citro and a buddy dared each other to search out the local hermit's cabin. The cabin wasn't difficult to find, but the riddles they encountered inside proved more incomprehensible, at least to a child: Why would someone save dozens of empty tobacco cans and stack them in a pyramid? Did the hermit think of the pretty girl standing in a windswept skirt on the front of an outdated calendar tacked to the cabin wall as a friend or a lover? Why were there women's dresses in the hermit's closet? Years later, these details from the hermit's cabin, along with the sensory imagery and physical details of that recluse's shack (especially the potpourri of scents he encountered—old man, wet dog, kerosene, wood stove, tobacco) graced the pages of his first novel, *Shadow Child*.[2]

Citro named his hermit Perly Greer, or Pearly Gates, as the natives in Citro's fictional town of Antrim called the recluse who meets a gruesome end in *Shadow Child*. The physical details come from Citro's memory; the rest comes from his imagination. Imagination is, of course, important to any writer—and vital to those who, like Citro, create stories beyond normal experience.

Citro's father was an old Yankee storyteller who worked as a machinist in Springfield. He was the major influence in Citro's early life, filling his imagination with tales of the old people who once lived in Vermont, stories of animals and plants and their properties, stories about haunted houses, deer cavorting drunk on fermented apples, specters that moved through trees, trees that parted before supernatural beings. Citro's mother, an avid reader of mysteries and novels, encouraged young Citro to read. Together, the parents created an environment in which a vivid imagination might grow. What fascinated Citro most was when he couldn't tell what was real and what was imagined. That dichotomy fascinates him still.

At the same time, Citro was busy collecting stories from other sources, although he didn't know it yet. He says, "I enjoyed talking to old people and picked up a lot of stories along the way. I can't remember ever consciously deciding to do this. I think I just grew up with this pride of place, this sense of Vermont and wanting to know more about it." Then, into the mix, in about grade five or six, came his "taste for the bizarre." Like other boys that age, he was fascinated with tales of the dark side and, so, into the storehouse of his mind, already crammed with Vermontiana and the Hardy boys, went Mary Shelley's *Frankenstein*, tales of Dracula, and the horror books of H. P. Lovecraft.

Even the Catholic Church played a role in his developing interest in the supernatural. "Being exposed to Catholicism at an early age programmed me and made me vulnerable to the idea of a 'supernature,'" he told Matt G. Paradise for *Not Like Most*.[3] "That notion remained part of my makeup long after conventional religion ceased making sense. The supernatural became a theme in what I wrote, from my first novel in 1987 until now." The Catholic Church also whetted his appetite to know more. When he questioned the nuns in school about mysteries Catholics must accept as articles of faith, he got in trouble. But it was just his innate curiosity at work; being denied answers and explanations for the unexplainable only made him ask more questions.

Citro started writing stories as a young boy, borrowing first from those he'd heard or read, then trying to write his own. He reads across the literary genres, not just the occult, horror, and the like. Over the years, he worked myriad jobs from landscape laborer to state bureaucrat. But, in 1987, when he published his first novel, he gave up his day job. He's reluctant to discuss his formal education, preferring to attribute his education as a writer to on-the-job training.

It's déclassé in certain suspense writers' circles to admit that one was influenced by H. P. Lovecraft, the writer whose mystery stories often took place in rural New England, including several located in Vermont. But Citro, true to his no-apologies nature, is not embarrassed to admit the influence. He still remembers the first Lovecraft story he read, "The Dunwich Horror," when he was in the sixth grade. Citro is proud that a story of his was included in *Lovecraft's Legacy*, a book honoring Lovecraft and the horror story genre.[4] In a footnote to his selection in *Lovecraft's Legacy*, Citro calls Lovecraft "my first writing teacher." He adds, "I owe a considerable debt to Lovecraft for my awareness of setting and atmosphere. Although I am a lifelong New Englander, it took Lovecraft to show me what was directly under my feet: that searchers after horror need not haunt strange, far places." Citro's story in the collection explores "what might grow unchecked behind the locked doors of some remote, forgotten country mansion in what Lovecraft called 'the wild doomed hills of Vermont,' the hills right behind my home."

It's not so much gore and mayhem that he's attracted to but more the myths that are repeated generation after generation, unexplained and unusual phenomena, odd behavior, disappearances, oddballs, and odd groups. In this way, he's a historian, recording for posterity the stories told in the dark around the campfire, the myths of villages and hamlets, odd facts and odder occurrences. He's always researching; like a detective, he follows tips and digs deep into archives, old diaries, newspapers, deeds, and histories. He gets to interview people who believe they've seen UFOs or whose cows have mysteriously died in the middle of the night. He wishes he had kept a journal back in the days when the old folks told him their tales but people are always willing to tell him more. "Did you hear the one about . . ." and off they go.

### Tips and Techniques

Environment is an important element in creating a story. Environment is best created using specific telling details. Naming a place is good; it gives it physicality. But a name—even a great one—is not enough. Employ descriptions that distinguish the place you're writing about from all others: describe the shape and color of the rocks, the specific plants and birds that live there, the weather, the shape of the land, the construction of the buildings, the furnishings in a room. Remember to use as many senses as possible: the smell of the nursing home versus the smell of the coffeeshop; the smell of a suburb versus the smell in an urban neighborhood. Sensory information causes the reader to reach back into her own sensory recollections; it ratchets up the reader's interest in the story.

Remember to include sound in your environment, as well. Music establishes time, class, and attitude. Sirens and horns denote a busy city but they also create a tone of stress. On the other hand, birdsong or rustling branches can connote peacefulness. Pay close attention to the noises in your environment so you can describe them artfully in your writing.

Remember too that environment is also atmosphere or mood. You can establish a scary mood by describing a dark wood in foreboding terms. Rather than writing, "It was a scary night," you can write something like, "The limbs of the bare trees towered over the child and rubbed together in the wind, sounding like old bony knees knocking in the darkness." Notice how the second example is constructed of simple sensory details that are easy to picture and evocative of experiences that most people share.

Think about the sound of the words as you write your descriptions. Vowels and long words can sound languorous and soothing, lazy or slow while quick words with lots of consonants can sound harsh or hurried, jarring or disruptive. All this detail, of course, doesn't occur in a first draft. It happens in revision when careful attention is paid to each word.

And remember to let the verbs in your sentences do the heavy lifting. They're the most important word in the sentence.

Citro has never seen a ghost. Nor has he encountered any of the other strange creatures that appear in his stories and are said to inhabit the lakes and valleys and forests of Vermont. He's never seen a UFO or been abducted. It's his imagination that allows him first to see the possibility in the stories he's told or created and then to re-create them on the page. Citro describes his writing process thus: "I don't know exactly how I do it but I know that setting is essential to the writing I do. Creating setting and environment is inbred in me from growing up in Vermont where I spent a lot of time outdoors alone or with a single friend, interacting with nature. If I'd grown up in the city and with lots of people interacting in my environment, my inclination would be toward characterization; but instead I grew up outdoors and in rambling old farmhouses. So I'm able to re-create these settings and explore what goes on in them. I know these places well. I'm trying to capture a uniquely Vermont landscape; it's been what's motivated me.

"If I'm working on a novel, all I do initially is compile information about my characters and what happens to them. The first draft is extremely labor-intensive; it requires a great deal of discipline and concentration. I write every day, from 9 to 12 noon, until the first draft is done. I usually do something else with the rest of the day. People don't realize how much business there is in the writing life.

"When I first started writing novels, I gave myself a quota of three pages a day, come hell or high water, until I finished a book. Now, writing is so much a part of my life that I have to write every day. When I'm revising, I put in very, very long hours at the keyboard. I love to revise. That's where the real pleasure kicks in, in my experience. I'm sort of terrified until I have a beginning, middle, and an end. I operate without an outline. I'm as much at sea as the reader. I'm always afraid I won't find the elegantly revealed ending. Sometimes, it takes endless revisions until I get it. Writing teachers talk about writing as finding one's voice; I think part of finding one's voice is finding a method that allows one to get words on the paper. For me, the struggle is in the first draft and then the fun, the play, begins.

"In the revision, I'm experiencing the book as I'm writing it. When it's working really well, I'm in an altered state. I'm sort of externalizing the dream experience. Some of the initial suspense is created in the first draft, but it becomes the task of the second, third, and fourth drafts to make it as suspenseful and real as possible. I've learned to trust my subconscious mind and let it deliver up twists and turns as I go along. It's the two things working together. As I revise, I'm backfilling with information and scenes that help support the drama. But my subconscious provides me with much of the material, rather than my conscious mind."

In his novels, Citro employs all the techniques available to mystery writers: foreshadowing, suspense, drama, and convincing narrative. *Deux-X: The Reality Conspiracy* blends typically electrifying elements of occult fiction with nightmarish contemporary themes.[5] The story begins with two seemingly unrelated events: a political prisoner is executed at a remote California government facility while, in Vermont, an elderly farmer vanishes, the victim of an out-of-this-world abduction. It takes three amateur and unlikely investigators, each with his own area of expertise to unravel the mystery. Together, a psychologist, a physicist, and a priest figure out the links between the two events as they encounter UFOs and bizarre religious phenomena. Like so many science fiction and horror novels, *Deux-X* explores the questions of good and evil, man against technology, and man against man.

In *Shadow Child*, the protagonist, Eric Nolan, returns to his grandparents' farm in rural Vermont to heal himself after a string of deaths and his brother's disappearance. There's no succor awaiting him here, however, as Nolan discovers that something terrible is lurking out there in the woods just out of reach of the farmhouse's lights.

Citro again explores the theme of horror waiting in a place once considered sanctuary in his novel, *The Gore*.[6] The title is a great play on words: "gore" refers simultaneously to bloody mayhem and to a parcel of unincorporated land left over when towns were laid out. Often these gores were considered too remote or uninhabitable because of the lay of the land. This time, it's an ex-journalist named Roger Newton who seeks a quiet retreat in Vermont; he picks the Northeast Kingdom, expecting that Vermont's most remote corner will provide the greatest amount of comfort. Instead, he encounters age-old secrets that threaten not just his life but the very peace of Vermont.

Even *Lake Monsters*, the novel that explores the myth of Vermont's Loch Ness Monster, discloses a dark and disturbing presence in the seemingly tranquil Vermont town where Harrison Allen takes up residence after he's downsized from his job and dumped by his girlfriend.[7] If he's looking for a fresh start, Allen gets more than he bargained for: an onslaught of malevolent forces. For Vermont fans of gothic tales and dark mysteries, there's nothing quite so much fun as reading a story that takes place in an environment you're familiar with.

After he had written several suspense novels, Citro realized that he also had accumulated a fascinating collection of stories about Vermont history—not the history you normally encounter in a textbook but the history of unsolved mysteries, of myths and hauntings. "Living in Vermont is like living in a storybook, filled with hundreds and hundreds of wonderful stories," he says. "When I was writing my novels, I did a lot of research to find facts for them and I began to collect all these wonderful stories. Then, I took a detour from writing novels into sharing some of the stories I'd collected. Now, it's something of a mission for me. I realized no one has done that in the entire history of Vermont. I realized I had a niche. I'm a conservationist, these stories will vanish if we don't record them." In writing his essays and stories about strange phenomena and unsolved mysteries in and around Vermont, Citro combines the tools of the journalist with the tools of the storyteller. Like a good journalist, whenever possible, he uses a person's own words, avoiding speculation as to the validity of their report. For Citro, if a person believes he saw a ghost, that's what he reports. He's heard enough spooky stories to believe that some of them are true; it's not up to him to judge the veracity.

Among the unusual stories he's researched, the tale of the Eddy brothers remains his favorite. Citro has written about their lives and the goings-on in their ramshackle house in Chittenden, a mountainous hamlet near Rutland, in several of his collected tales. The Eddy brothers were a national phenomenon in their time, shortly after the Civil War. To fully understand the fascination with the Eddy brothers, it's important to note that many Americans at this time were fairly obsessed with supernatural phenomena and spiritualism, the belief that human personality survives death and that people can commune with the dead. Beginning in about 1848 (with the Fox sisters of upstate New York, who claimed the dead communicated with them by rapping on the table; the "raps" were actually the sisters cracking their toe joints), people held séance parties at which they supposedly communed with the dead. Among the most confounding of the practitioners were the Eddy brothers, described throughout the literature as backwoods Vermonters with little social grace but the ability to stun skeptics with a full array of apparitions, noises, and other paranormal phenomenon that occurred in their rough Vermont farmhouse.

In *Green Mountain Ghosts, Ghouls, and Unsolved Mysteries,* Citro relates how the *New York Daily Graphic* sent a highly regarded reporter named Henry Olcott to Chittenden to investigate the reports that, in the presence of William and Horatio Eddy, material objects moved, and richly clothed apparitions (sometimes several at a time) appeared and talked, walking through one another and addressing people in the room.[8] Olcott spent many months with the Eddy brothers but was never able to figure out how these poor, humble men could have pulled off a charade of such detail. Here's an excerpt from the tale, taken from *Green Mountain Ghosts, Ghouls and Unsolved Mysteries.*

---

≥§ FROM *"Chittenden's Ghost Shop"*

It was a case of nineteenth-century ghostbusting. The year: 1874. The investigator: Henry Steel Olcott, on assignment from the *New York Daily Graphic*. The target: highly peculiar goings-on at a remote Vermont farmhouse in the tiny mountain town of Chittenden.

The house was a shunned place. Some locals called it "the ghost shop"; others swore it was "the abode of the devil." It was owned by William and Horatio Eddy, two middle-aged nearly illiterate brothers, and their sister, Mary.

Olcott, renowned for his rigorous investigations of corruption in military arsenals and naval shipyards after the Civil War, had been awarded the title of Colonel.

But it wasn't bandits in uniform the Colonel was after this time—it was supernatural creatures, ghosts and spectral phenomena of such magnitude as to be unrivaled before or since. The events at the Eddy farm were so powerful and strange that people came from all over the world to witness them. In some circles, Chittenden, Vermont, became known as "The Spirit Capital of the Universe."

Olcott's job was to determine whether William and Horatio were villains or visionaries, humbugs or heroes. If they were gifted clairvoyants, he would tell the world there was some validity to this "spiritualism" business. If they were ingenious charlatans, he'd expose them and let public contempt do its worst. In either event, Olcott was determined to be fair. . . .

Perhaps there was no better man for the job. But what about the mysterious Eddy brothers themselves? What type of men were they?

Sketchy records indicate they were descended from a long line of psychics. In Salem, their maternal grandmother four times removed had been sentenced to be hanged for witchcraft in 1692. She escaped with the help of friends.

Their grandmother had second sight; she'd often go into trances and converse with entities no one else could see.

Their mother, Julia Ann MacCoombs of Weston, Vermont, moved to the Chittenden farmhouse when she married Zephaniah Eddy in 1846. There she amazed and frightened the townspeople with predictions and visions. Her husband, an abusive, narrow-minded lout, discouraged further displays of her powers, convinced they were the work of The Evil One. After a while, Julia learned to hide her gifts.

But the unseen forces were impossible to conceal when the couple began having children. Inexplicable pounding resounded through the barren rooms of the ramshackle farmhouse. The parents and their visitors heard disembodied voices near the cribs. Sometimes the helpless infants were removed from their beds and transported elsewhere by unseen hands.

As the boys grew, occult forces strengthened to the point that spirits became visible. On several occasions, Zephaniah said he saw his sons playing with unfamiliar children, children that would vanish when he approached. Billy and Horatio couldn't go to school; their unobservable companions made it impossible. Loud hammering from nowhere disrupted the local one-room schoolhouse. There were tales of invisible hands yanking books away from terrified children. Objects—ink wells, chalk and rulers—were reported to fly around the room.

Zephaniah beat his sons, but the strange antics continued. He grew furious every time the boys fell spontaneously into a trance. First he'd accuse them of being slackers; then he'd declare they were in league with the devil. He'd try to wake them by punching or pinching them until their skin was black and blue. But the boys didn't waken.

Once, at the advice of a Christian friend, Anson Ladd, Zephaniah doused the boys with boiling water. When that indelicate approach failed, he allowed Ladd to drop a red-hot coal into William's hand to exorcise the devil. The boy didn't stir, but he bore a scar in his palm until his dying day.

Then, perhaps in a moment of twisted inspiration, Zephaniah realized he could profit from the "devil's" work. In exchange for a goodly sum of money, he released the sons to the custody of a traveling showman who took them on tour throughout the U.S., Canada and Europe.

They toured for fourteen years, performing their odd feats not only in front of audiences, but also before skeptics and self-proclaimed "psychic investigators" who tied them up to keep them from cheating, or filled their mouths with hot wax to prevent "ventriloquism." Punched, poked, prodded and pinched, they were left indelibly scarred and permanently misshapen—but their gifts were never discredited. The Eddys were mobbed in Lynn, Massachusetts, stoned in Danvers, even shot. William Eddy was irreparably disfigured by bullet wounds.

It is difficult to imagine a more horrible childhood. When the parents died, the brothers and (their sister) Mary retreated to the family place in Chittenden. It is no wonder they grew into cold, suspicious, unfriendly men who, Olcott reported, ". . . make newcomers feel ill at ease and unwelcome."

Clearly, these were not glib and affable con men.

They were something else.

But what?

It is at this point in 1874 that Colonel Olcott's adventure begins. Picture Olcott arriving by train in Rutland during the height of August's heat. Imagine the bumpy, dusty, sweaty, seven-mile journey by stagecoach into a "grassy valley shut in by the slopes of the Green Mountains." Here, Olcott entered the "plain, dull, and uninteresting town" of Chittenden. From there, he made his way to "the ghost shop," the Eddys' isolated two-and-a-half-story farmhouse on the road south toward East Pittsford.

And imagine meeting the Eddys for the first time. Somber, sinister and silent, they must have been an unnerving pair. Olcott wrote, "There is nothing about [them] to inspire confidence on first acquaintance. The brothers . . . are sensitive, distant, and curt to strangers. . . . [They] look more like hard-working rough farmers than prophets or priests [with their] dark complexions, black hair and eyes, stiff joints, [and] clumsy carriage. . . ." They also spoke in a thick Vermont dialect, which often made them difficult to understand.

But in the ten weeks Colonel Olcott spent with the brothers, it wasn't horrors that he witnessed. Instead, it was a fantastic display of mind-numbing spiritual phenomena that even now remains without explanation.

Nowadays, we're not used to spiritualist displays. We wonder just exactly what Olcott saw in that 17-by-35.5-foot "circle room" above the kitchen of the Eddy's mysterious farmhouse. Apparently the séances progressed something like this:

Every night of the week except Sunday, guests and visitors assembled on wooden benches before a platform lighted only by a kerosene lamp recessed in a barrel.

William Eddy, the primary medium, would mount the platform and enter a tiny closet known as his "spirit cabinet." For a suspenseful moment, all would be silent. Then far-off voices would speak or sing, often accompanied by music. Tambourines came to life and soared around the stage; ectoplasmic hands appeared, grappling, waving, touching the spectators.

Tension mounted.

Shortly, from behind the curtained door of the cabinet, ethereal forms began to emerge. One at a time or in groups. Twenty, even thirty in the course of an evening. Sometimes they were completely visible and seemingly solid. Other times they'd only partially materialize, or remain transparent. The figures varied in size from that of an infant to those well over six feet (William Eddy himself was only five-foot-nine.) Although the most familiar ghostly visitors were elderly Vermonters or American Indians (the sprightly Honto in her beads and moccasins or the sullen giant Santum) a vast array of representative nationalities appeared in costume: black Africans, Russians, Kurds, Orientals and more.

Where'd they all come from? Olcott was well versed in the methods of stage magicians and fraudulent mediums. His detailed examinations of the spirit cabinet disclosed only plaster and lathe. No trap doors, no hidden compartments, no room for anyone but the medium himself.

Then the apparitions would perform, singing, dancing, chatting with the spectators; they'd produce weapons, scarves and musical instruments. In fact, the wondrous Eddy exhibitions included all the manifestations known to psychic science at the time: rappings, moving objects, spirit paintings and drawings, prophesy, speaking in strange tongues, healing, spirit communication, human levitation, musical instruments playing, uncanny hands appearing, ghostly writing, remote vision, clairvoyance.

But most amazing were the materializations. Olcott concluded that such a show would require a whole troupe of actors and several trunks full of costumes. With the help of carpenters and engineers, Olcott made a thorough search of the premises. His conclusion: there was simply no place to hide people or props.

And such a show would be expensive to put on every night. The brothers were poor; they, along with their sister, did all the housework themselves. Half the visitors didn't pay, the rest gave only eight dollars a week for room and board. No charge was ever made for the séances. So how could the Eddys compensate actors, researchers, costumers and the designers of complicated "illusions?"

## Questions and Exercises for Reflection and Inspiration

In writing the section (above) on the Eddy brothers, Citro conducted a thorough reading into the available research on the subject, studying newspaper accounts from the time, books on the Eddys, and the broader subject of séances and apparitions. He interviewed people who knew Chittenden's history and pored through notations in the Rutland County Historical Society's files. He read Olcott's report. Essentially, he worked much as an investigative journalist or researcher might, culling through the yellowed pages of old newspapers and diaries for scraps of information. He finds this notation in a June 1875 issue of the *Rutland Herald*, an account by an eyewitness, Franklin Bolles of Hartford, Connecticut: "My wife's mother . . . deceased March 1859, at the age of 78 years, appeared to us in white clothing, looking so natural that we recognized her instantly."

But Citro's story is not told as a journalist or researcher would. A journalist would "report" what others said, writing something like, "People in the audience said they saw an apparition, speaking fluently in Russian" rather than stating directly that an apparition spoke in a foreign tongue. There's more than a subtle difference here. Citro leaves skepticism aside in his reports and writes the account through the eyes of those who experienced it. He employs the tools of the storyteller to create suspense and interest. Journalists necessarily distance themselves (or should) from conferring fact-status on events whose veracity might be hard to ascertain.

How does Citro create suspense and interest? He does so by providing details of Olcott's efforts to find out where the "apparitions" were coming from. He doesn't outright say they were actual manifestations but rather leaves the question open: how could these poor, barely educated brothers have created this show with the resources available to them just after the Civil War? And, of course, there's the more essential question: if they weren't faking these apparitions, then just what *was* going on at the Eddy house? Perhaps we'll never know but, as humans who seek to understand what happens after death, who wonder if there are parallel universes, or creatures living beyond the realm of normal human activity, or unidentifiable flying objects or any number of unexplored phenomena, we're fascinated still by the unexplained events occurring not so far from our own bedsides.

> **Exercise 1:** Remembering the sheer delight and terror of the campfire ghost story or your first viewing of a scary movie, spend some time trying to capture exactly what it was that scared you the most. For some people, terror takes the form of the unknown (alien beings, the walking dead, the devil); for others, it's the monster within. Write a list of attributes a creature or person should have to fit your definition of truly scary. Using the list of elements that make a character, whether real or imaginary, come alive on the page—description, dialogue, action, thought, and reaction—make an inventory of distinct attributes for the scary thing in a story you might write. Does your monster speak? Does it look human or very alien? Does it have a body at all? What, if any, supernatural powers does it possess? What makes it angry? What makes it gentle? What does it want? (As you may discover, monsters are not all that different from you and me; they have hopes and fears, strengths and weaknesses, too. And, in the case of the Eddys, who were the monsters? Or, better still, *were* there any monsters? What might the apparitions have been if not the spirits of the dead?) In writing your story, you may explore any of these themes, stretching reality as far as you can or leaving, as Citro does, the explaining to the reader's imagination. You may find it useful to draw a picture of the thing that makes you afraid or is inexplicable. Write a short piece, describing an hour in your monster's life. What does it do when it's bored or lonely? What is its witching hour? And what does it dream?

Smell is our oldest sense. Certain smells evoke strong memories in most readers. When an author introduces a smell into a piece, it calls upon both our ancient memory and our own singular associations. Smells have to be chosen carefully for their effect. The smell of a burnt out match can cause the reader to recall a birthday cake or a loved one who died from cancer caused by smoking cigarettes. When a writer evokes the smells of apple pie or wood smoke or Thanksgiving turkey, the reader supplies not only the smell but (for the most part) the accompanying pleasant memory. When a writer describes a hospital smell or, as in the case of Citro's Perly Greer, the smell of old man, the reader smells it. You can smell that awful combination, can't you? Old man, old dog, kerosene, cigarettes, the dank stuffy air in the hermitage? That smell carries with it other sensory responses: it puts us on guard, it signifies loneliness, and too many days trapped inside with only the habit of feeding the wood stove, lighting the kerosene lamp, petting the dog, and rolling cigarettes to pass the time.

> **Exercise 2:** Make your own list of smells for a story you are working on. What was the smell of your home growing up? Is there a special meal or event that evokes a specific olfactory memory? Do you have an experience that is recalled whenever you smell a particular odor: new car, gun powder, a particular perfume, roast beef, Toll House cookies, suntan lotion, citronella, the locker room? Notice how closely some of these smells are associated with food. Food is another sensory trigger. Your description of memorable meals will call to mind the reader's similar or dissimilar experiences. Writers use these sensory sparks to engage the readers at deep, sometimes primitive levels. This is especially important in mystery writing in which the author wishes to grab the reader's attention and sustain his interest.
>
> **Exercise 3:** Take a piece you have been writing and add one of your own sensory triggers to enhance the mood and atmosphere of the piece. You don't have to dwell long on the sense imagery if you use the right words: the inside of his locker smelled like a season of football games; as we walked into the party, we could smell the competing lotions and potions the singles had applied in hopes of luring a companion for the night; in spring, a Vermont road smells like all the skunks have committed suicide, hurling themselves by the dozens under passing truck tires. This exercise does not have to involve a scary story. It works with almost anything you may be writing.

Setting is especially important in mystery and horror writing; indeed, setting can almost be a character, creating mood and atmosphere that heightens the drama and our response to it. When creating setting, Citro draws on memories from his childhood. In *Shadow Child*, for example, there is a unifying device that runs through the book. It begins with two brothers flattening pennies on a railroad track. "It was something I did as a kid. When I was in the world of the book and a kid again, that process of flattening the pennies came back to me and I could re-create the scene—not just the sound of the train coming down the track and the feel of the woods just beyond the tracks, but the feel of the penny after the train has flattened it. Says Citro, "Who knows how that one memory came back to me but I'm glad it did. Those flattened pennies are important later on in that book. Stuff like that is just a gift from our subconscious."

**Exercise 4:** Take some scary memory from your childhood—stumbling upon a person sleeping in the woods, or trying to fall asleep on a dark night when the trees were scratching at your window—and re-create the scene as if you are back in the setting, recalling in slow motion the elements that made you scared. These might be the way the moon came and went from behind the clouds; lightning brightening the sky and then the long wait until the thunder's boom shattered the night; an eerie feeling that someone was watching you, and the like. Before you start writing, record as many physical details as you can, calling on as many senses as you can. Did the lightning have a smell? Could you taste your fear in your mouth? Did you have goose bumps or were you suddenly hot or cold? What did it sound like when the wind rubbed the limbs outside of your bedroom? Try to re-create the scene, either with yourself as a main character or using your own experiences with a fictional character. Avoid entirely the use of words like "scared," "terrified," "shaken," "spooked," and the like. Rather, show the setting and your response to it through direct action: "I pulled the blankets over my head but that wasn't enough. I needed more protection. So I took my blankets and pillow, raced across the cold bedroom floor and dug myself deep into the mound of clothes, shoes, and broken toys in the back of my closet."

# 5    Jeffery Lent
*Perseverance Furthers*

Born 29 December 1958 in North Pomfret, Vermont
Attended Franconia College and State University of New York
    at Purchase
Lives in Tunbridge
First publication: *In the Fall*
Novels: *In the Fall* (2000); *Lost Nation* (2002)
Awards: National Book Award finalist for *In the Fall* (2002)

A S THE YOUNG JEFFREY LENT honed his writing craft at Franconia College and, later, the State University of New York at Purchase, he felt confident that by the time he was twenty-five he would have published a best-selling novel. Fifteen years and five novels later, he finally published his award-winning novel *In the Fall*. Reviewers consistently called *In the Fall* a first novel that didn't read like one. The *New York Times* called it "a majestic, vital book." The *San Jose Mercury News* wrote, "*In the Fall* heralds the emergence of a fully formed writer, seemingly from nowhere."[1]

It certainly wasn't from nowhere. Lent had repeatedly almost gotten to the pinnacle of acceptance—that is, securing a contract with a mainstream publishing house. For about twelve years, he was often in communication with publishers, editors, and agents who were looking at his work. Over and over, there were serious nibbles but no contractual bite. Finally, on the fifth almost-sold novel, his agent offered to shop his latest book around at the second tier of publishing houses and smaller, university presses. Lent said no. He believed that where you start off as a writer determines how the industry will regard you in the future. He wanted to start at the top. At the time, he had yet another novel in the works and had written about eighty pages of it. His agent agreed with his decision not to try to sell low, saying, "I know what you're working on now is going to just wow them. Let's wait for that book then."

But Lent says he knew the novel he "was working on wasn't going to wow anyone. I told my wife that and I said I'm going to write the big novel I've been waiting for. Years ago, I heard of a union soldier who came home to Vermont with a black bride. That was the nut of the story, all I remembered. I took that image and went with it. I wrote every day. I made a conscious decision that, whatever came of it, I would put everything into this one novel. My family supported my decision. The punch line is, it had taken two years for me to write each of those 250-page short novels, the ones I almost sold. *In the Fall*, which was 860 pages in the original, took eighteen months."

The process he'd developed in writing his other books went like this: Lent and his wife would take a walk every morning and he'd tell her what he planned for the day; most evenings, he'd read her what he had written during the day. He didn't show anyone a word of *In the Fall*, or talk about it, until he had the first long chapter done. The book simply felt different, maybe because he'd been carrying it around in his head for years, maybe because it was the kind of book he wanted to write: long and evocative, poetic, epic, embracing three generations and one of America's most difficult issues, slavery, rather than the short, snappy, contemporary books he'd been writing. Whatever the reason, "the most amazing thing happened. In forty pages, my characters were up, fully dimensional and I was hard-pressed to keep up with them," he recalls. To slow the action down, he'd get up and pace, saying the story out loud, returning to his desk to capture it on paper. The end result is a novel that's been compared not just favorably but sometimes as being superior to Faulkner.

*In the Fall* begins at the end of the Civil War in war-shattered West Virginia with a wounded Union soldier from Vermont, Norman Pelham, awakening to being cared for by a runaway slave woman named Leah. Leah is fleeing a terrible situation in North Carolina, believing that she killed a white man, her half-brother, when he tried to rape her. When Norman is better, the two "marry" and begin the trip north to Vermont and Norman's farm, always traveling just a bit out of sight of the troops and the villages. Still, word of them spreads and, by the time they finally arrive in Vermont, Norman's mother knows something of her son's companion. The couple keeps to themselves, happy and busy with the chores of running the farm and caring for their three children. But Leah's past haunts her and she returns to Sweetboro, North Carolina, the town from which she fled. There, rather than putting the past to rest, she's told a story that kindles the torment already burning in her heart; leading her to take dramatic steps that further isolates the family. Throughout the years, Norman and Leah's daughters stay on the farm, living in the community but not part of it. In contrast, the couple's son, Jamie, who can pass for white, leaves home as a young teenager. He eventually settles down, marries, and has two children. When Jamie's wife and daughter die in the influenza epidemic of 1918, Jamie raises their son, Foster, without telling him of his racial heritage. After Jamie's death, Foster travels to Vermont in search of his family. From there, he's driven to set out for the South to learn the truth about his family's secrets.

*In the Fall* is a complex story that never loses its momentum. Each generation's story is important and convincingly told and, near the end, when the various loose ends and puzzles start coming together, it's like a magic trick where the magician pulls a string and all the pieces fall together. One of the things the critics praised most highly about *In the Fall* was the way all the elements of a good novel—character development, scene setting, plot, historical detail and the actual language of the book—are artfully presented.

Lent's prose language—so rich and entertaining—comes from several decades of writing and studying poetry. Before he started writing novels, he found himself writing long, long poems, fifty pages and longer. He also loves the classics and learned much from his reading. He says his "real teachers were the people I read—Faulkner, Tolstoy, Dostoevsky, the long early poetry of Robert Frost." From them he learned not just language but what he calls "the voices of a place."

The published version of *In the Fall* is 542 pages long, a very long book by contemporary standards. Yet, the book never drags. Instead, the reader feels lulled into the book's enjoyable passages and propelled into the disturbing ones. Lent does this by combining distinctive character building with compelling plot. But it is his language—at times mesmerizing—that propels the book along. Here's an example:

> Walking up that final half mile of rough track above Randolph with the farmhouse not yet in sight, the crown of the elms over the house stretched ahead where the road cut an opening through the trees, the girl already thought she knew something of the place to which she'd come, having walked through half the state just to get here, as well as all the rest of the north that lay behind them now. The boy paced slow with so much home after so long finally in sight, both with those long days and too-short nights behind them; those and the weeks they spent outside Washington where after Lincoln's assassination Norman waited with his company through a mourning for the president. They stayed through most of May to walk together one final time as a military force down Pennsylvania Avenue in the Grand Review of the Army of the Potomac, Norman waiting with great agita-

tion while Leah disappeared into the swamped springtime of the capital, a place at odds with itself, wildly festive with the war's end and murderously foul from the dead president. After four long days, she reappeared with lye-burned mottled hands and a pure gleefulness nothing could diminish; she was working in the basement of a hotel scrubbing linens and ironing them to a slick starched stiffness but earning cash money, in fact a sum that gave Norman pause; during the years of the war he'd come to think of money in the abstract and at those random intervals when his pay arrived he wired it through to his sheep account at the bank in Randolph. Those first six weeks passed and they went their own way, disregarding the packed trains leaving for Philadelphia or New York or Boston and walking up the country through the lush and easy summer, sleeping in woods or fields with hedgerow cover and buying food when they needed it. At times they had to fend off dogs and small boys with their name-calling and meaness strident and forgivable for their age and ignorance. Only once, outside Port Royal, New York, did a man on horseback block their passage, inquiring the price of the nigger whore. And Norman brought the man down from his horse, an easy job after that long-dead cavalryman, and thrashed him there in the dust of the road, three other men off in the distance watching and not involving themselves. It was not the watchers but Leah who stopped him, who began kicking him in the muscles on the backs of his calves and screaming at him until he gave way.[2]

Each sentence builds on the next as in the scene above in which the couple's ease together is contrasted with the growing signs of unease on the road, foreshadowing the couple's reception when they finally arrive home to Vermont. So much is telegraphed in these lines: Norman's deep commitment to protect Leah, her ingenuity and restraint, and their shared reluctance to face what awaits them.

Lent's sentences have a rhythm to them, almost an iambic pentameter pacing. The sentences are lengthy but they don't feel encumbered. It's as if we instinctively know when to pause for breath; Lent has signaled that by constructing his sentences of rhythmic parts, relatively short and evenly spaced, so that we don't feel like we're rushing to the end. Lent explains that this tempo is created both consciously and subconsciously. "The central thing to remember as a writer is you are first and foremost a storyteller. Finding the way to tell a story that is true to you is probably going to also resonate with the reader. You have to find the music of a novel, of your novel. I attribute much of my language and my way of telling story to my deep and ongoing immersion into poetry. Before we are born, from our mother's heartbeat we have an inner notion of rhythm, of the iambic. Good fiction has to have that same resonance that speaks to our common experience, along with musicality of language," he explains. Writing and reading out loud, crafting paragraph after paragraph, he "strives to work with preciseness in my mind," choosing the exact words and images that will bring the reader to understand not just the physical condition and action of the characters, but their psychology as well.

"I am a native Vermonter by birth and lifestyle," Lent says proudly. He was born in 1958 in North Pomfret. The family had come to Vermont via Lent's paternal grandfather, a senior vice president in a successful advertising agency in New York City. The family had a home in Connecticut and a country place in Grafton, Vermont. Lent's father fell in love with farm life. A favorite family story tells how Lent's father and uncle were both given ponies when they were boys. Lent's father scrounged around until he found harnesses and used his brother's pony to make a team. Both his father and uncle went to the Putney School and were expected to go on to college and then into business. But when graduation came, Lent's father moved onto the family place in Grafton and turned the place back into a year-round working farm. "He wasn't a trust-fund farmer," Lent says of his father. "He worked hard and enjoyed hard work." Lent's mother was cut from the same cloth. She wanted to be independent and had studied to be a schoolteacher. His parents shared an appreciation of life in a small community and of working close to the land.

Lent spent his early years on a Vermont hill farm where his father managed a small herd of cows and sheep, farmed with horses and sugared each spring. In the late 1960s, however, the family moved to the Finger Lakes region of New York where farming was easier and more profitable. Throughout his life, Lent's father's passion remained horses; Lent was riding by the time he was four.

The Finger Lakes were fine enough but Lent says of himself, "I never really left Vermont. I was just displaced for a while." After high school, he attended Franconia College in New Hampshire but the school was forced to close before he had graduated. A friend of Lent's told him about the State University of New York's branch in Purchase, a kind of alternative college that specialized in liberal arts. Lent thought it was just the place for him; he attended, taking as many literature courses as possible, reading and writing constantly without any desire to take the courses required to get a college degree. "I was fortunate in that I had very good teachers who let me indulge my independent streak with all the moronic self-certainty of a twenty-year-old. I was sure I'd be in print by twenty-five. I have no regrets about that course of action. I self-consciously set myself up by not getting a degree. I had to either work shitty jobs or write," he says.

Encouraged by his mother, Lent had read by age four and began writing by age five. His grandfather, the advertising man, had actually shown him how to be a writer—at least a part-time one. Over the years, as he traveled by train from Connecticut to New York City, Henry B. Lent had penned fifty or so books for children and young adults, many of them about businesses and industries with titles like *Diggers and Builders*, *Full Steam Ahead*, *This is Your Announcer*, *I Work on a Newspaper*, *PT Boat*, *Bombardier*, and *The Peace Corps*.

Lent's mother moved to the South in the mid-1970s; some years later Lent also relocated there, expecting to live there for just a little while. He had read the complete works of William Faulkner with much appreciation and wanted to understand the South. Over the next decade or so, he lived in the rural Piedmont region around Durham and Asheville, North Carolina. But he always expected to move back to New England. So did his wife Marion. She also had a Vermont connection, having spent summers in the Green Mountain state as a girl. But much as Budbill became an economic hostage to Vermont, Jeffrey Lent and his wife were economic hostages living in the South, longing to move back to Vermont but too poor to do so. As he cobbled out novel after novel, Lent and his wife held a series of caretaking jobs; his wife worked as a graphic artist and in a bookstore, but money was often tight. Lent believed he had to write a popular novel to break into the publishing world; once he'd done so, he reasoned, he could write the way he wanted.

"I wanted to write serious literature accessible to a variety of people but I was writing these short novels, thinking the idea was to sell one, and get enough money to write the longer, more expansive novel I wanted to write," he explains. Thus, when he finally set about writing *In the Fall*, it was with the sense that he was writing the way he'd always been meant to write. "I knew that book was either going to sell or that I was delusional. But, even if it meant dying with twenty-five unpublished novels under the bed, I knew I would never give up."

When the novel was completed, his agent sent it out to the top publishing houses in early December 1998. The following Thursday, she told him that Grove Atlantic, Knopf, and Farrar, Straus and Giroux had all expressed interest. The next day, he learned that Grove had asked for a second copy for the publisher to read. He spent an anxious weekend, telling himself, over and over, "You have a good life." That previous July, his first daughter had been born after many tries, miscarriages, and operations. He was thankful for a supportive family and for his daughter. "Don't be greedy," he told himself. But on Monday morning, when the agent called to say that Grove Atlantic had offered what he considered "a staggering amount of money," he was stunned. "My agent said, 'I think I can ask for more.' I said, 'Sure, whatever you think.' Later that day, the phone rang and it was her saying, 'They accepted our offer.' I thought, in an hour, I just made more money than I'd made in my life up to that point. . . . That was just weeks short of my fortieth birthday."

Six weeks later and the couple was living in Vermont. Lent used the advance to buy another Vermont hill farm, one that had been non-active for seventy or eighty years. They've been busy, ever since, clearing land and restoring pastures on their fifty-two-acre spread. Lent says simply, "We both love it here." It's easy to see why as you step into Lent's roomy, rustic writing studio, located in the barn across a dirt road from their farmhouse. An easy chair sits by the woodstove; shelves are neatly stacked with books, and CDs surround his desk; two big, gangly dogs keep him company. Just outside the door, in the pastures surrounding the house. Lent raises lamb for his own family; they also have a small flock of chickens and a vegetable garden. When he calls, two handsome horses come running. A lover of horses like his father before him, Lent sometimes sports around town in a carriage drawn by one of the horses.

He says the farm and the farm animals, the work of keeping up the farm, and the demands of the seasons, work well with the writer's schedule. Shoveling out the horse barn is just the right activity to clear the mind after too many hours hunched over paper or the computer. Writing is amorphous work. Some days you struggle at it for hours and have nothing to show at the end of the day. Farming is concrete. Lent has no illusions about full-time farming, however; he gave that up at age nineteen. But he's found happiness on his small piece of property with his wife and girls, the farm animals, and the writing. "For me, the greatest role Vermont plays is simply, I'm totally, absolutely a happy person here, every season of the year," he explains. "I accomplish something practical and it's done. It's necessary and it's done. There's something wonderful about that."

Unlike so many writers who find they do their best work in the mornings, Lent writes in the afternoons and into the evenings, usually spending the morning on correspondence and errands, followed by lunch and a nap, then the concentrated time in his writing studio. "This dates back to the first caretaking job," he explains. "Marion was working at a bookstore while I was supposed to be writing. I'd procrastinate all day long and realize I'd better get to it and start writing by mid-afternoon. It seemed to work for me and so that's the habit I've continued."

*In the Fall* is the story of three generations but it is also the story of America. In exploring the impact of slavery and its secrets—in particular, that white slaveholders often had sex with their slaves, fathering children that they in turn treated as second-class citizens or sold off, essentially making orphans of their own flesh and blood—Lent was tackling an important subject. But in locating much of his story in Vermont, he also explored the North's inherent prejudice. Children of mixed race weren't safe anywhere in America.

As with several other Vermont writers in this book, Lent is interested in Vermont's somewhat mixed handling of race issues. He says it's important that, as the fourteenth state, Vermont "modeled its constitution after the U.S. constitution but with one important difference, in that the Vermont constitution abolished slavery." Lent observes that the state constitution "was based on the notion of the freedom of the individual. It's that mentality that makes Vermont such as interesting place." Vermont, Lent says, "is not exactly a liberal bastion, as some people define it today, but rather old-school Republicanism, which means fiscally responsible, conservative when it comes to change, but socially progressive. That is why, throughout Vermont's history, this view of tolerance can be found. It allowed people of different stripes and colors to come in." He notes, of course, that because of the harsh weather, the lack of factory jobs and highways, the influx into Vermont has been slow and has resulted in few people of color, and of minorities in general, moving to Vermont. In *In the Fall*, Leah and her children are treated more with indifference than with scorn. They choose to be left alone, and are.

### Tips and Techniques

Prose rhythm is a combination of sound, pacing, repetition, and other grammatical tools. Sentences establish rhythm by their length and punctuation. Long languid sentences convey a different mood than short choppy ones. A short sentence that comes after several longer ones draws attention to itself, as if to say, pay attention. Lent employs several techniques to create a distinctive prose rhythm in his novels. His sentences are constructed using the iambic beat, which he compares to a mother's heartbeat. His careful use of commas helps the reader negotiate the sentences. The commas help to slow the reading down, which Lent does on purpose. He wants the reader to pay attention.

The best way to find your own rhythm is to write and then read out loud. Think about the mood you want to create and use words and patterns of words, sounds, and sentence lengths to reflect the mood you want to convey. Use short, choppy sentences and one- and two-syllabic words when you want to suggest speed, excitement, and chaos. Likewise, use multisyllabic words and words rich in vowels if you want to create a softer mood, one that conveys ease or the passage of time. Think about the sound of words and start collecting words that sound like their meaning. You'll find they'll come in handy someday.

Having pulled off a successful first novel, one with a large and important subject matter, Lent felt incredible pressure to write another. Atlantic Monthly Press had offered a two-book contract. What would the second book be about? Lent fooled around with several plots but kept coming back to a single image in his mind: a man pulling an oxcart, accompanied by his dog and a girl, walking into the North Country. He wrote a one-paragraph summary, essentially expressing that one picture. Atlantic accepted the book "proposal."

*Lost Nation*, the novel that began with that one image, is a dark tale that explores questions as deep and uncomfortable as those Lent asked in *In the Fall*. What is freedom? What is evil? Can a man be redeemed? Is something a sin if it occurs only in your imagination? The main character is a man known only as Blood, well educated but running from a secret past. The book opens with him trying to remake himself in the harsh uncivilized land of northern New Hampshire surrounding the Connecticut Lakes, an area still wild and fairly uninhabited. As he makes his way toward Lent's fictional town of Indian Stream, a refuge for the lawless and the luckless, Blood is accompanied by a sixteen-year-old girl named Sally that he won in a game of cards from the madam of a brothel. Blood opens a way station in the far north, selling rum or Sally to any customer, even after he and Sally develop a guarded affection toward one another. In this novel, however, as in *In the Fall*, there is no escape from the past. It catches up with Blood after a series of ever more violent clashes in Indian Stream that eventually pit Blood against everyone, even Sally.[3]

In this novel also, nothing is how it seems. Blood's demons turn out to be partly of his own making. But aren't those the worst? Even when he discovers that there may be a way to redeem himself, Blood remains a tragic figure. A dark tone is established from the opening paragraph of the novel:

> They went on. The man Blood in hobnailed boots and rotting leather breeches and a stinking linen blouse, lank and grease-grimed hair, tied at his nape with a thin leather binding cut from a cowhide, goad in hand, staggering at the canted shoulder of the near ox, the girl behind, barefoot in a rough shift of the same linen as Blood's shirt, her fancy skirt and bodice in a tight roll jammed down in the back of the cart atop her button-hook boots furred now with green slime, the girl's hair no cleaner than Blood's but untied and tangled, redblonde, her face swollen from the insect delirium that her free hand swiped against, unceasing ineffectual bat around her head. Her other wrist cinched by a length of the same stripped cowhide tethering her to the rear of the lurching groaning cart. The huge dog trotting on the off side, opposite Blood.[4]

It's few writers who can pull off a 116-word sentence, but that's exactly what Lent has done in the second sentence of the first paragraph of his book. Notice how the first sentence is quite short: "They went on." It sets up the book: a story of going on, of trying against odds, and trying some more. The second sentence, that 116-word one, does something else entirely: it provides information about the two people and their relationship while also communicating the full weight under which they operate. We know by the end of the first paragraph that this will be a story of struggle and attempts to overcome, to go on. The opening paragraph establishes the mood of the novel.

Lent says he writes with this degree of detail because he wants the reader to be "an active participant in the story." By constructing scenes in slow motion, he allows the reader to absorb each detail, to picture it in his mind's eye and consider the accumulated information. Lent says his approach deliberately goes against contemporary writing in which the authors seem hell-bent to get to the ending before we've gotten to fully know the characters. He says, "So many novels I read, I want to grab the person and say, 'Wait; you've squandered a fabulous story. You've rushed its telling.'" For Lent, after writing shorter novels that didn't allow him this freedom of language and character development, the permission to write *his kind of novel* seems like a rare gift. Yet, he realizes that, for any author, "you're only as good as your next book." He's written two more novels, now in draft form. Both should be out in 2006.

---

**◦§ FROM *In the Fall* · PROLOGUE**

The boy woke in the dark house and knew he was alone. It was knowing this that woke him. The house was not empty, he just was alone in it. He stood and dressed and went down through the house in the dark. From the kitchen, he could see the lantern light past the overgrown pasture beyond the barn. He took his jacket from the peg and held the door to settle it back into the frame without noise. Under the big hemlocks and tamaracks surrounding the house, he crossed the soft dirt track of the drive and stepped into the tangle of sumac and blackberries and young popples, keeping a clump of sumac between him and the light. He was not afraid of the dark. He was afraid of being in the house. The lantern sat on an upturned stone. His father was digging with a spade in the woods floor, piling the soil he lifted onto a canvas tarp laid next to the hole he was making. The boy heard the soft noise of dirt slipping off the spade. The hole was round, not wide but deep. His father worked carefully, prying free stones, small rocks, with the tip of the blade. When the handle disappeared halfway into the ground his father stopped, set down the spade and from the edge of the tarp took up one of three coffee cans and got down on his knees to position it in the bottom of the hole. Still on his knees, he packed handfuls of dirt around the can and only when it was covered did he rise to finish the job. He worked slowly, transferring the soil from the tarp back to the hole. When he was done, he tamped the soil with the flat of the blade, the sound gentle blows in the night. He set aside the spade and shook the tarp for the last traces of dirt and then took up a metal-tined rake and pulled the leaves and understory trash back over the hole, raking back and forth until he was satisfied with his job. Then he moved a short distance in the woods, the boy moving with him, a soft unwatched dance within the thicket. He watched as his father dug another hole, the same careful job as the first, another small grave for a coffee can. And when this was done, they both moved again and one more hole was dug and filled and finished, covered over, hidden. When his father was done, he sat on a stone, lighted a cigarette and smoked it. The boy watched, knowing he had to get back to the house before his father but only wanting enough time and no more. The cigarette tip made an orange flare in the dark as his father inhaled and the release of smoke from his lungs would come float through the brush where the boy stood and he'd breathe in all he could—as if it were his father's presence. The night after his little sister died and his mother still lay sick his father had sent him to bed but it had been his mother that woke him, standing at the foot of his bed with the girl held by the hand, his mother saying nothing but watching him while Claire waved to him. It was not long after this that his father came up the stairs to send the boy out with a lantern to shovel snow from the drive out through the hemlocks to the road, shoveling uselessly against the four-foot snowfall, crying as he worked, raging in an effort he already knew was for nothing. When his father came into the brittle orange and purple dawn to stop him, to still his shovel, to tell him his mother was dead, even then he would not stop, but dug at the snow as if into his own bursting heart. Seeing the two of them together, side by side in his room. A silent farewell. His mother and sister had come to him on their way out of the house to view him once more. This was enough then to be scared of being alone in the house. It was not the dark. He had no fear of the dark outside.

His father ground the cigarette against the sides of his trousers, broke the butt apart and scattered it, and still the boy waited. Then his father took up the tarp and passed it through his hands along one edge until he held the corners and draped it down before him, his arms spread wide. For a moment the tarp hid both father and lantern—a screen over the scene, the tarp backlit from the lantern—and then his father brought the corners together and folded the tarp against the length of his body, placed it under one arm and reached down with the other to gather up the rake and shovel. It was time to go. His father took up the lantern as the boy turned back to the house, moving swiftly through the dark, the house a blank silhouette against the night sky. He heard his father behind him his wind a ragged suck as if he pulled himself forward by drawing in the air—his lungs still weak with the winter's influenza which he'd carried into the house but risen from, just when Claire had sickened with it and then their mother. They didn't have it near as long as his father but both drowned in it. The boy had not been sick at all. With the noise his father was making he guessed he could have run, and not been seen or heard, but he wanted nothing more than just to beat his father back to the house. To lie in bed and hear him come in.

Whatever was in the coffee cans, whatever was buried in the woods behind him, he did not know. Something secret laid away, something hidden deep in the earth, out of sight, gone. Without ever having once been told, he knew it was his father's business buried out there, not his. Curious as any boy, he still knew to leave it be.

## Questions and Exercises for Reflection and Inspiration

Lent uses 1,034 words in this prologue to describe a scene in which a boy watches his father bury three coffee cans. The scene could have been told in far fewer words. But Lent seamlessly allows the reader to follow the movements of the boy and the actions of the father, intricately, almost step-by-step, while also telling the story of the boy's mother's and sister's death. The scene presented in the prologue refers to characters we don't meet until the middle of the book, long after the Vermont soldier whose actions set the book in motion comes home with his black bride. While we meet Norman and Leah in the first pages, the prologue to *In the Fall* forecasts events that occur much further on. The father and child in this scene are Norman and Leah's son Jamie and his son Foster, acting out their own story. Here Jamie is seen burying some secret; his son, Foster, knows to leave well enough alone. By beginning with this scene, however, Lent whets the reader's desire to dig up those secrets.

**Exercise 1:** Take a scene from a piece you are working on or one you hope to write and walk your characters through it, very slowly, step-by-step. Take something simple and almost mindless like washing the dishes or something mind-consuming like fixing a complicated gear on an old clock. It would be boring if you wrote the scene dryly, step by step, as if you were writing a how-to manual. Instead, follow Lent's example and interject the physical actions with emotional information. If Lent had merely told us the steps of the father digging the hole, that would not have held our attention. It is the drama of the boy watching secretly, the question of what is in the coffee cans and why they need to be buried, *and* the description of the mother and child coming to the boy's bedside as they were dying, that make this scene compelling . Maybe that boy doesn't want to know what's in those coffee cans, but the reader does. And that desire to know propels us through this long book. Write your scene going through the steps of your character's activity. Then go back and put in thought. Backfill with a significant scene from the past. Avoid a presen tation like "as he adjusted his wrench, he couldn't help thinking about the time when ..." When you remind the reader that your character is remembering something, you distance the reader from the action. Instead, move seamlessly between your character's actions and thoughts. Notice how Lent does this, moving from the description of the father's smoke, "float[ing] through the brush where the boy stood and he'd breathe in all he could—as if it were his father's presence," to the memory of his bedside visitation: "The night after his little sister died and his mother still lay sick his father had sent him to bed but ..." In this example, one of the activities being described in detail is a mundane physical task while the other is an unnatural or supernatural one. Lent doesn't distinguish between the two; he uses the same language and rhythm to describe both experiences. Try your hand at something similar, describing, for example, someone peeling potatoes or hemming a skirt while some other more important drama unfolds in her memory as if it were occurring at the same moment.

Blood's dog Luther plays a central role in *In the Fall*. He is big, black, loyal, and powerful. He's part companion, part bodyguard. His demise near the end of the novel does not bode well for Blood—and we know it.

**Exercise 2:** Give a character in something you're working on a pet or an animal protector. What would it be? How can you show that animal's relationship to his owner or companion without using words like "loyal," "mythic," "useless"? You can show a lot about a character, whether real or imaginary, through how he treats his pet. If you are just beginning a piece, perhaps you could describe your main character through the eyes of the character's pet. Then place the character and pet together in a scene. Is the pet an ally or a foe? What small and large dramas do they encounter together?

*Lost Nation* has been favorably compared to the classical Greek tales of trial and redemption. Like Ulysses, Blood sets off on a voyage; he's searching for himself; he encounters many hardships and tests along his dangerous voyage. The novel revolves around classical themes of the search for self and the search for the father. You'll have to read the book to see if Blood is victorious in gaining the prize at the end of the novel. Suffice it to say that the fate awaiting Blood is as unpredictable and difficult as the journey to it.

**Exercise 3:** Many writers adapt classical stories into modern tales and you can too. Take a fairy tale(Snow White, for example, or Humpty Dumpty) or a Greek myth (the story of Helen of Troy or that of Achilles, for example) and retell the story with modern characters, settings, and details. You do not have to be constrained by the original drama; Your princess can awake from the coma and reject the prince. Your Humpty Dumpty can have his body put back together again. Your beautiful maiden can be saved or lose herself to human frailties; she can do the saving. It's up to you and the convincing language you employ to make the scene .

# II · Finding Community and Nature

Photo by Vyto Starinskas

# 6     David Moats

## *Public Writing*

Born 3 October 1947 in Salt Lake City, Utah

Education: B.A., University of California at Santa Barbara

Lives in Salisbury

First publication: Article in his school newspaper, *El Gaucho*, in Santa Barbara, California

Newspaper articles, editorials, and commentary: *New York Times, Washington Post, The Advocate, Guardian of London, Rutland Herald, Valley Voice, Journal Opinion*

Nonfiction book: *Civil Wars* (2004)

Award: Pulitzer Prize in Journalism, 2001

WHEN DAVID MOATS began writing his editorials about civil unions, the legal ceremony by which same-sex couples in Vermont share in some of the legal rights of married couples, he knew that no matter what he wrote in the newspaper, someone wouldn't like it. He had an inkling how controversial the issue would become but no idea that the editorials he wrote would bring him a Pulitzer Prize, the top award in journalism and a first for his Vermont newspaper, the *Rutland Herald*. In its brief statement accompanying the award, the Pulitzer Prize committee wrote that the award recognized Moats's "even-handed and influential series of editorials commenting on the divisive issues arising from civil unions for same-sex couples."

Moats had been working at journalism for several decades when three same-sex couples requested marriage licenses from their town clerks, a move that eventually led to a lawsuit, a Vermont Supreme Court ruling, and the creation by the Vermont legislature of the first civil union law in the United States. For most of his journalistic career, Moats has written editorials rather than hard-news stories, although he has tried his hand at both reporting and editing copy. By nature a quiet person who does not relish the limelight, Moats had taken on contentious issues before and written about them forcefully. But no issue before or since has drawn the degree of response, pro *and* con.

Editorials are different from news or feature stories; they express the opinion of the writer (and sometimes the newspaper), rather than objective information gathered from interviews, documents, observation, and the like. While the best news reporters strive to remain objective on issues they write about (or, at least, keep their opinions out of their copy), editorial writers are traditionally given their publisher's permission to express positions, take stands, and sometimes argue a cause. As an editorial writer, Moats has consistently aimed for fairness and accuracy; nonetheless, he has taken strong stands on such issues as environmental protection, the rights of tenants, and freedom of the press. His own political leanings are liberal and most conservatives in Vermont view the *Rutland Herald* as left-leaning. For Moats, the issue of civil union was not so much one of left versus right, but one of fairness.

He had come of age at the height of the civil rights movement and the Vietnam War and he viewed civil union as another civil rights issue. For Moats, failing to allow same-sex couples the right to formalize their commitment to one another was tantamount to discrimination. Decades back, people of different races had been denied the right to marry; Moats viewed the restriction against same-sex partners from marrying as equally wrong.

Yet he knew that the issue was not that simple for many people, particularly those who viewed marriage as a sacred contract between a man and a woman. As the battle was fought out in the public arena, it was apparent to Moats that few debates would have the emotional impact of this one for Vermont residents. That realization filled him with a great sense of responsibility. Now, more than ever, the community could benefit from clearheaded, nonideological commentary that might create a climate where reasonable discussion could take place. Moats never questioned his own position but he wanted to understand those people who thought it was wrong for people of the same sex to marry, even if he disagreed with them. From 27 January 2000 through 26 April 2000, Moats published ten editorials covering the civil-union-laws debate in the Vermont House and Senate.

Many will disagree with his editorials, saying they were biased, but the Pulitzer committee felt that he had listened to criticism across the spectrum and shown sensitivity to the moral qualms of those opposed to the unions. Moats felt quite passionately about the issue, even more so over the days and months in which he, like many Vermonters, followed the debate in the Vermont legislature and listened to testimony both from those who supported the law and those opposed to it.He did not accept the argument that granting rights to same-sex couples threatened anyone else's marriage or moral stability; indeed he felt strongly that denying those rights harmed all individuals and families. Because the issue was so charged, he tried to take a very moderate and restrained tone. Some supporters found his tone too soft. Indeed, those who thought that Vermont ought to grant the right to marry to same-sex couples criticized Moats for lobbying for a civil union law. But Moats's goal was not to inflame the argument but rather to find compromise that might lead to less discord and represent "a wide variety of views, honestly arrived at, by Vermonters."[1] As the Pulitzer committee noted, the remarkable thing about the editorials is that, while they clearly state Moats's stand on the issue, they also give respectful voice to opposing views. In one written on 9 February 2000, Moats strove to separate bigotry from opposition based on long-held religious or moral belief—especially significant in Vermont, which has a large Catholic population. The editorial (see below) clearly defined the difference between opposition to civil unions based on bigotry and opposition based upon traditional views of human sexuality as a gift from God whose purpose is solely procreation. In this editorial, he expressed the hope that, as the debate moved forward, Vermonters "would cultivate a charitable view of those on the other side. That way, however the issue is resolved, Vermont will be a better place in the end."[2]

As already stated, it had all begun in the late 1990s when three same-sex couples requested marriage licenses in their small Vermont towns. When they were denied, they filed suits, alleging their rights had been violated. Eventually, the case ended up before the Vermont Supreme Court, which ruled in December 1999 that same-sex couples had the right to the "benefits and protections" associated with marriage. However, the state's highest court left it up to the legislature to decide whether or not to incorporate those rights into Vermont's marriage laws or create some other remedy. Although there were high passions all around, with many gays and supporters of gay rights urging the legislature to give same-sex couples the same rights as opposite-sex couples to marry, saying anything less was discriminatory, the legislature pushed for a compromise that would fall under the general category of a domestic partnership law. Thus, Vermont created the first civil union law, which gave same-sex couples many but not all of the rights guaranteed to opposite-sex spouses. After former Governor Howard Dean signed the bill, he and the bill's supporters faced a strong backlash and efforts to defeat them in the 2000 election. When it was over, several prominent politicians were out of office; new, more conservative members had taken their place. But Vermont's civil union law has remained in force.

Moats subsequently wrote a nonfiction book entitled *Civil Wars*, which told the personal and historical stories behind Vermont's civil union law.[3] Laws, after all, are merely words on paper that represent ideas, guarantee rights, or place restrictions on the people they apply to. Laws in and of themselves are relatively uninteresting; it's the impact of laws on people's lives that's important and makes for good reading. And it was the personal stories of the major players in the fray that make the book come alive as Moats tells the story through their eyes.

The players included Holly Puterbaugh and Lois Farnham, who had lived together as a couple for nearly thirty years, most of the time in Milton; the two ran a Christmas tree business together, were active in the United Church of Milton, and had, over the years, taken in fifteen foster children—and in 1994, adopted one of them. There were Stan Baker, a psychotherapist at the Counseling Service of Addison County, and his partner, Peter Harrigan, a professor of theater. And there were Nina Beck and Stacy Jolles, whose son had died from the effects of a heart defect at two years of age and who now were parents to another young child. There were also Beth Robinson and Susan Murray, lawyers with one of Vermont's most prestigious law firms, Langrock Sperry & Wool in Middlebury, who had been working on the "freedom-to-marry issue" for years. These lawyers represented the same-sex couples who brought their suits against the towns when they were denied marriage licenses. Others whose lives were impacted included Bill Lippert, a Democrat House member from Hinesburg who was the only openly gay member of the legislature; Tom Little, a Republican who chaired the House Judiciary Committee; and Nancy Sheltra, a Republican House member from Derby and ardent opponent of legalized abortion and gay rights.

So many others were impacted: politicians, religious leaders, ordinary people, parents of gay children. Moats's book effectively captures the intimate stories and drama behind the battle, combining traditional journalism with narrative storytelling that illustrates the experience here in Vermont and puts it in a national framework as well.

### Tips and Techniques

Look at a newspaper to see how journalists traditionally present different kinds of information. The stories on the front page are usually ones editors feel are the most important stories of the day. They are usually news stories. Occasionally, a human-interest story or a feature story that's particularly well written or engaging will also be put on the front page. News stories are traditionally gathered together in two or three sections, such as national, regional, and local news. Feature stories—soft news, people stories, how-to articles— generally are presented in their own sections labeled to signal to the reader that these sections are service-oriented or entertainment pages rather than news sections. Columns are generally accompanied by a writer's photograph and represent a writer's personal take on a subject, from business and sports to culture and politics. Again, readers have come to recognize that, when there is a photograph of the writer accompanying an article in the newspaper, the words in that column represent the writer's point of view.

Most papers devote at least two pages to editorial and commentary. Look at these pages carefully. Usually, there are editorials written by the paper's staff or purchased from other papers such as the *New York Times* or the *Boston Globe*. There are usually also editorials and commentary made by people in the community. These pages often print letters to the editor, written by people across the diverse range of the region. The editorial/commentary pages often also carry a political or other subject cartoon.

Moats was born in Salt Lake City, Utah, and grew up in California, graduating from Hillsdale High School and the University of California at Santa Barbara. In the 1970s, he joined the Peace Corps in part to get out into the world and in part because it offered a deferment from the draft and having to serve in the Vietnam War, which he opposed. Initially, he hoped to go to Iran because he had a college friend who was Persian. Moats had been intrigued by what he'd heard of the country. He was assigned instead to two years in Afghanistan, which he describes as "a formative experience and a great challenge." Moats completed much of his education in Afghanistan, reading many of the classics that had gone unread in college, getting to know people of different religions and cultures, and learning how to live away from home in an environment that, while not uncomfortable, was certainly more rugged than northern California. After his time with the Peace Corps, he traveled widely through India, Pakistan, and Thailand, eventually making it back to the Bay Area and in need of a job. Other Peace Corps friends had found work in journalism and Moats, who'd had no formal training in that discipline — or much else — felt "drawn to journalism because of my interest in politics and history and because it provided a way to be a writer and make a little money at the same time." Knowing nothing about journalism, he still managed to get a job as a copyeditor at *Saturday Review* magazine. Within two months, he'd submitted his own piece. The magazine ended up not using the piece but Moats received encouragment from an editor. Those kind words inspired him to write again. He began to study and develop a journalistic style. About that time, he met his (now former) wife, Kathy, who had attended Royalton College (now the Vermont Law School) and fallen in love with Vermont.

"She was always telling me about Vermont and urging us to go there," he recalls. And so, like so many other young people at the time, the couple set off in a van to drive to Vermont. The trip began inauspiciously enough when they totaled their vehicle in the Sierras, rolling down an embankment. But someone took them in, a move not all that uncommon in the counterculture days of the late 1960s and early 1970s; by the summer of 1975 they were back on the road. Once in Vermont, Moats got a job selling ads for a give-away newspaper in Lebanon, New Hampshire. He gave them a few freelance feature stories as proof of his writing ability and began writing stories of local interest. That was followed by a job with the *Journal Opinion* in Bradford where he was hired as an assistant editor in January 1976. A year later, he became the managing editor at the *Valley Voice* in Middlebury. He came to the *Rutland Herald* in 1982, first as a wire editor, then state editor, then assistant managing editor, then editorial writer.

Moats believes that he might have become a journalist regardless of where he ended up living. It's just his nature to be curious about places and people, especially those around him; journalism provides a living for those who are curious and want to write. Moats has had opportunities to go to bigger papers, but he asked himself early on: "Do I want to be a journalist who moves up and up and ends up in a city?" The answer was always: "No, I want to raise my kids here. It's the choice of community that determines that. This is the community I've chosen."

Moats starts his day by reading newspapers: all the major papers in Vermont, the wire service, and the *New York Times* and *Boston Globe*. He's educating himself about the issues that affect Vermonters, near and far. Most of the time, he concerns himself with issues close at hand but he also writes about broad issues that affect the economy, the position of the United States in the world, and the average Vermonter—such as the 9/11 tragedies and the war in Iraq. "As I'm studying the news and talking to people, I'm always looking for something that catches my eye and gets me thinking about its impact. Sometimes, it's two unrelated stories," he says. "As I begin writing, my subject matter clarifies itself. Initially, I might not know exactly what I'm going to say or how I'm going to say it but I have a general idea of the point I want to make."

Over the years, Moats has also worked assiduously on another form of writing: drama. He has written eleven plays, four about events in small New England towns, one that takes place in a Cape Cod–type environment, and several based on intriguing historical events. "Writing a play is so very different from writing editorials; it's an entirely different process," he says. Editorials come from items in the news and public issues—issues that Moats experiences because he's a person living in Vermont but, by and large, still outside of his personal experience. Moats says the ideas for his plays come "from something within me. The plot comes from something I develop that allows the character to wrestle with a conflict, a change. I tried writing fiction but I couldn't find the right narrative voice. In a play, you just have the characters and what they say and do. You don't have to worry about narrative voice."

And, he says, writing a play is a great antidote to balance the energy-charged and sometimes confrontational world of daily journalism. He would not trade genres, even if one of his plays received the attention or accolades his editorials have received. He loves journalism with a passion. Few jobs, he says, offer more satisfaction.

◆§ A sampling of David Moats' editorials on same-sex marriage
EXCERPTED FROM THE *Rutland Herald*

## A charitable view

The House Judiciary Committee heard moving testimony last week from one of the lawyers who brought the suit that led to the Supreme Court's decision requiring the state to provide equal benefits to gay and lesbian couples.

The lawyer, Susan Murray, described the pain of people who must listen to frequent and repeated public denunciations of their morality and character. "It's really painful to hear people say, 'You're immoral. You're an abomination,'" Murray said.

Gay and lesbian Vermonters have heard a full range of denunciation in the past several weeks. It is something they have heard all their lives, beginning with common school yard taunts and culminating in the passionate condemnations heard at the two public hearings inside the State House.

Murray used the words of Episcopal Bishop Mary Adelia McLeod in saying, "Gays and lesbians are the only group that are still politically correct to kick."

Sometimes, the attacks on gays are plainly mean-spirited and oblivious to the pain they cause. In some cases an unholy mix of anger and fear suffuse the language of those who condemn gays and lesbians as immoral. These attacks are the equivalent of the fire hoses and police dogs that were turned on civil rights workers in the South in an earlier day. They are a reminder that seeking justice exacts a price.

But opposition to same-sex marriage or domestic partnerships comes in many shadings, and it is useful to distinguish those who hate from those whose opposition has other origins.

Bishop Kenneth Angell has prompted resentment in asserting the Roman Catholic opposition to same-sex marriage. It's helpful, however, to realize that the Catholic position arises, not from bigotry, but from a specific teaching about sexuality, a teaching that a lot of people have difficulty with, including millions of Catholics.

It is the Catholic teaching that sex is a gift meant for the purposes of procreation and that sex indulged in for other reasons is a misuse of that gift. Thus, sex outside of marriage is not condoned. Even sex within marriage when the possibility of procreation has been blocked by birth control is not condoned. Gay sex, in this view, does not fall into the category of permissible sex.

It is possible to disagree with this view while still recognizing it to be a legitimate doctrine of a major religion aimed at providing guidance in the chaotic realm of human sexuality. It may offer some comfort to supporters of same-sex marriage to see through to the humanity of the opposition and to recognize the reasons for opposition are not always founded in bigotry.

At the same time, opponents of same-sex marriage have an obligation to see through to the humanity of a vulnerable minority. Anyone tempted to condemn homosexuality as other than normal ought to consider that it is quite normal that within our population 5 to 10 percent—the number is not important—happen to be gay or lesbian. For each of us, it is normal to be who we are, whether we are heterosexual or homosexual. It has always been that way, and the sooner we recognize it the better.

There are among us already those eager to sharpen the swords of conflict on the issue of same-sex marriage.

But the people of Vermont are in this together. Opponents and supporters of the Supreme Court's ruling are part of the same community, and as the discussion moves forward it is important to cultivate a charitable view of those on the other side. That way, however the issue is resolved, Vermont will be a better place in the end.

—*February 9, 2000*


### *A conscientious start*

Ever since the Supreme Court issued its ruling on same-sex marriage in December, it has been clear the state's political leadership hoped to forestall the wrath of the people by pursuing the option of domestic partnerships for same-sex couples.

The House Judiciary Committee took that step on Wednesday, deciding by a vote of 8-3 to support domestic partnerships as it begins the job of drafting legislation.

Supporters of same-sex marriage are disappointed, reasoning that any option short of marriage treats gays and lesbians as second-class citizens. But the president of a group opposed to same-sex marriage had a different view. In describing why she also opposed domestic partnership, she said: "If it looks like marriage, acts like marriage and talks like marriage, it's marriage."

Domestic partnership ought to look like marriage. It could even be connected to marriage. The Legislature could provide that one of the means of securing legal standing as domestic partners would be a marriage certificate from one of the religious faiths now willing to marry same-sex couples.

In choosing to pursue domestic partnerships, the committee is aware of the disappointment that will be felt by those who believe that treating heterosexual and homosexual couples differently creates a stigma. The sting of that disappointment may be lessened by considering the pluses and minuses of each approach.

It is likely that either domestic partnerships or marriage would satisfy the substance of the demand by the Supreme Court that same-sex couples receive benefits equal to those enjoyed by heterosexual married couples. Marriage, however, would go further than domestic partnerships, granting a victory of principle and using the imprimatur of the state to erase the stigma attached to same-sex unions.

But the stigma, at least in some people's minds, won't be erased so easily. Resistance to same-sex marriage among Vermonters is widely felt and deeply ingrained. Some of it is grounded in homophobia, ignorance and fear. Some of it is grounded in good faith differences about sexuality and marriage.

The court left the burden of choice to the Legislature. By opting at this stage for same-sex marriage, the Legislature would bequeath to gay and lesbian Vermonters the equal benefits they seek and a victory of principle, plus an atmosphere of exaggerated bitterness and hate. By opting for domestic partnerships, the Legislature provides the benefits, minus that victory of principle, but minus also the bitterness.

There will be bitterness in the fact of compromise. But a domestic partnership law should be seen as a vehicle for eliminating inequity rather than as a vehicle for imposing discrimination. Laws creating separate schools for African-Americans were a ruse designed to perpetuate discrimination. Vermont's domestic partnership law could be a wedge to open up the laws for greater equality.

Compromise on a matter of principle is harder if one believes one's opponents are absolutely wrong. But if one can accept the fact of honest differences, then compromise is more palatable.

On the idea of gay marriage legislators would be hard-pressed not to recognize a wide divergence of views, honestly arrived at, among Vermonters. For them to ignore those differences would leave them open to charges of arrogance, and they would be vulnerable at the polls.

Political survival, of course, should not be the highest priority when it comes to matters of principle, but the perception of arrogance could lead to a destructive backlash.

The brilliance of the ruling by Chief Justice Jeffrey Amestoy was that it allowed the people themselves to address head on these questions of politics and principle as they resolve the issue of same-sex marriage. The House Judiciary Committee has made a conscientious start.

—*February 11, 2000*

*A courageous step*

The Vermont House of Representatives took a courageous step Wednesday in giving preliminary approval to a bill providing for civil unions between same-sex couples.

The events of the past two and a half months have been an example of extraordinary lawmaking. Republicans and Democrats joined together to respond to a constitutional mandate. The confidence of their own convictions ought to serve as their best shield against criticism. The swift, sure action they have taken ought to serve as the best protection against the deep division that a protracted conflict would create.

Two people stood out in the debate that preceded the vote Wednesday evening. One was Rep. Thomas Little, the Shelburne Republican who shepherded the bill through the House Judiciary Committee and to the floor of the House. His reasoned, low-key approach to the task kept the debate focused and properly restrained. His conviction in the rightness of his course can only have helped to stiffen the courage of fellow House members.

The other was Rep. William Lippert, a Democrat from Hinesburg, who spoke before a vote was taken, defeating an amendment that would have diluted and weakened the bill.

As Lippert began to speak Wednesday, the House fell silent. Lippert, who is gay, spoke with dignity and with passion. He began by saying it was important for his fellow House members to understand reality.

Gay relationships, he said, are in some ways "miracles" because they manage to take shape within an atmosphere of unremitting prejudice. He asked his fellow House members to imagine how difficult it would be for them to form lasting relationships in such circumstances. He said gay relationships represented a "triumph against discrimination and prejudice."

Lippert said that until two and a half months ago he believed Vermont had made great progress in guaranteeing gay rights. But in the last two and half months, he said, "I have been called names in this chamber and in this building the likes of which I have never seen in my life." He understood that his fellow House members had been subjected to a similar barrage of hate. "I wouldn't have wished this on any of them," he said.

He said he felt, in these circumstances, it was strange to ask, "Should we get our rights now, or should we wait a little longer, or should we ask all the people whether we should get our rights."

He spoke of the burden that the AIDS epidemic had placed on gays. "Don't tell me what a committed relationship is and isn't," he said. The emotional power of Lippert's message combined with Little's reasoned approach to the task were hard for the House to resist.

The House turned aside amendments that would have delayed their decision, either by calling for a constitutional convention or an advisory referendum. Opponents said the people wanted a say on the issue.

But House members already know that a majority probably opposes the action they have taken. Two extraordinary public hearings allowed the public an unprecedented opportunity to express its views, and the volume of mail to the Legislature and to the press has provided the Legislature with a full spectrum of opinion. Votes on Town Meeting Day showed continuing opposition to same-sex marriage or civil unions.

What the House required was not more finely calibrated gauges of public opinion, but the power to weigh the opinion it heard against the requirements of the law. In the end, that is what the House did.

It is likely that, if this bill becomes law, Vermonters will recognize they have lost nothing by extending fair treatment to neighbors who have had to conduct their personal lives in a shadow of discrimination. Vermonters, in the end, will appreciate the leadership shown by the House on Wednesday.

—*March 16, 2000*

### Questions and Exercises for Reflection and Inspiration

Journalistic writing is controversial; there's simply no two ways around it. Information is in the news not because nothing happened and no one was concerned but because something happened or might happen or didn't happen but, whatever happened, people wanted to know about it. Sometimes young writers try their hand at journalism and discover uncomfortably that they're not equipped to deal with the realities of covering the news. Whether it's a city board of aldermen meeting or a shooting in a rural community, journalists cannot avoid writing about issues that will instill passions.

When David Moats came to the subject of civil unions, he made a decision to write in favor of the unions but at the same time to use language that respected the beliefs and feelings of readers across the spectrum.

**Exercise 1:** Without getting into your personal feelings about the subject of civil unions, think about whether or not Moats succeeded in trying to create a civil atmosphere around the issue. Read one of his columns, jotting down words whose purpose it was to convey reason. Now, take your own issue that you feel strongly about and make a list of words that you believe would be convincing but not inflammatory when used to make your argument. Write an editorial, no longer than seven hundred words, that you think could appear in a newspaper. Remember to use simple, declarative sentences and to express your views in as straightforward and clear language as possible. Avoid absolutes—words like "everyone," "always," "never"—and inflammatory language.

**Exercise 2:** In debate class, instructors teach you first to write a debate speech that supports the opposite argument to yours. Then, write your speech to counter the opposition's argument, making sure to hit on the essential points that are likely to be used in disagreement. Try this: Take the exact opposite argument from the one you have made in exercise 1. Write as fairly and passionately against your own position as possible. When you have done your best effort, writing fairly and accurately, go back and revise your original editorial, paying close attention to the places where you are most likely to have to defend your position.

Letters to the editor are traditionally quite short—four hundred words or so. As a result, the crafter of these sentences must get to his point quickly and succinctly. They are the public equivalent to an editorial because they allow the writer to state his opinion or make his argument without interruption. They may be cut for space or clarity but most papers follow a practice of not censoring letters unless they contain egregious misrepresentations, libelous or offensive language, or are insulting to a group or person. One of the obvious differences between a letter to the editor and a paper's editorial, however, is that the letter is signed whereas the editorial generally is not. Many readers don't even know who writes a paper's editorial. In this, there's something of a risk for the writer of a passionate letter on a controversial issue. Sometimes, it takes great courage (or foolhardiness).

**Exercise 3:** Write a letter to the editor about an issue you've been following in the news and want to comment on. Keep it short and, remember, don't say anything you wouldn't want your neighbor to read.

Photo by Bruce Paul Richards

# 7    Sydney Lea
## *Writing the World We Inhabit*

Born 22 December 1942 in Chestnut Hill, Pennsylvania, and grew up in
    the rural countryside nearby

Education: B.A., M.A. and Ph.D. from Yale University

Lives in Newbury

First publication: a poem in *Creative Moment*, a short-lived magazine, in
    1973

Poetry: *Searching the Drowned Man* (1980); *The Floating Candles* (1983);
    *Prayer for the Little City* (1989); *The Blainville Testament* (1992); *To the
    Bone: New and Selected Poems* (1996); *Pursuit of a Wound* (2000);
    *Ghost Pain* (2005)

Essays: *Hunting the Whole Way Home* (1994); *A Little Wildness: Some
    Notes On Rambling* (2005)

Novel: *A Place in Mind* (1989)

He was the founder and for thirteen years the editor of the *New England
    Review*

Awards: Finalist for the Pulitzer Prize in Poetry for *Pursuit of a Wound*; *To
    the Bone: New and Selected Poems* was cowinner of the 1998 Poets'
    Prize. Lea has received fellowships from the Rockefeller, Fulbright, and
    Guggenheim foundations.

S YDNEY LEA made himself a promise long ago. "For a long while, I
pledged I'd never inhabit ground I couldn't pee on in broad daylight
without worry over observation."[1] Lea's home in Newbury is about as free
from human observation as one can hope to find on the East Coast. His
house, a structure that looks a little like a country castle, overlooks a private

pond and big, hilly fields where his children have played and his dogs have sunned themselves over the years. It's a place that feels grand and rustic at once, one with the land and made from it, the right kind of place for a man whose writing and thinking lives (are they two separate things?) have been entirely concerned with nature and man's relationship with it. Lea is a complex man with simple loves: family, friends, the land, peace, health—and his dogs.

On the side of the pond, a former cabin has been converted into a kennel for Lea's many hunting dogs—wiry, obedient animals that run for pure pleasure and in whom Lea takes great pleasure. Not far away, he's built his studio in a small house that was the original dwelling on the property when he bought it. He and his wife, Robin, a lawyer, and Lea's five children, born over a twenty-year-period in two marriages, fitted themselves into the smaller house while the big house was being built more than fifteen years ago. Now, the studio is spartan but comfortable with bathroom, bookshelves, computer, and a spare room for visitors. A place apart yet one with all else that goes on around him.

Lea and his family came to Vermont in part to get away from human intrusion and to find a community that offered genuine kinship. Before then, the family had been living across the Connecticut River in the town of Orford, New Hampshire. The move had been difficult; Lea had come to know intimately his own property in New Hampshire and the surrounding terrain though years of hiking, hunting, and fishing. In doing so, he was fulfilling a childhood desire. "From an astonishingly young age, I'd vowed to find a region—some beautiful and intriguing country, home to fleet, wild things—and marry it," he wrote in *Hunting the Whole Way Home*. "Thought how I'd courted the wilder parts of Maine, New Hampshire, and Vermont all through my adolescence and then, in my twenties, tied the knot with upper New England.

"For a long stretch, I'd remained so in love with this Grafton County that even on the worst day of mudtime my heart would stutter at the simple sight of a certain slope or tree or stream. The stubborn green of an October sidehill surrounded by darkening woods seemed a marvel that all by itself proved life worthwhile."[2]

But then his love affair grew troubled. The trouble came in the guise of a developer intent on building luxury "estates" on the mountain; Lea considered the idea a travesty. What would happen to the creatures already living there and why would someone want to bring civilization into a place so perfectly wild? He poured considerable time and money into fighting the development proposal and caused the town's planning commission to reconsider the housing development. But Lea could read the writing on the mountain. If this project went unapproved, another would come along. Eventually, roads would crisscross the mountain. The mountain would be tamed, his isolation violated. He felt that New Hampshire residents were not so concerned about environmental protection, especially in relation to unroaded wilderness, as they should be. Other projects would be proposed; he knew he could not fight them all. He looked across the Connecticut River to Vermont, where Act 250, the state's land-use law, protects valuable environments and essential wildlife habitat and where Act 200 requires regional planning that looks at benefits beyond the narrow confines of one man's or one generation's fortunes. He and his wife made the decision to move to Vermont.

"The day the developer filed his plan with the town, we vowed we'd resist it to the end; but we also put our Stonehouse Mountain home on the market and went looking for a bigger spread somewhere else, outside the gentrifying web, something affordable," Lea wrote.[3] While the move was difficult, the result proved worth the difficulty. Here's how he describes the Vermont property: "The spot we found sits a good way upriver, and in one respect I should be satisfied for good: with nearly three hundred acres of scrub and ledge to choose from, I'll relieve myself where I damned well please.

"I want to live where a meeting with a brown-phase fisher is never a commonplace, but always a possibility," he continued. "I'd rather wander a path across the very landscape I dwell in, certain that by such mere circulation, however stealthily undertaken, I might slip among its secretive, metaphysical wonders, as I've done for so much of my life."[4]

*Hunting the Whole Way Home* combines two seemingly disparate occupations: hunting and philosophizing. Lea's poetry and poetic prose is not confined to subjects usually ordained "poetic." He writes as a man who likes to fish and hunt and trail behind his gun dog's bell or follow the trail of the buck that got away. He's a man whose various vocations and avocations are not compartmentalized; rather, they run over and inform one another, so that the story of the father he lost too young is also the story of the boy finding his way in the natural world, learning what he can from the father but eventually having to develop his own connections.

Lea is a big man, powerful of muscle and formidable of intellect but he's not afraid of emotion. One of the loveliest of his essays, "Goodbye Boy," recounts a day spent out on the water with his decoys, his gun, and his dog.[5] His dog thinks the two are going hunting and so too does Lea when he sets out. But memories of other days have their way with Lea on the river. Lea brings us into his thought process as he walks along, writing "[T]here was . . . the plain gratification of being in a beautiful place when the sun first comes to it, a white stain seeping down the high palisade on the Vermont side opposite. The shouts of unroosting crows jostled memories of my boyhood self, crouching in weeds near a papier-mâché owl, hoping to outsmart what I then considered the wariest animal on earth. I'd seen so many warier ones since that that old headiness seemed nearly unimaginable. Yet I could and did imagine it after all, together with the pure, youthful compulsion to what I then called success."

Of course, the success of the hunter depends on many things that include the hunter's own diligence as well as the availability of prey. Lea uses his story in part to express his concern that some waterfowl, especially the varied species of ducks that frequent Vermont in fall and spring, have become fewer over the years while other species, such as the Canada goose, have extended their range. He's lost in his own reverie and doesn't notice that "a pair of drake wood ducks, who should long since have been gone from this territory, was paddling in among my blocks; lost in reminiscence and morose prophecy I'd missed their arrival." His dog, however, has not.

"Topper's trembling was strenuous yet controlled. Briefly rolling his eye back, as he does for example whenever the little dippers cavort unmolested before us, he mutely questioned me: For God's sake, will you *shoot?*"

Right about here, the reader might be squirming in empathy for the handsome drake ducks. Would Lea shoot? Writes Lea: "Just then I mutely answered: No." Instead, he yelled to the wood ducks, "Get out of here," and they did.

Of course, the hunter's reason for *not* shooting—for releasing the fish or letting the buck go unmolested—is more interesting than his reason *for* shooting. Lea explores here the antihunting argument as well as his own sense that there is something quite contractual in the relationship between the hunter and the hunted, something central to what it means to be human. He's not abandoning that contractual relationship by shooing away the wood ducks—and later a gaggle of geese who failed to take to the sky when he approaches them. Rather, he suggests, the ducks looked too pretty on this particular morning for shooting. His decision not to shoot the geese, however, is a more complex one: "It wasn't the birds' beauty and grace, nor their conformity to the land—and riverscape—even more stunning than the ducks—that had dissuaded me. Or at least none of these things entirely. It was simply that I'd exercised no skills; rather, the game had atypically failed to exercise *its* skills, its keen senses, its native wariness. A kill, so far from defining anything, would have done just the opposite, ratifying the accidental, the random. It would have left me no better than the oaf who, driving by in his car, blasts a grouse off a roadside wall, shooting merely because he's happened on something shootable. Or I'd have been the fool who, looking for deer, murders the bear he blunders across. In a child we may partly forgive such moral idiocy, but not an adult."

### Tips and Techniques

A memoir is not an autobiography; it's a slice of life, a moment in time. That moment in time may be central to the character's life but it must also resonate with the reader. It needs to have universality. We are interested in other people's lives, of course, but we are most interested when we can learn something essential from that person's history. Sydney Lea's memoirs take the form of poetry and essay. In them, he captures small moments: a chain saw injury and the immediate days afterward, a day with his father, a hunting trip with his dog in which nothing was shot. If we only read that he did-n't shoot the ducks, we might applaud that decision or consider him over sentimental or lacking courage. But, in sharing his thought process, Lea writes of larger issues: that contractual relationship be-tween man and prey and its inherent responsibility.

Memoirs can be written in any format. They usually are written in prose style but not necessarily. Regardless of the format, there's an intimacy to a memoir, a laying bare of the soul, often a confessional style. The writer both writes about the event that inspired the recol-lection and muses upon it; his contemplative thoughts and conclu-sions often are expressed in the memoir, as Lea has done in his story, "Goodbye Boy."

The memoir is currently one of the most popular genres. People who study literary trends suggest that the format is most popular during difficult times, times of change or struggle, times in which people look to others for clues on how to get by.

In all of Lea's work, there is this careful dissection of the moral dilem-mas inherent in everyday decisions, whether those decisions are those of the hunter or the father. If Vermont (or nature) is his material, then so too is man's (and woman's) place in it, as well as Vermont's place—both wild and civilized—in the greater world. And the world's place in our hearts.

The title poem of his collection *To the Bone: New and Selected Poems* is a long, narrative excursion through his mind and memory in the moments and weeks after Lea cut his leg quite nastily in a chain saw accident. The ac-cident occurred during a mission of mercy when Lea was trying to cut some wood for a woman friend "whose husband had left her dirty / as hell    no car    no cash      two kids    no fuel."[6]

The poem puts us in the poet/injured man's head in the early moments after the accident as a nurse, Susan Kennedy, does the smart thing and splints Lea's leg in a way that keeps the muscle from "roll[ing] up like a window shade." We share Lea's derangement as he is taken to the emer-gency room, as the morphine dulls the pain while simultaneously unleash-ing a disorganized non sequitur barrage of memories and scenes from the past, presented in the poem much the same as they imposed themselves on his drugged mind. In this drugged state, he recalls that a tooth was shat-tered in the accident. His friend Earl Bonness comes to him, imposing him-self into Lea's delirium, over and over. Lea recalls the death of Earl's daughter, followed closely by the suicide of Earl's grandson. These thoughts are interrupted by the recollection that just a few days previously Lea had picked up and then decided not to buy Kevlar trousers that would have protected his leg. We're with Lea as the images and thoughts unfold, riding the morphine drip with story after story. Days later, after Lea was out of danger, his wife finally told him that Earl had died the very day of Lea's accident.

It's a remarkable poem in that Lea is able to capture the feel and rhythm of the delirium, its nonsense and its clarity. Throughout its telling, there are the constants that keep the reader and the speaker grounded: the wife and children by his bedside; the wound itself, a violation and a sober reminder of mortality; that sense of imbalance, of otherness, whenever our bodies have been dramatically violated. There is loss throughout the stanzas, repeated over and over through the various images and stories. But what remains is not loss or despair, but rather gratitude, as expressed in these lines:

> the wound sealing itself such that again I'd refer to me
> as being entire  and such that this ceaseless current bearing every
>     desire
> we name it life  would come out all right
> it would be all right  it would be all right
> whatever it might be[7]

Lea says he wasn't actually back in the delirium when he wrote *To the Bone,* but rather "re-imagining the delirium. Something happened in that poem and in the poem, 'The Feud,' in that both poems came to me almost fully packaged. I did very little revising. I don't know how to account for that. Those are the two longest poems I've written. The one thing they have in common is they broke the ice after a fairly long period for me of not writing," he says, adding that perhaps the poems came to him whole because they'd been percolating in his mind during the long period of not writing.

Robert Penn Warren wrote that Lea "converts factuality into a poetry of depth (an attempt that has become a fashion but that usually fails), small observations into something as deep as ritual. He is a poet who knows where to find the poetry that suits his nature—and a poetry of which we would not be happily deprived. He has the subtlety of mind, emotion, and ear to achieve this in a genre in which many fail."[8]

Lea came to the writing life late, having lived the first fifteen years of his adult life primarily as an academic. He explains: "I had dreams of being a writer since a child but never started writing until age thirty-five. Writers were something different. I thought there was something magical about writing; I didn't know what it was." After college and graduate school at Yale, he was hired to teach at Dartmouth College. After he'd been there seven years or so, the chair of his department told Lea that, if he ever wanted to be considered for tenure, he'd best publish some scholarly writing, the old "publish or perish" advice. Lea went to the Baker Library at Dartmouth and took a look at "my inscrutable PhD dissertation on supernatural literature of the nineteenth century." He thought he might turn some section of the thesis into an article for one of the literary magazines that publish scholarly works. He recalls standing in the stacks with the dissertation in his hand and actually saying out loud, "This is not what I want to do when I grow up."

Although he had not been pursuing his writing seriously, he had always hoped that at some point he would become a writer. As he told Marie Jordan Giordano in an interview for the *Writer's Chronicle* in September 2004, "Some little genius inside me said, 'Well if you want to be a writer, you'd better write.'" When he gave some thought to it, he knew immediately what he wanted to write about and it had nothing to do with scholarly research and his dissertation. "I was captivated by a generation of men and women I knew in New England, virtually all of them gone now, at least the ones that I knew well. They were essentially pre-industrial people who made their own entertainment, and the entertainment tended to take the shape of narrative, and I loved to hear those voices, male and female, as they rolled on and spun stories. I just loved the rhythms and the cadences of that language, and I said I'd like to write about them. I wanted to capture that quality.

"I had this notion that I could do it better in poetry than I could do in prose, because in prose I'd have to be a genius like Mark Twain and write dialect which was at once convincing and not condescending. Without having to imitate these old folks, I thought, rightly or wrongly, that I could get a little bit of the heft of their language if I used verse. Of course, since a lot of the stuff I heard from them was narrative, it's unsurprising that the poems took on a narrative direction. I was very lucky very early and got poems prominently placed and had a book out pretty soon. I worked a lot harder on my poetry then than I do now. I mean, I was a tiger. I worked every day from very early in the morning and I arranged my teaching schedule in the afternoons."[9]

By "prominently placed," Lea is referring to his first published poem, published in 1976 in the *New Yorker* and followed quickly by poems in the *Atlantic* and the *New Republic*. Over the decades, Lea has taught at Dartmouth, Yale, Middlebury, Wesleyan, Vermont College, and the National University of Hungary in Budapest, but he takes ample time off for his writing, which, along with his family, remains his priority over teaching.

Lea's writing process is inextricably linked to his ramblings in the woods. "I'm an early riser," he says. "I get out of bed and head for the woods first thing—maybe 5:00 in the morning. I'm not necessarily looking for material for a poem. Things just seem to be given to me and I come back and write. Getting off by myself is part of my writing process." His friend, the late Bill Matthews, used to compare Lea's writing to the 1932 song, "The Teddy Bears Picnic," which has the line, "If you go down in the woods today, you're sure of a big surprise." Lea almost always has a surprise when he wanders through the woods. "It's that surprise that hooks you," Lea explains. "Last winter, for example, I was walking along and came across the carcass of a dead deer and I said to myself the words, 'winter kill.' Something in those words intrigued me and I played around with them when I got back home. Out of that came four poems in four days, all from going into the woods and encountering a big surprise."

When he first started writing, Lea kept a little notebook in his pocket and scribbled down notes as ideas and images came to him. He also found himself writing thoughts to himself while driving, so much so that his wife got him a Dictaphone. He's trained his mind so that he can now recall those images on demand and doesn't need the notebook so much as he once did. Still, he urges beginning writers to record their thoughts before they disintegrate into the frustrating memory of the memory.

In the interview with Giordano, Giordano asked Lea how he felt to be so frequently called the "poetic heir to Robert Frost." For Lea, that is the ultimate compliment as he considers Robert Frost "the great American poet. . . . You can take a Robert Frost poem into almost any venue and people will get something out of it. It's what I hope for in my writing. The common reader, if the creature still exists, should be able to get something out of my work, and she or he does not have to have gone to a graduate program to get a sense of what's on my mind."[10] Yet, he notes, there are great differences between him and Frost. "One thing Frost was able to do that I am constitutionally unable to do is to leave the almighty fetid, squalid 'I' out of the poem. I think when people call me an heir to Frost, what they're talking about is where I live, but I'm not really very much like Frost. Frost, God bless him, would never have written anything like my poem, *To The Bone*, which is kind of a blues rant," he says.

You can hear the blues in Lea's writing. Indeed, he says if he'd been 10 or 15 percent better a musician, he might have pursued music as a career rather than writing and teaching. Like the black jazz musicians who influenced the rhythm and pacing of Budbill's poetry, Lea says, "The rhythms and cadences of what I call black classical music are probably more influential on my psyche than anything I've ever read. The heft of the old twelve-bar blues is always in my mind to some extent."

But, like Frost, Lea is deliberate about writing for the average person. He notes that some writers purposefully make their work too difficult for the average person to read, never mind comprehend. He points out that Ezra Pound once said, "'The man in the street is there because he doesn't deserve to be let in.' Well, the hell with that, I say! I want to invite as many people into my poetry or fiction as I can. Is that a lightweight aspiration? Not to my hero, Frost, it wasn't."[11]

And, as it was to Frost, place is central to Lea's work. As he told Giordano, "I live in a town in New England where I know everybody. I mean I know absolutely everybody. The town in Maine in which *A Place in Mind* is based and a lot of my poems are based, is a town of 180 souls. I know family histories. I know local gossip, and that kind of thing. I suspect it may very well be a failing in me, but if I lived in Los Angeles or New York City, I'd write poetry, to be sure, but I don't know what kind of poetry it would be. I think it would be less beholden to the concept of character just because it would be difficult for me to sift out people I wanted to write about with intimate knowledge. Sure, I could write a poem about gang members or drug addicts or street people or whatever, as many people do, but I'd have to write about them as a complete stranger and I certainly wouldn't want to write about them, as some do, as seen through the window of the bus on the way to a faculty meeting."[12]

As a writing teacher, Lea tries "to dismantle some of the misunderstanding of poetry that my students get from English teachers, that somehow or other, literature is a cryptic way of relaying ideas. I try to suggest that poetry is simply another way of knowing things. Although a poem contains ideas, it is not exclusively intellectual. I tell them, 'Don't worry so much about what it means.' I try to indicate to them that poems are really ways of making unforeseen connections. That whole 'To the Bone' poem is just a whole bunch of stuff coming at me. If I made a list of the [people and events that are mentioned in the poem], they'd seem disconnected. The poem is what makes those connections."

Writing a novel, of course, is a different experience from writing a poem. Lea wrote his first novel, *A Place of Mind*, in less than a month while on a fellowship in Ireland. He was living out in the countryside without a car, away from his family. It rained most of the time. He had intended to write a nonfiction story that would recall a tale that had lodged in his mind, a story told to him by an old man up in Maine who was a wonderful raconteur. "The next thing I knew I was a hundred pages into this manuscript. It just sort of took off on me. I had hundreds of memories of going to Maine and the stories of these old guys and somehow these stories just got linked together into a novel," he recalls. Against his usual habit, he found himself working on the novel all night long and sleeping late into the morning. He can't explain why the process was so different but says that, unlike writers who know where they are going, even in a novel, he lets the story unfold, lets it come to him.

Says Lea: "I don't do the plotting until much later. I'm probably not a novelist at all. I just keep writing while the writing's coming. I don't think about the timeline until I have a lot of it written. Then I start making a little chart of dates and places and stuff like that. Any kind of writing I do I just get into it and immerse myself in the material."

---

◆§ EXCERPT FROM "To the Bone"

In memory of Earl Bonness
and for Susan Kennedy, R.N.,
who did the right thing

and I    I wanted to do the right thing
for the woman whose husband had left her dirty
as hell    no car    no cash        two kids        no fuel

and wanted as well    it being Labor Day    to get it done and go home
wife    sons    daughters        the first tartness of autumn seeming
to tang the mist above our pond        and so I hurried

"up like a windowshade otherwise" said the surgeon
meaning what the quadricep saw to the bone might've done
if Sue hadn't done    yes    the right thing and splinted and bound
my left leg so that the muscle would not precisely
roll up that way        and what sort of god
has blessed me all my days that the nearest one

to me was one who knew what to do
which is not to mention that there were six stout men to bear me
from among those trees and down to where Mary and Louise
lived    and that        though it did plunge to        the blade did not
        plunge through
bone nor artery nor ligament nor center of inscrutable nerves nor
        tendon
and that the whole thing was so eerily

painless but for a moment
on the ER table when the intern
noting that the cut was a mess        decided to dress
the thing and shoved two packets of Betadined gauze to the bone
and I passed out and coming to heard somebody say *morphine*
which at first burned

and then through its haze the saw I saw took out my right
        bicuspid
porcelain crown and all and I watched the shards leap into woods
and there Earl Bonness stood ancient eloquent        understanding
        good
Earl Bonness of Washington County Maine
who had known more pain than any intern could conjure
his girlchild    long since        at seventeen    having plain dropped
        dead

no one knew why    and one of his boys born with muscular dystrophy
and what of the grandson he and Tecky raised who raised a pistol and
        pointed
at the soft palate and felt of the trigger and pulled it
and here Earl scooched down to duck these tatters
of tooth that rattled into the woods
with a sound of rain    then he started

to speak as always he did because a story
gives shape to a life and I just let my brain drink it like lifeblood
and    as to myself I always would say when I heard him say

a story   he spoke with the voice of many waters       old river-driver
*it was good times you see but not all good*

*that river trip was a mighty tough job if I'm to be honest*
*we drove a billion board feet clear to the sea*
and I woke because it was absurd that word
*billion*   but of course that was just morphine talking
not Earl who    as my wife would not tell me till a good while after
knowing the way I loved him had died on the very day

of this wound and the wound
being dirty as hell       I'd stay in the hospital five days hooked up
to the damned IV       all the while    needless to say
imagining Earl still alive       but just then    once I got past
the word *billion*       even if I knew it was closer to that
than to the measly six cord we meant to cut

for the abandoned woman    after I got past the billion I fell back in
 and Earl recalled that an old fella cooked for thirty-eight men on an
       open fire
he had three cookees    helpers which dried the pans and platters
by sticking them all in a flour sack and working them back and forth
by golly that cook was quite a man    I did like him
we worked all the daylight there were

and then Earl was gone
I did like them       those friends    and what would've happened
       otherwise
without the men and the woman who splinted and bound my big limb
with the trunk of a third-year maple
without which as I was told on the steel
table    my wife beside me    and the drug seeming to make my very eyes

sweat as my brain went hot
what would've become of the muscle
yes—"up like a windowshade"—so I was more than glad
for morphine    less for killing pain than freeing me to think without
       muscle
and so to lapse under again
and hear Earl

say don't let me say there wan't ever no hard feelings of any kind
*but a lot of them comical too I'll tell a tale    a true one*
*we had us a boy back then in these parts       Jim Foy*
he lived out on Tough End same as I do
and was he a character
and there'd come this peddler with a horse and wagon

about twice a month. Reuben the peddler
which had various things for sale on his cart but mainly clothes
and Reuben was up one evening at Grand Lake Landing
*yes    a bright red evening time*
*when Jim and I come in from guiding*
*and pulled up our canoes*

*and Jim's pants being bedraggled somewhat he went over*
*to Reuben and said I need trousers*
*and they both sorted through till Jim Foy found a pair that'd do*
*we was paid five dollars a day as guides then*
*so when he asked of the peddler the price*
*and when he heard four dollar*

*why Jim looked around and said god almighty for four dollars*
*I'd sell my moccasins hat    shirt    everything I own*
*and Reuben just coughed    once    and then he said take 'em off*
but how did this all come out I wondered as the last clap of tooth
sounded against the understory
all sweet fern and witch hazel frost-browned

by now        and the world as after a beating        went silent
but for something that hummed outside the OR
did Jim get those trousers    I wondered    and wondered
whatever became of my own pants    irreparably rent
above the knee
the ones that should've been the pair

made of Kevlar that I'd looked at across the river
at Deb's Wheel & Deal the very day before    only to decide
not just then to buy because my own winter's supply
of cordwood was already bucked up
and all I needed
was to split the bigger chunks and stack the logs inside

and had only this little good deed to do with good people
and had cut about a billion board feet of wood with a power
saw in my        now    half a century    good God no
so was long on experience    *but there is always a trap*
set for you in the woods
or anywhere at all around lumber

said Earl        *one job I had was hanging boomstock*
*for    you see    on the west river is many big flowage areas above the dam*
*at Grand Falls and they had to boom them logs off each and all*
*to keep them from getting in among the stumps*
*because it was so costly*
*to pull them out of there again*

eighty bucks for the Kevlar trousers at Deb's
and I told her    well    another time
old Bill Park was the boss on the upriver work
and he said I don't know how you can do it
I was green
he said you walk clear out about to the end

of one of those sticks
then hop onto another and you ain't fallen in yet
I told him give me time and said it again    give me time
I was green
as I say        of course
I had a pair of good cog boots

*made by the Bass Company    and still have them today in my shop*
*stepped over a lot of timber they did    you know*
*in all them days        but finally*
but finally what        I don't know
well finally in came my children        or four of the five
the big one away at graduate school    good God no

and they looked at me funny
well likely I looked funny too not funny ha-ha as my grandma
        used to say
but funny peculiar    peculiar    forgive me    reader
if now I must say
I didn't know whether to laugh or cry
I shouldn't put it so banally because I am supposed to have this
        way

with words but every time
push comes to shove    hate    love    joy    disease        trouble
words fail me    at least at first as you can plainly
see and it's not a good feeling
it's like when I studied math in school
forever lost in the shuffle

but never mind math    never mind figures    it is hard
just to write your mind        and Earl to my mind was alive
        who was ninety
who once told me    his old eye twinkly
that in the Depression times got so bad and my deer dog so weak
he had to lean against a bank to howl
but in my dream he never finished the story

26 September–11 October 1994

## Questions and Exercises for Reflection and Inspiration

Until you are quite adept at remembering key words that will allow you to re-create a scene in your mind, you should keep a journal in which you record observations of the world around you, conversations you overhear, conversations you have with yourself, and certain words that strike you as interesting either individually or in combination with other words, such as Lea's words "winter kill." If you find yourself coming up with ideas for poems or stories throughout the day, get a tape recorder that is easy to manage and record your thoughts while driving, doing the dishes, or other tasks. Once you have about a week's worth of journal entries, try the following exercise, which Lea often gives to his writing students.

> **Exercise 1:** After you have accumulated any amount of notes, in any shape they want to be, take any three entries from your journal and use them to write a poem that connects them. Lea says that the three subjects may not seem connected on first contemplation but "you can believe they are connected because you wrote them down." He says this kind of exercise allows the writer to "discover what has been in your own mind that you didn't know about." Allow the connectedness between the three items from your journal to come to you of its own accord rather than thinking too hard about what it might be. Just start writing on one of your themes and let the other two in when the time seems right. You may be pleasantly surprised.

Lea's friend compared his style of writing to the "Teddy Bears Picnic" song. Try your own hand at going down to the woods one day to have a big surprise. Take your walk in a real woods, one in which you are apt to be fairly alone for several hours. Try to let go of thoughts about daily chores and responsibilities—the "I have to get back to do the laundry" thinking. Pay close attention to the natural world around you but let your mind wander to its own destinations and pick at what it wants to nibble. Try to be of two minds—one paying close attention to your surroundings; the other giving attention to your inner dialogue—without paying too much attention to your paying attention. That's hard to do, especially if you're not used to being outside in the woods; other thoughts, such as fears or anger at yourself for being out of shape, may creep in. But there are no taboo subjects, other than things you have to do. Even those might later be recalled and included in the essay you will write.

> **Exercise 2:** When you get home, go immediately to your study or place of writing and begin recording what you saw and felt, letting your thoughts about other issues quite naturally fall into your narrative. Try to weave your way through the two, spending some time with a description of what you saw and some time describing your reaction

to it and the thoughts that came to you as you walked and observed the natural world. If you were frightened of uncomfortable, you might explore why and connect your recent fear with an older one. Throughout this exercise, try to be as free to associate as possible. Be vivid and specific in your descriptions of what you saw but don't stop to look up the names of plants or birds now—do that later. Just keep writing, trying as best as possible to get into the mind-set you had in the woods and to relate that external and internal experience as best as possible.

Lea's poem *To the Bone* is written as if he were still in the delirium. He re-creates the sense of brokenness and the logic of the illogic that we experience under medication or after a trauma. He has cut himself very badly with a chainsaw. He could have lost his leg. He could be dead. He doesn't say any of these things directly but these thoughts fuel the poem. In it, he's visited by remembrances of one after another dead person, as real and vital to him almost as the wife and children who sit and worry next to his bed. By using the language and pacing of the delirium—re-creating its choppiness, the way the mind goes in and out of focus, the way the brain tosses up new images with little sense of logic—Lea puts the reader in his mind and body. We're there with him through this journey from the moment of the accident to his being able to stand and accept that life might come out all right after all. The poem's power comes not only from the imagery but from its form, the way that Lea has constructed a series of stanzas that are set apart from one another yet flow together just as reality and delusion flow together in the dream or delirium. What is real? What is not? Why are all these people with him, especially Earl Bonness, who has died on the same day as Lea's accident? He doesn't answer these questions; we know the answer as surely as we know why he weeps. He is alive. His family loves him. A smart nurse saved him from having a crippled leg. His friend is gone and so many others. But he is here.

**Exercise 3:** Have you had a similar experience where you endured an illness or injury or trauma and were in and out of consciousness for an extended period of time? Can you recall any of the dreams you had? Did they seem real to you, more real than actual life? Sometimes these dreams and deliriums remain vivid years later, such as the nightmares of childhood or the waking dreams after a loved one has died and you think she has come back to you. Try your own hand at writing a dream poem. Should your poem contain short, declarative sentences or fragmented snippets of scenes, salvaged from your subconscious? Think about the format as much as the words. Construct a format that seems to echo your experience. If the dream or the image came to you all in a rush, write the poem that way. If you floated in and out of consciousness with seemingly separate images coming to you, then fading, try to create that same feel and mood in the format and structure you use. Try, as best you can, to put yourself back into the mind-set you were in at the time, writing perhaps with your eyes closed, and your fingers on the keyboard or simply speaking into a tape recorder. Don't try to make sense of the experience but rather let the poem (or story) tell itself. Stay as close as you can to the original experience that you are trying to capture, using the language of the dream itself, even quoting people who spoke during the dream or hallucination.

Photo courtesy of Gentl & Hyer/Arts Counsel, Inc. © 1994

# 8 Grace Paley

*Angelic-looking Grandmother*
*with Revolution in her Heart*

Born 11 December 1922, the Bronx, New York

Education: Attended Hunter College and New York University

Lives in Thetford

First publication: "Goodbye and Good Luck," published in a small literary
magazine and later republished in *The Little Disturbances of Man:
Stories of Women and Men at Love*

Short story collections: *The Little Disturbances of Man: Stories of Women
and Men at Love* (1959); *Enormous Changes at the Last Minute* (1974);
*Later the Same Day* (1985); *Grace Paley: The Collected Stories* (1994)

Poetry: *Leaning Forward* (1985); *Long Walks and Intimate Talks* (1991); *New
and Collected Poems* (1992); *Begin Again: Collected Poems* (2000)

Essays: *Just As I Thought* (1998)

Awards: Guggenheim Fellowship; American Academy and Institute of
Arts and Letters Award in Literature; Jewish Cultural Achievement
Award for Literary Arts; Vermont Award for Excellence in the Arts;
REA Award for Short Stories; and the Edith Wharton Citation of Merit
for Fiction Writers. She was named New York's first state author in
1986 and Vermont State Poet in 2003.

THE ROAD TO GRACE PALEY'S HOUSE is uphill and muddy—
the proper kind of road for an octogenarian, bantam-sized champion
of peace and the planet, women and minorities to live at the end of. For
more than forty years now, Paley has been questioning authority: sitting on

tarmac in heat and cold, getting bashed over the head, and going to jail for any number of causes from nuclear proliferation to American involvement in the Middle East. Simultaneously, she has written hundreds of short stories, poems, and essays that remain among the most memorable and admired in contemporary literature. Many consider her America's greatest living short story writer. In 2003, she was chosen Vermont State Poet.

A few years ago, while Paley's book, *Just As I Thought*,[1] was being praised from shore to shore, she and her husband, the writer Robert Nichols, shared the pages of Vanity Fair magazine with Madonna and Courtney Love. While Madonna, Love, and a bevy of other beauties bared bodies and flashed pearly whites, Paley and Nichols were photographed in their humble Thetford cabin, sitting on either side of a round, wooden table beneath a shelf laden with canning jars. In contrast to the bare midriffs and bleached coifs of Madonna and Love, there were Paley and Nichols with their halos of wild, white hair, boots upon feet, sweaters and wool pants covering their bodies. Soup was undoubtedly bubbling on the stove, although you couldn't tell from the photo. There was no talk of fashion or foolishness from either Paley or Nichols reported in the article. Rather, it read like excerpts from their ongoing dialogue on the plight of political prisoners, the beauty of language, and the Quaker belief in the intrinsic goodness in each man and woman. It contained remarkable—one might say unusually intelligent—observations for a mainstream magazine, but it also reflected Paley's ability, in person and in print, to disarm and charm even the most jaded listener.

*Vanity Fair* called Paley "the angelic-looking grandmother with revolution in her blood" and called her work "required reading" for all contemporary writers and thinkers. Paley chose to say simply, "I'm kind of lucky to be old at a time when it's getting a better name."[2] That's vintage Paley: simultaneously self-deprecating and funny, a woman with amazing energies that she dispenses with equal generosity upon her much-loved grandchildren and young writers seeking a few writing tips.

Paley didn't come to Vermont to write. She could write anywhere although she considers writing a hard job no matter where she's at. Her short stories are usually grounded in the people and places of Greenwich Village and the Bronx where she grew up and raised her children. But her poems are as often as not rooted in Vermont. "I'm here for Bob," Paley says, referring to her second husband, a writer who worked as an engineer and community organizer in New York City for many years. The house that Nichols and Paley live in is a family property where he always planned to retire. The couple began coming here about thirty-five years ago and moved here for good in 1987. Says Paley: "I hear people say of me, 'She divides her time between Vermont and New York.' That's not accurate," she says. "I go to New York, but I live here."

As Vermont State Poet, an unpaid position with no guidelines, Paley has tried "to bring poetry to where it isn't spoken." Her goals are simple and democratic: to demystify the idea of poetry and storytelling in general: to provide an opportunity for poetry to enrich average people's lives and to share its powerful ability to help us understand the incomprehensible and speak the unspeakable. Here's a good example of how a Paley poem is easily digestible while rewarding the reader who takes a second or third helping of her words with unanticipated depths of meaning:

### The Poet's Occasional Alternative

I was going to write a poem
I made a pie instead—it took
about the same amount of time
of course the pie was a final
draft—a poem would have had some
distance to go——days and weeks and
much crumpled paper

the pie already had a talking
tumbling audience among small
trucks and a fire engine on
the kitchen floor

everybody will like the pie
it will have apples and cranberries
dried apricots in it—many friends
will say——why in the world did you
make only one

this does not happen with poems

because of unreportable
sadness I decided to
settle this morning for a responsive eatership—I do not
want to wait a week—a year—a
generation for the right
consumer to come along

—from *Begin Again*[3]

There's irony and humor in Paley's works, whether poetry or fiction. One of the remarkable things about both the poems and short stories is that the reader feels like he's just stepped into a life. In the short story "An Interest in Life," for example, the opening line is engaging and funny and pathetic all at once—and so real that you are immediately drawn to the narrator's story.[4] It begins:

My husband gave me a broom one Christmas. This wasn't right.
No one can tell me it was meant kindly.

"I don't want you not to have anything for Christmas while I'm away in the army," he said. "Virginia, please look at it. It comes with this fancy dustpan. It hangs off a stick. Look at it, will you? Are you blind or cross-eyed?"

"Thanks, chum," I said. I had always wanted a dustpan hooked up that way. It was a good one. My husband doesn't shop in bargain basements or January sales.

Still and all, in spite of the quality, it was a mean present to give a woman you planned on never seeing again, a person you had children with and got onto all the time, drunk or sober, even when everybody had to get up early in the morning.

I asked him if he could wait and join the army in a half hour, as I had to get the groceries. I don't like to leave kids alone in a three-bedroom apartment full of gas and electricity. Fire may break out from a nasty remark. Or the oldest decides to get even with the youngest.

"Just this once," he said. "But you better figure out how to get along without me."

The story brings us into a world populated by the narrator; her neighbor in the apartment building, Mrs. Raferty, whose kindest comments carry an intended sting; and Mrs. Raferty's son John, whose marriage has its own disappointments. John's visits to the narrator initially flatter her, then proceed to the next stage. It's a story of all the trapped mothers who struggle to feed their kids after the father walks out. When Paley's narrator accepts the fact that her husband isn't coming back, she calls on the welfare people but "in no time I discovered that they're rigged up to deal with liars, and if you're truthful it's disappointing to them. They may even refuse to handle your case if you're too truthful."

The story ends with a dream (or is it?) of the husband's return. He hasn't been seen or heard from in two and a half years yet there he is at the door, using his old key. Paley, who has written the story up until now in past tense, suddenly changes to present tense. This device disarms us; is it a dream or has the husband actually returned to start the cycle all over again? That simple change in verb tense creates the uncertainty. First we are in the past tense, with the narrator reminiscing about this hard time and that hard time in her life; then we are on the kitchen floor with the narrator and her husband, "and the truth is, we were so happy, we forgot the precautions."

Along with the world that Paley creates in this fifteen-page story is the world left unwritten, the world that continues after the story has ended. We're left wondering what actually happened that day. Yet, we know the story: people endure; they make fresh mistakes; they fall in love; they are foolish; someone gets hurt; sometimes they get over it; life goes on.

*Just As I Thought* gathers together two of Paley's primary activities—writing and working for peace and justice. At the time of its publication, Paley, at almost age eighty, was traveling on a fact-finding mission to Vietnam to see firsthand what had happened to the Vietnamese people and the country since the Vietnam War. She had been involved with the Joiner Center for the Study of War and Social Consequences (which provides educational and other services to veterans) in a writing project with poets from the United States and Vietnam. She had been in Vietnam in the 1960s; in her return visit in the mid-1990s, she revisited many places where she had first observed the war. As she had previously, she spent her time interviewing people for articles and stories she might want to write, and working on the joint publishing venture.

Immediately upon returning home, however, Paley found herself visiting schools, libraries, and an occasional bookstore, wherever people had asked her to speak about her new book. Even those who know her are often surprised by her tremendous energy, her maternal earnestness, her humor and humility. Despite fatigue and the press of creative work she longed to devote herself to, she turned each speaking engagement into an unforgettable dialogue in which she shared her observations about the damage her country had done to a people who had done us no harm and about the resilience of the human spirit. She also read from a body of work that spans the genres.

Those in the audiences who hadn't met Paley before were ill prepared for the impact she would have on them. She gets you thinking about the huge problems of war and hate and zealotry by talking or writing about them in the most human of terms. Besides her essays on war, famine, and discrimination, *Just As I Thought* also includes essays that give us small glimpses into her own life, here in Vermont. In the essay entitled "Life in the Country: a City Friend Asks, 'Is it Boring?'" Paley writes:

> No! Living in the country is extremely lively, busy. After the gardens have gone to flower, to seed, to frost, the fruits canned, frozen, dried, the days and evenings are full of social events and human communication. Most of it dependent on the automobile or phone, though a few tasks can be accomplished on foot or ski. Even if you are not worried about the plain physical future of the world, there's a lot to do.[5]

There follows a lengthy and funny list of the meetings that people in the country attend: planning boards, conservation committees, historical societies, food co-ops. The essay concludes with this observation about living in Vermont:

> And of course there is standing in the front yard (or back) staring at the work time has accomplished in crumpling the hills into mountains, then stretching them out again only a few miles away into broad river plains, stippling white pink rust black across the

wooded hills, clarifying the topography by first aging, then blowing away the brilliant autumn leaves. Although here and there the wrinkled brown leaves of the oak hold tight, and the beech leaf, whose tree will die young, grows daily more transparent, but waits all winter for the buds of spring.[6]

Paley's approach to writing is as diverse and unpredictable as her interests: "I have the idea that I'll write every day but sometimes life doesn't let you. I often write at night, or at least I look at things I'm working on and make changes," she says. "Sometimes I begin writing and I don't know what it will be—a story or a poem. Sometimes, I have just a few lines. I have lots of paper—pages and pages and odds and ends, beginnings that I look at all the time.

"I'm like the painter Miró who said 'I work like a gardener. I'm never so happy as when I'm rich with canvases. I water this one; I prune another.' Bob says I have no habits. But I tell him I do. I either water this piece or prune it until I get it right."

Life in the Paley/Nichols household does look a little like controlled chaos: the mail to be answered, piled high on the kitchen table, stacks of books to be read, the answering machine blinking with messages still unheard. Nichols sometimes follows behind Paley at some point in the day, gathering up the various scraps of paper upon which she's jotted notes and putting them in a box that might be labeled "ideas for writing," or "writing in progress." He lectures her about taking better care of herself, slowing down, taking time for herself. But Paley would rather go to bed exhausted than give up any of her interests and causes or say no to yet another request for a reading. She might have been more prolific if she had attended to her writing more, rather than being pulled in so many directions. Yet she says she doesn't think of what she does as a balancing act. "You're better off if you don't think of it that way. I just went with whatever was going to drag me one way or the other. It's not such a bad way to live a life. I can't imagine any other," she says.

She recalls that the inspiration for her very first story, "Goodbye and Good Luck" came from one line uttered by her first husband's aunt during a visit a few years after the two were married. Something about Paley and her first husband, Jess Paley, who were in their thirties, the prime of their lives, annoyed the aunt, who said to them, "'I was popular in certain circles, and I wasn't no thinner then.'"

"That wonderful sentence resonated in my mind, probably for a year, before I wrote anything. I'd ask people, 'You know what his aunt said?' and I'd repeat it," recalls Paley, who eventually started constructing a story around that sentence. In the story, a young and buxom woman named Rosie Lieber becomes involved with a married Russian actor while working in a Yiddish theater on New York's Lower East Side. It's a mistake, of course, to take up with a married man, but this is no morality play and

Rosie ends the story with few regrets. The story isn't based on the aunt; but the aunt's sentence gave birth to it.[7]

Paley has a very distinctive voice. In all her work, it's as if she is speaking directly to the reader. The tone is natural, conversational, even when the meaning is layered. Paley explains how she developed this voice—or, rather, how her voice came naturally to her. When she was young, she wrote poetry that sounded a lot like the poets that she had been reading—Auden, in particular. "Those poems meant a lot to me when I wrote them," she says. But she came to see that the voice of the poets she had studied, the voice of the classic writers, was not her own voice. Her voice was of a Jewish woman who grew up in New York, was an activist and mother, and listened to a lot of women (and men) who struggled with real-life issues. That's the voice she writes in.

"I've come to think about it this way: you have two ears. One is the literary ear, the one we train when we study writing and read the greats. It's a good ear, an essential ear, but it's not our own. Your own ear is the language of your own people, of your home, your street, or whatever is your true, closest environment and way of talking.

"I discovered this during that time I had off, when I was sick, and using both ears. I was trying to write a story and I had a kind of breakthrough. I had enough poetry from this ear, the literary one, and I suddenly broke through into the language that I knew, my own language, the language I continue to write with. That was an important hour in my life," she says.

As she writes, she reads aloud, as much for consistency as to keep herself going. She can hear her voice and hear when it isn't right. "When I write that first sentence, I don't know if I'm making a poem or a story. But by the time I'm at my third line, I know what it's going to be. The poem or story makes its own form. Some stories begin in the third person; some with the 'I.' I don't know why one is a 'she' story and another an 'I' story. But as I write and read out loud, I can hear if it goes wrong. That happens when you get blocked. You can hear that you have the wrong voice or the wrong person telling the story. When the wrong person is telling a story, sometimes it takes me a long time to get it right. Sometimes, you don't; you just know it's wrong."

Born in 1922, Paley grew up in a home in which intellectual and political thought were integral to daily life. Russian and Yiddish were spoken alongside English. In the Russia of her parent's youth, before the turn of the century, dinner was accompanied by heated debate as her father, a socialist, argued with an anarchist uncle while an aunt, a Zionist, traded barbs with another aunt who was a Communist. Paley grew up hearing these stories in the Yiddish of her ancestors.

Her parents, Isaac and Manya Gutseit, seemed heroic to her. As a young couple, they had been arrested and charged with holding anti-czarist beliefs. After a period of exile in Siberia, they were released unexpectedly when the czar's wife bore a son. Fearing the czar might change his mind, they and other political prisoners fled to the United States just weeks before the Russian Revolution. In America, their name was anglicized to Goodside. Her father, a doctor, and mother settled among other Russian Jews in a neighborhood where the flavors and scents of the motherland permeated the air.

As a very young girl, Paley joined the Falcons, an organization for Bronx socialists under twelve. Falcons wore blue shirts and red kerchiefs, sang the "Internationale," learned about "real suffering," and studied prejudice. Even though she lived in a Jewish neighborhood, Paley had already felt the bite of discrimination When she was eleven, neighbors in Mahopac, a socialist bungalow colony Paley's family frequented in summer, were alarmed by rumors that the Ku Klux Klan planned to burn crosses on their front lawns; Paley joined her father and others as they patrolled the area that summer.

At age nineteen, she married Jess Paley, then a young member of the Army Signal Corps, and traveled with him to various military camps for two years before returning to New York. There, the two lived in a basement apartment in Greenwich Village. He launched a career as a cinematographer while Paley set about raising their daughter, Nora, and their son, Danny. She didn't know it at the time but, as she sat in Washington Square with other mothers and traded troubles and recipes, she was also collecting the real-life stories that would find their way into her books: *The Little Disturbances of Man, Enormous Changes at the Last Minute*, and *Grace Paley, The Collected Stories*, which was a finalist for the 1994 National Book Award.

In the introduction to the *Collected Stories*, Paley tells of how she got discovered as a writer. She attributes her "discovery" to two strokes of good fortune: "In 1955 or '56 I decided to write a story. I had written a few nice paragraphs with some first-class sentences in them, but I hadn't known how to let women and men into the language nor could I find the story in those pieces of prose.

"I needed to speak in some inventive way about our female and male lives in those years. Some knowledge was creating a real physical pressure, probably in the middle of my chest—maybe just to the right of the heart. I was beginning to suffer the storyteller's pain: Listen! I have to tell you something!

"Then the first of two small lucks happened. I became sick enough for the children to remain in Greenwich House After School until suppertime for several weeks, but not so sick that I couldn't sit at our living-room table to write or type all day. I began the story 'Goodbye and Good Luck' and to my surprise carried it through to the endl"[8]

The second good thing happened after an ex-husband of a friend came by her apartment to pick up his children, who were playing with Paley's children. This man sat in her kitchen chair and said his former wife had been pestering him to read Paley's stories. Paley put him off. He persisted on several subsequent visits and, eventually, Paley gave him a couple of stories to read. As it turned out, the man was the Doubleday editor Ken McCormick.

When he returned to Paley's apartment a week or two later, he again sat at her kitchen table and announced that, if she could write seven more stories, he would publish the book. That book, *The Little Disturbances of Man*, launched her career.

But Paley says the biggest luck of all in her life "has to do with political movements, history that happens to you while you're doing the dishes, wars that men plan for their sons, our sons." By this, she means that she came into her writing years just as the feminist movement was coming into its own and women were discovering the power of their own voices. She had already been active in community organizing, in working to keep buses out of Washington Square, in supporting neighborhood schools, and fighting nuclear proliferation. She had already discovered the inter-relatedness of many of the causes she was concerned with. Her characters, mostly women, were already talking about these issues, mixing worldly concerns into the talk of husbands and children and bills. There is Faith, a recurring figure in her stories, saying in the short story "Like All the Other Nations:"

> For happiness, she required women to walk with. To walk in the city arm in arm with a woman friend (as her mother had with aunts and cousins so many years ago) was just plain essential.
>
> For happiness, she also required work to do in this world and bread on the table. By work to do, she included the important work of raising children righteously up. By righteously, she meant that along with being useful and speaking truth to the community, they must do no harm.
>
> By harm, she meant not only personal injury to the friend the lover the co-worker the parent (the city the nation) but also the stranger; she meant particularly the stranger in all her or his difference, who, because we were strangers in Egypt, deserves special goodness for life, or at least until the end of strangeness.[9]

These had been her subjects for years but suddenly these concerns were also alive in the land and, more and more frequently, it was women who were giving them voice. Paley became one of the spokeswomen for her gender, not a strident voice full of blame at the men of the world but a mother's voice, saying motherly things: Stop fighting. Share. Leave your brother alone. Eat your vegetables. The power of the feminist voice was hers, but it also belonged to many. "Every woman writing in these years has had to swim in that feminist wave. No matter what she thinks of it, even if she bravely swims against it, she has been supported by it—the buoyancy, the noise, the saltiness," she says.

### Tips and Techniques

Writers tend to feel more comfortable writing scenes, whether fictional or real, in past tense. However, writers often discover that when they use the present tense, as if the reader is there as the action is unfolding, that the prose has more immediacy and resonates more deeply with the reader. When you write, experiment with different tenses to see which works best for a particular story.

Regardless of what tense you use, think about how your choice affects the telling. Ask yourself how the story changes if the reader knows it happened in the past rather than as the story unfolds on the page.

Writers also find that if they manipulate tenses, sometimes using past tense; other times using present, that the reader pays more attention.

Changing tenses can be confusing; it must be done with absolute control. The writer must know precisely what she is trying to convey by placing some actions in present tense and others in past. But, when it's done right, as in the excerpt below, "Traveling," or in several of Grace Paley's short stories, manipulation of tense gives the story added depth and resonance.

Paley's work is not memorable soley because she has the gift of telling stories of individual relationships in context with the great causes of her day. Also noteworthy is her voice: so distinctive and strong that we instantly recognize it, regardless of the setting or context. So says Evan Boland, the Irish poet and director of the Wallace Stegner Creative Writing Program at Stanford University, which gave Paley a lifetime honor for her achievements in 1998.

At the ceremony honoring Paley, Boland praised the natural rhythms, irony, humor, and authenticity of Paley's words, how she delights us time after time with stories of women who are clear-eyed about sexual relationships and power as they fail to resist the men in their lives who take advantage of them and of the situations both parties find themselves in.

Paley tried to shrug off Boland's praise and the enthusiastic applause of the audience as she made her way to the podium, walking more like a truck driver than a poet. Once on the huge stage, she looked into the audience, barely perceptible from the bright stage. "Turn on the lights out there," she commanded as she peered over and around the podium. "If you're telling people stories, you ought to be able to see your audience," she said, taking her 4-foot-9-inch self to the side of the podium so she could see and be seen.

"Don't give me so much credit," she admonished the audience that seemed reluctant to stop clapping. "I'm no different from you. You write about what has to be written."

◄§ FROM *Just As I Thought* · "Traveling"

My mother and sister were traveling south. The year was 1927. They had begun their journey in New York. They were going to visit my brother, who was studying in the South Medical College of Virginia. Their bus was an express and had stopped only in Philadelphia, Wilmington, and now Washington. Here, the darker people who had gotten on in Philadelphia or New York rose from their seats, put their bags and boxes together, and moved to the back of the bus. People who boarded in Washington knew where to seat themselves. My mother had heard that something like this would happen. My sister had heard of it, too. They had not lived in it. This reorganization of passengers by color happened in silence. My mother and sister remained in their seats, which were about three-quarters of the way back.

When everyone was settled, the bus driver began to collect tickets. My sister saw him coming. She pinched my mother. Ma! Look! Of course, my mother saw him, too. What frightened my sister was the quietness. The white people in front, the black people in back—silent.

The driver sighed, said, You can't sit here, ma'am. It's for them, waving over his shoulder at the Negroes, among whom they were now sitting. Move, please.

My mother said, No.

He said, You don't understand, ma'am. It's against the law. You have to move to the front.

My mother said, No.

When I first tried to write this scene, I imagined my mother saying, That's all right, mister, we're comfortable. I can't change my seat every minute. I read this invention to my sister. She said it was nothing like that. My mother did not try to be friendly or pretend innocence. While my sister trembled in the silence, my mother said, for the third time, quietly, No.

Somehow finally, they were in Richmond. There was my brother in school among so many American boys. After hugs and my mother's anxious looks at her young son, my sister said, Vic, you know what Mama did?

My brother remembers thinking, What? Oh! She wouldn't move? He had a classmate, a Jewish boy like himself, but from Virginia, who had had a public confrontation with a Negro man. He had punched that man hard, knocked him down. My brother couldn't believe it. He was stunned. He couldn't imagine a Jewish boy wanting to knock anyone down. He had never wanted to. But he thought, looking back, that he had been set down to work and study in a nearly foreign place and had to get used to it. Then he told me about the Second World War, when the disgrace of black soldiers being forced to sit behind white German POWs shook him. Shamed him.

Almost fifteen years later, in 1943, in early summer, I rode the bus for about three days from New York to Miami Beach, where my husband in sweaty fatigues, along with hundreds of other boys, was trudging up and down the streets and beaches to prepare themselves for war.

By late afternoon of the second long day, we were well into the South, beyond Richmond, maybe South Carolina or Georgia. My excitement about travel in the wide world was damaged a little by a sudden fear that I might not recognize Jess or he, me. We hadn't seen each other for two months. I took a photograph out of my pocket; yes, I would know him.

I had been sleeping waking reading writing dozing waking. So many hours, the movement of the passengers was something like a tide that sometimes ebbed and now seemed to be noisily rising. I opened my eyes to the sound of new people brushing past my aisle seat. And looked up to see a colored woman holding a large sleeping baby, who, with the heaviness of sleep, his arms so tight around her neck, seemed to be pulling her head down. I looked around and noticed that I was in the last white row. The press of travelers had made it impossible for her to move farther back. She seemed so tired and I had been sitting and sitting for a day and a half at least. Not thinking, or maybe refusing to think, I offered her my seat.

She looked to the right and left as well as she could. Softly she said, Oh no. I became fully awake. A white man was standing right beside her, but on the other side of the invisible absolute border. Of course, she couldn't accept my seat. Her sleeping child hung mercilessly from her neck. She shifted a little to balance the burden. She whispered to herself, Oh, I just don't know. So I said, Well, at least give me the baby. First, she turned, barely looking at the man beside her. He made no move. So, to my surprise, but obviously out of sheer exhaustion, she disengaged the child from her body and placed him on my lap. He was deep in child-sleep. He stirred, but not enough to bother himself or me. I liked holding him, aligning him along my twenty-year-old young woman's shape. I thought ahead to that holding, that breathing together that would happen in my life if this war would ever end.

I was so comfortable under his nice weight, I closed my eyes for a couple of minutes, but suddenly opened them to look up into the face of a white man talking. In a loud voice he addressed me: Lady, I wouldn't of touched that thing with a meat hook.

I thought, Oh, this world will end in ice. I could do nothing but look straight into his eyes. I did not look away from him. Then I held that boy a little tighter, kissed his curly head, pressed him even closer so that he began to squirm. So sleepy, he reshaped himself inside my arms. His mother tried to narrow herself away from that dangerous border, too frightened at first to move at all. After a couple of minutes, she leaned forward a little, placed her hand on the baby's head, and held it there until the next stop. I couldn't look up into her mother's face.

I write this remembrance more than fifty years later. I look back at that mother and child. How young she is. Her hand on his head is quite small, though she tries by spreading her fingers wide to hide him from the white man. But the child I'm holding, his little face as he turns toward me, is the brown face of my own grandson, my daughter's boy, the open mouth of the sleeper, the full lips, the thick little body of a child who runs wildly from one end of the yard to the other, leaps from dangerous heights with certain experienced caution, muscling his body, his mind, for coming realities.

Of course, when my mother and sister returned from Richmond, the family at home wanted to know: How was Vic doing in school among all those gentiles? Was the long bus ride hard, was the anti-Semitism really bad or just normal? What happened on the bus? I was probably present at that supper, the attentive listener and total forgetter of information that immediately started to form me.

Then, last year, my sister, casting the net of old age (through which recent experience easily slips), brought up that old story. First, I was angry. How come you never told me about your bus ride with Mama? I mean, really, so many years ago.

I don't know, she said, anyway you were only about four years old, and besides, maybe I did.

I asked my brother why we'd never talked about that day. He said he thought now that it had had a great effect on him; he had tried unraveling its meaning for years—then life family work happened. So I imagined him, a youngster really, a kid from the Bronx in Virginia in 1927; why, he was a stranger there himself.

In the next couple of weeks, we continued to talk about our mother, the way she was principled, adamant, and at the same time so shy. What else could we remember . . . Well, I said, I have a story about those buses, too. Then I told it to them: How it happened on just such a journey, when I was still quite young, that I first knew my grandson, first held him close, but could protect him for only about twenty minutes fifty years ago.

1997 [10]

## Questions and Exercises for Reflection and Inspiration

Paley's style has a natural prose rhythm; stories are often told in fragments that reassemble into a single voice. The voice is both wise and humorous, without trying to be. The wisdom and humor comes from her nature. So too do her toughness and compassion. What attributes and knowledge gained from living inform your writing? Sometimes a person is a natural storyteller; her stories are spontaneous, funny, and suspenseful. But then when the person goes to put the same story on paper, it loses its magic. It becomes heavy with trying, too deliberate, or the writer rushes to her point. This happens when a writer hasn't developed her own personal voice but rather writes in the voice of "literature." For most of us, that voice is inappropriate; it just doesn't work.

> **Exercise 1:** Record on tape a family story or an account of something you experienced that has both universal and personal significance: "the time I ..." Pay attention to your voice as you talk, to how you quite naturally tell stories. Pretend you're telling the story to someone. Be as natural as possible. Then, using the tape as a guide, try to reproduce your individualistic voice and tone on paper. Write your story, speaking out loud as if you were addressing your best friend or grandchild as you write.

Paley says one aspect of life informs another. She doesn't regret the time she spent with the other mothers and their children in Washington Park. Those hours and days provided her with deep relationships and material that later translated into fictionalized stories. Says Paley: "The gift of that subject matter was made to me while I watched my kids." It was also given to her on that bus trip to Florida when she went to meet her first husband and in the story her older siblings told of their mother's trip south. Stories are given to us all the time. The writer sees the larger significance in these stories. When Paley holds the small black boy, she not only "sees" her own unborn grandson but all the innocent children whose lives will be affected by other people's prejudice. When she writes of the mother left by a husband who blames her for the children, she may be inspired by a particular person's drama but the story reaches out to all the mothers who have been left in the lurch.

Do you have a similar experience that provided you with material you'll be telling the rest of your life, stories that have rich moral and social significance: tales the other kids told you the summer you spent working as a lifeguard at a camp for rich kids; stories you gathered during the five years you lived in an ashram in California; stories you heard during the afternoons you volunteered at a nursing home or the humane society?

> **Exercise 2:** Meditate on an experience in which you came to see the heroism and pathos in some everyday experience and the ways in

which people can either make one another's lives happier or more miserable. Take two or three characters (real or imaginary) and have them act out a situation such as that in Paley's story "Traveling" in which there is a personal drama and a big story. Avoid preaching; rather, let the story show the moral point that you want to make. This is another example of how to practice the writing teacher's dictum: "show, don't tell."

Verbs are the most important word in each sentence. They propel the sentence; they're the engines driving it. In "Traveling," as in her story "An Interest in Life," Paley plays around with verb tense, making time fluid; in so doing, she adds rich layers of meaning to her story. Past tense is perhaps the easiest tense to write in, but something different happens when a story is told in present tense. When it works well, the reader is more deeply engaged in the story, as if she is there in the action, viewing and hearing the characters as they act. Writers with command of the language manipulate tense to do their will. When, as in these two examples, the action shifts from past to present tense, the reader is put off balance. Our interest is heightened. What's going on here, we ask. What's real? What is past and what is present?

Exercise 3: Take a story that you've written in past tense and rewrite it in present tense. How does it change? Or, try your hand at playing around with the tenses, manipulating them both to foreshadow the future and to suggest that the past can be altered or reassessed.

Did you notice in the memoir piece, "Traveling," that Paley uses the language of the time to refer to her African American traveling companions, using the word "Negro" in the first reference and the word "colored" in the second. These reflect the language of the times. By the time she is referring to her own grandson, she uses no label; she merely refers to "the brown skin of my own grandson." Labels are very dangerous. It's important when you write not to stigmatize any group. Stereotypes and racist words should be avoided; yet, it's often equally important when quoting someone to use their exact language so that people can hear the speakers' words without an author's censorship. Language is constantly evolving. Writers must think carefully about the words they use and understand their reasons for employing a particular word. This rule applies to many other situations when writing about minorities or people who have been disenfranchised, such as people with disabilities, gay men and lesbian women, and people whose religious beliefs or cultural mores have made them subject to ridicule, discrimination, misrepresentation, or misunderstanding.

Exercise 4: In your notebook, as you travel, pay attention to the people around you and the manner in which you instantly categorize them by race, religion, sexual identity, handicap, and so forth. Write honestly in your notebook, paying close attention to your own prejudices. You don't have to write a piece as a result of this exercise. Its purpose is to show you how you react to people who may be different than you and how you react to people who are like you. At all times, writers should be aware of their own biases and strive to think and write without preconceptions.

# 9    Ellen Bryant Voigt

*Song and Spirit*

Born 20 March 1943 in Danville, Virginia

Education: B.A.: Converse College; M.F.A.: The University of Iowa

Lives in Cabot

First publication: Four poems, "Beauty Bound," "Centennial," "Harriet,"
    and "Low Monday," in *South and West* (Spring 1966)

Books of Poetry: *Claiming Kin* (1976); *The Forces of Plenty* (1983); *The Lotus
    Flowers* (1987); *Two Trees* (1992); *Kyrie* (1995); *Shadows of Heaven*
    (2002)

Essays on craft: *The Flexible Lyric* (1999)

Awards: National Book Award finalist; National Book Critics' Circle Award
    finalist, Teasdale Poetry Prize, Vermont State Poet

WHAT DO YOU DO if you have two wonderful talents and interests, both demanding in their need for attention, training, exercise,
and precision? Ellen Bryant Voigt has that lucky problem. A serious student
of piano and music all her life, Voigt is also an accomplished poet whose
writing has earned her the title of Vermont State Poet. She balances her two
loves by bringing her sense of rhythm and sound to the making of poems,
reconciling song and story through the writing of extraordinarily eloquent
poetry. Her six books of poetry and her collection of essays on craft have
won her widespread acclaim. But she hasn't abandoned music entirely.
Although no fan of public performances, she enjoys being part of a close-
knit artistic community in and around Vermont's capital of Montpelier and

occasionally plays for community theater and other regional performance groups.

The word "lovely" springs to your lips after reading a poem by Ellen Bryant Voigt. There's a melancholy in almost each one, and a hopefulness as well, as she writes of the death of millions from influenza or the dying neighbor, the dog on the front lawn and the hawk in his domain, language and logic, the lifeline in a hand or the lifeline of the human race. Readers with a keen ear for the poetry of song and the musicality of poetry will recognize that these two artistic endeavors are not opposites but, rather, relatives. Voigt's marriage of the two is both subtle and satisfying. She writes in *The Flexible Lyric*, a collection of essays on the art of the lyric poem, that "poetry's first allegiance is to music."[1]

Her poem "Song and Story" tells of the power of music to comfort, to inspire, to weave connections between humans, to record our troubles and our triumphs.[2] It's an exquisite poem, one that begins with an image of one child, sick in a hospital bed, and that of the mother singing the "song of the sea, song of the scythe." Here are two excerpts:

> The girl strapped in the bare mechanical crib
> does not open her eyes, does not cry out.
> The glottal tube is taped into her face;
> bereft of sound, she seems so far away.
> But a box on the stucco wall, wired to her chest,
> televises the flutter of her heart—
> news from the pit—her pulse rapid and shallow,
> a rising line, except when her mother sings,
> outside the bars; whenever her mother sings
> the line steadies into a row of waves
> song of the sea, song of the scythe
>
> > old woman by the well, picking up stones
> > old woman by the well, picking up stones

. . . . . . . . . . . . . . . . . . . . . . . . . . . . . . .

> The one who can sing sings to the one who can't,
> who waits in the pit, like Procne among the slaves,
> as the gods decide how all such stories end,
> the story woven into the marriage gown,
> or scratched with a stick in the dust around the well,
> or written in blood in the box on the stucco wall—
> look at the wall:
> the song, rising and falling, sings in the heartbeat,

sings in the seasons, sings in the daily round—
even at night, deep in the murmuring wood–
listen—one bird, full-throated, calls to another,
*little sister,* frantic little sparrow under the eaves.

—from "Song and Story"[3]

The poem connects this mother with others who have struggled with loss and pain; it reaches down into our mythic consciousness, bringing to life similar longings and losses among mythical beings, Orpheus and Euridice and Procne.[4] Despite its reference to Greek myths, now centuries old, the poem embraces each one of us. You don't have to know the story of Procne and her "little sister" to understand this poem. Those words *little sister* have the magical effect of instilling sympathy in the reader, of drawing the reader into the small and large tragedies of existence, both those alluded to in the poem and those that are not. It's this combination of the external with the deep-rooted that makes reading Voigt so enjoyable; there's the poem on the surface and the under-poem, the deeply layered meanings waiting to be unearthed.

An aspiring poet could be both inspired and intimidated after spending a few hours with one of Voigt's books. If poetry is a magic act, Voigt is an adept magician, weaving the familiar with the unfamiliar. With each poem, much is revealed and yet much is left to ponder. That's part of what makes reading her work so satisfying; each reading brings fresh understanding.

Voigt was born in southern Virginia in 1943 and grew up on a small farm with lots of relatives around from both her father's and her mother's families. From an early age, music and the life cycle of the farm provided her with a rich sensory landscape, one that resonates in her poetry. From her earliest years, she found the company of family (and their scrutiny) claustrophobic and developed a strong need for time alone, something that music first provided her with. She tells the story of how she became a student of music. "I had an older sister who started taking piano lessons. At about four years of age. I wanted to be just like her. No, I wanted to *be* her. I would play by ear the songs that she had been practicing; it was probably pretty annoying. Her piano teacher was a little old lady dressed in black who kept the blinds drawn, a stereotype of an old spinster. My sister was very dramatic, very volatile. One day when my sister was at her lesson and for some reason the teacher got on her nerves, my sister said, 'Well, you have bad breath,' and she ran out of the room and biked home.

"I was in the next room and had to take her lesson. But the two of us were done with that teacher. My parents got me another teacher, a real 'Music Man,' a music teacher for all of the county high schools. He was marvelous; he so loved what he did," Voigt recalls. By high school, he was taking her with him to perform at different schools and programs where he was directing.

"Music was a door to solitude, which I desperately needed." Voigt explains. "My parents loved music and had come from musical families. As long as they could hear the music coming from the piano, I was excused from other duties. It was really about the only time I could be alone. Playing piano was an occasion for solitude that was socially sanctioned, which I think is really important in terms of my notion of music, or my relationship to it." Later, poetry took up "the friction between that solitary individual—that need to be alone—and the pressure to be a social person."

After high school, she attended Converse College, in part because it had a conservatory of music. Voigt wanted to escape small-town life and thought she might do so by studying to be a high school band director. Today, she reflects that if she'd gone to a different college, she might be composing music today. Instead, her college, like many others, trained for performance. But Voigt had discovered early on that she didn't really have the temperament to perform on stage or to be a concert pianist: "At about age twenty, I worked in resorts where the waiters and waitresses sang and performed. Seven days a week I played music, mostly junk, and I came to hate it." Unfortunately, she'd also concluded that she didn't have the patience to be a high school band director.

Meanwhile, a friend who loved poetry showed her some poems by writers who were still alive: ee cummings, Rilke, Yeats. "I was smitten by these new writers my friend introduced me to. Their poems had music, words, ideas. I juggled my schedule about to take English courses. I took *Beowulf* and loved it, started writing poetry, mostly as an imitative act, and quite literally fell in love with poetry. I experienced a cosmic shift," she says, "the art that had been mine since the age of four was merging into poetry."

Music had given her order and structure—and now poetry did: "I'm a formalist; that's part of my makeup. I don't have much tolerance for disorder, and of course the world is full of disorder." Initially, she didn't expect to become a poet, but just to read and enjoy poetry. "I started to write poetry as an act of homage," she says. Over the years, she came to see that her love of music was essentially a love of harmony, of pattern, of repetition and of ideas, and that this love could well be explored in words.

After attending graduate school at the University of Iowa (famous for the quality of writing produced by its graduates) and teaching at a small college in the Midwest, Voigt and her husband Francis, a political scientist, came to Vermont in 1969 to teach at Goddard College, a small experimental college in Plainfield. (Francis Voigt went on to cofound the New England Culinary Institute with John Dranow, a novelist.) "We fell in love with the place," Voigt says of Vermont. "But we had to decide periodically whether to stay or not, particularly as Goddard's problems came and went."

Voigt created the idea of a low-residency program for writers at Goddard, a system by which students attend classes intensely for two weeks each semester but do most of their work on their own, working one-on-one with a mentor between campus visits. When Goddard experienced funding problems, she moved the program to Warren Wilson College. (The low-residency program has been successful all over the country, allowing people with busy lives to get advanced degrees while still living with their families and working.)

Voigt says Vermont has been important to her writing life. Although she misses "a real spring" in which many flowers bloom in succession, rather than a few almost all at once, the way they do in Vermont, she says Vermont provides a writer with the same kind of "opportunity for solitude" that she longed for as a child. Vermont residents have a temperament that allows a person to embrace solitude without being considered odd, she says. Simultaneously, there's an attendant opportunity to "cultivate community. But you can withdraw from it without cost. No one tries to bring you out of your solitude. There's a much greater tolerance for solitude and idiosyncrasy here," she says. "It's hard for poets to find a place in the world. Our culture does not encourage literacy. Vermont also offers a more congenial pace of life. I find myself depleted and exhausted by the contemporary world, by all that comes at you. The most routine things can be debilitating. Emerson said, simplify, simplify, simplify. You can do so here. There's a history for doing so."

"Part of it, of course, is the hard winters. There's a time to do everything. It feels steady. Living here doesn't take so much from you; you have got more brain cells for contemplation, for poetry, for sewing a quilt, for being part of the rhythm of life. On top of all that, you live with this glorious landscape, close to the circadian rhythm of life. You stay at poetry because your life allows it." Voigt adds that Vermont is a wonderful place for writers because of "the wealth of independent bookstores," observing that, in a half hour's drive, she can shop at three or four wonderful small, independently owned bookstores.

Voigt was one of the most active state poets since the program was reestablished in 1990. Her term ran from 1999 to 2003. Before being chosen, Voigt was already involved in a program called The Poet Next Door, which was supported by a Lila Wallace–Reader's Digest Fund grant administered by the Vermont Center for the Book. Under the program, 180 high school students from thirty schools each year were given books written by three poets. Through interactive television, the students could ask the poets questions directly after reading their poetry. "The thing I like best about this project," Voigt told Stephen Whited, a writer for *Book Magazine*, "is that teachers teach from the books of the three poets, and we give books to the students. So each kid gets three books of poetry to have and to keep by Vermont poets, and so, presumably, one of those three is going to be from some area of the state similar to where the students are from. And there will be poems on subject matter or they will use imagery that should be recognizable to them. And by using the interactive TV, we're able to get to kids in these little rural schools, and we can serve more of them."[5]

As poet laureate also, Voigt helped to make poetry meaningful and accessible, not to just Vermont high school students but to residents throughout the state and far beyond. As she told Whited, she used the role of state poet "to say you don't have to be afraid of poetry. It's not necessarily obscure or stuffy, and it's made by people just like you. That general message, I think, is a very effective way to get people to try it." It's a theme she has explored in both poetry and prose. In 1999, she told Steve Cramer in an interview in the *Atlantic Monthly*[6] shortly after *The Flexible Lyric* was published that her "sense of readership has changed over the years. I now imagine a reader—maybe one I haven't found yet—who is intelligent but perhaps thinks he or she doesn't like poetry, not having read it for a long time, and thinks of it as a kind of 'clue hunting.' That's the reader I'm most concerned about and would like to reach, to whom I could say, 'Look, just read this and see what you think.' So, increasingly, clarity has risen to a higher place in my pantheon of virtues. When I first started writing poems, I put musicality above clarity, although I didn't think of it as musicality. I thought of it as nuance. But how much do you risk in ambiguity? These are just choices every poet makes all the time, self-consciously or not."

### Tips and Techniques

Lyric poetry is generally referred to as that which focuses on and explores the poet's personal emotions or sentiments; it's often song-like. Lyric poetry is distinguished from narrative or epic poetry, in which a story is told. Narrative poetry generally has a beginning, a middle and an end. It follows a story line. In contrast, lyric poetry can enter an event at any point of time; it makes its impact in a very brief space. It often uses internal repetitions. The word "lyric" comes from the Greek instrument, the lyre, which produces a flexible, lilting sound. Hence, the inspiration for the title of Voigt's collection of essays on poetry, *The Flexible Lyric*.

Poets who are drawn to this kind of writing, much different than the narrative poetry of writers like Sydney Lea, can contemplate the impact of a trailer from a movie, contemporary songs, and TV commercials. These forms of media rely on quick emotional impact and, often, a repeated slogan or stanza. One should realize, however, that the lyric poem's quality requires concentrated control on the part of the author. She is in charge of the language and pacing. But if trying your hand at this wonderful format, you might recall how quickly an emotion can be telegraphed to a viewer simply by putting the right images on the screen, accompanied by the right words. The lyric poet's job is to do the same in the poem.

Voigt is especially conscious about the decisions she makes, not only about subject matter but also format. She doesn't write every day but when she's involved in a project, she's involved in it fully, morning, noon, and night, all the time, in the bed, in the car, walking the dog, or making a meal.

Each project takes on a life of its own and Voigt finds herself engaged in it thoroughly, unable to think about much else until a work is complete. Voigt writes slowly, composing fifty or sixty or even seventy drafts of each poem, "working on each with a certain doggedness. Some are quite bad. I may write each poem over each time, fixing one small thing at a sitting, working on revision after revision until I run out of things to be fixed. I get it as close as I can get it to perfect; if I fail it's because I didn't have the vision, the proficiency," she says. After completing each work, she sets herself assignments. She asks herself, "What's missing?" "What do I need to know?" "What haven't I written?" When she observed after several books of introspective work that her poems did not have much irony, she set out to write with an ironic voice. She explains, "I'm a very earnest person. No one over fifty should be so earnest. I felt there was no irony in my work and, thus, I wanted to create a piece with irony. I wanted to develop a piece with an ironic voice and point of view."

As she pondered her interest in writing with an "ironic vision," Voigt began thinking about one of the now most famous (but at the time of Voight's writing, forgotten) pandemics, the influenza of 1918, which killed more than twenty-five million internationally (combat deaths in World War I totaled only nine million). Explains Voigt of her generation: "Most of our parents lived through this flu epidemic. My father had told the story of how his mother had died in childbirth when he was eight and his father had sent the children to live with relatives until he remarried and brought four of the five children, not the infant, back home. This was the fall of 1918." As it turned out, her father's family had barely been back together in Southside, Virginia, "when the whole family was struck with what was called the Spanish influenza. During a terrible November snowstorm, all of them boarded up in the house, the country doctor came by. But he had no medicine, no relief. The doctor asked my grandfather, 'Do you have any corn?'—meaning corn whiskey. He did. The doctor took a swig, passed the jug to my grandfather, then told him to give each person in the house a swig. They all survived. His name was Doctor Gilmore Reynolds. What interested me was the story of Doctor Reynolds. What would it be like to be a doctor with sick patients and nothing to offer them? Doctor Reynolds provided me a voice in which to explore irony—the kind of worldview irony conveys, and the kind of utterance it accommodates and requires. The sonnets began out of that intense, heightened moment in the center of the epidemic: everybody's dying and there's nothing you can do. I had no particular interest in the epidemic itself. But I had written a sonnet in which a young boy stands by his mother's deathbed. And having written that, it occurred to me that its circumstance—my father's circumstance—had been multiplied thousands of times during the epidemic. Most of the victims had been adults between the ages of eighteen and their early thirties. My father's was a generation of orphans.

"Once I made that connection, I began to hear other lines, lines with a fairly ironic tone, such as, 'Oh yes I used to pray. I prayed for the baby.' And I would think, who would have said that? So, I made up other voices. I wrote sixteen or seventeen sonnets that satisfied me. And then I did some research about the flu epidemic. I discovered little had been written about it, except the book by Alfred Crosby called *America's Forgotten Pandemic*. I think that knowing how little had been written about such a big thing encouraged me to write more sonnets," she says.

The book-length series of poems that resulted, *Kyrie*, required Voigt to do things with her writing she hadn't done before.[7] A lyric poem stands alone. The writer captures a moment of intensity and holds it. Each poem can inform its neighbors but there is no obligation to tie them together, to provide fluidity between the poems. In a book-length sequence, the writer has to move through time, create many voices, and provide opportunities for the reader to follow the story line. Voigt solved the dilemma by creating Price, one of the "speakers" in *Kyrie*, a young man who writes to his betrothed, a schoolteacher named Mattie, as he goes off to war, ships off to France, gets wounded. In his travels and observations, Price not only provides a story line throughout the book; he also brings the outside world into the poems.

Here are a few selections from *Kyrie*. As you read them, listen for how Voigt tells one story while also telling the human story of loss and the human will to carry on:

> After the first year, weeds and scrub;
> after five, juniper and birch,
> alder filling in among the briars;
> ten more years, maples rise and thicken;
> forty years, the birches crowded out,
> a new world swarms on the floor of the hardwood forest.
> And who can tell us where there was an orchard,
> where a swing, where the smokehouse stood?[8]

> All ears, nose, tongue and gut,
> dogs know if something's wrong;
> chickens don't know a thing, their brains
> are little more than optic nerve—
> they think it's been a very short day
> and settle in the pines, good night,
> head under wing, near their cousins
> but welded to a lower branch.
> Dogs, all kinds of dogs—signals
> are their job, they cock their heads,
> their backs bristle, even house dogs
> wake up and circle the wool rug.
> Outside, the vacant yard: then,
> within minutes something eats the sun.[9]

> Dear Mattie, You're sweet to write me every day.

The train was not so bad, I found a seat,
watched the landscape flatten until dark,
ate the lunch you packed, your good chess pie.
I've made a friend, a Carolina man
who looks like Emmett Cocke, same big grin,
square teeth. Curses hard but he can shoot.
Sergeant calls him Pug I don't know why.
It's hot here but we're not here for long.
Most all we do is march and shine our boots.
In the drills they keep us 20 feet apart
on account of sickness in the camp.
In case you think to send more pie, send two.
I'll try to bring you back some French perfume.[10]

When does a childhood end? Mothers
sew a piece of money inside a sock,
fathers unfold the map of the world, and boys
go off to war—that's an end, whether
they come back wrapped in the flag or waving it.
Sister and I were what they kissed goodbye,
complicitous in the long dream left behind.
On one page, willful innocence,
                         on the next
an Army Captain writing from the ward
with few details and much regret—a kindness
she wouldn't forgive, and wouldn't be reconciled
to her soldier lost, or me in my luck, or the petals
strewn on the grass, or the boys still on the playground
routing evil with their little sticks.[11]

This is the double bed where she'd been born,
bed of her mother's marriage and decline,
bed her sisters also ripened in,
bed that drew her husband to her side,
bed of her one child lost and five delivered,
bed indifferent to the many bodies,
bed around which all of them were gathered,
watery shapes in the shadows of the room,
and the bed frail abroad the violent ocean,
the frightened beasts so clumsy and pathetic,
heaving their wet breath against her neck,
she threw off the pile of quilts—white face like a moon—
*and then entered straightway into heaven.*[12]

Dear Mattie, Pug says even a year of camp
would not help most of us so why not now.
Tomorrow we take a train to New York City,

> board a freighter there. You know how the logs
> are flushed through the long flume at Hodnetts' Mill,
> the stream flooding the sluice, the cut pines,
> Crowding and pushing and rushing, and then
> the narrow chute opens onto the pond?
> I'll feel like that, once we're out to sea
> and seeing the world. I need to say
> I've saved a bit, and you should also have
> my Grandpa's watch—tell Fan that I said so.
> Keep busy, pray for me, go on with Life,
> and put your mind to a wedding in the yard[16]

Nature has a strong presence in Voigt's work. Her metaphors and rich pastoral sensibility take their roots from her days growing up on a farm and continue all the way to her current home on a lovely stretch of land outside of Cabot. Here, with the green of rolling hills all around her comfortable farmhouse and the wild animals not far off in nearby pastures and forests, observations of the natural world on a day-to-day basis fuel her work with both tragic and consoling elements. Her collection *Shadow of Heaven* is imbued with both nature's wonder and its cruelty.[14] Indeed, it is the juxtaposition of these two observations with equally fierce statements about the power and frailty of human life that the reader feels so passionately. It is the life outside our door and the life inside our hearts.

Nature, both in Vermont and far away, links the poems in her collection *Shadow of Heaven* but it is not nature in and of itself, but rather nature in relation to the human. In the poem "Apple Trees," for example, when Voigt writes of the "surgeon's chainsaw" trimming a diseased tree, she links the tree's determination to survive—"from one stubborn root / two plumes of tree now leaf / and even blossom"—to her own life:[15]

> whereas on my left hand
> not a single lifeline
> but three deep equal
> channels—
>    O my soul,
> it is not a small thing,
> to have made from three
> this one, this one life.[16]

Most of us have had to struggle to balance life's demands: of work, family, vocation, art, hobby, religion. These balancing acts sometimes make us feel as if we're living many lives simultaneously (and, in fact, many of us do live not only several lives simultaneously, but sometimes secret lives as well). The poem speaks to these struggles. It also provides solace to those who have had to cut themselves off from pursuits or loves they've longed for, to those whose sacrifices may seem too great in retrospect, and to those who continue to mourn a life that might have been. And because we all know and love that tree (or any living thing) that starts over from nothing, that, once amputated, grows new life, the poem gives solace to our daily struggles. Yes, life goes on.

But, while Voight's subjects are often local—the backyard, the dog on the front lawn, the family plot, the children, the husband—her overriding concern is a universal one. Regardless of whether she is writing historical narratives, lyric poems, or sonnets, Voigt is exploring the questions central to the human spirit: What is free will? What is fate? How does each individual life and the life of the planet and its inhabitants depend upon and evolve out from the tension between the two? Regardless of the format, Voigt has consistently grappled with the same issues throughout her life—human character and human destiny, childhood and adulthood, mortality and immortality, innocence and man's fall from grace—in poems that are at once accessible while also so richly layered that one can discover fresh meanings with each new reading. In so doing, she teaches the would-be poet and the proficient writer of poetry alike how to combine the issues of the individual heart with the problems and successes of the human race. It was for these gifts that the American Academy of Arts and Letters honored her with its 2000 Award Citation, saying, "With stoic commitment to meaning, and with immense technical resources, Ellen Bryant Voigt has fashioned an art of passionate gravity and opulent music, an art at once ravishing and stern and deeply human."

---

◄§ EXCERPTS FROM *Shadow of Heaven*

### Largesse
*Aix-en-Provence*

Banging the blue shutters—night-rain;
and a deep gash opened in the yard.
By noon, the usual unstinting sun
but also wind, the olive trees gone silver,
inside out, and the slender cypresses,
like women in fringed shawls, hugging themselves,
and over the rosemary hedge the pocked fig
giving its purple scrota to the ground.

What was it had made me sad? At the market,
stall after noisy stall, melons, olives,
more fresh herbs that I could name, tomatoes
still stitched to the cut vine, the soft
transparent squid shelved on ice; also,
hanging there beside the garlic braids,
meek as the sausages: plucked fowl with feet.

Under a goose-wing, I had a violent dream.
I was carrying a baby and was blind,
or blinded on and off, the ledge I walked
blanking out long minutes at a time.
He'd flung a confident arm around my neck.
A spidery crack traversed his china skull.
Then it was not a ledge but a bridge, like a tongue.

From the window over my desk, I could look down
at the rain-ruined nest the *sangliers*
had scrabbled in the thyme, or up, to the bald
mountain in all the paintings. I looked up.
That's where one looks in the grip of a dream.[17]


### Dooryard Flower

Because you are sick I want to bring you flowers,
flowers from the landscape that you love—
because it is your birthday and you're sick
I want to bring the outdoors inside,
the natural and the wild, picked by hand,
but nothing is blooming here but daffodils,
archipelagic in the short green
early grass, erupted
bulbs planted decades before we came,
the edge of where a garden once was kept
extended now in a string of islands I straddle
as in a fairy tale, harvesting,
not taking the single blossom from a clump
but thinning where they're thickest, tall-stemmed
from the mother patch, dwarf to the west, most
fully opened, a loosened whorl,
one with a pale spider lugging her thread,
one with a slow beetle chewing the lip, a few
with what's almost a lion's mane,
and because there is a shadow on your lungs, your liver,
and elsewhere, hidden,
some of those with delicate green
streaks in the clown's ruff (*corolla*—
actually made from adapted leaves), and more
right this moment starting to unfold, I've gathered
my two fists full, I carry them like a bride,
I am bringing you the only glorious thing
in the yards and fields between my house and yours,
none of the tulips budded yet, the lilac

a sheaf of sticks, the apple trees
withheld, the birch unleaved—
it could still be winter here, were it not
for green dotted with gold, but you won't wait
for dogtoothed violets, trillium under the pines,
and who could bear azaleas, dogwood, early profuse rose
of somewhere else when you're assaulted here, early May,
not any calm narcissus, orange *corona*
on scalloped white, not even its slender stalk
in a fountain of leaves, no stiff coronets of the honest
jonquils, gendered parts upthrust in brass and cream:
just this common flash in anyone's yard,
scrambled cluster of petals
crayon-yellow, as in a child's drawing of the sun,
I'm bringing you a sun, a children's choir, host
of transient voices, first bright
splash in the gray exhausted world, a feast
of the dooryard flower we call butter-and-egg.[18]

## Questions and Exercises for Reflection and Inspiration

Poets use metaphor and imagery to create mood, provide information, set tone, and embrace myth and history. In poetry, what is unsaid and unexplained is as important as what is said. We are often left to accept that we can understand the poem just so far; another reading may bring us closer to understanding. And yet another reading. More often, it is the experience, the sentiment of the poem that brings us back. We have felt the intensity of a moment, the passion of the voice, and seek to understand more. In "Largesse," Voigt creates a sense of vulnerability and restlessness in the choice of words and images she employs: rain has caused a gash in the yard; the sun is unstinting; the women in their fringed shawls hug themselves; the pocked fig gives its purple scrota to the ground. (By the way, isn't that a fabulous image? Once you've heard it, it's impossible to think of purple figs otherwise.)

These physical images set us up for the question: What was it had made me sad? Yes, we were already wondering what portent was being broadcast in the wind, the sun, even the figs. On one level, the poem is a response to the largesse of the world, the market, the constant supply of sensory emotion, dreams that replenish themselves in our imagination, repeatedly, bringing their own sadness. It's on the deeper level where the under-story goes on that the larger meaning of the poem can be found. It won't be held or expressed in words, but it has something to do with the transience of time, the uncertainty of the future, the persistence of the past, the largeness of human vulnerability. In part, because the poem was written in Aix en Provence, a place famous not just for foreign language schools but as an inspiration to many writers and artists, it suggests both the burden of all that creativity and the pleasure of it. Little of this, of course, is said in so many words. That's why we have poetry: to express such emotions and observations without saying them directly. We experience the emotion between the words.

> **Exercise 1:** Make your own list of images from your surroundings, carefully choosing elements of nature and the physical world that will express a particular mood. You may combine these with more details from either a waking or a sleeping dream. Begin playing with these words or writing just one line inspired by one of the images. Then add another, seeking to express a frame of mind primarily through physical details outside of yourself. Rely on as few facts regarding the emotion you're trying to understand as possible; garner, rather, from the world around you items and responses that connote the emotion you want to express. As you are writing your poem, pay attention closely to your language. Notice, for example, how Voigt says "under a goose wing," rather than under a goose-down blanket. Her image evokes several responses; there's a protectiveness about the phrase as well as a sense of being high above the fray, but brought down by it nonetheless. This desolation becomes more evident later in the poem when the narrator speaks of looking down upon the sangliers' nest. Yes, even the nest is ruined.

In her collection, *Kyrie*, Voigt used her family's myth as a jumping-off point to tell a human tragedy, one that had then been nearly ignored by historians. In so doing, she tells so many stories: the story of the orphan, of the soldier, of the frail and the sick, of those who have lost loves and those who are lost, of difficult choices, of fate and destiny, of the human capacity for love, and the human capacity for suffering. Read the following poem from *Kyrie*:

> To be brought from the bright schoolyard into the house:
> to stand by her bed like an animal stunned in the pen:
> against the grid of the quilt, her hand seems
> stitched to the cuff of its sleeve—although he wants
> most urgently the hand to stroke his head,
> although he thinks he could kneel down
> that it would need to travel only inches
> to brush like a breath his flushed cheek,
> he doesn't stir: all his resolve,
> all his resources go to watching her,
> her mouth, her hair a pillow of blackened ferns—
> he means to match her stillness bone for bone.
> Nearby he hears the younger children cry,
> and his aunts, like careless thieves, out in the kitchen.[19]

Can you see how this poem tells both a particular and a universal story? It is the story of a particular mother's death, as seen through the eyes of her son, as well as the story of the world's children who have suffered incomprehensible losses from disease, war, and natural disasters. It's easy to see how a poet's exploration of this kind of subject matter leads to a fuller exploration of the larger dilemmas of human existence. Yet there's a specificity about this poem that sets this death apart from all the others, a vividness captured in images: the child standing by a bed "like an animal stunned in the pen;" "the grid of the quilt," the hand, already unreal, appearing "stitched to the cuff of its sleeve." It is as if we are there in that bedroom on that sad day, and from that, of course, our mind goes to our own bedside dramas, our own sad goodbyes.

> **Exercise 2:** Take some historical event that affected your own family strongly enough that people still tell stories about it. It can be a historic flood or snowstorm, a war, or some other important event in history. Conduct some research so you have big-issue information and factual data about the event, as well. Try writing about the event from both a historic and a personal point of view, interweaving big themes with ones from your own life or that of your family. In so doing, create a few characters through whom you can tell both the smaller and larger stories. Pay close attention to how the story changes and grows as you find the universal elements in your family tale. Write several poems from several points of view, meditating on how the human community is both affected by a singular death and becomes inured to death.

In the poem "Dooryard Flower," a first-person speaker wants to bring flowers to a sick friend. From this simple impetus, the poem progresses to the real issue at hand: the friend "assaulted here" and the powerlessness of the speaker either to hurry the spring or to heal the friend. Still, the human impetus is to try, "bringing you the only glorious thing / in the yards and fields between my house and yours."

There's a meditative quality to this poem that we recognize in the best lyric poetry. How much time passes in the poem? No time at all yet all the time that we bring to such spiritual questionings. The time of this poem is measured by the intensity of the moment that is captured as the speaker gathers a bouquet and ponders that, even though the tulips had not yet budded and the birch unleaved, there were still these daffodils to offer, "a sun, a children's choir, host / of transient voices, first bright / splash in the gray exhausted world, a feast / of the dooryard flower we call butter-and-eggs." That is to say, hope.

> **Exercise 3:** Try your own hand at a lyric poem, taking an intense moment and honing in on its emotional energy. As you write, look for images

that capture the emotion, interweaving them with more narrative or factual elements that provide enough information for the reader to enter into the experience—but just enough. Remember, poetry is as much about what is unsaid as what is said. Poets use not all the words, but the right words. Experiment with this form of poetry, using the experience at the same time to broaden your meditative capabilities.

# 10  David Huddle
## *The Writing Habit*

Born 11 July 1942 in Ivanhoe, Virginia

Education: B.A.: University of Virginia; M.A.: Hollins College; M.F.A.: Columbia University

Lives in Burlington

Short story collections: *A Dream with No Stump Roots in It* (1975); *Only the Little Bone* (1986); *The High Spirits: Stories of Men and Women* (1989); *Intimates* (1993)

Poetry collections: *Paper Boy* (1979); *Stopping by Home* (1988); *The Nature of Yearning* (1992); *Summer Lake* (1999); *Grayscale* (2004)

Novella: *Tenorman* (1995)

Novella and story collection: *Not a Trio* (2000)

Novels: The Story of a Million Years (1999); La Tour Dreams of the Wolf Girl (2002)

Essays: *The Writing Habit: Essays* (1991, 1994)

Fiction and poetry collection: *A David Huddle Reader* (1994)

D AVID HUDDLE'S yellow house with green shutters, nestled in a quiet neighborhood near the University of Vermont in Burlington, seems almost too orderly, too ordinary for a Vermont writer. Huddle has chosen to live in Vermont's largest city rather than a mountaintop refuge or cozy farmhouse like so many of Vermont's other writers. Most mornings, he writes on a laptop computer, sitting in an easy chair in his living room, under a wonderful painting of Huddle himself, younger, standing casually against a patterned wall. Sarah Swenson of Johnson, Vermont, painted it as one in a series of portraits of Vermont artists.

Huddle came to Vermont not as the fulfillment of a lifelong dream to live in the Green Mountain State but rather through serendipity. After earning his graduate degree from Columbia University in 1971, Huddle sent out thirty job applications and got two offers. One was for a one-year appointment with no opportunity of gaining tenure; the other was for a tenure-track position at the University of Vermont. He took the job without ever having been in New England, let alone Vermont. After a quick trip to Virginia to say goodbye to their parents, on the first of April (a month in which Vermont often does not look its best) Huddle and his wife drove a rented car north to Burlington with Huddle's wife weeping all the way.

Now, three decades later, he's still at UVM, still married to Lindsey Massie, an attorney with whom he has two grown daughters. Although Huddle still experiences the same "seasonal disorder" when his inner clock says it should be spring but it's still winter outside, he has no desire to leave Vermont. The Appalachian culture he grew up with is no longer his, neither socially, nor intellectually, nor politically. Much as he ridicules the brusqueness of Yankees and wearies of the winter, he says, "I fit more into Burlington than I ever would at home." That said, Huddle says, he'd be a misfit in Budbill's Wolcott or Mosher's Irasburg. It's not that he dislikes nature or country; quite the contrary. It's just that he likes the size and pace of Vermont's largest city. And also, Huddle found in Burlington and at UVM a small but satisfying coterie of like-minded people and an environment that lets him be a writer without too much fuss or hubbub. When he arrived, there was already established a wonderful cadre of young writers who welcomed him and made him feel at home. The group included Leland Kinsey, Tinker Green, Red Lawrence, and Bob Caswell; they called themselves "the Mimeo Poets," because one of them had a mimeo machine and had self-published a book of poems, long before self-publication's current fashion. Burlington was smaller in 1971, less chic, and certainly less well known around America. It made a perfect place for Huddle to hunker down to teach. And write. In the intervening years, he has been one of Vermont's most prolific writers, publishing five short story collections, five books of poetry, a novella, two novels, a book on writing, and a book of his selected works.

With the freedom that distance can bring, Huddle was able to explore his childhood experiences and the place where he had grown up, especially in his first book of poems, *Paper Boy*.[1] He explains: "I don't think I would have written so much about Virginia if I didn't have that need. . . . I was a little off in Vermont—not quite fitting in, which is good. Writers need that not quite fitting in. Vermont is artist-friendly because it doesn't make a big deal about someone being an artist, a writer. That was good for me, too. I might have been respected and given too much attention as a writer in my old environment." That said, he's "grateful I haven't had to make my living as a writer. That puts a pressure on you. Because I'm an academic, I have more freedom to do what I want. Whatever I do as a writer is my choice. Of course, we [college professors] have some pressure to publish but I don't have to make my living from it. And it's allowed me the freedom to have one thing lead to another, to try something new."

And, try new things he has. Readers of Huddle's work are delighted with the span of his subject matter from the early biographical poems to the rich blending of seventeenth-century French culture and contemporary life in his novel *La Tour Dreams of the Wolf Girl*.[2] His novella *Tenorman* not only provides delightful insight into the minds of the watched and the watcher; it also displays a formidable understanding of jazz music and the human psyche.[3] And Huddle's book of craft tips, *The Writing Habit*, has proved valuable to writing students for more than a decade.[4]

By his own account, Huddle was not always a good student. When he came to the University of Virginia in the early 1960s, he thought of himself as a mountain boy who wanted to be a writer. Like many young people, however, he wasn't very confident about his writing and found the university not very writer-friendly. Fortunately for Huddle, a professor named John Coleman, an outcast among other faculty members, was assigned to teach creative writing. He encouraged Huddle's writing and set him on a path of writing daily. Despite this reassurance, Huddle flunked out that semester and, wanting adventure, joined the army. After a stint in Germany, he was assigned to Vietnam—an experience he does not like to dwell on. He explains that his assignment was in intelligence rather than combat. As a result, he never fired a weapon in Vietnam, nor did he know anyone who was killed, or even shot. He does not regret that he was spared the firsthand horror that many other Vietnam-era veterans experienced and acknowledges that the war did not come to define his writing, as it did so many others of his generation. Nonetheless, the first two stories he published ("Rosie Baby," in the *Georgia Review* in the fall of 1969; and "The Interrogation of the Prisoner Bung by Mister Hawkins and Sergeant Tree," in *Esquire*, in January 1971) may have been taken because they were set in Vietnam. "So, essentially and oddly enough, I owe my writing career to having been in Vietnam."

Huddle returned to the University of Virginia after Vietnam. Again and again, Huddle found among the marginal figures on campus mentors like James Croft and Peter Taylor, who accepted him as an undergraduate in graduate classes and took an interest in him. Huddle babysat for Taylor and got invited to dinner when famous writers like James Dickey came to visit. Anxious to learn, he soaked up as much as possible from these chance meetings.

In 1968, Huddle and Lindsey married and he began graduate school at Hollins College. There, George Garrett, a "gentleman of letters," became Huddle's next mentor. Garrett's philosophy was that it wasn't a big deal to be a poet and people shouldn't behave as if it were or be intimidated by poetry. Huddle hadn't written many poems up until then. But, thanks to Garrett, "I gave it a try with the idea that I didn't have to belong to some sort of literary elite," says Huddle (in a soft, melodic voice softened by a Virginia accent that at times carries the inflection of the Scottish folks who settled the region where he grew up). He found, much to his surprise, that he liked writing poems. After Hollins, Huddle entered the Master of Fine Arts program at Columbia University in New York. To make ends meet, his wife worked for the telephone company and Huddle worked as a man Friday at Simon and Schuster. It was there, in cold, busy New York, that Huddle began to discover the freedom that came with separation from family, friends, and all those who knew him intimately and placed both their expectations and preconceptions upon him. Moving farther away to Vermont deepened that experience.

Huddle's poetry is deceptively simple. Written in narrative style, pared down, it's as if we are in the writer's head as images, reactions, memories spill forth. There's controlled pacing and deliberate manipulation of language, but the reader is unaware of these devices on first reading; the lines propel us forward. In a heartbreaking poem, "Wytheville Hospital, February 1985," we are there in the hospital room as the age-old struggle between father and son is compounded by the weight of mortality, of fatigue, of frustration, of need:

FROM **Summer Lake**

we'd driven a thousand miles to his bedside
and our assignment was to make him wear

this corset he'd want loose and then decide
it wasn't tight enough, and he got the word
Velcro on his mind, would say it every five

seconds. "Get this Velcro fixed, Dave," or weird
things like, "I gotta go to Velcro now."
about the sixty-seventh time I'd heard

"Fix the Velcro, Dave," I gave him a scowl
and told him I guessed he could live with it
the way it was. It was late, I was out

of patience, having been his good servant
all afternoon. (Charles would take the morning
shift.) Hallway noise made the room seem quiet,

and the blank, beige wall was occupying
his attention like a text he was about
to be quizzed on. But then he was eyeing

me in that sideways way of his, and out
of the corner of his mouth, he said, "If

I were a little stronger, I'd kick your butt."

I wish I could say I stuffed a handkerchief
in my mouth, but for most of my life we'd
been arguing. "You could fix it yourself,

If you were a little stronger," I said,
And he said yes, he guessed that was the truth.
Not much dialogue after that.[5]

There's a whole novel in those words, "Not much dialogue after that."

Huddle credits Vermont poet Ruth Stone with helping him feel comfortable with writing about his childhood. One summer, early in his time in Vermont, she heard him read some narrative poems inspired by memories. "She really heard them and encouraged them. That opened up my childhood to me," he recalls. What characterizes Huddle's poetry—the spare, direct, yet loaded pacing and wording coupled with a determination to speak the truth—also gives his short stories, novellas, and novels a surprising depth. The "autobiographical impulse" he brings to his poetry translates into an almost ruthless honesty on the part of his characters. It's not so much Huddle's plots that keep us turning the pages (although they are often interesting and quirky) but his ability to write of both the outer actions and the inner lives of his characters.

Huddle says he has come to understand that his "true form . . . is the long short story. I don't write a novel naturally or ever go with a plan. I write a nugget, then another. I begin to put them together, then finally make a shape of it." Sometimes, the shape comes in the form of telling the story from different angles, as in *Tenorman*, a deceptively complex novella in which at least two or three things are going on at all times, even though the language is quite direct and simple. He says he's been fortunate with an editor, Janet Silver at Houghton Mifflin, who has helped him work on the longer projects. With great candor, he describes the process of constructing his novellas and novels: "Mine is a very primitive way of doing things, sort of placing rocks on the floor until you come up with an arrangement that seems right. The long pieces were serious hard work, work that caused a kind of crisis for me, in which I was not exactly weeping but walking about the house, cursing and yelling and feeling generally miserable until I figured out how to put all the pieces together into a story."

In the following excerpt from the short story "The Undesirable," the reader can begin to grasp the relationship between a father and son in the opening paragraphs. Right from the opening words, telling details provide us with information about the two characters and a strong sense of place.

I got over to the side of the road as far as I could, into the grass
and the weeds, but my father steered the car over that way, too.
Through the windshield I could see his work hat, the shadow of

his face and shoulders, the specks of light that were his glasses. I pushed right up against the fence, squeezed into the honeysuckle vines. In a bright haze of sunlight I watched him come at me, the green hood of the Ford growing huge as it came close enough for me to see waves of heat rising from it. Then he swerved the car over to the middle of the driveway and stopped it beside me. I could see him, in his khaki work clothes, shifting to neutral, pulling the emergency brake, sliding over to the passenger side of the front seat, picking up his dinner bucket to hold in his lap. He waited for me while I scuffled in the vines and trash beside the fence to reach my glasses.

"'You weren't scared, were you?" he asked when I opened the door. There was that sharp smell in the car with him. Sometimes I imagined, when he came home from work, there was a coating of grey dust all over him. I got in behind the steering wheel and slammed the door. Every day now I met him at the head of our driveway and drove the car the quarter of a mile into our house. I was practice driving with him.

"I knew you wouldn't hit me," I said. When I said it, I knew it was true, sitting there beside him with the sunlight coming down through the trees onto the gravel road in front of us. My father scooted down to rest his head against the back of the seat. He took off his glasses and rubbed the two spots they dented into the bridge of his nose. He wasn't going to hit me with the car. He'd never even hit me with his hand except once, when I was eight and I'd splashed bathwater on him. I said it again, "I knew you wouldn't hit me." I put the car into low and started it moving.[6]

Huddle believes that some of "the success of fiction depends on the recognition of place." In the excerpt above, we may not know the exact place of the story but we recognize both its physical and emotional landscape. This story, like so many of Huddle's, takes us to unexpected places within each of the characters; it's their interior lives and their interactions that propel the story forward.

Having lived all his life in places where the environment demands notice, Huddle says he just naturally weaves strong elements of place into his works. But it's not place simply as setting: it's always in relation to character, as in this description of Vermont in the short story, "In the Mean Mud Season."

This northern season helps me understand my daughter's personality. It's mid-March. Last weekend the temperature went up to sixty. Dirty snow rotted before our eyes. Where the ground appeared it was a soggy greenish brown, but the rivulets that ran down our driveways and street gutters sparkled, and the sunlight inspired even some old people from the neighborhood to try the treacherous sidewalks. But before daylight on Monday a wind came up, the thermometer started dropping and by ten in the morning the windchill factor was five below zero. Now the snow is a hard shell of ice; it promises to stay that way for weeks to come. At night the stars glisten meanly. In a hard place like this, you can't be surprised when your daughter turns into a rock.[7]

Huddle says when he first came to Vermont, he only wrote when he had something he wanted to say. Now, he tries to write a couple of hours a day, preferably early in the morning, with his coffee. "A bit of writing every day gives me a better attitude. Without writing, I get impossible," he says. Sometimes, necessity dictates format. In an interview with Dan Wickett in March 2002 for the online magazine *Emerging Writers Forum*, he explained that the format he chooses to write in is often dictated by time and other constraints: "Writing poems is a comfort in a time when I'm distracted by duty and internal chaos. But whenever I'm lucky enough to have more than a week of 'free time,' then I'd rather be working on a short story or an essay. Of course the best of all possible writing times for me—and I suspect for any writer—is when I can see my way clear to finishing a novel. In that situation, there can be many days of exhilaration and a sense of learning something and getting somewhere with your life. But getting to that point requires so much anxiety and painful effort that I doubt that novel-writing will ever become my favorite format."[8]

To make time for his writing, he sometimes gets up very early; otherwise, he says, he misses "the peace of the writing desk," borrowing a phrase from the poet Robert Hass. "When I tell people I get up at 4:30 or 5:00 to do my writing, they often praise my discipline," Huddle writes in the wonderful opening chapter of his book of essays on writing, *The Writing Life*, "but now that my writing life has been established, discipline has nothing to do with it. Getting up to do my writing requires no more discipline than sitting down to eat a meal or going to bed at night to get some sleep. It's natural and necessary."[9]

Sometimes, a piece begins in one format and ends in another. *Tenorman* began as a poem and ended up a novella. The family stories he wrote in *Only the Little Bone* were a logical extension of the family poems for *Paper Boy*. He says writing the poems "opened up the territory. Once I took hold of that somewhat intimate material, I found it so engaging that I stayed with it for a long while." It's easy to see why Huddle likes the long short story so much and the novella and the novel—his work in all three genres has an edge to it, a depth that comes from his "desire to know other human beings and have access to their experience," to the point of making it up.[10] That desire is explored in part in *Tenorman*, a novella in which a crew of professional voyeurs rescue a brilliant tenor sax musician from the streets of Stockholm and set him up with an apartment, studio, and all manner of necessary human enticements, under the condition that they are allowed to tape him—not just his musical experimentations and conversations about music, but his daily comings and goings. The book is spooky in an understated way; the reader too is a voyeur but we have access not just to the tenorman's words and music but also to the people who are watching him.

Relationship is at the center of Huddle's work. In *Tenorman*, there's the oddly symbiotic yet dysfunctional relationship between musician Eddie Carnes and his "keepers," primarily Henry McKernan, the director of the NEA program that pays for Carnes's keep and supervision, and McKernan's wife. That relationship is compounded by the potential relationship between Carnes and a dedicated schoolteacher named Thelma Watkins, who escaped from an abusive first marriage and is courted by Carnes. In the simple act of sharing stories of the relationship from their pasts, Carnes and Watkins achieve an intimacy that McKernan and his wife can only imagine. In his novel, *The Story of a Million Years*, Huddle explores the relationship between two couples as they trade histories in which they, like so many of us, portray themselves as the heroes of their own stories while protecting the secrets they'd never reveal in a million years.[11]

His novel *La Tour Dreams of the Wolf Girl* was inspired by a trip to the National Gallery of Art in Washington, D.C., in 1996, where Huddle saw several paintings by the seventeenth-century French artist, Georges de La Tour. The paintings sympathetically portrayed peasant life, but Huddle subsequently learned that in his real life La Tour tyrannized the peasants in his own town and once beat one poor neighbor quite severely. The book grew out of that seeming contradiction. In it, art professor Suzanne Nelson becomes obsessed with La Tour and invents a whole life for him as he undertakes his final painting of a local girl whose parents allow her to pose for money. Again, secrets are at the heart of the relationships Huddle writes about. As the village girl disrobes for LaTour, he sees upon her back a glistening patch of hair that she is unaware of, her parents having kept it secret. The narrative deftly alternates between Suzanne Nelson's failing marriage to Jack, Jack's clandestine relationship with a musician named Elly, and the relationship between La Tour and his beautiful teenage model who, during their modeling sessions, tells fictions of her life and that of the village for La Tour's entertainment.

Huddle says, "Character has always been the element of fiction that interested me most. The other elements—language, structure, and plot—seem to me clearly to belong to Art. Character is the company of other human beings, the experience of living. I love gossip. I like to talk and hear and think about people . . . I like to be told or to be able to guess what people are thinking and feeling. I am interested in the scandalous and the foolish, the brutal and fiendish, the brave and intelligent things people do."[12]

It's this curiosity that both fuels his imagined stories and propels those inspired by real events. In *The Writing Habit*, Huddle defends the use of autobiographical material in writing, claiming that it "brings forth [an author's] best writing. This is an instinctive, a necessary choice, because finally what the serious fiction writer—of whatever inclination—aims to do is to make art that embodies his or her best self."[13]

---

◀§ FROM *Tenorman*

When Carnes got out of the hospital in Stockholm, we offered him the horn of his choice, the studio of his dreams, and luxurious support for as long as he stayed clean. At the time, Carnes was 59 years old, but he looked closer to seventy. During the worst winter of his life, a couple of days before somebody checked him into the hospital, he had hocked his old horn. When we talked to him, he still vividly remembered having almost died on the streets of Göteborg. He was ready to consider what we had to offer him.

The first condition of our agreement was that he had to move back to the States—we wanted him in the Washington area, within driving distance of the museum's main office. He wasn't eager to come back to "Ol' Virginny," as he put it, but our deal must have seemed like his own customized version of paradise: a comfortable place to live; whatever he wanted in the way of food, clothes, books, records, and so on; along with an ideal working circumstance and all the time he wanted to spend with this replacement tenor he had asked for.

He already had that horn on his wish list, a Selmer Mark VI, vintage 1957, that Getz had played for a couple of years and that some private collector in Stockholm had picked up and let Carnes try out one afternoon some years back. How much of the American taxpayers' money we had to pay for that saxophone is still a confidential matter. . . .

There was no shortage of young musicians who wanted a chance to spend time around Carnes, to study with him, as it were. We turned away lots of them who'd just heard about our project, people whose names you probably would know if you listen seriously to jazz. Carnes was this living landmark of the music, an artist already of forty years' consequence, who had reached the apex of his genius here at the end of his life. We had our pick of the New York prodigies, the kids who'd been brought along by Wynton Marsalis and his dad. Our grant provided money to pay musicians top wages just to be available to Carnes when he wished for their assistance in his composing, his arranging, his noodling around in his art.

So when Carnes said, "Send in that piano man," Cody Jones, our gifted twenty-two-year-old pianist, presented himself at the studio door. Then Carnes and Cody would work on a piece as long as the old man wanted to. If Carnes decided they needed a bassist, they summoned Wil Stanfield, who appeared with his instrument, pleased to have been called and eager to jam with Carnes. Ditto with Curtis Wells, our Julliard dropout drummer. And so on. Wynton himself came down from New York occasionally and sent word in to the old man that he was available; Carnes appreciated that and always asked him to step right in. He liked Wynton, respected what he'd done for jazz. The two of them spent as much time talking as they did playing music.

When he had tired them out—he himself was apparently indefatigable—Carnes thanked the young musicians, laconically advised them to stay away from drugs, drink, and loose women; raised a gnarled old hand; and told them "later." Then he played to himself and the empty studio for another hour, or two hours, or all night if he wanted. Some nights—or early mornings—he set down his compositions or made notes for them, a kind of scoring only he seemed to understand. But usually he relied on his memory and set down nothing. He did exactly what he wanted to, and whatever it was, it suited us. We videotaped and recorded everything he did, every sound he made. Except for when he went to the bathroom. We could have done that, too, if we'd wanted; Carnes didn't care about the recording and videotaping of the project; he seemed happy doing what he was doing, living inside his music.[14]

### Questions and Exercises for Reflection and Inspiration

In the above excerpt, a proposition is established. A down-and-out musician/genius has agreed to allow every aspect of his life to be recorded and studied as part of a research project. In return, the musician is given a place to live and other creature comforts, a studio, a saxophone and other accoutrements necessary to "live inside his music." There's a funny scene in the Steve Martin movie, *The Jerk*, where Martin is down on his luck and he's broken up with the love of his life. As he leaves, he says, "This is all I need . . ." and he starts grabbing various items from around him: a lamp, a thermos, his dog. (Of course, the dog refuses to go with him.)

> **Exercise 1:** What items would you need to make a perfect situation where you could work on your art or most cherished hobby, whether it's fly-fishing or writing? Make a list of what you would need. What would you be willing to give up to gain those items? Are they all material items or is there something immaterial that you would have to give up to pursue your dreams? Would you let someone record your actions and reactions — like on those TV shows where people are

thrown together and videotaped day and night? Write a story in which you either

- get what you want and then have to produce something of importance for public review,

- make a deal to get what you need to pursue some project in return for giving up some essential element of your freedom or privacy,

- or, get what you need to pursue your dreams and then discover something essential about yourself that makes that dream less than desirable.

In the excerpt from "Wytheville Hospital" above, Huddle writes from his own material. The emotions in that hospital room are visceral. One can feel the desire to be a good son coming into conflict with old resentments and behavior. In *The Writing Habit*, Huddle maintains, "Writing autobiographically involves not only revealing ourselves to the world—which although frightening is also a little bit thrilling—but also writing about others, our family-members, our friends, our enemies."[15] He advises the would-be writer to avoid hurting other people's feelings but, in the end, "he cannot allow the opinions and feelings of others to stop or to interfere with his writing."[16i] He's not revealing the most horrible things about himself or his relatives. The father in the poem is not a mass murderer but he is a curmudgeon. The son is not a bad son but he does succumb to impatience. The poem reveals even deeper emotions: the fabric woven of a lifetime of things said and those unsaid filling the silence of that hospital room. There's an important lesson in this: the drama of family, of pain, of disappointment, of succor and release, can be told in the smallest of scenes.

Would reading this passage hurt the father? Would someone reading it think less of the author? Huddle says these are not his concerns. The first concern is "to make the thing beautiful," he says, "No matter who sees it."[17]

**Exercise 2:** Take some simple memory from your past, one that has great emotional impact but, on the surface, might appear insignificant to others: a boyfriend buying the wrong kind of present, thereby signaling he didn't really know or love you; a husband inadvertently saying the wrong thing in the delivery room; the time you missed the train or bus and ended up having an experience that changed everything; the time your mother didn't say she was sorry for talking about you in front of her best friend. Write a poem or short story in which the emotion you experienced is at the center of the piece but never specifically mentioned. Let the reader experience the emotion through your description of events leading up to the crucial moment and following it. Avoid abstract statements such as, "I felt disappointed" or "I was so unhappy." Rather, let the dialogue and the actions and reactions between the characters show these emotions. Aim for understatement rather than overstatement.

Huddle talks about the difference between making time for one's writing and writing's being essential to one's life so that it becomes natural, for example, to get up early or to give up some other activity (TV, for example, or playing golf or video games) to do one's writing. What is your best time of the day for mental and creative activity?

> **Exercise 3:** Try getting up one hour earlier to write, then try staying up one hour later to write. Try taking a nap at midday and then writing. Try all sorts of different sleep/writing arrangements, giving each about a week, if possible. Keep a journal in which you record your experiences, the quality of your concentration and writing. This is an exercise that might take you as long as six months or even a year to do. What you're after is discovering what works for you so that you can develop your own routine and learn when your brain and imagination work best together to produce your best work, given your busy schedule and the demands of others. In doing this exercise, you should first do two things: tell your family members, roommates or others who depend on you and might need you during your writing time what you need and ask them to help you with your goal to find an hour or two each day for your writing life; make a pledge to yourself that you will stick to your goal and your various schedules, no matter what. That might mean getting up long before everyone else in the family. It might mean eating a yogurt for lunch and spending the time in the bathroom stall at work with your notebook. It might mean going to the library for a quiet hour or two alone every evening after dinner. It can be done. In this exercise, you'll probably discover two things: your right pattern for writing and the one your life allows you to have. Do what you can with whatever time you can cobble out. But remember: if writing is essential to who you are, those who love you—and you yourself—need to give you the space and time to be your best self.

Photo by Maude Kinnell

# 11  Galway Kinnell
## *Man's Place in the Universe*

Born 1 February 1927, Providence, Rhode Island

Education: B.A., Princeton University; M.A., University of Rochester (New York)

Lives in Sheffield

First publication: a poem in the Princeton University student literary magazine, *The Nassau Lit*, in 1947

Collections of poetry: *What a Kingdom It Was* (1960); *Flower Herding on Mount Monadnock* (1964); *Body Rags* (1968); *First Poems, 1946–1954* (1970); *The Book of Nightmares* (1971); *The Shoes of Wandering* (1970); *The Avenue Bearing the Initial of Christ into the New World: Poems, 1946–1964* (1974); *Three Poems* (1976); *Mortal Acts, Mortal Words* (1980); *Selected Poems* (1982); *The Past* (1985); *When One Has Lived a Long Time Alone* (1990); *Imperfect Thirst* (1994); *A New Selected Poems* (2000)

Novel: *Black Light* (1966)

Nonfiction: *Walking Down the Stairs: Selections from Interviews* (1978)

Children's Book: *How the Alligator Missed Breakfast* (1982)

Translations: Novel: *Bitter Victory* by Rene Hardy (1956); Poems: *The Poems of François Villon* (1965); *On the Motion and Immobility Of Douve* by Yves Bonnefoy (1968); *Lackawanna Elegy* by Yvan Goll (1970)

Awards: Bess Hokin Prize from *Poetry Magazine* (1965); Shelley Prize from the Poetry Society of America (1974); Pulitzer Prize (1982); National Book Award (1982); Vermont State Poet (1989–93)

GALWAY KINNELL'S house in Sheffield, a town of 727 residents in Vermont's Northeast Kingdom, is out in the middle of nowhere — quite literally. It's a handsome red structure built around 1750, with views into the interior of Vermont on one side and onto Mount Wheelock on the other. Inside the old house, the living room has a brick fireplace big enough for half a tree. With wide plank floors and low, beamed ceilings, Oriental rugs, a bent-wood rocker and comfy couch, a worktable and Aladdin's lamp, an odd assortment of bird feathers and a hornet's nest for decoration, and books crammed into wall-to-ceiling bookcases, the place is as homey a retreat as you could hope to find. He has owned the house in Sheffield for more than forty years. He bought it and a few surrounding acres with the eight hundred dollars he had in his pocket when he was in his early thirties and looking for a place to store his books and write when he wasn't traveling or teaching. Over the years, he purchased more acreage.

As a young man, Kinnell trekked all over the country and many parts of the world, living in many beautiful places. But he came to believe that "the human presence had adapted itself to the other animals and to the contours of the land and vegetation" better in Vermont than almost anywhere else. And that was why he chose to live here. The cheap cost of the property helped; he's living so far north in part because he quickly figured out that the further north he went, the cheaper land and housing became.

But, it's a lot more than affordability — or beauty, for that matter. Place is important to a writer but there are many places on the planet that can brag of physical beauty, natural wonders, and other attractions that make them distinct and desirable. As Kinnell explains, "When it's an intriguing and appealing presence in your life, you're drawn to see it, to experience the place you're in, all the time. That's why Vermont, like many other places, is almost a character in your life and your work. But one of the reasons one chooses Vermont over some other place that is also wonderful, like some western states, for example, is the politics of Vermont. It's good to live in a place where you're not entirely disapproved of, where you're in some sort of basic agreement with most of the people about how the political life should be organized, about what is the role of the human in the environment. These things are dealt with more or less in a satisfactory way in Vermont. That makes it particularly good to live here. There's a general respect for the land and the other creatures, which in my mind is essential."

Despite his love for Vermont, Kinnell has spent many months teaching around the world — in Grenoble, France; in Teheran, Iran; in Manoa, Hawaii — and more than twenty years in New York, where he taught creative writing at New York University. He retired in 2003 but still spends time in New York City. He loves having both New York and Vermont in his life: "People who live all the time in New York don't know what they miss; they miss the world that may be the best, the natural world, the world we try to accommodate ourselves to. Without this world, I would feel eventually half alive," he says. "But in the same way, I feel that if I lived here [in

Vermont] indefinitely, I would forget, not intellectually, but emotionally, how much of humanity lives, for better and for worse."

And so he spends as much time as he can in Vermont. "I take stimulation from the extreme winter. I feel more akin to the spaces beyond us. This is a very perilous planet in God knows what universe. To be reminded of its fragility is useful and makes us have to take care of it. Surely somewhere else, there's conscious life but never in this conscious life will humans make contact with it. To go out at night when it's forty below and all the stars are out and somehow the air has been cleansed, and the stars are brighter, and you feel part of something that is not the world. It's a big part of the origin of religion."

Kinnell shares his feelings with the reader, putting into words that sense of being tiny and alien, of our being both part of the earth, responsible to it, and at the same time totally inconsequential, as in this excerpt from the poem "Middle of the Way":

> I wake in the night.
> An old ache in the shoulder blades.
> I lie amazed under the trees
> That creak a little in the dark,
> The giant trees of the world.
>
> I lie on earth the way
> Flames lie in the woodpile,
> Or as an imprint, in sperm, of what is to be.
> I love the earth, and always
> In its darkness I am a stranger.[1]

The poem is so utterly and surprisingly simple and complex, all in one. That second line, "an old ache in the shoulder blades" states the human condition in tangible terms while simultaneously linking our humanity to the trees, "the giant trees of the world" that creak in the night. And just as the fireplace's flames lie dormant in the woodpile, so too does our own swift end lie dormant in our beginning, the possibility of life swimming in sperm, unbidden, while the earth goes about its business. It's the kind of poem one can imagine him writing after a night of meandering around his own pastures and hills in Sheffield.

Kinnell is particularly delighted that the town is "a little out of the way. You can't get anywhere by driving through the town. It's off by itself, unassuming." His neighbors are working class; they make little to-do about the fact that he is a poet. "They respect poetry but don't idealize it," he says, "and that's the way it ought to be."

Kinnell was born 1 February 1927 and lived in Pawtucket, Rhode Island, until he was fifteen, when the family moved to New Hampshire. About that time, he began reading an anthology of poetry, poring over the different authors and studying their formats and styles. "I really liked the whole idea of poetry," he recalls, "that it was about the inner life and almost, in some cases, almost another realm of existence entirely." His early love of poetry coupled with his appreciation of nature set in motion instincts that drive his poetry all these decades later. Scholars often observe that Kinnell's poetry derives from his own experiences and awareness of his inner self in relation to the world that exists quite outside of man. As Kinnell puts it, "Poetry is the singing of what is to be on our own planet."

The ability to be outside in nature made a big impression on him but so too did learning. He had begun writing poetry in high school, just writing for himself, what he characterizes as "not terribly serious poems." That changed when he arrived at Princeton University. His roommate was W. S. Merwin, already a serious poet. With the influence of Merwin and several faculty members who were writing verse, poetry came alive for Kinnell. He began to realize that "it was something one could do. I wrote quite a lot of poems, long poems; they were kind of over the top in a way, emotionally speaking. I lacked skill and composure and control. But it stuck with me, that notion of writing something, of capturing one's inner experience, but I never actually dreamed, I still didn't imagine I could be a poet."

After graduating with highest honors from Princeton University in 1948, he was unsure what he wanted to do. Without even applying, however, he got an offer of a full scholarship to study at the University of Rochester, where he earned his master's degree. It was, he recalls, " a wonderful time. There were just ten grad students in English; we formed a close bonded group. Some of our professors there gave a lot of time and attention to their graduate students. I could see that the kindness of my teachers meant a lot to me, so I've always tried to be a kind teacher to my students.

"From that point on, wherever I was, I always found a poet friend," he says. But his career was far from traditional. After graduate school, he served in the United States Navy and then visited Paris on a Fulbright Fellowship. Returning to the United States, he worked for the Congress on Racial Equality and then traveled widely in the Middle East and Europe. He worked in Chicago as the director of the downtown center of the University of Chicago for four years, organizing poetry readings and other cultural events. "I met a lot of poets from all over the country when they came to Chicago. It was really quite wonderful. Then I started sending out poems to magazines. I had a lot of bad luck and a lot of good luck. The *Beloit Poetry Journal* took a liking to my poetry. Anything I sent to them, they took and published. Also *Poetry Magazine*. Anything I sent to them, I knew they would publish. Those two publications shared the same delusion, that my work was worth publishing," he says with a wry smile.

"I was making money living by my wits. I eventually married, had children, had to work very hard to keep things together. I noticed some of my friends got jobs in universities but I didn't go that way full-time for a long time. At first, I taught all over, earning a pittance as an adjunct professor. One semester I taught at four different schools—Columbia and Sarah

Lawrence, Holy Cross and Brandeis. I would drive at night to get to my various places. I usually taught three days a week. On the fourth day, I would give a reading. Weekends, I spent with my wife and children. I wrote in airports and motel rooms."

No wonder that Vermont house was a godsend.

Kinnell didn't publish his first collection of poetry, *What a Kingdom It Was*, until 1960 although he had been writing for quite a long time before that: "I didn't feel any hurry to produce a book. Instead, I felt the opportunity for a book will come or it won't."[2] Rather than feel pressured to publish a book—a freedom that he experienced in part because he was an adjunct professor rather than someone seeking tenure as a full-time employee—he "made no effort to get a book contract."

Instead, the publishers came to him—three top-shelf publishing houses requested manuscripts in the same year. He sent manuscripts out to the three, explaining his dilemma. All three wanted to publish his book. He eventually chose Houghton Mifflin, which has published most of his work since. He says it might be better if more writers resisted the urge to publish too soon—or too young. "I thought it would be better to have a book that was strong than have a book with some weak poems in it. I kept what I called 'the book manuscript' with me all the time but I kept substituting new or stronger poems for ones I felt were weaker. In the end, it makes a better impression on people than the juvenilia you would have published a few years earlier." Still, he says, in that half self-deprecating style of his, when he looks back at his early collections, he wishes he'd cut or revised more. Indeed, he's constantly reworking poems. His collection, *A New Selected Poems*, published in 2000, contains selections from volumes dating back to the 1960 collection. He says in a foreword, "I wish it were in my nature to stop working over these old poems and accept that they will never be perfect."[3]

Kinnell does not have a system for creating poetry. He doesn't write at a certain time every day. He doesn't keep a schedule. He just tries to write a little bit every day—or, rather, to work on a poem every day. He says, " A poem takes me a long time to finish, years maybe. I might produce one poem in a year. They might say, 'Well, he wasn't working very hard.' But I was working every day on that poem." He doesn't keep a journal, but he keeps "sheets of paper folded in four parts in my pocket, just in case I feel something I'd like to write down. Memory is not reliable. It might hold the general idea but the specific words are hard to keep. Whitman wrote down so much of *Leaves of Grass* as notes, Ginsberg wrote *Howl* as notes. That's why all their observations are so fresh. I walk a lot. It's good for a writer. Walking is a rhythmic activity that doesn't bounce you too much. It keeps your head moving in that level line, instead of bouncing up and down. You can still be in tune with the things around you. If you're bouncing up and down, you're seeing things out of sync." That belief does double duty as a good excuse for not taking up jogging.

Kinnell is known as an inspirational teacher with a legion of appreciative students. "If someone's writing something I don't really like at all, I don't try to criticize them. It's kind of a laissez-faire teaching. What I really like to do is talk to people one on one in conference. Then I can tell them everything I think about their poems. I don't like to tell them things that could be seen as harsh before a whole class. In conference, it's possible to make it clear you're trying to make it helpful." He says he "never gives exercises. The process of writing is the origin of the poem; the idea comes from the poet. Telling someone what to write about short-circuits the process, eliminates the first and most important part of the process, which is getting the idea. It would be harmful tampering. I wouldn't regard it as tampering if a student gave him or herself some exercises to do, if a student were to say, for example, I want to write a poem just like William Butler Yeats or ten poems just like William Butler Years. That would be following one's own instinct and I think that would be a wonderful thing to do. Instead, when I talk about writing, I talk about alertness, about having all one's antennae on as much as possible so that you're aware of what you're walking through. Your connection with some things you pass becomes clear to you and you want to write about that thing."

Kinnell's earliest poems had their roots in traditional religion and authority but he quickly turned from conventional notions, coming to believe in a kind of religion of nature. He has said, "If you could keep going deeper and deeper, you'd finally not be a person . . . you'd be a blade of grass or ultimately perhaps a stone. And if a stone could read, poetry would speak for it."[4] That notion is there repeatedly in subsequent volumes, some with obvious references to Vermont places, such as *Flower Herding on Mount Monadnock*[5] or ones that feel hatched alive from Vermont places, such as the long poem "The Striped Snake and the Goldfinch," which includes this contemplation:

> How much time do I have left of the loyalty to earth,
> To human shame, and dislike of our own lives,
> And others' deaths that take part of us with them,
> Wear out of us, as we go toward that moment
> When we find out how we die: clinging and pleading,
> Or secretly relieved that it is all over,
> Or despising ourselves, knowing that death
> Is a punishment we deserve, or like an old dog,
> Off his feed, who suddenly is ravenous,
> And eats the bowl clean, and the next day is a carcass.
>
> . . . . . . . . . . . . . . . . . . . . . . . . . . . . . . . . . . . . . . .
>
> Yet I know more than ever that here is that true place,
> Here where we sit together, out of the wind,
> With a loaf of country bread, and tomatoes still warm

From the distant sun, and wine in glasses that are,
One for each of us, the upper bell of the glass
That will hold the last hour we have to live.[6]

When his collection, *Selected Poems*, won both the Pulitzer Prize and the National Book Award in 1982, reviewers and critics alike praised Kinnell's ability to share the dilemmas of human existence in language that was at once private and universal. Kinnell often employs simple declarative statements, repetition, and rhythm, along with distinctive physical observations to create his montage of images and meaning, as in this poem, "Sheffield Ghazal 4: Driving West":

A tractor-trailer carrying two dozen crushed automobiles overtakes a
    tractor-trailer carrying a dozen new.
Oil is a form of waiting.
The internal combustion engine converts the stasis of millennia into
    motion.
Cars howl on rain-wetted roads.
Airplanes rise through the downpour and throw us through the blue sky.
Computers can deliver nuclear explosions to precisely anywhere on
    earth.
A lightning bolt is made entirely of error.
Erratic Mercurys and errant Cavaliers wander the highways.
A girl puts her head on a boy's shoulder; they are driving west.
The windshield wipers wipe, homesickness one way, wanderlust the
    other, back and forth.
This happened to your father and to you, Galway—sick to stay, longing
    to come up against the ends of the earth, and climb over.[7]

The poem "Fergus Falling," one of Kinnell's best known and best loved, grew out of the near tragedy that occurred in nature but was compelled by human curiosity. The poet, whose son escapes a horrible death, knows life—for both the trees and the fish, as well as the iconic fisherman of his poem—will go on while both his and his son's will not.

**Fergus Falling**

He climbed to the top
of one of those million white pines
set out across the emptying pastures
of the fifties—some program to enrich the rich
and rebuke the forefathers
who cleared it all at once with ox and axe—
climbed to the top, probably to get out
of the shadow

not of those forefathers but of this father
and saw for the first time
down in its valley, Bruce Pond, giving off
its little steam in the afternoon,

pond where Clarence Akley came on Sunday mornings to cut down
the cedars around the shore, I'd sometimes hear the slow
    spondees of his work, he's gone,
where Milton Norway came up behind me while I was fishing and
stood awhile before I knew he was there, he's the one who put
the cedar shingles on the house, some have curled or split, a
    few have blown off, he's gone,
where Gus Newland logged in the cold snap of '58, the only man
willing to go into those woods that never got warmer than ten
    below, he's gone,
pond where two wards of the state wandered on Halloween, the
National Guard searched for them in November, in vain, the
next fall a hunter found their skeletons huddled together, in
    vain, they're gone,
pond where an old fisherman in a rowboat sits, drowning hooked
    worms, when he goes he's replaced and is never gone,

and when Fergus
saw the pond for the first time
in the clear evening, saw its oldness down there
in its old place in the valley, he became heavier suddenly
in his bones
the way fledglings do just before they fly,
and the soft pine cracked . . .

I would not have heard his cry
if my electric saw had been working,
its carbide teeth speeding through the bland spruce of our time, or
burning
black arcs into some scavenged hemlock plank,
like dark circles under eyes
when the brain thinks too close to the skin,
but I was sawing by hand and I heard that cry
as though he were attacked; we ran out,
when we bent over him he said, "Galway, Inés, I saw a pond!"
His face went gray, his eyes fluttered close a frightening
moment . . .

Yes—a pond
that lets off its mist
on clear afternoons of August, in that valley
to which many have come, for their reasons,

from which many have gone, a few for their reasons, most not,
where even now an old fisherman only the pinetops can see
sits in the dry gray wood of his rowboat, waiting for pickerel.[8]

That theme of the fundamental frailty of life, of how death and life hold
hands and accompany our every moment, infuses most of Kinnell's work.
It is, he says, at the core of his own existence, especially now as he nears his
eightieth year. For him, however, there is comfort, albeit grudging comfort, that those stars and the cycle of life, whether it is one that includes the
human or not, will continue, long after he and all who read his words are
gone. It's a poignant belief, but it's the one he lives with. Age, responsibility, fatherhood, love—all these make each day more precious, more fleeting. That notion is expressed in a father's poem from *New and Selected
Poems*, "Little Sleep's-Head Sprouting Hair in the Moonlight":

### 1

You scream, waking from a nightmare.

When I sleepwalk
into your room, and pick you up,
and hold you up in the moonlight, you cling to me
hard,
as if clinging could save us. I think
you think
I will never die, I think I exude
to you the permanence of smoke or stars,
even as
my broken arms heal themselves around you.

### 2

I have heard you tell
the sun, *don't go down*, I have stood by
as you told the flower, *don't grow old*,
*don't die*. Little Maud,

I would blow the flame out of your silver cup,
I would suck the rot from your fingernail,
I would brush your sprouting hair of the dying light,
I would scrape the rust off your ivory bones,
I would help death escape through the little ribs of your body,
I would alchemize the ashes of your cradle back into wood,
I would let nothing of you go, ever,

until washerwomen
feel the clothes fall asleep in their hands,

and hens scratch their spell across hatchet blades,
and rats walk away from the cultures of the plague,
and iron twists weapons toward the true north,
and grease refuses to slide in the machinery of progress,
and men feel as free on earth as fleas on the bodies of men,
and lovers no longer whisper to the presence beside them in the
dark, *O corpse-to-be* . . .

And yet perhaps this is the reason you cry,
this the nightmare you wake screaming from:
being forever
in the pre-trembling of a house that falls.

## 3

In a restaurant once, everyone
quietly eating, you clambered up
on my lap: to all
the mouthfuls rising toward
all the mouths, at the top of your voice
you cried
your one word, *caca! caca! caca!*
and each spoonful
stopped, a moment, in midair, in its withering
steam.

Yes,
you cling because
I, like you, only sooner
than you, will go down
the path of vanished alphabets,
the roadlessness
to the other side of the darkness,
your arms
like the shoes left behind,
like the adjectives in the halting speech
of old men,
which once could call up the lost nouns.

## 4

And you yourself,
some impossible Tuesday
in the year Two Thousand and Nine, will walk out
among the black stones
of the field, in the rain,

and the stones saying
 over their one word, *ci-gît, ci-gît, ci-gît,*

and the raindrops
hitting you on the fontanel
over and over, and you standing there
unable to let them in.

### 5

If one day it happens
you find yourself with someone you love
in a café at one end
of the Pont Mirabeau, at the zinc bar
where white wine stands in upward opening glasses,

and if you commit then, as we did, the error
of thinking,
*one day all this will only be memory,*

learn to reach deeper
into the sorrows
to come—to touch
the almost imaginary bones
under the face, to hear under the laughter
the wind crying across the black stones. Kiss
the mouth
which tells you, *here,*
*here is the world.* This mouth. This laughter. These temple bones.

The still undanced cadence of vanishing.

### 6

In the light the moon
sends back, I can see in your eyes
the hand that waved once
in my father's eyes, a tiny kite
wobbling far up in the twilight of his last look:

and the angel
of all mortal things lets go the string.

### 7

Back you go, into your crib.

The last blackbird lights up his gold wings: *farewell.*
Your eyes close inside your head,

in sleep. Already
in your dreams the hours begin to sing.

Little sleep's-head sprouting hair in the moonlight,
when I come back
we will go out together,
we will walk out together among
the ten thousand things,
each scratched too late with such knowledge, *the wages
of dying is love*.⁹

## Questions and Exercises for Reflection and Inspiration

Galway Kinnell doesn't believe that teachers should give students exercises.
He says that eliminates the first part of the writing process—the coming up
with the idea. It's okay if students give themselves exercises. Read through
his poetry again and think about your own work. If there are exercises you
could give yourself, particularly ones that rely on having those antennae
fully turned on, please assign them. Otherwise, just walk around with a
piece of paper folded in fourths in your pocket and jot down ideas as they
come along. Maybe you'll decide to do something with them; maybe you
won't.

Photo by Oliver Parini

# 12   Jay Parini
## *The Writing Life*

Born 2 April 1948, Pittston, Pennsylvania

Education: B.A., Lafayette College; M.A. and Ph.D., the University of Saint Andrews in Scotland

Lives in Weybridge

First publication, a collection of poetry, *Singing in Time* (1972)

Collections of poetry: *Singing in Time* (1972); *Anthracite Country* (1982); *Town Life* (1988); *House of Days* (1997)

Novels: *The Love Run* (1980); *The Patch Boys* (1986); *The Last Station* (1990); *Bay of Arrows* (1992); *Benjamin's Crossing* (1997); *The Apprentice Lover* (2002)

Textbook: *An Invitation to Poetry* (1986)

Essays: *Some Necessary Angels* (1993)

Biographies: *Theodore Roethke: An American Romantic* (1979); *John Steinbeck* (1995); *Robert Frost: A Life* (1999)

He also edited many books, including *Gore Vidal: Writer Against the Grain* (1992); *The Columbia History of American Poetry* (1995); and *The Norton Book of American Autobiography* (1999)

Awards: *Chicago Tribune*-Heartland Award for the best work of nonfiction for 2000; John Ciardi Lifetime Achievement Award from the National Italian American Foundation; Josepha Hale Award for Literature; Guggenheim Fellowship

IT'S NEARLY IMPOSSIBLE to categorize Jay Parini. He writes and publishes successfully across the genres of poetry, fiction, essay, and biography and pens articles for both the scholarly and popular press. He

spends long hours in libraries and on the computer poring over dense manuscripts and doing literary research, but most weekday mornings he break-
fasts at Steve's Park Diner in downtown Middlebury, where for an hour or
so he writes poetry in longhand with the chatter and commerce of neighbors surrounding him. Between the depth of his literary knowledge and his
own output—more than twenty books and hundreds of articles—one wonders how he has a spare moment. Yet, he manages to spend his lunch hour
at a gymnasium in Middlebury playing full-court basketball and to find
time to ski, hike, and motor his boat around Lake Champlain. And, despite
the demands on his time from Middlebury College students, where he has
taught since 1982 and is known as a remarkably accessible mentor to developing writers, he still finds time to attend one of his three sons' sporting
events or make dinner with his wife.

Perhaps the best lesson the aspiring writer could garner, therefore, from
Parini is an answer to the question, How do you do it all. How do you balance the demands of work, home, and hobbies—and still have time to
write? Parini says it's a matter of priorities. "There's really considerably
more time available in a day than most people think. To begin with, if you
just don't watch TV, you can add several hours a day to your schedule. But
it's not simply a matter of doing without certain activities; it's more a matter of using the time you are devoting to your writing, research, or reading
as efficiently as possible. Focus is the main thing. Don't spend a lot of time
looking out the window. Daydreaming is good when you're out on the lake
or doing some tedious job; in fact, it's an essential part of the writing
process. But when you're sitting down to getting the writing done, put
your mind to that. And if you get blocked and find you're wasting a lot of
time, get up from the desk or computer. Do something else, something entirely different. Go for a walk, weed the garden. Of course, writer's block
can also be an indication that you're letting the internal critic in your head
get in the way. Send the critic away. Just write. You can always revise. But
if you don't have anything on paper after an hour or two of work, you'll be
more discouraged and it will be even harder to write the next time. Just
begin. That's the most important part."

Parini grew up in a small mining town near Scranton, Pennsylvania, a
place he does not describe with much affection. Besides the slag heaps and
the pollution of the mining industry that ruined the environment, the area
felt "finished, an industrial wasteland, a beautiful place turned foul by un-
bridled capitalism." Then, when he was ten, he got to spend a week in Vermont. Before the week was over, he told his parents he would live here
someday. Vermont's landscape "spoke to me in a kind of spiritual way. I've
never taken it for granted," he says. Parini spent many years studying and
traveling through Europe before returning to the Green Mountain State.
In a way, he was apprenticing for a career as a writer, a career that would
ultimately lead him to Middlebury, where he has written and taught for
more than twenty years.

Like several other successful writers profiled in this book, he was the first in his family to go to college. Back home, his father and uncles operated a construction business; it had been assumed that he too would work in the family business, even though his interests in literature certainly differentiated him from those around him. He chose to go to college rather than join his father's business. Lafayette College, a small liberal-arts institution in Easton, Pennsylvania, afforded him just the right environment to grow as a thinking person: it was small enough that he wasn't overwhelmed, and its focus on the humanities allowed him to gain a firm footing in a wide range of subjects. And the town had a small café where he could spend part of each day writing, a habit that he has pursued throughout his writing life (more on that later). Parini took his junior year abroad at the University of Saint Andrews, Scotland's most ancient university, founded in 1312.

After college, he returned to Scotland, in part to avoid and protest against the Vietnam War, and also because he wanted to immerse himself in the intellectual and community life of Saint Andrews. Although he didn't know it yet, Parini had begun his love affair with small-town life. In his collection of essays on writing and politics, *Some Necessary Angels,* Parini describes Saint Andrews as "an idyllic coastal town on the East Neuk of Fife . . . The medieval city walls are still, here and there, intact, and the university's granite towers dominate this town beside the North Sea."[1]

The writing life, like so many other disciplines, often takes its shape from chance occurrences and meetings. Parini's first blessings came in the form of a mentor, a brilliant writer whose influence is reflected in the versatility of Parini's writing projects, his passion for the classics, his dedication to his craft, and his willingness to share what he knows with others. Because Parini benefited so much from his friendships with older, more established writers (who include Alastair Reid, Gore Vidal, and Robert Penn Warren), he encourages students and developing writers to find a mentor, preferably someone whose sensibilities are similar to your own, someone you can admire and want to please. The best mentor will be tough and honest about your failings but supportive of your successes. Most of us won't have the great good fortune to find such luminaries in the field as Parini had, but that's not necessary. What you want in a mentor is someone whose understanding of writing you respect and someone who can guide you to do better work without destroying your own distinctive voice.

Here's how Parini found his first mentor: Upon hearing that Parini wanted to be a writer, a history tutor at Saint Andrews said quite emphatically, "Then you should meet Alastair Reid." Parini went to the library to read the works of Reid; he immediately felt both awe and trepidation. Nonetheless, Parini telephoned Reid to request a meeting. He was quite surprised to get an immediate invitation to meet Reid at a nearby pub. "Bring a poem," Reid instructed.

"I still remember how tremblingly I went to see him. I had never met a 'real' writer," Parini recalls in *Some Necessary Angels.* "I had checked his books—the slim volumes of idiosyncratic, pellucid, gorgeously musical verse, the collections of essays on travel and ideas . . . I had never encountered a prose manner like that before, so deeply personal in syntax, image-centered, at times almost singing. The tone was so infinitely worldly wise, with a flicker of Celtic charm at every crucial turn. I knew at once that I wanted my poetry and prose to look like that."[2]

Reid took Parini under his wing, using with him the same methods that the famed writer Robert Graves had used in mentoring Reid. In the late 1960s when Parini was studying under Reid, Graves had something of a cult following in America. Graves's *White Goddess*, which (in the vein of Joseph Campbell's books) traces the similarities among myths from widely disparate cultures as well as the mythological and psychological sources of poetry, was especially popular with American intellectual youth of the time. So, to be sitting in the home of Graves's student, himself a well-respected writer, was a privilege not lost on Parini who came to think of himself as the literary grandson of Robert Graves:[3] "Between stirrings of soup, he [Reid] would sit beside me and do what Graves did for him: add or chop a word, a phrase. Sometimes whole stanzas [of Parini's poems] would disappear or get moved up or down. Once he crumpled a whole poem without a word. He said little. I watched and learned." Parini's poetry "began to sound extremely like Alastair's. I knew this, of course, but it did not worry me. I knew that one day, if lucky, my voice would blend with his, would gradually separate, and become distinct. This happens naturally."[4]

Reid also guided Parini's intellectual life, suggesting books and leading him through the literary landscape, albeit one that reflected Reid's own tastes in history and the classics. Parini—who describes himself at the time as someone who read only the books that *weren't* on the required reading list—became a willing student. He also studied Reid's personal life, an itinerant one and cavalier toward relationships. Reid had never married, acquired few possessions, and wrote in one poem, "Change is where I live." Parini came to think of Reid as a cat person, someone who could make himself at home wherever he landed.

"I [found] this admirable but terrifying," Parini wrote later. "I quickly realized that my own instincts worked against Alastair's here and that I preferred a doglike existence: one house, one wife, a permanent landscape, which for me is always northern New England. But the cat person still calls to me, and—perhaps in obeisance to something I learned from Alastair—I can't resist my forays into the larger world. My wife, Devon, and I regularly go abroad, to Italy or England, where we rent a house for a month, a year, at a time. I entertain fantasies of villas in Mexico or Sicily. I too am drawn to the exhilaration of impermanence, though I retreat for daily life to my wood-frame farmhouse on a hill overlooking the Green Mountains."[5]

While still a graduate student in Scotland, Parini published his first book of poems, *Singing in Time*[6] and began contributing essays and reviews to various journals, such as *Lines Review* and *Scottish International*. He returned to the United States after earning his doctorate. His first teaching job was at Dartmouth College in Hanover, New Hampshire, in 1975, close to the Vermont border. There, he sought another mentoring relationship, this time with Robert Penn Warren, the nation's first poet laureate, who had a house nearby in West Wardsboro.

In a 25 February 2002 article in the *New York Times*, Parini tells the story of his apprenticeship under Warren: "He was . . . quite ruthless with his pen and could be harsh with his critiques of a poem or piece of fiction. But he was generous, too, and understood that praise and censure have to be carefully meted out so that the younger writer doesn't lose hope. It is just so miserably easy to lose hope." Once, during a walk through the woods near Stratton Mountain, Warren asked Parini why he hadn't shared any of his writing in a long while. "I explained that my life had become overwrought. I had been unable to complete a poem or story for months. Everything I wrote seemed secondhand, boring and impossibly crude. He looked at me sternly and said, 'You must cultivate leisure.' I knew instantly what he meant: I had neglected my own essential laziness, that mental place where you have to spend, or to waste, a lot of time. For a writer there is no such thing as wasted time. It doesn't work that way."[7]

Parini took Warren's advice and lightened up on himself. He began to understand that physical exercise and social diversions were essential to a writer and began to plan time in each day for both forms of leisure.

A few years later, Parini also developed a lasting friendship with Gore Vidal, the self-exiled American author of twenty-three novels that range from historical fiction to contemporary satire, several Broadway hits, and nearly one hundred teleplays, eight volumes of essays, and innumerable articles and reviews. Vidal lives in a small village in Italy where Parini happened to be staying in 1985. Again, Parini learned by chance that Vidal lived nearby. Again, with some trepidation, he left a note for Vidal at a café that Vidal frequented, requesting a meeting. Again came the invitation for a visit. And, again, a long friendship based on a love of writing blossomed. Vidal is often an outspoken critic of American foreign policy; he calls his native country The United States of Amnesia, for what he considers our collective ignorance of history. He believes that writers have a duty to comment upon the history surrounding them and to use their gifts to make the world a better place. It's a notion Parini shares, writing in *Some Necessary Angels*, "writers do, in fact, have a responsibility to society. . . . Those who have language and analytical skills at their command have an obligation to use them."[8]

Parini learned from all three mentors—Reid, Warren, and Vidal—how to move easily between genres, while also carrying a teaching schedule. At Dartmouth, Parini used Warren as a model, "to see how the pieces of his life's puzzle had been fitted neatly together." His innate instinct to write all sorts of things rather than restrict himself to one genre, as has been the tradition here in the United States, was legitimized by Warren, who said, "literary specialization in America has actually hurt our literature." Parini accepted this, acknowledging, "while I have kept poetry at the center of my writing and reading life, I have found useful expression in various prose forms, including the novel and the critical essay."[9]

Also, following his mentors' example, he's gone out of his way to help developing writers "with their manuscripts, their questions and their hopes. If the chemistry is right, amazing conversations will ensue. There is so much to talk about. And I often feel as though I'm taking part in a much larger conversation, one that reaches back as far as Athens and has kept the lamp burning in many windows down the centuries, wherever young writers have gone for advice, for inspiration, for 'correction' and—of course—for love."

Thus, the aspiring writer can learn a second lesson from Parini. Setting one's priorities and cobbling out time for writing is important; so too can be having a mentor. You can find many accomplished writers and writing teachers, as well as students of great literature, in your surrounding area whose advice, company and inspiration might prove valuable. As Parini's life indicates, some of the best writers are quite generous with their time; the worst that can happen to you if you seek a relationship with a writer is that he'll say no. If you receive no answer or an impolite one, the person probably wouldn't have been much help to you anyway. Another way to seek mentors is to join a writing group. Look for one that has writers at your level and above so that you can support and learn from one another. If there isn't already a writing group in your town or county, form one. The local library and bookstores are the best places to ask about writing groups or to find like-minded writers (and readers) who would like to join together. The important thing about mentors and writing groups is that they get you writing, commenting on other's writing, and receiving response in return. There's nothing like an audience to make one actually finish that piece that's been locked inside your hard drive for a few months or years.

Another lesson Parini shares revolves around the *where* of writing. Some writers hole up in their attic or a studio far from distractions; Parini writes in several settings but his favorite is a café—first in Scotland, then Italy, then Hanover, and now in Middlebury. He writes, "Apart from the vaguely social aspects of writing in restaurants—the delicious sense of being alone within a communal center—there is a further advantage. In a public place, one doesn't normally use a writing machine more complicated than a pencil. In the age of word processing, diners are an ideal place for the rediscovery of this remarkable product of our civilization. The pencil is surprisingly efficient, in fact. You can delete what you don't like with a quick horizontal stroke that both rids you of the unwanted phrase and simultaneously preserves the deletion—just in case it was better than the revised version, which is often the case. Also, the strange visceral connection between hand and brain is somehow lost in the subliminal click of keyboards and the computer screen's unyielding gaze."[10]

During his years at Dartmouth College, from 1975 to 1982, Parini published the first of his many biographies of important literary figures, *Theodore Roethke: An American Romantic*,[11] his first novel, *The Love Run*,[12] and a second book of poems, *Anthracite Country*.[13] He contributed poems, essays, and reviews to numerous journals, including the *Atlantic*, the *New Yorker*, *Poetry Magazine*, the *New Republic*, and *The Nation*, and cofounded the *New England Review* (with Sydney Lea) in 1976. In 1982 he moved to Middlebury College, where he is the Axinn Professor of English and has continued to publish nearly a book a year.

As with so many writers, Parini's life experiences often make their way into his writing but in different ways in different formats. His poetry spans the Scranton years all the way to the present, a sometimes sly and sometimes transparent record of a man's inner life and outward responses. Poetry is an intimate form of writing, as if the poet is communicating emotion and response in his or her unique and sometimes peculiar language directly on to the page. Indeed, the word "communicate" might be inaccurate. On the most primary level, poetry has no audience; it is the poem itself and the writer's relationship with the poem that matters. For many readers (and some poets), poetry seems like a magic act: a miraculous transformation of emotion or sentiment or memory from the brain (or muse) to the page in language that is at once familiar yet strange, rearranged, made whole and yet dismembered. Parini's poetry reflects his evolution as young man escaping the mining country to his current roles of husband, wife and community member. We read of events, large and small, that have gnawed at his consciousness over the years, such as this funeral scene in the poem entitled "The Miner's Wake":

> The small ones, in suits and dresses,
> wrapped their rosaries round the chair legs
> or tapped the wall with squeaky shoes.
>
> But their widowed mother, at thirty-four,
> had mastered every pose of mourning,
> plodding the sadness like an ox through mud.
>
> Her mind ran well ahead of her heart,
> making calculations of the years without him
> stretching before her like a humid summer.
>
> The walnut coffin honeyed in sunlight;
> lilies blossomed over silk and satin.
> Nuns cried heaven into their hands.
>
> I was just a nephew with my lesser grief,
> sitting by a window, watching the pigeons
> settle onto slag like summer snow.
>
> —from *Anthracite Country*[14]

The poem takes us to that place where the widow calculates her future. The language is simple yet beautiful, and it creates a haunting and complex understanding of grief. Simultaneously, we see that the first-person speaker in the poem has already left this world, has recognized the slag for what it is and himself as an outsider. The poem contrasts the widow's future with the narrator's. His is unspoken but we understand unconsciously that it is not here: in his act of looking out the window and making his own calculations (pigeons and slag equals settling for something lesser than), the narrator of the poem will chose a different fate.

The language is lovely, poetic, multilayered, and yet available. And, because Parini's poems draw upon his life experiences, their intimacy makes the reader feel included in the internal dialogues that inspired the poems in the first place. That's one of the most wonderful things about poetry; the best of it leaves us contemplating all that is unspoken. Poetry both gives us information and refuses us information; poetry is simultaneously intimate and secretive. It is as much about what is revealed as what is left out. That's why it's endured through the ages. It satisfies our longing for shared experiences while making it clear that each of us is a mystery to his fellow human beings.

Some of Parini's apprenticeship days are retold in fictional form in his novel, *The Apprentice Lover*.[15] The novel takes place on the Isle of Capri in 1970 when a young writer named Alex apprentices himself to an older, accomplished writer named Rupert Grant—an unlikable mix of Robert Graves and Alastair Reid. Grant's villa is a haunt of literati and artists, such as W. H. Auden, Graham Greene, and Gore Vidal, people Parini actually has known. The novel, although highly readable, is considered a "writer's novel" because there are so many reflections about writing in it. It's also a classic coming-of-age novel as the main character, Alex, equally shy about his sexuality and writing ability, is thrown into Grant's ruthless world. It's a great read, especially for would-be writers or those who think the writer's life is glamorous. It can be, of course, as the book amply illustrates; but it can also be vicious and self-centered and, ultimately, self-destructive as well. You'll read in an excerpt later in this chapter how cleverly Parini uses simple domestic scenes to create character—a valuable lesson for developing writers who often think, erroneously, that one needs earth-shattering drama to create interest on the page. Life-and-death decisions and realizations occur more often across the dinner table or over cocktails than on the sinking ocean liner.

Among Parini's important biographies of literary figures, perhaps the most notable to New England writers and readers is his *Robert Frost, a Life*. Samuel Hazo, founder of the International Poetry Forum, wrote of the work:

> Biographical writing is an art unto itself. Not only must the facts of a life be known and understood (to the limits of the possible),

but they must be re-created in a style that transcends a mere factual retelling. . . .

To write a literary biography is doubly difficult since the biographer must also be something of a literary critic, not reading the
poetry (as is the case with Robert Frost) as extensions or revelations of factual biography but as texts whose worth does not
have a one-to-one relationship with the author. This relationship
is metaphorical, not literal.

Jay Parini's work seems to me definitive as literary biography.
True, there have been previous literary biographies and studies of
Frost and his poetry (and Parini's postscript openly acknowledges and evaluates the most significant of these and presumes
that there will be others), but I doubt if they will rival Parini's for
thoroughness, fairness and poetic insight.[16]

What Hazo means is that, while the reader can learn much about Frost as
poet and human being from Parini's book, the book also serves as an ex-
cellent example of how to write a biography. The book reads like a novel,
so much so that readers find it hard to put down. That's because Parini is
also a novelist. And, because he is also a poet and a literary critic, the book
is imbued with many layers of understanding and instruction—not to mention sensitive revelations about Frost's life. Many biographies of Frost make
it clear he was no saint; Parini's doesn't gloss over the less attractive aspects
of Frost's life; at the same time, however, it makes the man come alive in a
way that is especially dear to Vermont readers.

The book took Parini twenty years to write. He began researching it at
Dartmouth after he discovered a treasure trove of archived material on
Frost in the college library. But it wasn't until Parini was firmly ensconced
in Middlebury and had also spent considerable time at Middlebury College's Bread Loaf Writers Conference (where Frost had spent so many
years) that he was able to piece the work together. Being in the place where
Frost spent so much of his life, surrounding himself with the same inspirational material, helped make Frost come alive for Parini. In his own life—
both the writing life and the personal life—Parini feels a reverence toward
his environment. He loves both the natural aspects of Vermont and village
life and takes inspiration from each. In writing his book on Frost, he felt a
kinship with Frost's own love of nature and village life, a kinship that makes
the book especially revealing.

Parini often ends his day walking in the fields surrounding his house in
Weybridge or out on the water of Lake Champlain or Lake Dunmore, mo-
toring his boat, with one of his three sons or wife, under a star-spangled
sky. He believes these opportunities—to spend time easily in both natural
and man-made environments—explain why Vermont has long been "the
main place for literature. I count myself so lucky to be here, to be in the
place of so many literary giants and just wonderful, ordinary people too. I

never take it for granted. It would have ruined me to be a writer in the city. They're living in an external place, one of concrete details. In Vermont, one lives in a spiritual place, a spiritual embodiment that embodies me. It keeps us honest and direct. No one's ever ironic in the middle of the woods."

---

◆§ SELECTIONS FROM *House of Days*

**Nature Revisited**

A sparrow hawk has swooped,
a field mouse failed behind the Kmart
in the empty lot where dandelions sprout
in blacktop cracks.

The sun's gold kite is flying overhead,
monotonously high;
heat hangs like someone's bright idea
gone awry;

*Hello, it's summer,*
and the world is full of fiberoptics.
Everyone's on-line, their e-mail begging
for a rapid answer.

Mothers with their pudgy, fevered children
wait in corridors, in plastic chairs.
The intercom is talkative today.
The mothers pray

as fish are drying in the local stream,
and billboards shimmer.
Tarboils pop in fresh-laid roads
as cars slur by.

There's new construction going on quite near;
white glass and cinder block and steel.
The trucks like yellowjackets buzz;
they sting and disappear.

The sky is falling, piece by piece,
like weakened plaster.
It is hard to find the wilder world,
what nature was.

Look in thickets of a thousand sorrows,
under bridges or behind the malls,
in hedgerows leading nowhere in the dust,
or over walls

for what is missing. It is there.
You'll see.
*Hello, it's summer.*
It is there. You'll see.[17]

## I Was There

I say it, I was there.
No matter what the yellow wind has taken,
I was there, with you.
We have walked out early in the spring
beside the river, when the sun's red shield
was caught in branches
and the bud-tips bled.
We have plucked ripe berries from a hill of brush
in mid-July,
and watched the days go down in flames
in late September,
when the poplar shook its foil.
We have walked on snow in January light;
the long white fields were adamantly bright.
I say it, I was there.
No matter that the evidence is gone,
we heard the honking of the long black geese
and saw them float beyond the town.
Gone all those birds, loose-wristed leaves,
the snowfire, days
we cupped like water in our hands.
So much has slipped through fragile hands.
The evidence is lost, but not these words.
You have my word;
I say it, I was there.[18]

## The Small Ones Leave Us

The small ones leave us, and the leaves are blown,
It doesn't matter what we do or say,
there's nothing in the end that we can own.

The facts, of course, are all well-known.
We should have understood that come what may
the small ones leave us, and the leaves are blown.

There's nothing in the world that's not on loan:
young children, trees, this house of days.
There's nothing in the end that we can own.

So why regret that each of them has grown?
Why grieve when grasses turn to hay?
The small ones leave us, and the leaves are blown.

This accidental harvest has been sown
and willy-nilly reaped in its own way.
There's nothing in the end that we can own.

What little we can make of skin and bone
unsettles us, who watch and sometimes pray
as small ones leave us and the leaves are blown.
There's nothing in the end that we can own.[19]

---

◆§ FROM *The Apprentice Lover*

That night, in the dining room, I met Holly Hampton, Grant's English assistant, for the first time. She was elegant in a distinctly English way (although her mother was from Philadelphia), with pure but understated features. Her blond hair was silky, parted in the middle, and cut just above her shoulders. She wore a simple white dress with a high neckline. Our eyes rarely met, but I found myself excited by her presence, and wishing I could study her face at leisure.

To welcome me, Vera had made one of her favorite dinners: tagliatelle al prosciutto for the first course, or primo, then salt cod alla romana, served with long green beans marinated in olive oil and garlic. This was followed by a cheese tart covered in pine nuts and raisins—crostata di ricotta. The wine, from Grant's cellars, was Bianco del Vesuvio—"a whorish little vino," he said, filling glasses around the table, "but suitable for us, I fear." He obviously relished the position of arbiter bibendi.

Grant introduced me as "a Latin scholar fresh from the New World."

"My brother is a Latinist," said Holly. "At Balliol."

"That's an Oxford college, Lorenzo," Grant said, when I didn't respond at once.

"I know," I said.

"Sorry, old boy. That ignorant look of yours rather deceived me."

A grandfather clock stood against one wall, ticking loudly.

"Please Rupert," said Vera. "It's his first night."

"He's a strong chap," Grant said. "And we're already friends, aren't we?" His nostrils appeared to flare.

"Malefico," said Marisa, clucking her tongue.

"Oh do speak English, Marisa," Grant told her. He turned to

me. "She's spent a year in Liverpool, and she's perfectly fluent."

"I hope you will like us when you get to know us," said Vera, tentatively.

"For God's sake, Vera, let it go," said Grant, with a detectable slur in his phrasing. I guessed that he had been drinking since our meeting in his study.

"Rupert is drunk," said Holly. "He's not always so frightful."

Maria Pia and a delicate-looking young man called Alfredo, a cousin of hers, were serving the first course. There was nothing elegant about their presentation as they dropped plates before each person at the table with a clatter.

Grant leaped from his seat, moving around the table putting his arms on Holly's shoulders. "She is my prize," he said. "I believe she will be a fine novelist one day."

I noticed that Marisa blanched, looking down.

Holly shook off Grant. "I'm writing my first novel, and so are a billion other people."

"I'm a fairly reliable reader," said Grant, "and I like what I see." He kissed her on the back of the head.

"I must be not good," said Marisa. "You have never told me anything of this kind Rupert."

"How could I, since I've read almost nothing of yours? Unlike most reviewers, I insist on reading a work before judging it."

Vera quickly poured herself a second glass of wine, agitated by her husband's performance.

"Our new friend, Lorenzo, is himself a poet," Grant announced. "Why don't you recite something? Acquaint us all with your work." He folded his arms, as if waiting for my recital to begin.

I said, "I'm not much of a poet."

"But you sent me poems. I rather liked them."

"I don't remember any," I said.

"Dementia, what? Brain cells washed away by alcohol? I sympathize."

"I just never bothered to memorize them," I said. "They're not good enough."

"Oh dear," he said.

"Do sit down, Rupert," Vera said. Looking sternly at her husband.

"Shut up, Vera. You're becoming a bore," he said. I had never heard that word carry so much negative weight.

Walking slowly around the table, he glanced at each of us in turn, eventually taking a seat. Munching a piece of bread, he told us he'd heard from a producer at the BBC that morning that one of his novels, *Siren Call*, was being considered for a serial. "There will be money in it," he said. "Especially if I get to do the scripts."

"Those projects never pan out," Vera said. Dampening the flame of his enthusiasm. "Or they take decades to materialize."

"You're always so refreshing, Vera," said Grant. "It's no wonder I love you."

"I fear Alex will get the wrong impression of us," she said. "We don't always carry on like this."

"I have an idea," said Grant.

"Shall we alert the press?" Vera quipped.

Grant ignored her. "There's a marvelous game," he said. "A way to introduce us properly to our new friend, Lorenzo d'America." He wiped breadcrumbs from his mouth, as everyone waited. "Let's assume it's my turn. My dear wife must state the least likely thing that could be said about me. Go ahead, Vera. What would no rational person in the galaxy ever say about me?"

"Rupert Grant has no idea how clever he is," she said, without hesitation.

"Bravo!" He clapped his hands, then turned to Holly.

"I'm not much for games," she said.

"Do be a sport," Vera said. "We used to play this game at school."

Holly put a finger to her lips, thinking. "Rupert Grant," she said deliberately, "always lays his cards on the table."

"Very nice," said Grant.

Marisa didn't have to be prodded. "Mister Grant," she intoned, "does not care too much what people say about him."

"A dagger, dear girl, an absolute dagger," he said. "I must work to correct this misapprehension on your part. You see, Alex, the game has many positive aspects. It's better than psychotherapy." He gestured toward Vera. "The focus will now shift to my wife of many years, and I shall go first." He wrinkled his nose, in deep thought. "Vera Grant does not have a jealous bone in her body."

"How ludicrous," said Vera. "He's reversing the game."

"I stand corrected," said Grant.

Holly did not wait a moment. "Vera should employ a cook. The food at the Villa Clio is rubbish."

Grant was expressionless. "You're clever, Holly, but I detect a lack of wit in that response. It does not speak well of an Oxford graduate."

"You take your games too seriously," said Holly.

"Poetry is a game," I said.

"A game of knowledge," said Grant. "That's Wystan's formulation, I believe."

"How literary we are," said Vera. I really should have invited the press."

Marisa said, "Vera does not care what he makes, her husband."

"I should hope not," said Grant. "I do whatever I please."

"Bollocks," said Vera.

Grant sighed. "As you see, this is a game of knowledge, too. But humankind cannot bear too much reality."

I recognized the last line as a quotation, but could not locate the source.

"Marisa Lauro is a serious journalist," said Grant, portentously.

"Marisa Lauro doesn't care what people say about her," said Holly, glaring at Grant.

"Marisa Lauro paints her toenails only to please herself," said Vera.

"Every girl is painting her toenails except Holly," said Marisa. "I am not so intelligent as these," she said to me. "I am sorry for my confession. But you will not tolerate me for long. I am going to bed." She rose and left the room, her pasta course untouched.

No one spoke till she was gone.

"Tetchy girl," said Grant, reaching for her glass of wine, which he gulped.

"She's very sensitive, Rupert," his wife said. "I wish you'd be more careful."

"Life is too short for that," he said. "Truth is all that matters."

"I'd have voted for Beauty," she said.

Grant turned to Holly, "It's your turn, I suspect. We aren't letting you off the hook."

"I'm tired of this game," Vera said.

"Come on darling. Play up, play ball, and play the game," said Grant.

This was, I suspect, another quotation.

"All right," said Vera. ""Holly Hampton is perfectly transparent. What you see is what you get." A permanent-looking smirk formed on her lips.

"But one sees so little," said Grant. "Or, perhaps, one sees so much. I'm not sure."

"Let's say that I'm a mystery," said Holly, "even to myself."

"We like you as you are, my dear," said Grant. "Make no adjustments for our sake. " He said tapping his fingers on the table, formulating a line. "Holly Hampton is desperately in love with Rupert Grant," he said, suppressing a grin.

"I do love you Rupert," she said flatly. "Why else would I sleep with you?"

Vera's smirk vanished.

"What about you, Lorenzo?" Grant wondered. "We don't really know you, but if we did, what would we never say about you?"

I didn't hesitate. "Alex Massolini is a hard sell," I said.

Vera crinkled her brow. "You're a pushover in a shoe shop, is that what you're telling us?"

"He's what Americans call a wimp," said Holly.

"I see," said Grant. "Lorenzo will be good fun for all of us, what? Gullibility an endearing flaw. But we shall do our best to correct it, I daresay."

## Questions and Exercises for Reflection and Inspiration

Parini often begins his day at a local diner in Middlebury, drinking coffee and writing poetry with the chatter of his neighbors about him. He writes in a notebook, usually in pencil, "writing by hand, taking notes. I often transfer the notes to a computer later. My poems are *always* written by hand, and then typed onto a computer for revision. Prose I find I can write directly onto a computer screen . . . and revise on the computer. I'm not a systematic writer, in fact; my work moves along in various ways. I'm fairly practical, so I do whatever I need to do to get my work accomplished."

**Exercise 1:** Spend an hour each morning in a quiet corner of your local café or diner; choose a place where you can observe the comings and goings of the clientele while also being unobtrusive about your writing—a back booth, for example, or the corner table. Bring a notebook of your choice but be advised to purchase one that's light enough to carry in your bag or knapsack, that's inexpensive enough to not cause you any guilt over spilled coffee or egg yolk, one that feels good under your pen or pencil. Get to the diner or restaurant early—by 6:00 or 7:00, if it's open that early—so you can take advantage of that time in your brain when you're still in a semi-dazed state, on automatic pilot, before the business of the day has taken over with its reminders to pay the bills and get to work. Begin writing. If you don't have anything in mind, just start recording your thoughts as you watch your fellow customers come and go. Don't worry much about what you're writing; as Parini says, this is a first draft. It can be revised later. If you're really stuck for something to write about, pick some physical item in your environment: the dirty snow on the sidewalk; a parking ticket on a car left overnight on the street; the plaid jacket hanging on a nearby peg; daffodils opening in a window box outside the window; the waitress's apron; the menu; your omelet; the diner bathroom. You'll find in a few days that your words will come more easily. Regardless of what format you're using, keep your writing loose and spontaneous. Leave the self-censors at home. After a week of writing thus, evaluate what you've accomplished and determine if you are a candidate for public writing. How did being in a public place contribute or hinder your writing? Did you find yourself stimulated by the daily exchange of food and conversation? Or, did you conclude that you belong to that group of solitary writers?

In the three selected poems above, we see the stuff of daily life: the killing of a field mouse, dandelions sprouting in cracks on the blacktop, e-mail chatter and hot roads in one; sunshine and ripe berries, poplar leaves and snow, the geese overhead in another; more leaves, aging children, skin and bone in the third. Yet the poems are not about these things. They are about the universal questions: What remains? What matters? What is there to hold onto when everyone ages and eventually dies, in a world that is forever changing, dying and being reborn? These are, of course, the questions at the heart of almost all poetry, perhaps at the heart of all literature. Why else write if not to express our own astonishment with the universe, to try to unravel the mysteries of birth and death, the impermanence of life itself. As you can see in Parini's poetry—and in some of the work of other writers in this book—readers respond to poetry that is rooted in the understandable. In Parini's poem, "Nature revisited," we first see the field mouse that dies so that a hawk can live. As the poem progresses, however, we feel the ever-encroaching world of man onto the world of nature. The poem ends with the statement that it is growing harder and harder to "find the wilder world / what nature was." The poet reminds us in the last words that, despite the chatter of fiber optics, the shimmering billboards, the new construction and the mall, the thing that is missing is still there. You just have to look and listen harder to see and hear it. The poet does not say these things directly but the message is there, made more significant through the use of poetic language, loaded with meaning. Examples are words like this: "The sun's gold kite is flying overhead"; "Look in thickets of a thousand sorrows"; and "the trucks like yellowjackets buzz."

Writing poetry is fun. The examples above contain metaphoric language. A metaphor is a literary device in which something becomes something it is not: the sun is a gold kite, the thickets are the repository of sorrows. A simile is a literary device in which one thing is compared to another: Trucks like yellowjackets. Poets play with words, with metaphors and similes, to express themselves. You can too.

> **Exercise 2:** Back at the café, make a list of images, sensory details, and ordinary things in your environment. Try to give each a fresh metaphor or comparison. What mood are you feeling? Make another list of words that describe your mood. What question would you like to ask the universe: Does God exist? Will I find someone to love? Will I get the job? Now, using your everyday words and corresponding metaphors, mood words, and the questions in your heart, begin to weave a poem that speaks singularly to you as the poet but also can be read and appreciated by others. Have fun. Don't settle for clichés. Let serendipity bring unplanned combinations of words. The looser you are, the more risks you take, the better the result will be.

Writers use many devices to show the interaction of characters. It's a way of showing the individual personalities of each character while also illustrating how the characters react and interact with each other. Often, the dynamics in a group can be wonderfully demonstrated by putting the characters together in a scene, such as a dinner party or playing a game. In the excerpt from *The Apprentice Lover*, Parini uses a dinner party in which the dominant character, Rupert Grant, pits one person against another for his personal entertainment by having them play a game in which each player gets to say what another person would be least likely to do. The game allows us to accumulate material about each character quickly and what the others think of them. The reader is in on the game, gaining insight into the various players' hopes and fears. Our sympathies and aversions are stimulated by the interplay.

What do you know about each character from this one simple scene? What do you know of the various relationships: Vera and Rupert? Rupert and Marissa? Rupert and Holly? Which of the women is the strongest? What do you think Marissa's departure signals? Which of the characters has survivor instincts and which could be a victim? Do you like or dislike any of the characters by the end of this scene? And what do you think Alex is making of all this? How do you think he will fit in?

> **Exercise 3:** If you have a work in progress with already established characters, have them play a game—tag football, Scrabble, Trivial Pursuit, or something more daring (like your own version of the game that Rupert Grant invents)—and use it to show the relationship between your characters. Who will win at any cost? Who is willing to concede rather than compete? Who establishes a secret alliance with another player to defeat a common enemy? If you don't already have a piece in progress, create some characters and place them in a scene where their characters are revealed through their actions in a competitive situation. They could be characters who don't know one another: contestants on a quiz show, for example, or finalists for a Foreign Service job who are being tested in a group situation. Or, they could be people who chance to meet in a highly charged situation: their children have been involved in a car accident together or are competing against one another in a chess tournament. As much as possible, use no adjectives to describe your characters but rather let them show their personalities through their actions and reactions to one another.

# III · Finding Sanctuary

# 13　Aleksandr Solzhenitsyn
## *Making Sanctuary*

Born 11 December 1918 in Kislovodsk in the North Caucasus of Russia

Lived in Cavendish, 1976–1994

Education: University of Rostov-on-Don in Mathematics; Litt.D., Harvard University

First publication: *Odin den' Ivana Denisovicha* (1962). Published in the United States as *One Day in the Life of Ivan Denisovich* (1963)

Novels: *One Day in the Life of Ivan Denisovich* (1962); *We Never Make Mistakes* (1963); *For the Good of the Cause* (1964); *Cancer Ward* (1968); *The First Circle* (1968); *August 1914* (1972); *The Gulag Archipelago* (published in three parts) (1974–1978); *From Under the Rubble* (1975); *Lenin in Zurich* (1976); *Prussian Nights* (1977); *World Split Apart* (1978); *The Oak and the Calf* (1980); *Detente: Prospects for Democracy And Dictatorship* (1980); *October 1916*, *March 1917*, and *April 1917* (published collectively as *The Red Wheel: A Narrative in a Discrete Period of Time* (1989); *Invisible Allies* (2003)

Awards: Nobel Prize for Literature, 1970; Freedom Foundation Award, Stanford University, 1976; Templeton Foundation Prize, 1983

C AN YOU IMAGINE being so poor that you and your mother have to live in unheated, rented rooms and huts until you are fifteen years old and your mother finally finds a cold and drafty stable where the two of you can bed down? Can you imagine knowing from the time you were a small child that you wanted to write but living in fear that your words could send you to prison? Can you imagine that actually happening? All this adversity and more forged the spirit of Aleksandr Solzhenitsyn, one of the world's greatest writers who had spent much of his adult life as a political prisoner before being exiled to West Germany. In 1976, at age fifty-nine, Solzhenitsyn finally found asylum and the refuge he needed to write—in Vermont.

Thanks to the efforts of Vermont Senators Patrick Leahy and James Jeffords and an international support system for Soviet dissidents and political exiles, Solzhenitsyn bought property on Windy Hill Road, a remote, narrow, and winding dirt road about two miles from the center of Cavendish. Here, the Russian writer was able to produce three of his famous historical novels—*October 1916*, *March 1917*, and *April 1917*[1]—and to live, perhaps for the first time in his life, in relative peace and tranquillity. In his few public speeches, he made a point to thank his Vermont neighbors for their acceptance but, even more so, for protecting his privacy from the swarms of media, admirers, and curiosity seekers who sought his time and distracted him from his work. Indeed, for seventeen years—until the fall of the Soviet Union and Solzhenitsyn's return to Russia—the sign in the general store in town read, "No restrooms. No bare feet. No directions to Solzhenitsyn's."

Solzhenitsyn's life was difficult from the beginning. Just six months before his birth in 1918, his father died. His mother, well educated and English-speaking, worked as a shorthand-typist and raised him in a series of humble abodes in Rostov-on-the-Don. In an autobiography written upon receiving the Nobel Prize in Literature in 1970, Solzhenitsyn said, "Even as a child, without any prompting from others, I wanted to be a writer and, indeed, I turned out a good deal of the usual juvenilia. In the 1930s, I tried to get my writings published but I could not find anyone willing to accept my manuscripts. I wanted to acquire a literary education, but in Rostov such an education that would suit my wishes was not to be obtained. To move to Moscow was not possible, partly because my mother was alone and in poor health, and partly because of our modest circumstances."[2]

Rather than writing, Solzhenitsyn studied mathematics at the University of Rostov-on-Don. After graduation, he fought in World War II, during which he wrote a letter to a school friend in which he expressed disrespectful remarks about Stalin, whom he disguised with a pseudonym. Despite the pseudonym, these writings came to the attention of the authorities and, in February 1945, Solzhenitsyn was arrested and sentenced to eight years in a detention work camp. (His experiences as a miner, bricklayer, foundryman, and occasional mathematician in the camp are told in fictionalized form in several novels, including *One Day in the Life of Ivan Denisovich*[3] and *The First Circle*.)[4] During his time in the work camp, he was diagnosed with cancer.

One month after his sentence was supposed to be over, he was informed that he was not to be released but exiled for life to southern Kazakhstan. Altogether, he spent eight years in prisons and labor camps, then three more years in enforced exile. In 1953, he was very near death from cancer and sent to a clinic in Tashkent where he was cured. In 1956, he was "reha-bilitated," and allowed to settle in Ryazan, in central Russia, where he taught mathematics and began to write. He considered his cure a miracle and believed God had spared him from death because he had a mission: to tell of the human rights abuses that had and were continuing to occur in his country and to work to restore Russia to its place of spiritual and intel-lectual ascendancy. Solzhenitsyn tells the story in his marvelous novel *Can-cer Ward*.[5]

Solzhenitsyn had only a brief period of favor with Soviet officials. En-couraged by the loosening of government restraints on cultural life, he sub-mitted his short novel *Odin den iz zhizni Ivana Denisovicha* (One day in the life of Ivan Denisovich) to the leading Soviet literary periodical, *Novy Mir* (*New world*). The novel met with immediate popularity and made Solzhen-itsyn an instant celebrity. Writes Solzhenitsyn, "During all the years until 1961, not only was I convinced that I should never see a single line of mine in print in my lifetime, but, also, I scarcely dared allow any of my close ac-quaintances to read anything I had written because I feared that this would become known. Finally, at the age of 42, this secret authorship began to wear me down. The most difficult thing of all to bear was that I could not get my works judged by people with literary training. In 1961, after the 22nd Congress of the U.S.S.R. Communist Party and Tvardovsky's speech at this, I decided to emerge and to offer *One Day in the Life of Ivan Denisovich*."[6]

Nikita Khrushchev allowed the book to be published because he was anxious to discredit Stalin. As Khrushchev's power waned, however, Solzhenitsyn found himself attacked as "an enemy of the USSR" and could not get his next two books, *The First Circle* and *Cancer Ward*, published in his native country; his manuscripts and private archives were confiscated. He had been hiding his novel *The Gulag Archipelago* from the authorities, afraid that the people mentioned in it might face reprisals. But he became convinced that he had to publish it after a former assistant, Elizaveta Voronyanskaya, committed suicide by hanging herself following an inter-rogation by the KGB during which she revealed where a copy had been hid-den. When *The Gulag Archipelago* was published in Paris in 1973, it outlined some 1,800 pages of Soviet abuses from 1918 onward.[7] As feared, Solzhen-itsyn was arrested, stripped, interrogated, and charged with treason. The next day, he was told he was going to be deported to West Germany. For Solzhenitsyn, who deeply loved his country despite the abuses he had suf-fered, this exile proved to be a terrible loss. He finally moved with his wife Natalya, three children, and stepdaughter to Zurich, where he continued to publish. Two years later, he was offered sanctuary in Vermont.

Initially, his property consisted of fifty acres but Solzhenitsyn purchased several surrounding properties until he had a rather large domain. Even be-fore the family arrived, they had caused a stir in the community as a six-foot-high, fine-mesh fence was erected around the property and two rows of trees planted inside the fence as a visual barrier. Guard dogs patrolled the property; a loudspeaker and camera were mounted in front of an iron gate so that visitors could be viewed and communicated with from within the estate. Most callers were ignored. Only a few people were allowed inside the compound.

There, they found that the estate consisted of five buildings: a main house, two cabins, a bathhouse, and Solzhenitsyn's extensive studio. The main house, which had eight bedrooms and a big traditional American kitchen, connected to Solzhenitsyn's study through an underground tunnel. The studio consisted of a four-story building that seconded as a repository for Solzhenitsyn's extensive archives. These included documents that had been smuggled out of the Soviet Union during years of repression and collected by other expatriates who wanted to preserve their country's history and culture. The building was made of brick and heated by wood. Solzhenitsyn kept his studio purposefully cold, saying he worked best in near-frigid temperatures.

Anyone who reads *One Day in the Life* might wonder how Solzhenitsyn could stand to be cold after his years of frigid imprisonment. Yet, above all, Solzhenitsyn was a man of self-denial and discipline. The ostensible purpose of the fence, the dogs, and the cameras was self-protection; he feared for his life. But it was also to keep people from disturbing him in his work. Solzhenitsyn knew that his body had been strained by the rigors of his childhood, his imprisonment, and his fight with cancer. Nonetheless, he had great personal strength and determination; he often plunged himself into the frigid water of a pond located near his studio so that he could keep writing and often slept on a simple cot in the studio during long hours of productivity.

Locals, however, knew little of this upon the Solzhenitsyns' arrival. They'd been besieged by reporters and photographers and wondered what all the fuss was about. They wondered why a man would come from behind the Iron Curtain and years of imprisonment to mountainous Cavendish (a community of 1,355 people, where few locked their doors) and build a prison for himself. If anything, however, his neighbors were more upset that his fences blocked their access to once-popular hunting territory and skimobile trails. In March 1977, almost a year after moving here, Solzhenitsyn attended a Cavendish annual town meeting to explain himself, his need for security and privacy. Addressing a crowd of about two hundred for twenty minutes, he wooed his new neighbors by telling them he had chosen Cavendish purposefully after much research because "of the simple way of life of the people, the countryside and the long winters with the snow which reminds me of Russia." Then he said, "I have been reading in the newspaper that some of you were disturbed I put up a fence."

The crowd got very quiet, as if they were almost embarrassed. But Solzhenitsyn—a physically impressive man with a large head that seems to be half forehead, penetrating eyes, a dark beard streaked generously with gray, and flaring eyebrows—smiled for a moment before adding softly that, during the years that he lived in Zurich after leaving the Soviet Union on 13 February 1974, he was constantly harassed by Soviet agents, journalists, and people who just wanted to see him. "So, for hundreds of hours," he told the attentive crowd, "I talked to hundreds of people and my work was ruined. I had no means of stopping them. . . . All my life consists of only one thing—work. And the characteristic of my work does not permit sudden interruptions and pauses. Sometimes a five-minute interruption, and the whole day is lost." Besides, he said, it was hard to tell the curious from the dangerous. Already, in the brief time he'd been in Vermont, "messages had been put under my gate with threats to kill me and my family."

It was then that he asked his neighbors to help him with his life's work by keeping his whereabouts private. No doubt, some would find him out, he said, but he urged Cavendish residents not to give directions to his home. And the townspeople readily agreed. For the next seventeen years, they kept their end of the bargain. It worked fairly well. The house was in such a remote location and the woods around it so thick, that even when you knew where it was, it was hard to find. And Solzhenitsyn kept his part of the bargain, too; he wrote and he worked on the archives. His three sons went to public school in town and had their friends; Natalya was sociable enough, shopping in town and getting to know some people. But Solzhenitsyn was rarely seen off the compound.

Joe Allen, who owned the Cavendish store with the famous sign, explains that residents protected Solzhenitsyn's privacy, not because of who Solzhenitsyn was, but because he had asked them to. "At times, there has been a constant parade of people coming here looking for directions," Allen said in 1994, as Solzhenitsyn was preparing to return to Russia. "People were protective of him but it wasn't because he was Solzhenitsyn. We would do that for anyone who asked to be left alone. That's the way Vermonters are. They respect people's wishes, even when they seem a bit odd."

Solzhenitsyn's second public appearance in Vermont occurred at Cavendish's Bicentennial Celebration on 15 September 1991. He stood with his son, Stephan, and Natalya in the viewing area, watching the parade, then spent several hours shaking hands with more than one hundred well-wishers. A section of the public library had been set aside as a place where Solzhenitsyn could retreat if he needed to get away from the crowd. He didn't take advantage of the offer and seemed to enjoy the rare social exchange.

He had a real appreciation of the Vermont town meeting, the practice whereby residents gather together, usually on or around the first Tuesday of March, to vote on local issues, pass school and town budgets, and elect local officials. After the collapse of the Soviet Union, Solzhenitsyn used the town meeting forum again to address his neighbors—this time to say good-bye and thank them for their years of support. More than once, he said he had found a spiritual strength from the Vermont countryside and the rhythmic nature of the four seasons. These things gave him hope for mankind and the planet, as did the small and large considerations of the people of Cavendish. He said he would miss the tranquillity and power of Vermont in his "tortured" homeland. But he said the memory of his years here would sustain him through the difficult times that lay ahead.

At this time, his publisher, Roger Straus, president of Farrar, Straus & Giroux in New York City, said in an interview that Solzhenitsyn always had a strong sense of place in his life and work. He brought the expectation of that to Vermont. To some degree, place defined who Solzhenitsyn was, Straus said. Thus, it was natural for him to feel comfortable in such a rich place as Vermont. But, Straus said, this benefit went beyond the geographical amenities of Vermont. Solzhenitsyn might not have had a daily relationship with his adopted neighbors, but his work was enriched by their willingness to protect him from intrusion from the outside world. Solzhenitsyn's time in Cavendish was "productive beyond imagination," Straus said. "Being there, allowed to work in privacy, permitted him to be one of the most prolific writers among the all-time great writers of the world. All the world owes Vermonters a debt of gratitude for taking care of this man and allowing his creativity to flourish." Besides the three novels he completed in Vermont, Solzhenitsyn had overseen the publication of better translations of his previous books and, as glasnost had come to the Soviet Union, had seen many of his books finally published in his own country.

On the family's last day in Vermont, his sons came to the fence that guarded the Solzhenitsyn fortress to talk to the press. They were Americanized youths who played classical music, drove fast cars, and dressed in leather. Many of the journalists, who had written about Solzhenitsyn over the years, including myself, had come to know the sons. We asked a favor. We agreed not to barrage Solzhenitsyn with questions, microphones, or cameras, if he would step from the car before departure for one last photograph in Vermont. The sons said they would do what they could, but made no promises.

It was a raw, gloomy day and the departure came hours later than planned. Trucks had already taken crates of archival material away to be shipped back to Russia. Now, as the line of cars drew to the gate, which opened slowly, Solzhenitsyn stepped outside the car, apparently agreeing to the photographers' request. He was solemn but there was no way to read whether this was his usual demeanor or whether he was feeling especially sad or torn by mixed emotions. Solzhenitsyn walked heavily to the gatepost and, quite dramatically, posed for photos, looking like the aging philosopher among the hardwoods of Vermont. True to form, he declined to answer questions, saying confidently, "My sons have answered all your questions, I believe."

The isolation of the Soviet Union meant that many Soviet writers were not overinfluenced by Western literary developments. Instead, during the Communist era, many Soviet writers felt compelled to promote and glorify the values of communism and the Soviet Union. Solzhenitsyn chose not to do so. Instead, he followed the path of the great nineteenth-century Russian authors who wrote emotionally charged novels in which the characters demonstrate through deeds and determination how much they truly loved Russia and their fellow countrymen. Like those great Russian writers, Solzhenitsyn laments the fate that has befallen his country and carries a strong admiration for the peasant and for village life, along with a moral sense of right and wrong. Scholars generally agree that Chekhov, the great Russian novelist and short story writer, was Solzhenitsyn's closest literary predecessor. Like Chekhov and the other great Russian writers, he carried a deep concern for human suffering and felt a responsibility to offer solutions to his country's moral dilemma rather than take the safe route of mouthing communist dogma.

Solzhenitsyn's novels offer wonderful examples of the dictum "Show, don't tell." He doesn't preach or grandstand about the horrible conditions in the gulag or the decline of life in the village. Rather, he creates believable characters and places them in settings that show the conditions he wants to expose. His protagonist in *One Day*, Ivan Denisovich Shukhov, doesn't whine or complain about his fate. He doesn't have time or energy for that. His resources must be focused on survival: on getting one more crust of bread or finding one more scrap of wood to keep warm by.[8]

The prisoners' hopelessness in *One Day* echoed the hopelessness of the Soviet people. But beyond that, the book has universal appeal because of its simple, convincing depiction of human suffering and perseverance. By creating a peasant unjustly imprisoned in the Soviet system rather than telling the story as a memoir or creating a character based upon himself (a university-educated intellectual), Solzhenitsyn creates a sympathetic character whose suffering is all the more real for its absurdity. We can see through Shukhov's small acts of generosity to others, even in the most dire of situations, that he is a good man.

Yet it's clear that the experiences that are contained in this and his other books are based on Solzhenitsyn's own experiences, and his novel *The Cancer Ward* is based upon his own experiences in a Soviet hospital and his miraculous recovery. Knowing this makes Solzhenitsyn's life even more important to us. He has survived to tell the survivors' stories—but also to inform us that many did not survive, that humans continue to be cruel, that governments can go wrong, and that ideology is often the cruelest of weapons.

Solzhenitsyn rarely speaks of his writing style or approach. Clearly, he worked on his novels and memoir in his mind for many years before being able to put his thoughts and creations on paper. What the developing writer can learn from him, however, is discipline and perseverance. It's not necessary to wall oneself behind a chain-link fence, or jump into icy water when sleep beckons, to be a great writer. But it is essential to be disciplined. Books do not write themselves. The lesson we can learn from Solzhenitsyn is that determination and faith, belief in one's power of expression, respect for the power of the written word, and the responsibility of artists to speak out against atrocity can conquer the direst adversity. Struggling writers might reflect on Solzhenitsyn's life when they get discouraged—and try again.

---

**◆§ FROM *The Cancer Ward***

On top of everything, the cancer wing was Number 13. Pavel Niko-layevich Rusanov had never been and could never be a superstitious person, but his heart sank when they wrote "Wing 13" on his admission card. They should have had the ingenuity to assign number 13 to some kind of prosthetic or intestinal department.

But this clinic was the only place where they could help him in the whole republic.

"It isn't, it isn't cancer, is it, Doctor? I haven't got cancer?" Pavel Nikolayevich asked hopefully, lightly touching the malevolent tumor on the right side of his neck. It seemed to grow almost daily, yet the tight skin on the outside was as white and inoffensive as ever.

"Good heavens, no. Of course not." Dr. Dontsova soothed him, for the tenth time, as she filled in the pages of his case history in her bold handwriting. Whenever she wrote, she put on her glasses with rectangular frames rounded at the edges, and she would whisk them off as soon as she had finished. She was no longer a young woman; her face looked pale and utterly tired.

It had happened at the outpatients' reception a few days ago. Patients assigned to a cancer department, even as outpatients, found they could not sleep the next night. And Dontsova had ordered Pavel Nikolayevich to bed *immediately*.

Unforeseen and unprepared for, the disease had come upon him, a happy man with few cares, like a gale in the space of two weeks. But Pavel Nikolayevich was tormented, no less than by the disease itself, by having to enter the clinic as an ordinary patient, just like anyone else. He could hardly remember when he had been in a public hospital last, it was so long ago. Telephone calls had been made, to Evgeny Semenovich, Shendyapin, and Ulmasbaev, and they rang other people to find out if there were not any VIP wards in the clinic, or whether some small room could not be converted, just for a short time, into a special ward. But the clinic was so cramped for space that nothing could be done.

The only success he had managed to achieve through the head doctor was to bypass the waiting room, the public bath and a change of clothing.

Yuri drove his mother and father in their little blue Moskvich right up to the steps of Ward 13.

In spite of the slight frost, two women in heavily laundered cotton dressing gowns were standing outside on the open stone porch. The cold made them shudder, but they stood their ground.

Beginning with these slovenly dressing gowns, Pavel Nikolayevich found everything in the place unpleasant: the path worn by countless pairs of feet on the cement floor of the porch; the dull doorknobs, all messed about by the patients' hands; the waiting room, paint peeling off its floor, its high olive-colored walls (olive seemed somehow such a dirty color), and its large slatted wooden benches with not enough room for all the patients. Many of them had come long distances and had to sit on the floor. There were Uzbeks in quilted, wadded coats, old Uzbek women in long white shawls and young women in lilac, red and green ones, and all wore high boots with rubbers. One Russian youth, thin as a rail but with a great bloated stomach, lay there in an unbuttoned coat which dangled to the floor, taking up a whole bench to himself. He screamed incessantly with pain. His screams deafened Pavel Nikolayevich and hurt him so much that it seemed the boy was screaming not with his own pain but with Rusanov's.

Pavel Nikolayevich went white around the mouth, stopped dead and whispered to his wife, "Kapa, I'll die here. I musn't stay. Let's go back."

Kapitolina Matveyevna took him firmly by the arm and said, "Pashenka! Where could we go? And what would we do then?"

"Well, perhaps we might be able to arrange something in Moscow."

Kapitolina Matveyevna turned to her husband. Her broad head was made even broader by its frame of thick, clipped coppery curls.

"Pashenka! If we went to Moscow we might have to wait another two weeks. Or we might not get there at all. How *can* we wait? It is bigger every morning!"

His wife squeezed his hand in an effort to transmit her courage to him. In his civic and official duties Pavel Nikolayevich was unshakable, and therefore it was simpler and all the more agreeable for him to be able to rely on his wife in family matters. She made all important decisions quickly and correctly.

The boy on the bench was still tearing himself apart with his screams.

"Perhaps the doctors would come to our house? We'd pay them," Pavel Nikolayevich argued, unsure of himself.

"Pasik!" his wife chided him, suffering as much as her husband. "You know I'd be the first to agree. Send for someone and pay the fee. But we've been into this before: these doctors don't treat at home, and they won't take money. And there's their equipment, too. It's impossible."

Pavel Nikolayevich knew perfectly well it was impossible. He had only mentioned it because he felt he just had to say something.

According to the arrangement with the head doctor of the oncology clinic, the head nurse was supposed to wait for them at two o'clock in the afternoon, there at the foot of the stairs, which a patient on crutches was carefully descending. But the head nurse was nowhere to be seen, of course, and her little room under the stairs had a padlock on the door.

"They're all so unreliable!" fumed Kapitolina Matveyevna. "What do they get paid for?"

Just as she was, two silver-fox furs hugging her shoulders, she set off down the corridor past a notice which read: "No entry to persons in outdoor clothes."

Pavel Nikolayevich remained standing in the waiting room. Timidly he tilted his head slightly to the right and felt the tumor that jutted out between his collarbone and his jaw. He had the impression that in the half hour since he had last looked at it in the mirror as he wrapped it up in a muffler, in that one half hour it seemed to have grown even bigger. Pavel Nikolayevich felt weak and wanted to sit down. But the benches looked dirty, and besides, he would have to ask some peasant woman in a scarf with a greasy sack between her feet to move. Somehow the foul stench of that sack seemed to reach him even from a distance.

## Questions and Exercises for Reflection and Inspiration

Solzhenitsyn's eighteen years in Vermont were among his most productive, something he attributed to the peacefulness of the natural environment and the security he felt after his long years of repression in the Soviet Union and in exile in West Germany, to which he had been deported in 1974. Solzhenitsyn worked so hard that he rarely took time to greet visitors, refused most interviews and eschewed most social occasions. He took cold dunks in a pond he had built on his compound early each morning and worked late into most evenings. Solzhenitsyn placed himself in self-exile, essentially cutting himself off from human intercourse, so that he could do his work. What do you think about this decision?

> **Exercise 1:** Write a piece about the kind of sanctuary you would create for yourself if you decided to dedicate yourself primarily to your writing for several years. What elements would you require to help you concentrate on your work? What would you be unwilling to give up? Describe the setting in great detail, and then write a scene in which you are there, doing your work.
>
> **Exercise 2:** Solzhenitsyn's writing tip would probably have something to do with sacrifice and work; what do you think of such dedication?

Should one remove oneself from society to write about society? Write an essay on the pros and cons of writer's retreats and their potential impact on a writer's work. In contemplating your thesis, consider whether there is such a thing as too much isolation.

In the short excerpt from *The Cancer Ward*, above, Solzhenitsyn creates a very vivid picture of a Soviet hospital and the plight of people who are ill and need to rely on medical treatment under a financially strapped, socialist state. We are at once sympathetic to Pavel Nikolayevich's condition and repelled by his sense of superiority. None of this is expressed in direct words; we comprehend Pavel Nikolayevich's personality and elitism through his response to his surroundings. Notice how Solzhenitsyn cleverly and vividly creates the environment through just a few details: the boy screaming in pain on the bench, the slovenly peasant woman with her greasy sacks. Despite his own situation, Pavel Nikolayevich notices every one of these details.

When we need to create an environment that may not be familiar to readers everywhere but is essential to the telling of a tale, writers use the familiar to help readers see and feel the unfamiliar. As you re-read the excerpt in *Cancer Ward*, make two lists. In one, write down details that are familiar; in the other, note how these details are used to show the desperation of the scene and the unfamiliar elements. For example, the list of what one might expect to find in a hospital ward might include people in dressing gowns or patients sitting on benches; the list of the unusual would note that the dressing gowns are dirty and that the waiting room is so busy, people are sitting on the floor.

**Exercise 3:** Imagine a setting that is unfamiliar to people living in America today: a Central American coffee plantation; the hull of a slave ship; a space station in the year 3000. Make a list of everyday items one might find in your setting; make another list in which these everyday items appear, but changed, in relation to your setting. Now, write a three-page scene in which you show some action: a crewmate putting on makeup; a captive slave trying to fall asleep; farmers harvesting beans without high-tech equipment. Re-create your scene by relying on known and unknown elements of setting, looking back on Solzhenitsyn's excerpt for inspiration and instruction.

Photo by Rob Woolmington

# 14  Jamaica Kincaid
*Finding Your Voice*

Born 25 May 1949, Saint John's, Antigua.

Attended Franconia College and the New York School for Social Research

Lives in North Bennington

First publication: An interview with Gloria Steinem, "When I Was Seventeen," *Ingénue* (1973)

Novels: *At the Bottom of the River* (1984); *Annie John* (1986); *A Small Place* (1988); *Lucy* (1990); *The Autobiography of My Mother* (1996); *My Brother* (1997)

Memoir: *My Brother* (1997); *My Garden Book* (1999); *Talk Stories* ( 2001); *Seed Gathering Atop the World* (2002); *Among Flowers* (2005)

Awards: 1985 International Ritz Paris Hemingway Award finalist; Anifield-Wolf Book Award; Lila Wallace–Reader's Digest Fund Award; Morton Darwen Zabel Award of the American Academy of Arts and Letters

FOR NEARLY TWO DECADES NOW, Jamaica Kincaid has mined her personal history and that of the people of her native island of Antigua in novels and nonfiction works that allow a narrator (often a woman) to vocalize an anger that is at the center of much of human history: anger at colonizing countries that show little respect for the conquered, anger at men for begetting then forgetting children; anger at people who allow themselves to become victims or who cooperate in their own victimization. Hers is not the voice of mainstream Western civilization. She does not seek to provide a happy ending in her tales. Rather, hers is the voice of someone born at a time when Great Britain still controlled much of the world and had dominion over people living far from Britain's shores. Even though Kincaid long ago left her island home and eventually found refuge in Bennington, Vermont, the scars of her childhood remain with her.

Kincaid was born in 1949 as Elaine Potter Richardson on the island of Antigua, a spit of land in the West Indies. Her mother's family had been landed peasants from the nearby island of Dominica. Her maternal grandmother was a Carib Indian, the people Columbus encountered when he "discovered" the Caribbean islands. Few Caribs survived their encounters with the early Europeans. Kincaid's family was poor, but when she was a girl, she had little to compare her own life to and she did not feel poor. In some ways, she says, her earliest years were nearly idyllic. She was a very bright child, learning to speak before she could walk. Her mother doted on her and taught her how to read by age three. When she was nine, however, the first of her three brothers was born and her relationship with her mother began to change, setting in motion events that would lead Kincaid to eventually turn her back on her family.

It's hard for a person from Vermont to imagine Kincaid's life as a child, growing up on a tropical island, surrounded by the stunning Caribbean ocean. Yet in some ways, her living conditions on Antigua were similar to those of poorer Vermonters not that long ago. Kincaid's family had no refrigerator, no modern appliances. Clothes were washed by hand. Food was fish from the sea, vegetables from the market or garden. One marked difference: the history of Vermont has long been taught in its schools (although until recently Vermont education ignored its earliest residents, the Abenaki people); the children growing up on Kincaid's island were taught little about their native culture. Along with studying the history of Europe, so foreign and distant, Antiguan children like Kincaid were expected to memorize the words of long-dead British poets and novelists rather than the works of their own people.

A child like Kincaid, a bright child who quite naturally questioned authority, a child in love with books and learning, quickly learned that her questions would get her into trouble. But Kincaid is not passive. At a very young age, she learned to accept that trouble was unavoidable if one had an inquisitive mind, as she did. There was trouble at home, too; as her responsibilities grew, so too did her resentment at being treated as an inferior because she was female.

Kincaid hardly knew her father. She lived with her stepfather (a carpenter), mother, and brothers until 1965, when at age seventeen she was sent to Westchester, New York, to work as an au pair, taking care of a rich couple's four daughters. She was supposed to send money back home to Antigua but she resented that responsibility and instead concentrated on learning how to be an independent young woman in the very foreign culture and climate of New York. She explains that she hated the circumstances of her servitude: "not the family I worked for. It was that I had to send all my earnings to my own family, that is what I hated." She found a way to strike out on her own after not quite a year in this country. She had already separated from her own family, neither opening nor responding to letters from home. She chronicled this experience in a fictional form in her novel *Lucy*.[1]

From 1966 to 1973, Kincaid earned a high school diploma, attended a community college and studied photography at the New York School for Social Research. She won a scholarship to Franconia College in New Hampshire, but only attended for a year. That might have been the end of that, and Kincaid might have made her way through a series of menial jobs—receptionist, typist (although her typing skills weren't very good), or salesclerk—and then returned home or married someone and stayed here in the States. But Kincaid has a distinct and honest way of looking at the world and saying what others may be thinking (or wished they had thought) and this trait helped her change her fate. When she returned to New York from New Hampshire, she decided that she wanted to be a writer and set out to become one.

Her first writing assignment involved a series of articles for *Ingénue* magazine, a publication aimed at sophisticated teenagers. Her idea was to profile well-known women at the age of the magazine's readership—Gloria Steinem, Barbara Walters, and Yoko Ono, among them. What were these women like as teenagers? What were their hopes and fears? Her articles reflected her curious nature and showed an early ability to ask questions that others might feel uncomfortable asking. She also wrote reviews for the *Village Voice* and began to freelance for women's magazines.

In 1973, she changed her name to Jamaica Kincaid as a way of reinventing herself and further separating herself from her family and past. "I didn't want them to know about my writing," she explains. "I was afraid I'd fail and they would laugh at me. I needed a bit of anonymity." She also needed that anonymity because, more and more, she wanted to write about her life and family in Antigua, a subject that her family would not be happy to hear her views on. She wasn't being intentionally political in the choice of first name; however, she's pleased that Jamaica is an English corruption of Columbus's name for Antigua, Xaymaca.

While working for *Ingénue*, Kincaid met Michael O'Donoghue, one of the founding writers for *Saturday Night Live*, in an elevator. O'Donoghue was immediately struck by Kincaid's forthrightness and originality, and recognized that hers was an original voice. O'Donoghue thought that a friend of his, George W. S. Trow, a writer for the *New Yorker*, might find her entertaining. O'Donoghue introduced her to Trow and Trow began taking Kincaid around to social events in New York and writing "Talk of the Town" pieces about her and her reaction to people and events going on around her. The "Talk of the Town" section of the *New Yorker* is a highly visible collection of essays on a variety of subjects from local gossip to world affairs, written by different authors, often quirky, usually entertaining, and much read in and outside of New York City. At the time, the pieces were unsigned, leaving the reader to guess who wrote them. At first, Trow began referring to Kincaid as his "sassy black friend," a woman who saw the world differently than most people, bringing her distinctive mix of disdain and fascination with life to her observations. Her comments were sometimes outrageous, often funny, and rarely predictable.

Eventually, Kincaid met the editor of the magazine, William Shawn, who offered her a job and she became a regular featured contributor to the section. "It really was quite remarkable because I was not OF the *New Yorker*," recalls Kincaid. "I was not male. I was not white. I was not from Harvard or Yale, which were all the things that I think the *New Yorker* was about. But, it's true. William Shawn showed me what my voice was. He was the first person who made me feel that what I thought had value. My writing is so much my thought—or, at least, it was beginning to be—and no one had really appreciated that before. That's when I began to write the stories that later were collected together in my first book, *At the Bottom of the River*. I owe him a great debt of gratitude."

In 1979, Kincaid married Shawn's son, Allen, a composer and Bennington College professor, and moved to Bennington where she and her husband both taught at the small, private Bennington College. Eventually, the couple acquired the house where she currently lives, a wonderful, rambling building filled with books and memorabilia. The couple has two children. Kincaid and Shawn have divorced, but she continues to live in Bennington where her gardens and her writing about them have brought her considerable fame and respect in the horticultural world, not to mention the wonderful pleasure of growing things, learning the names of the flowers, and seeking out and preserving rare and beautiful plants. Kincaid now teaches writing at Harvard University.

Kincaid's house in Bennington is set back a bit from the road, offering privacy. The property affords Kincaid both sunny and shady areas for both formal and natural gardens. A visit might involve a horticultural tour in which Kincaid can tell you the Latin names of the plants growing in her gardens, their country of origin, where she acquired them, who gave them to her, and whether or not she still likes them. A visit might also involve a hunt on all fours for a woodchuck's various holes and a discussion of plots to eradicate the varmints. She hates woodchucks and wants to shoot the one who's digging up her garden. In all things—whether gardening or writing or food or people—Kincaid is a woman of distinct tastes, a clear and direct way of saying what she likes and what she doesn't, and a wonderful ability to change her mind "when I think it needs changing."

Because Antigua was a British Colony until 1967, Kincaid had completed her secondary education under the British system. She speaks with a lilting British accent lessened only slightly by her time in the United States. A tall, stately woman, Kincaid concedes that her work is highly autobiographical. She writes in a spare style that is deceptively simple, often repetitive. The effect is of a long prose poem in which the repetition of information and words becomes a kind of incantation. Kincaid says she writes this way as much for herself as for the reader: "I write to understand myself," she says. Often her narrator is a woman much like herself: outspoken, unpredictable, difficult, exasperating even. The themes come from her own life too: what it's like to grow up under the pressure of poverty and colonialism, under the burden of race and gender, to experience loss and be raised by a powerful mother—all this and the emotional onset of adolescence as well. These issues are at the heart of both her fiction and nonfiction work.

### Tips and Techniques

*Fact or fiction?*

The word *fiction* is used to describe a written work in which some or all aspects of the story are made up. The word fiction comes from the Latin word *fictus* for false, counterfeit, or feigned, but the word is also closely associated with creativity and transformation. Fictions are the creation of the author even when they take their inspiration from real events or people in the writer's life. By calling a piece "fiction," the writer signals to the reader that some or all of the facts, ideas and quotes in the book have been made up. Some writers consider fiction a freer form of writing than nonfiction because they are not forced to adhere to the literal truth. In not being constrained by actual events, some authors feel they can achieve a deeper truth, a more universal truth. Often, stories or poems begin with the memory of a real event but take on a life of their own and become fictions in the imagination of the writer.

Nonfiction is the term applied to works whose essential facts are true. The word itself, "nonfiction," is a bit problematic as it literally means "not false." Works of nonfiction traditionally include memoirs, in which a writer relies upon his or her memory for the facts, biographies and autobiographies, histories, reference books, true-life accounts, factual explanations of how things work, and other written material that is based on a strict adherence to fact.

It is not necessary for a writer to explain why she uses the term fiction for one piece and nonfiction for another, even if there is great similarity between the two. A writer's impetus for designating a piece fiction or nonfiction is complex, one that requires clear knowledge of purpose and an understanding of the different ways that readers approach the two formats.

Kincaid's book *At the Bottom of the River* is actually a series of prose poems in which a young girl becomes increasingly aware of the patriarchal politics of oppression and struggles against an onslaught of expectations and demands from both her family and her culture. The short story "Girl" is perhaps the most famous in the collection. The entire story consists of a single ongoing sentence of two pages' duration in which a mother gives her daughter a list of numbing orders and criticisms, delivering them in chant-like fashion.[2] The effect is quite powerful. The rhythmic pacing of the sentence, re-creating the mother's voice as a series of everyday admonitions to a daughter, build one upon another. The reader quickly understands that while the mother is telling her daughter how to prepare food and take care of herself, she is actually putting the girl down with the most fatalistic insults as she links these everyday tasks to the daughter's inevitably becoming "the slut you are so bent on becoming." The story is another brilliant example of "Show, don't tell." There are in this case no physical descriptions of the characters; yet, we can see and hear them and understand the essentials not only of their personalities but also of the central conflict that fuels their relationship.

*At the Bottom of the River* was nominated for the PEN/Faulkner Award and won the Morton Darwen Zabel Award of the American Academy of Arts and Letters, one of the more prestigious awards available to writers. Two years later, in 1985, Kincaid published her first novel, *Annie John*, which further develops the themes of teenage pain and isolation.[3] Her heroine, ten-year-old Annie John, is, like Kincaid herself, strong-willed and smart. Like Kincaid in real life, Annie John is deeply confused and hurt as her mother takes back her love and the support that Annie John took for granted when she was younger. But the story is more than Kincaid's story. She uses the relationship between mother and daughter as an allegory to explore the relationship between a colonial people and the "mother" country. *Annie John* was selected as one of three finalists for the 1985 International Ritz Paris Hemingway Award.

In the novel *Lucy*, Kincaid further explores biographical information in fictional form.[4] Lucy's full name is Lucy Josephine Potter. Kincaid's given name is Elaine Potter Richardson; Potter is Kincaid's biological father's name. Kincaid gives Lucy her own birthday. As in Kincaid's life, Lucy's mother marries an older man, a carpenter, and has three sons by him. Like Kincaid, the character Lucy travels to New York to work as an au pair. The story tells of Lucy's growing awareness of her appetites—for freedom, for sexual experience, for independence—while also allowing Kincaid to express her opinions and observations about a certain class of people who seem on the surface to live very perfect, well-ordained lives but often disappoint themselves or one another. It's not a stretch of the imagination to assume that these people are reflections of the family members she was working for or a general classification of people who have children but employ others to raise them. The narrator of her novel is often unapologetically cold, even cruel in her observations of the family with whom she lives and the friends she makes. The reader must remind herself that the book is fiction. It may have elements that come from Kincaid's real life but its themes and explorations are universal ones: the need for autonomy and independence, the despoiling effect of power and money, self-realization versus other people's expectations, privilege versus servitude.

A subsequent novel, *The Autobiography of My Mother*, is set on Kincaid's mother's home island of Dominica.[5] It tells the story of seventy-year-old Xuela Claudette Richardson—again, Kincaid shares a family name with a fictional character—who struggles to find her identity in a country depleted by colonialism. Xuela's father is uncaring; her mother, unknown. Again, while some elements of Kincaid's life are present or altered, the reader must approach the material as a fictional account.

On the other hand, *My Brother*, a gripping chronicle of Kincaid's relationship with her youngest brother Devon during his losing battle with AIDS, is presented as nonfiction.[6] The memoir is one of Kincaid's most riveting and controversial books. Critics have called her depiction of the brother she hardly knew until his death coldhearted. And some are puzzled as to why she calls some books that are based on the facts of her own life fictional works while identifying *My Brother* as nonfiction. Kincaid is not especially interested in explaining the decisions behind her choice of category. Perhaps *My Brother* adheres closer to reality than some of the other books; perhaps she felt its obvious theme of a life wasted by passivity needed to be presented as nonfiction. These are decisions that Kincaid chooses not to elaborate on and we, as readers, must accept.

*My Brother* teaches us important facts about Kincaid's life, facts that inform our understanding of the other books and Kincaid herself while also casting new light on several age-old themes: of girl children sacrificed for boy children, and of gifted people who waste their talents and die too young, out of passivity as much as anything else. When Devon was born, Kincaid was forced to quit school even though her grades were among the top in her class. Her father was ill and her mother needed her at home. Quite naturally, Kincaid resented the assumption that her life and education were less valuable than the needs of others. The irony of his birth and her parent's decision—at least in her eyes—to place more value on Devon and his brothers' lives than hers is obvious. Devon was quite young when Kincaid left for the United States. She describes the risks he subsequently took with his health and his seeming inability to direct his life in positive directions. She was sacrificed for her brothers, yet the decision to send her to New York to earn money for the family set her on her journey to becoming a writer. Because Devon was so young when she took that journey and because she cut herself off from her family, she does not know Devon. Yet, at the end of his life, Kincaid finds herself returning to Antigua to ensure Devon has the care and medicine he needs. Along with exploring the passivity of her brother's life and death, she also uses the story to meditate on the ways in which his fate might have been hers had she stayed on the island.

As with so many of the other books, the subject of *My Brother* is as much Kincaid's mother as it is Devon. Kincaid describes her mother as "bitter, sharp" after Devon's birth. . . . "She and I quarreled all the time. . . . Her features collapsed, she was beautiful in the face before . . . but that wasn't true anymore after my brother was born."[7] No wonder Kincaid wanted to change her name; these are harsh things for any mother to read. In the memoir, Kincaid weaves stories and observations across time, from the years when she lived in Antigua to her present life in Vermont as wife, mother, and successful writer. Then we are back with her in the hospital ward where her brother lies dying, alone, shunned by the other patients, the staff and his old friends. "I shall never forget him," she writes of Devon, "because his life is the one I did not have, the life that, for reasons I hope shall never be too clear to me, I avoided or escaped. . . .I could not have become a writer while living among the people I knew best, I could not have become myself."[8]

This idea—that one can save one's own life, or not—is also central to *Mr. Potter*, a novel in which Kincaid tries to understand the father she never knew.[9] Mr. Potter cannot read. He is a chauffeur in Antigua who spends his days traveling the only roads he will ever know. The daughter he didn't raise became a writer and professor at Harvard University. It was books and the magic of story—and persistence and luck—that separate the two of them. And, of course, much more. Thus, the book's message is simply that reading and writing are incomparable prizes and gifts; literacy can bring salvation. Kincaid explains that she uses the real events of her own life in her stories because this is the information available to her and because it is what interests her. Writers often say they write "for the work"—to find a truth and share it with the reader—but Kincaid unabashedly says she writes for herself first.

Books have always been important to Kincaid. As a child, she could hardly part with a book once she'd read it. Sometimes, she'd take a book back to the library, then steal it and hide it under her house, where she accumulated quite a pile of texts. One of Kincaid's mother's most grievous deeds involved books. Once, when Kincaid was babysitting Devon, she became so engrossed in a book that she forgot to change the baby's diaper. When her mother returned home and found Devon with a dirty bottom, she took Kincaid's books away from her and burned them on the stone pile outside the house. Books, says Kincaid, are passports to knowledge, to understanding, to adventure, to the imagination. She says if she had one tip to give to would-be writers of any age it would be read, read, read: "Fill your head with words. Look up words in dictionaries. Read all sorts of books—nonfiction books on subjects that you know nothing about, encyclopedias, and histories. Live with words and ponder sentences."

Kincaid cannot keep a writing schedule. She doesn't write at the same time every day "because most days I don't have the anything to write down in my head." She says she's too busy living life for a schedule: there might be weeds to pull or children to attend to. Yet she is almost always working on her writing. She spends a lot of time thinking out everything she wants to say before she sits down to write, sometimes working on a single passage in her head for many weeks.

The lesson to be learned from Kincaid's writing is to be true to your particular voice, to strive to discover your particular way of thinking and viewing the world, then find the words that most closely communicate those thoughts. She urges writers to spend time seeking their own words, expressions and patterns of speech, their own rhythms. On the surface, Kincaid's simple and repetitive language mirrors the patterns of nature as they were ingrained in her conscious and subconscious day after day, night after night, growing up in Antigua. Her language resonates with the repetitious ebb and flow of tides and seasons; the singsong patterns of her mother's patois can be heard in the recurring incantations of Kincaid's sentences. But as much as the language itself, it is her own unpredictable response to the world and her opinions—even unpleasant ones—so matter-of-factly spoken that make people read her written works. You just never know what she's going to say.

Kincaid calls her coming to live in Vermont in 1985 "a happy accident." As a young woman developing her career, she had friends who owned a home in Vermont and sometimes invited Kincaid to housesit. Something about the lushness of Vermont's green valleys and mountains reminded her of home. Yet much about Vermont was so *not* home and she took pleasure in that as well. Interviewers have often asked her if she, a West Indian woman with coffee-colored skin and a strong British accent, stands out in Vermont and if she has experienced prejudice. They are curious about how her biracial children are treated in Vermont, one of the whitest states in the union. Kincaid says she has not experienced prejudice here; indeed, Vermonters have been wonderful to her: "I remember asking the children a question on this very subject once, seeking to understand how they have been treated. They didn't really know what I was talking about. I think if you are a decent person and you act properly and don't bring disgrace upon yourself and others, if you are forthright and respect other's privacy, people here respect you in return. Disrespect comes from bringing disrespect upon yourself." She says, "Vermonters, I imagine, have a long memory; they do not suffer fools easily. But then, neither do I.

"Winter is a wonderful time for reading and for writing. I'd get much less done if I could garden and look at my gardens and fight with the woodchuck all year round. In winter, I study plants and plant catalogues. I plan and redesign. I read and write. I think. It's all part of the creative process. And the seasons are a constant reminder of our own mortality. They keep us humble."

---

◄§ FROM "Girl"

Wash the white clothes on Monday and put them on the stone heap; wash the color clothes on Tuesday and put them on the clothesline to dry; don't walk barehead in the hot sun; cook pumpkin fritters in very hot sweet oil; soak your little clothes right after you take them off; when buying cotton to make yourself a nice blouse, be sure that it doesn't have gum on it, because that way it won't hold up well after a wash; soak salt fish overnight before you cook it; is it true that you sing benna in Sunday School?; always eat your food in such a way that it won't turn someone else's stomach; on Sundays try to walk like a lady and not like the slut you are so bent on becoming; don't sing benna in Sunday School; you mustn't speak to wharf-rat boys, not even to give directions; don't eat fruits on the street, flies will follow you; *but I don't sing benna on Sundays at all and never in Sunday School*; this is how to sew on a button; this is how to make a buttonhole for the button you have just sewed on; this is how to hem a dress when you see the hem coming down and so to prevent yourself from looking like the slut I know you are so bent on becoming; this is how you iron your fathers khaki shirt so that it doesn't have a crease; this is how you iron your fathers khaki pants so that they don't have a crease; this is how you grow okra far from the house, because okra trees harbor red ants; when you are growing dasheen, make sure it gets plenty of water or else it makes your throat itch when you are eating it; this is how you sweep a corner; this is how you sweep a whole house; this is how you sweep a yard; this is how you smile to someone you don't like too much; this is how you smile to someone you don't like at all; this is how you smile to someone you like completely; this is how you set a table for tea; this is how you set a table for dinner; this is how you set a table for dinner with an important guest; this is how you set a table for lunch; this is how you set a table for breakfast; this is how to behave in the presence of men who don't know you very well, and this way they won't recognize immediately the slut I have warned you against becoming; be sure to wash every day, even if it is with your own spit; don't squat down to play marbles, you are not a boy, you know; don't pick people's flowers, you might catch something; don't throw stones at blackbirds, because it might not be a blackbird at all; this is how to make a bread pudding; this is how to make doukona; this is how to make pepper pot; this is how to make a good medicine for a cold; this is how to make a good medicine to throw away a child before it even becomes a child; this is how to catch a fish; this is how to throw back a fish you don't like, and that way something bad won't fall on you; this is how to bully a man; this is how a man bullies you; this is how to love a man, and if this doesn't work there are other ways, and if they don't work don't feel too bad about giving up; this is how to spit up in the air if you feel like it, and this is how to move quick so that it doesn't fall on you; this is how to make ends meet; always squeeze bread to make sure it's fresh; *but what if the baker won't let me feel the bread?*; you mean to say that after all you are really going to be the kind of woman who the baker won't let near the bread?[10]

## Questions and Exercises for Reflection and Inspiration

Kincaid's stories succeed because they are told on two layers: first, there are the particulars of her own life and the island on which she grew: the stone heap, *benna, dasheen,* Sunday school, bread pudding. These elements are the elements of the obvious story, the story of a particular girl who feels wronged by a particular mother. But there is an under-story in each of her works, an unspoken but universal tale of the coming-of-age struggle between all mothers and daughters, the fight each one of us must wage to be our own person. How does Kincaid tell this second but more important story without ever expressing it directly? What elements make the story accessible, and therefore understandable, to readers from other cultures? What details—age, gender, class, and race—do you perceive about the characters in her story, "Lucy," without actually being provided with the information?

What do you think should be the rules on what to call a piece of writing—fiction or non-fiction? When writing about difficult subjects or family matters, does calling a piece fiction make it easier to write? Many of us carry scars from youth and unexpressed anger at a relative or loved one. Sometimes it feels quite cathartic to write out these angers, essentially to dump them out. But they can be quite hurtful to people who might recognize themselves in our words. At some level, what difference does it make if a writer calls a piece fiction or nonfiction if another person recognizes himself or herself in the words? Do you think a writer should concern himself with the feelings of others?

> **Exercise 1:** Write about a difficult time in your life, telling the story as accurately as possible in first-person from your point of view. Remembering all you've already learned about creating character, strive to show emotions and emotional responses, rather than telling us how the characters felt. You may also use Bohjalian's technique of drawing your setting to refresh your memory about sensory details of the scene you have chosen to write about. How does the exercise make you feel? Do you feel that you are breaking unspoken (or perhaps expressed) rules when you reveal painful personal stories? Or did it feel good to write about this event from your past? Do you think others would be interested in reading your piece? Does it have universality? Does it have an overt story and an under-story? Did you show, rather than tell?
>
> **Exercise 2:** Craft the same story as above in third-person, writing it as objectively as possible with as few loaded words as possible, as if a

person outside of the emotions and conflicts of the situation had observed it and was now telling the story. How does that change the tone and impact of the piece? Do you like it better? Does the process seem more comfortable? Is it easier to tell the under-story in third-person than in first-person or vice versa?

**Exercise 3:** Write the same story in fictional form, changing the names of the characters, including yourself, and some of the identifying details. You may alter the facts, combine characters, merge incidents, or change the scene, but try to capture the emotion of the original event. Again, work to show, not tell, and try to give your story universality by using details that any reader can relate to. Which of the three versions of your story do you feel gets closer to the real truth of the event, the emotional core of the experience?

Photo by Bill Eichner

# 15   Julia Alvarez
## Bridging Two Worlds

Born 27 March 1950, New York City

Education: B.A., Middlebury College; M.A., Syracuse University.

Lives in Weybridge

First publication: a poem, "My People" in *Soulscript*, an anthology published by Doubleday in 1970.

Poetry: *Homecoming: New and Selected Poems* (1996); *The Other Side / El Otro Lado* (1995); *Seven Trees* (1998); *The Woman I Kept to Myself* (2004)

Fiction: *How the García Girls Lost Their Accents* (1991); *¡Yo!* (1997)

Books for young readers of all ages: *The Secret Footprints* (2000); *A Cafecito Story* (2001); *How Tía Lola Came to Visit Stay* (2001); *Before We Were Free* (2002); *finding miracles* (2004)

Historical novel: *In The Time of the Butterflies* (1994); *In the Name of Salomé* (2000)

Autobiographical essays: *Something to Declare* (1998)

Awards: 1991 Pen Oakland / Josephine Miles Award; Finalist, National Book Critics Circle Award in Fiction (1995); Américas Award for Children's and Young Adult Literature from the Consortium of Latin American Studies Programs (2002); Hispanic Heritage Award in Literature (2002); American Library Association's Pura Belpré Award (2003)

JULIA ALVAREZ TRACES her writing life to her "radical uprooting from my culture, my native language, my country" when she was just ten years old. In 1960, Alvarez's family fled their island home of the Dominican Republic after the secret police learned of Alvarez's father's involvement in an unsuccessful attempt to overthrow the dictatorship of Rafael L. Trujillo. Trujillo was a prominent Dominican Army commander who had established absolute power in the Caribbean island-nation after a coup in 1930; he held power for the next thirty-one years. His reign was characterized by ever-increasing repression of human rights until his assassination in 1961, a year after the Alvarez family's self-exile to the United States.

Alvarez was actually born in New York City but her family had returned to the Dominican Republic shortly after her birth and it was there that she spent her early formative years. Her family's political situation was quite complicated. Her mother's family was also involved in the underground political movement. Her maternal uncle had been rounded up and put in La Victoria prison for nine months. Yet her family had deep roots in the community. They lived in an extended network, in houses that abutted one another or were quite close by. Here, Alvarez and her sisters were raised as part of a large, extended family made up of her mother, grandmother, aunts, and cousins. The men were around, of course, but the children's primary contact was with women.

The family was also highly influenced by American values and goods—often eating American food, wearing American clothing, and using American appliances. In this mix of Latin and American culture, the compound was an accepted haven of love and security while America was seen as a fantasyland, a place of virtually limitless opportunity and material richness. Alvarez's family had close ties with America; her uncles had attended Ivy League colleges and her grandfather was a cultural attaché to the United Nations. These ties had kept her family safe from Trujillo for many years and, later, helped the family escape to New York.

America, however, proved to be no fantasyland. Alvarez felt isolated from her family, homesick, alienated by prejudice and anonymity as they squeezed into a city apartment quite different from either the loving family compound in the Dominican Republic or the America of her dreams. She was cold that first winter and her schoolmates taunted her and her accent. The lack of welcome, the sense of being so "other," turned her inward. While at home, she remained the family ham and entertainer, at school she turned to books for company and solace: "My love of storytelling came from the oral culture around me but I was not a reader as a young child. When I came to this country, imagination became a portable homeland for me, a place I could go for comfort, a place I didn't have to leave. I began to love reading and, like many readers, I wanted to write as well, to tell my story."

And she had quite a story to tell: not just hers, but that of her fellow countrymen and women. With the death of Trujillo, she and her sisters began spending summers back on the island, further compounding Alvarez's sense of living in two worlds. Initially she found writing in English difficult. As the mother in her novel ¡Yo! says, "the hardest thing about coming to this country wasn't the winter everyone warned me about—it was the language. If you had to choose the most tongue-twisting way of saying you love somebody or how much a pound for the ground round, then say it in English. For the longest time I thought Americans must be smarter than us Latins—because how else could they speak such a difficult language."[1] Alvarez made up her mind to conquer the language barrier. By the time she was in high school, several teachers had recognized her writing talents. Poetry was her first avenue of expression, the genre that allowed her to express the mixture of emotions that accompanied her teenage years.

Alvarez began her college career at Connecticut College for Women, but in her junior year transferred to Middlebury College, from which she graduated summa cum laude in 1971. She received her M.A. in 1975 from Syracuse University, where she won a prestigious American Academy of Poetry prize. Over the years, she had many teaching assignments and a fellowship from the National Endowment for the Arts but kept coming back to Vermont, attending both the Bread Loaf School of English and the Bread Loaf Writers Conference, where, in 1979, she was named the John Atherton Scholar in Poetry. She returned to Bread Loaf again in 1986 as a fellow in poetry and the following year as a fellow studying fiction. Throughout this period, she received numerous awards: the Benjamin T. Marshall Prize in poetry two years in a row at Connecticut College (1968 and 1969), and then the Creative Writing Prize at Middlebury College in 1971.

After teaching at the University of Illinois, the University of Vermont, and George Washington University, she joined the faculty of Middlebury College in 1988. Several years ago, she gave up tenure—a position at universities that is difficult to achieve but is worth the trouble because it almost guarantees continued employment—so that she could have more time to write. She continues to teach as a visiting writer at Middlebury and is a member of the rotating staff at Bread Loaf.

Alvarez writes across the genres. She's equally adept in poetry, fiction, literature for children, and nonfiction. Poetry was her first love. On her website, *www.alvarezjulia.com*, she uses the publication of a recent collection of poems, *The Woman I Kept to Myself*, as an opportunity to discuss the role that poetry has played in her life and to provide something of a definition of poetry for her readers. Writes Alvarez: "For me, poetry is that cutting edge of the self, the part which moves out into experience ahead of every other part of the self. It's a way of saying what can't be put into words, our deepest and most secret and yet most universal feelings."[2]

She began writing the collected poems "as a birthday poem for my fortieth birthday. A way of assessing where I had come from, where I was going. But after I had thirty poems together, and my fortieth birthday had come and gone, I kept writing. I thought, well, I'll write forty poems for my fiftieth. . . . At any rate, here are seventy-eight poems of a woman, trying to understand this moment in the middle of our lives by looking back with new perspectives at my younger years and looking ahead at the unknown I have to sing to understand."[3]

Alvarez is best known for a series of unforgettable novels that, while they have their roots in her Dominican culture, are imbued with an insight that comes from living in many cultures and traveling widely. She says, "I am a Dominican, hyphen, American. As a fiction writer, I find that the most exciting things happen in the realm of that hyphen—the place where two worlds collide or blend together." Like Kincaid, Alvarez writes to understand her life, to know what she is thinking about the events that formed her. Although their styles are dramatically different, Alvarez and Kincaid explore similar themes: the story of exile; the story of women struggling to find autonomy in a society that accepts male dominion (and, by extension, political tyranny); the story of the [Catholic] church's role in aiding and abetting despots; the story of the few religious leaders who dare to see themselves as servants of the people; the story of courage over immeasurable odds; and the ultimate question of the worth of sacrifice.

Alvarez's first book of fiction, a collection of linked stories entitled *How the García Girls Lost Their Accents*, which was published in 1991, is semi-autobiographical. Like the Alvarez family, the García family was forced to flee the Dominican Republic for America, where the shock of secret police at the door was traded for another shock, that of prejudice and of feeling like foreigners in a place once considered fantasyland. And not only that: the world as a whole was changing and the García girls (like the Alvarez girls) struggle through the freewheeling American culture of the 1960s (then the 1970s and 1980s), with all the dizzying choices and challenges that young people all over the world were facing. Alvarez brings all of this to her novel. The *New York Times Book Review* praised the book, saying Alvarez had "beautifully captured the threshold experience of the new immigrant, where the past is not yet a memory and the future remains an anxious dream."[4]

Her second novel, *In the Time of the Butterflies,* was published in 1994 and made into a movie produced by and starring Salma Hayek. It is written in multiple points of view. The novel recounts an actual event in Dominican history. On 25 November 1960, Patria, Minerva, and María Teresa Mirabal were murdered by the Trujillo regime for their efforts to overthrow the hated dictator. The three Mirabal sisters, whose code name was Las Mariposas (the Butterflies), were returning from a visit with their husbands, who had been incarcerated as political prisoners, when they were killed. A fourth sister, Dede, had decided not to make this particular trip. She is left to cope with the guilt and sadness caused by this tragedy, the anniversary of which is now observed by the United Nations as International Day Against Violence Toward Women.[5]

The Mirabal sisters held special significance for Alvarez and her family; her father had been a member of the same resistance group as the Mirabal sisters, who were assassinated just four months after the Alvarez family fled the Dominican Republic. Indeed, it was the fact that the secret police had broken the code for this resistance group that led to her parents' flight. The Alvarez family was living in New York City when *Time* magazine eulogized the Mirabals. Julia and her sisters were not allowed to read the article but she sneaked a look at it. Later, she pondered how disturbing the murders must have been to her parents who "were still living as if the secret police might come to our New York apartment at any moment."

In 1986, a women's press was preparing a series of postcards about Dominican women and asked Alvarez to contribute something about the Mirabal sisters. She traveled to their hometown, where she knew that the surviving sister had raised the six orphans left behind. While there were no books written about them, everyone she met knew their story. Quite by chance, Alvarez met Noris, the daughter of the oldest sister, Patria. Noris took her to the museum that Dede had established in their mother's house. Here were displayed the sisters' favorite things and their photographs, along with items they had worn on the day of their murders. Alvarez saw Patria's bloodstained dress; the long braid of the youngest sister María Teresa's hair, laying in a glass case; the smart purses the sisters had splurged on guiltily during their last trip.

María Teresa's braid of hair haunted Alvarez. Later that night, she wrote in her journal: "There are still twigs and dirt and slivers of glass from her last moment tumbling down the mountain in that rented jeep. When Noris heads out for the next room, I lift the case and touch the hair, it feels like real hair." Alvarez wrote her postcard paragraph and thought of writing a biography of the women but "it was too beautiful, too perfect, too awful. The girls' story didn't need a story. And besides I couldn't yet imagine how one tells a story like this." But in 1992, during a trip to the Dominican Republic, Alvarez finally got to meet Dede: "She had suffered her own martyrdom: a living death; the one left behind to tell the story."

Alvarez realized she had to tell the sisters' story. But she had a problem. The sisters were dead and with them the intimate details of how they had developed from ordinary women living a very traditional Latin lifestyle to members of an insurrection. She could talk to people who knew the sisters. She could read their love letters. And she could study the facts of their death. She could look at their pictures, unlikely-looking heroines in their 1950s hairdos, their Latin-style dresses, and sweet smiles. But even those who knew the sisters best would have limited access to what they actually thought and felt.

In the end, Alvarez relied upon her own Latin roots to tell their story. In the Caribbean, Central America and South America, there is already a strong understanding that history is a fiction, that people create versions of history for themselves. Alvarez came to understand that sometimes, to tell a truth, you have to make parts up. Alvarez chose to tell the Mirabal sisters' story not as a biography but as a fiction based on fact. After all, it was the drama of their story that she was after, not a blow-by-blow recounting of events. To capture that, she realized, she would have to tell the story through the sisters' voices. In the fictionalized account of their lives, Alvarez imagines the sisters as ordinary women, who, once politicized, each in her own way, place themselves in extraordinary peril. Using the facts she could garner, she fills in what she doesn't know with what seems likely.

Alvarez likes to quote the poet Novalis, who said, "Novels arise out of the shortcomings of history." The official story of the Mirabal sisters wasn't "true"; the government tried to turn them into traitors. And the myths that arose about them were also not true but rather glorified accounts. Alvarez felt that to get at their truth, she needed to understand their characters. Her approach allows the reader to see the women as real people. Their hero status notwithstanding, the risks these women took were not any easier for them than they would have been for anyone else. Alvarez is so adept at making this point that the reader comes to both associate with the sisters and appreciate the difficulty of their sacrifice. She did this by developing singular personalities for each sister, drawing on their real-life stories to differentiate them from one another. Her success can be measured by the fact that Minou Tavares Mirabal, the daughter of Minerva, one of the slain sisters, read the book and urged Alvarez to use the sisters' real names. Minou Mirabal later became involved in the government of Leonel Fernández, a former leader of the Dominican Liberation Party who was president of the Dominican Republic from 1996 to 2000. When Minou Mirabal traveled abroad on state functions, she often took as a gift the Spanish translation of Alvarez's novel. Dede Mirabal and Alvarez remain close friends; Dede still sells copies of the Spanish translation of *In the Time of the Butterflies* at the museum dedicated to the sisters.

### Tips and Techniques

Biographies and histories are important documents. The best are page-turners; the worst are dull. Too often biographies or histories read as if they are a chronological telling of events; the emotional development of real-life characters can be hard to show when the writer is hampered by chronological facts. Even one's own story can be difficult to tell in a manner that is consistently engaging; real lives *aren't* consistently engaging. Often, however, the dull parts are essential to the whole story and must be included in a strict biographical or historical account.

Readers want to be provided with enough information to form mental pictures and wonder what happens next as they turn the pages. This active engagement allows the reader to make an emotional and intellectual investment in the work. Quite frankly, it's much easier to cause this emotional engagement in a fictional account than in a long nonfictional one. It's hard to explain why this is so, but if you think of your favorite books, it's likely that the list includes more novels than nonfiction books. There are, of course, exceptions, but most writing teachers concede that people make a bigger emotional commitment to fictional accounts than nonfiction ones. Alvarez puts it this way: "A novel is not, after all, a historical document, but a way to travel through the human heart." And, she adds, sometimes that journey reveals deeper truths than a factual account ever could. It's part of the magic of fiction, why we like a good epic novel so much.

The essential element, of course, is integrity. In nonfiction, the writer must stick to the truth or as close to the truth as research and talent allow. In a fiction, the writer has more leeway; she can blend events or merge characters. This blending, of course, is trickier when the fictional account is based upon real events known to many readers. In all cases, the writer must be clear about her goals and methods; the reader must know whether he is reading a true account or a fictionalized one.

One of Alvarez's more satisfying literary pursuits has been writing a series of books for what she calls "young adults of all ages." The books often address difficult issues similar to those she experienced as a child. For example, in her book *Before We Were Free*, the secret police takes a young girl's father away. The girl, named Anita in honor of Anne Frank, keeps a diary of her time in hiding with her mother. The book was inspired by Alvarez's uncle's imprisonment and its impact on his family.

*How Tía Lola Came to Visit Stay* addresses the issue of what it means to children of immigrants to be Latino.[6] In writing it, Alvarez was thinking of her nephew and of the new generation coming up, the children of the first immigrants like herself. On her website, Alvarez says she also lets the story bring "my memories of my wonderful aunts, tías, to the snowy landscape of the blank page." She was also tired of reading children's books about "our perfect 'little house on the prairie' Latino families, portraits that didn't accurately reflect the fact that our familias are as complex and riddled with problems and divorces as those of any other population group. I wanted a kid like my nephew to read a book that might reflect a family that seemed authentic to his own experience."[7]

As a little girl, Alvarez would lie awake at night, trying to catch a glimpse of *ciguapas* (see-GWAH-pas), a tribe of beautiful women who lived underwater and only came out at night to hunt for food. A special secret kept them from being seen by people. In *The Secret Footprints*, she brings this cultural story to life. In her book, one little girl ciguapa, Guapita, almost gives the special secret away after befriending a human boy.[8]

Alvarez's interest in writing children's books grew out of her frustration with finding good books to read to the people who live on and near a coffee farm she and her husband, ophthalmologist Bill Eichner, established several years ago in the Dominican Republic. She wanted to tackle illiteracy through books that appealed to both young readers and adults. She knew that the best books speak to our own experiences. Alta Gracia, the farm Alvarez and her husband established, is part of a cooperative of small farmers who have banded together to grow coffee and other crops sustainably, in a way that protects the land. On 1 June 2004, the farm was turned over to several groups, including Plan Sierra, a green movement that has had great success in combating deforestation. Alvarez set the farm up as a model project to teach sustainable methods to small farmers throughout the Dominican Republic. She thinks of it as "a green university." She and her husband will remain involved but, she points out, running a farm is like writing: you have to do it full-time or it doesn't get done well. She quotes the popular Spanish saying: "el ojo del amo engorda al caballo," (the eye of the owner fattens the horse). Just as she has given up her tenure at Middlebury College so that she has more time for writing, she also came to realize that she couldn't both run a coffee farm and devote herself to her craft. Alvarez tells the story of sustainable farming in another of her books for young adults of all ages, *A Cafecito Story*.[9]

When Alvarez is in the Dominican Republic, she uses a gas lamp and writes by hand. Most of the time, however, the everyday demands of life in the Dominican Republic—of the farm, the students, and the family—mean she does no writing. Sometimes, it's hard even to do her journal entries every day. That's why Vermont is so important to her. In Vermont, she writes in her roomy, country home in Weybridge, a village not far from Middlebury. She took to the computer late but now finds it essential to the writing process, although she prints out version after version of her creative work so she can read it on the page.

Vermont, she says, allows her to connect with her feelings about the events around her. It represents a kind of safety for her, a safety that allows her to relive the experiences of her childhood while also pondering the difficulties and rich heritage shared by many groups of people of whom the Latinos are a much-represented group. The quiet and solitude of her home provides the peace she needs to explore those sentiments and to translate her thoughts and emotions into stories, poems, and essays. She says "Vermont [is] a perfect space, very quiet, out in the country, very solitary. In fact, it's the quiet here—the absence of those voices that back 'home' on the island call to me to become involved in the immediate work to be done—it's that absence, that silence, which allows me to hear what my characters have to say."[10]

As she told the *Atlantic Monthly*'s Hilary McClellan, "The single most important thing I can help writers to do is to acquire the habit of writing. It becomes a way of life; it's what you do. You have a lot of good skills and some days everything you write you will throw away, but it's a matter of how you live your life."[11]

◆§ FROM *A Cafecito Story*

Joe finds Miguel's farm. You can't miss it. In the midst of the green desert, Miguel's land is filled with trees. Tall ones tower over a spreading canopy of smaller ones. Everywhere there are bromeliads and birdsong. A soft light falls on the thriving coffee plants.

Perched on a branch, a small thrush says its name over and over again, chinchilín-chinchilín. A flock of wild parrots wheel in the sky as if they are flying in formation, greeting him.

Miguel's house is made of pinewood, the roof is zinc, the door is opened. There are no electric wires, no telephone poles. Miguel smiles in welcome, half a dozen kids around him. Carmen, his wife, is out back, boiling rábanos for their supper.

A buen tiempo, Miguel says. You have come at a good time.

Supper is a bowl of víveres, the boiled roots that the family is accustomed to eating in the evenings. Afterwards, Joe learns about Miguel's farm, planted with coffee the old way, under shade trees that offer natural protection to the plants, filtering the sun and the rain, feeding the soil and preventing erosion. Not to mention attracting birds that come to sing over the cherries.

That makes for a better coffee, Miguel explains. When a bird sings to the cherries as they are ripening, it is like a mother singing to her child in the womb. The baby is born with a happy soul.

The shaded coffee will put that song inside you, Miguel continues. The sprayed coffee tastes just as good if you are tasting only with your mouth. But it fills you with the poison swimming around in that dark cup of disappointment.

So why doesn't everyone farm coffee in the old way? Joe asks.

The new way you can plant more coffee, you don't have to wait for trees, you can have quicker results, you can have money in your pocket.

Miguel keeps pointing at Joe when he says "you."

The next morning, Miguel shows Joe the line on the mountain where the shaded coffee ends and the green desert begins. He and his small farmer neighbors are about to cave in and rent their plots and grow coffee for the company using the new techniques.

La compañía has the mercado, Miguel explains. If we work for them we will get 80 pesos a day, 150 if we are willing to spray the poison. I get 35 pesos for a caja of beans, Carmen can pick two cajas a day. It takes three years to get a coffee harvest. On the plantation, with their sprays, they have coffee in a year.

Sipping his coffee, Joe becomes aware of how much labor has gone into this feast of flavors, how little trickles down to the small farmer. But an idea is percolating in his head. What Miguel needs to do is to write his story down, spread the word, so coffee drinkers everywhere will learn of his plight.

I cannot do that, Miguel says quietly. I do not know my letters.

Later that morning, Joe tests Miguel's kids. Standing in the vivero where the new plants are growing, he asks them to scratch their names in the soil with a stick. They shake their heads shyly. The little one, Miguelina, takes the stick and draws a circle on the ground, then looks up smiling, as if her name is zero.

By evening, Joe has decided to spend his whole vacation up in the mountains. All day, he works alongside Miguel and his children. At night, as he reads, he looks up and sees the family watching him.

What is it the paper says? Miguel wants to know.

Stories, Joe explains. Stories that help me understand what it is to be alive on this earth.

Miguel looks down at the book in Joe's hand with new respect and affection. Joe has noticed this same look on Miguel's face as he inspects the little coffee plants in his vivero.

Every day as they work together, Miguel tells Joe the story of coffee. How before the coffee can be planted, the land must be prepared in terraces with trees of differing heights to create layers of shade: first, cedros: then, guamas and banana trees.

Meanwhile, Miguel starts the coffee seeds in a germination bed. It takes about fifty days for the shoots to come up.

From the germination bed, the little transplants go into a vivero for eight months. Finally, when they are bold and strong, Miguel plants them on terraces.

Then comes the weeding and the feeding of the plants with abonos made from whatever there is around. We say orgánico, Miguel explains, because we use only what nature provides for free.

After three years, si Dios quiere, we have a first harvest. We pick four times during the season which goes from December to March. Only the red cherries, of course.

Then the rush is on: we must depulp the cherry that same night or early the next morning. The pulp goes to our worm bed where we are producing natural fertilizers.

The wet granos, we take to the river for washing. They must be bathed with running water for eight or so hours—a watchful process, as we have to get the bean to just the moment when the grains are washed but no fermentation has begun. It is not unlike that moment with a woman—Miguel smiles, looking off toward the mountains—when love sets in.

And then, the long drying process in the sun. Some of us, who cannot afford a concrete patio, use the paved road. The grains have to be turned every four hours. At night, we pile them up and bring them under cover. Woe to us if there is rain and we do not get our granos covered quickly enough! Wet coffee molds and ends up in the abono pile.

After about two weeks, if the weather is good, we bag the coffee.

Joe sighs with relief. I didn't realize so much work went into one cup! he confesses.

I am not finished, Miguel continues, holding up a hand. Once the coffee is bagged, we let it rest. A few days, a few weeks. We have only taken off the pulp but the bean is still inside the pergamino. So, after the rest, we haul the bags down to the beneficio to have this pergamino removed. Then we sort the beans very carefully by hand, since one sour bean in a bag can spoil the taste for the buyer. The seconds we keep for ourselves.

You mean to tell me that great coffee I've been drinking is seconds? Joe asks, shaking his head.

Miguel nods. The export grade is, of course, for export.

But your coffee is so much better than anything I've tasted in fancy coffee shops in Omaha, Joe notes.

That is because—as you told me yourself—you are a farmer's son, Miguel explains. You taste with your whole body and soul.

Until this moment of Miguel saying so, Joe did not know this was true. He remembers his father planting corn in rows so straight, God Himself might have drawn the lines with a ruler. While he worked, Joe's father would whistle a little tune as if he were in conversation with a flock of invisible birds.

Sometimes, as Joe works alongside Miguel, he finds himself whistling that same tune.

You can't sell your land! Joe tells Miguel that evening. You need to keep planting coffee your old way. You need to save this bit of earth for your children and for all of us. You've got to convince your neighbors before it is too late.

Easy enough for you to say, Miguel says. You don't have to live this struggle.

That night, Joe decides.

The next morning, he rides the truck down with farmers and chickens and goats and hogs. In town, he enters the Codetel trailer and dials the place he used to call home.

Joe buys a parcela next to Miguel's. They make a pact. They will not rent their plots to the compañía and cut down their trees. They will keep to the old ways. They will provide a better coffee.

And, Joe adds, you will learn your letters. I myself will teach you.

Every day, under Miguel's gentle direction, Joe learns how to grow coffee. They make terraces and plant trees.

Every night, under the light of an oil lamp, Miguel and his family learn their ABCs. They write letters and read words.

By the time Miguel and Carmen and their children have learned to write their names, the little seeds have sprouted. When the trees are a foot high, the family has struggled through a sentence. All of them can read a page by the time the trees reach up to Miguel's knees. When the coffee is as tall as little Miguelina, they have progressed to chapters. In three years, by the time of the first coffee harvest from trees Joe has planted, Miguel and Carmen and their children can read a whole book.

It is amazing how much better coffee grows when sung to by birds or when through an opened window comes the sound of a human voice reading words on paper that still holds the memory of the tree it used to be.

## Questions and Exercises for Reflection and Inspiration

Julia Alvarez came to writing as a poet first. As a result, her work resonates with a deep poetic voice. It's there in the particularity of the words she chooses and the strength of her verbs, especially in her children's stories. You can see this clearly in the opening paragraphs of *A Cafecito Story*. Trees tower, light falls, birds wheel. These strong, specific verbs help the reader not just to see the action but also to *feel* it. It's important to use strong verbs and telling details when you are relating a personal story on paper, especially one you've told and retold again. That's because when you know a story very well, you tend to shortcut its telling and rely on quick and easy words of expression. But to share an experience with a stranger, you need vivid details and the right verbs. These are tools that help a story come alive on the page.

In her stories—both fictional and real—Alvarez juxtaposes ordinary and extraordinary events to show the value of family, honor, and personal integrity. Consider your own response to different genres. Are you a person who prefers to read fiction or nonfiction?

> **Exercise 1:** Write a story based on a memory of how you or your family reacted to some event outside the home that affected the family's sense of safety or identity. It can be something as ordinary as a storm or as powerful as a bad accident. Think about Alvarez's comments about capturing emotions through physical detail, the old "show, don't tell" dictum. Look back on the verbs in Alvarez's simple story to see how well they convey the specific emotion she wants to express. Make a list of verbs that you might use in your story, verbs that will capture the specific emotions that you want to express. Try to avoid words like "he felt" or "she was" when introducing emotions.

Instead, show yourself and your family members' emotions in scenes. Use your list of verbs to inspire you to write clearly and effectively.

Now, rewrite the story as if it happened to someone else. Change the names and some of the events while remaining true to the drama and emotions of the event. To help you fictionalize it, try changing the narrator to a person who is a different sex from you. Or change the location of the events. Or change the time in history: moving your story to another century or into the future. Or you might create a new character and bring that character into the drama to change the outcome of the real events.

Which version of the story do you like better? Which felt more comfortable to you?

**Exercise 2:** Diaries are a neat tool for allowing a character to express herself or himself directly to the reader. Take a real story you know or a fictional account that you are interested in writing and have one of the characters keep a diary, as Alvarez's character Anita did in *Before We Were Free*.[12] Pretend you are that person and write a diary account every day for two weeks, not telling the events of your own life but those of your character, whether real or imaginary. If the character is a real person, you will have to rely as closely as possible on events and sentiments that the person you are writing about would actually experience or feel. If your character is imaginary, you can make up the diary notations but make sure that you know some things about your character, such as age, occupation, place of residence, time when he or she is living, hobbies, hopes, and fears. You can make a list of these details as you go along and use them to help you write the diary. When you are done, try creating a story around some of the diary excerpts, using them as ways of showing your character's emotions and responses to events.

Historical fiction is a very complex genre. Writers have the same freedom as fiction writers to create scenes, make characters come alive on the page, and move the characters through dramatic events. Writers who base their stories on actual historical facts, however, especially ones known well to people still living today, must also rein in their imaginations and use as much factual information in the telling of their tale as possible. Often, there are huge gaps in what is knowable. When this happens, writers have to rely on a combination of research and imagination to fill in the unknowns, to be as true as possible to truth. It's a daunting task, but one that Alvarez accomplishes very deftly in her novel about the Mirabel sisters.

**Exercise 3:** You may not want to write a historical novel; that's a large undertaking. But many short stories are based on true events. Study some event from past or recent history that involved many unnamed people: a Civil War battle, an antiwar demonstration, a historic flood, the Loma Prieta earthquake. Learn as much as you can about the real event. Then invent a character and plop her or him right into the action, with little fanfare or introduction. Just get your character into the fray, a normal person caught up in an abnormal event. Play "what happens next" with your character, imagining in small increments his or her involvement (hero, coward, bystander, heckler, streetperson caught up in history—or whatever your imagination serves up). Just stay with the person from beginning to end, whether it's a battle or a historic snowstorm, and find out exactly what he or she does.

Photo by Chuck Clarino

# 16  Ruth, Phoebe, and Abigail Stone
## *Creating the Creative Home*

### Ruth Stone

Born 8 June 1915, Roanoke, Virginia

Lives in Goshen

Education: University of Illinois

First publication: A poem at age five in the *Indianapolis Star*

Collections of poetry: *In an Iridescent Time* (1959); *Topography* (1971); *Cheap* (1975); *Second Hand Coat* (1987); *Who is the Widow's Muse* (1991); *Simplicity* (1997); *Ordinary Words* (1999); *In the Next Galaxy* (2002); *In the Dark* (2004)

Awards: Shelley Memorial Award, two Guggenheim Fellowships, Delmore Schwartz Award, Whiting Writer's Award, the National Critics Award, Paterson Poetry Prize, the National Book Award, and the Academy of American Poets' Wallace Stevens Award

### Phoebe Stone

Born 12 December 1947, Boston, Massachusetts

Lives in Whiting

First book both written and illustrated by her, *When the Wind Bears Go Dancing* (1997)

Children and young adult books: *When the Wind Bears Go Dancing* (1997); *What Night Do the Angels Wander?* (1998), *Go Away, Shelly Boo* (1999); *All the Blue Moons at the Wallace Hotel* (2000); *Sonata #1 for Riley Red* (2003)

**Abigail Stone**
Born 27 June 1953, Champaign, Illinois
Lives in Middlebury
First publication: short story in the *Atlantic Monthly* at age sixteen.
Books: *Maybe It's My Heart* (1989); *Recipes from the Dump* (1996)

R EFUGE COMES IN MANY FORMS. While Vermont provided Kincaid, Alvarez, and Solzhenitsyn a safe setting from which they could write of painful experiences that occurred in their homelands far away, poet Ruth Stone found a different kind of sanctuary in the Green Mountain State. She didn't know that, of course, that day in 1956 when she saw a little ad in the *New York Times* for a country place and called the realtor right up, making arrangements to immediately see the house advertised in Goshen, Vermont.

She didn't even look inside the rambling white house framed by lilacs, a babbling brook, and an apple orchard before agreeing to buy the property. Stone knew it was hers from the moment his car left the paved road. "It was very unlike me," she recalls of her impetuous act. "But I knew with some certainty that I needed this place. It had everything one could ask for—nature all around and lots of privacy and quiet. Of course, it was spring when I saw it. I had no idea about the long winters. I don't think knowing about the worst of winter would have dissuaded me. To me, it was paradise." Privacy was a big part of it. Ruth and her husband, the novelist Walter Stone, were part of an elite group of writers that sometimes included Sylvia Plath, Ted Hughes, and Dylan Thomas. Life was exhilarating and exhausting. Vermont offered respite from the heady competition, an environment conducive to writing, and a setting where the couple's three daughters could play outside in nature.

Shortly after she purchased the house and property, the family traveled to England where Walter planned to spend part of his sabbatical year from Vassar College researching a novel he was under contract to finish. He seemed beset with concerns about publishing and had hit his head quite hard in a freak injury. Still, Stone was completely unprepared for the call she received from police, saying her husband had been found dead, hanging from a cord thrown over the doorway of a London rooming house once inhabited by Keats. His death remains something of a mystery that couldn't be explained by a simple ruling of suicide. When he was found, Walter's feet touched the ground; a window was open onto the street below. What had happened in that room where Walter Stone had planned to do his research?

Without the answers, bereft and broke, Stone retreated to the Goshen house to raise the couple's three daughters, and to write out, again and again, the pain and anger and utter frustration she felt about her husband's incomprehensible deed. To supplement her meager income from publishing, she worked off and on over the years as a kind of wandering teacher of creative writing, with appointments at Indiana University at Bloomington; the University of California, Davis; New York University; Old Dominion University; the University of Kentucky; Brandeis; and the University of Wisconsin at Madison. Indeed, Stone taught at so many schools that Abigail Stone, the youngest of her three daughters, calculates she attended twenty-seven schools by the tenth grade when she stopped attending to devote herself to traveling, writing, and singing.

Throughout their migrations, the Vermont house remained at the center of the family's universe; here Stone created an environment in which her daughters could each develop their creative talents and try their hands at a variety of artistic endeavors. You can still see the remains of their early experimentations here in the ramshackle building: Phoebe Stone's artwork decorates a porch beam; Abigail's musings are scribbled on a staircase wall. Tragedy—not just understanding it but using it and getting beyond it—was the fuel that drove Ruth Stone and her daughters to express themselves in words, music, and art. And because the house attracted so many other artists who came to visit or to work in a small cabin also located on the property, the Stone children's environment was one in which words were honored above things. In their household, art was revered. Spontaneity and cleverness were celebrated and someone—often a famous writer—would actually listen to the little song a child had made up in her head as she walked through the woods on a cool, spring morning.

"We spent some long winters up there, hauling wood, snow blowing in through the walls onto our pillows. We were forced into ourselves by hardship. Hardship can be a good thing, unless it wins," Abigail Stone says. "It didn't win because mother wouldn't let it. We didn't have a TV. We played the Poetry Game, where everyone—children and adults alike—provides a word and you write a poem incorporating all the players' words, including your own. We drew and made music. My kids grew up the same way. When we all get together we still play the Poetry Game." Ruth Stone had adopted a theory after Walter's death: that art could heal. She never had much money but the family always had art, music, and words. And, if the proof is in the pudding, Stone's children and grandchildren provide confirmation of her belief in the value of a creative environment and its power not just to heal but also to make something lasting and universal from pain.

Writer Mary McCallum calls the Stone women "The Quarry," in recognition of their collective talent. Abigail published her first story in the *Atlantic Monthly* at sixteen. She has published two novels, *Maybe It's My Heart* and *Recipes from the Dump*[1] and several of her published short stories have been included in anthologies. She's a talented musician and songwriter. Middle daughter Phoebe Stone has been successful in both art and writing. Her paintings—huge canvases filled with luscious poppies, floating people and animals, scenes from her childhood overlaid with imagination—have been shown in New York galleries, and her books for children have brought her an ever-increasing audience of admirers. Phoebe Stone says her mother continues to be her primary editor and supporter. "I've read every one of my books to my mother, in draft after draft," she says. "Sometimes we're on the phone for hours, talking about the works. She's 100 percent supportive." Stone's oldest daughter, Marcia Croll, has channeled her creativity into landscape gardening and helping children deal with trauma by working as a school therapist and championing humanitarian causes around the world.

Much as Abigail, Phoebe and Marcia grew up playing the Poetry Game and entertaining themselves by writing, performing plays, and painting on the walls, they sought to foster a creative environment for their own children. It seems to have paid off. Abigail's daughter Hillery is a writer who teaches at New York University; daughter Bianca is a songwriter, musician, and founder of the feminist magazine *Speedsmear*; and son Walter is a published poet, musician, and recording artist. Phoebe's son Ethan is a photographer whose book in progress, "The Honorable Outsider," portrays his solitary wanderings through China. Marcia's daughter Nora is a poet; son Ehsan is a filmmaker.

But, back in 1956, what an oddity the Stone family must have seemed to their mountain neighbors—three long-haired, beautiful girls and their equally long-haired mother, shades of red and auburn streaming behind them as they ran through the orchard behind their house or frolicked in the brook, famous authors coming and going, playing the Poetry Game. Some would have considered the Goshen of the late 1950s and 1960s as not quite idyllic, especially if one were a single mother living on poet's wages. First off, the town is neither a chi-chi Woodstock nor bucolic Warren but rather a hardscrabble, backwoods hamlet that had fewer than eighty people living there when Stone arrived. The town had no general store, no post office, no true center. There was one working (just barely) farm and five families who ran the town, fought over town business, and occasionally married one another. Phoebe and Abigail attended the one-room schoolhouse where the children of these families ruled; although they were outsiders, the sisters have fond memories of the friends they made among the neighborhood children.

Today, much of the town is part of the Green Mountain National Forest; there's still no general store or post office. The town office is located in the former one-room schoolhouse. Nonetheless, Goshen continues to provide a comfortable refuge for Ruth Stone, who turns ninety in 2005. She still spends the summer at the Goshen house, which still has no central heating and few modern amenities. "It's the place I belong," she says simply.

Photo by Chuck Clarino

## RUTH STONE, POET

Celebration of art came naturally to Ruth Stone. Born in 1915 in Roanoke, Virginia, she grew up in a family of poets, painters, teachers, and musicians. She claims to remember her mother reading Tennyson to her while she nursed. She read by age three, climbing into the stacks of her grandparents' library to fetch "the big books." Her father was a drummer who often practiced at home. If he wasn't away, working or gambling, he would spend the night at home with her, sharing an elegant box of chocolates and new classical records. Stone says the rhythm of poetry and music are interlaced into the oldest recesses of her brain. Later, the family moved to live in her paternal grandparents' home in Indianapolis where her grandfather was a state senator and her Aunt Harriet played drawing and writing games with her. The family doted on Stone's earliest creative endeavors; she published her first poem at age five, and then published regularly in the *Indianapolis Star,* the *New York Times,* and *Golden Book Magazine.*

She met Walter Stone at the University of Illinois and fell hard. He loved words, listened to her work and typed the poems that eventually appeared in her first book, *In an Iridescent Time.*[2] They married after he returned from fighting in World War II. In 1953, the couple and their daughters moved to Vassar College in Poughkeepsie, New York, where Walter had a teaching position. That year, she won *Poetry Magazine*'s Bess Hokin Prize and a Kenyon Review Fellowship in Poetry and used her prize money, roughly four thousand dollars, to buy the house in Goshen.

Over the years, Stone has published countless poems in literary magazines and nine volumes of poetry. She won many prestigious awards but national recognition had eluded her. Finally, at the age of eighty-eight, she hit the jackpot. Her eighth collection of poetry, *In the Next Galaxy*, won the National Book Award in poetry in the fall of 2002.[3] A few weeks later, the Academy of American Poets awarded Stone its Wallace Stevens Prize, among the most prestigious awards given in the art of poetry. Given annually, the $150,000 award recognizes outstanding and proven mastery in the art of poetry. Those who had long admired Stone's work acknowledged the bittersweet element of her winning these prizes so late in life. She's nearly blind. Laser surgery several years ago to improve fading eyesight only exacerbated the problem. She's lost quite a bit of her hearing, too. But Stone, no stranger to adversity, produced another brilliant collection of verse in 2004, appropriately titled *In the Dark*.[4]

From childhood on, Stone's poems often came to her whole, "riding in like a freight train, the words appearing at full speed in my mind, sometimes from the bottom up." But, like a traveler rushing to catch a departing train, she has to write the lines down fast before they pass on by. That doesn't mean the poems arrive as complete entities. Occasionally, the poem might need only a little fiddling after the first draft; most often, they need careful attention to word choice, syntax, rhythm, sound and meter, depth of meaning, interweaving of simile, metaphor, and imagery. "What I'm after is the right words. I like to live with a poem for a while, get to know it, get to know its language," Ruth Stone explains of her writing process. She says she worked on one poem for a decade and, then, while doing some menial task, the perfect ending finally came to her. Inspiration is a necessary partner, she says, but you have to write it down.

This process used to happen much more simply; she'd write down a few lines or a draft and keep it around, reading it, contemplating it, thinking of it as the hours or days transpired, changing this, moving that, undoing an edit, scratching out the whole thing and starting over. Now, because of her failing eyesight, the process has become more tedious. So she can see her words, Stone writes in large script on pieces of paper as the poems—or parts of poems—come to her. As she works on them, she sometimes types them into a computer, again using very large type.

Poems have an internal structure that develops as the poet discovers its deeper and deeper meanings; fortunately, Stone can feel the internal architecture (its structure) as it evolves; eyesight has nothing to do with that. The external architecture (how it looks on the page) is a different matter, entirely. That very large type she needs to use distorts the shape of the poem on the page. Here's where her daughters come in. As she works on the poems, she tells her daughters how they should be arranged on the page— how she sees them in her mind. One of her daughters then types the poems for her as she wants them to appear. Abigail, in particular, has worked meticulously with her mother, line by line, poem by poem, to ensure that the structure Stone wants for each poem gets translated onto the pages of her book and that the poems themselves follow one another in proper order.

Stone says the recent loss of sight and sound translates into another loss. Sensory material is the food of poets; she acknowledges that hers has been diminished. She misses reading as she once did. She can still read but it's arduous; magnification alters the experience, she says. A hearing aid helps with the hearing loss but she complains that it also distorts background noise and there's always the problem with batteries and tuning. Still, she's taken these losses in stride and manages to listen to lots of books on tape and the recorded readings of other poets. Music gives her great pleasure also. And she's found that her other senses have become more alert. Nonetheless, she laments that the chipmunk gathering seeds right outside her porch door is only a blur to her now. In her old age, she says, the old Goshen house with all its familiarity, from the layout of the rooms to the flowers she planted around it decades ago, provides enormous comfort even though the wooden structure has also suffered the ravages of time. She knows the place by heart, in more ways than one.

*In the Dark,* like all of Stone's work, provides entry to a life in which sadness has been compounded by poverty, but there is no defeat in her words. Stone's work, like the woman herself, is fueled by an uncanny combination of perseverance, curiosity, and humor. There is pathos in her writing but there is never self-pity. Instead, without ever being preachy or condescending, her poems provide small lessons into the large conundrums of life—the suicide of a lover, parents who pollute the planet for profit, the persistence of violence—and the moments that are always worth cherishing: daughters and grandchildren, songbirds outside the window, nature's mysteries and miracles, poetry.

Stone's ability to inspire and mentor goes far beyond her immediate family. *The Oxford Companion to Women's Writing in the United States* calls Stone the "mother poet" to many contemporary women writers.[5] Willis Barnstone, the poet and scholar who co-authored *A Book of Women Poets from Antiquity to Now*,[6] one of the Bibles of women's poetry, described Stone in an interview as "a legendary teacher of poetry like no one on this side of the century, which has led to many ardent converts to poetry. . . . Her poverties have, like all adversity, kept her lean and real and made her wealthy in her profession," while also making her a wonderful teacher.

And, in an interview just prior to his death in 2003, the prolific (and sometimes outrageous) literary critic Leslie Fiedler observed, "Sometimes you find someone who's brilliant but they're selfish with their genius. Not Ruth. Wherever she went, she created a warm spot in the world, a place where other writers could come."

It's the inconspicuous elegance of lines like "the birch trees are wrapped in their white bandages" or Stone's ability to describe silence as "a glitch, like a pause / in abnormal breathing; and the large comfortable casket of snow." that readers find so engaging. Because Stone uses the stuff of daily life, describing, for example, a Midwestern sky as "fractured clouds like cotton wipes," or the job of a poet as inventing the universe with a handful of alphabet letters written on a few blocks, the average person does not feel intimidated by her poetry. Even when the subject is death and the loneliness of the person left behind, Stone's poetry remains accessible and rich in tangible meaning while also being fresh and inventive. You can see this in this poem from the collection *In the Dark:*

### I Walk Alone

Along the street at night,
sometimes the rain;
its bodiless déjà-vu,
random street,
the rain's velvet scrim.
Almost the whisper of your voice,
as I remember
your elegant fingers
in the flare of a match,
as we paused on the edge
of that illusion
that now rises from the dead,
that returns years from then
without warning,
on this dark street
where I stand transfixed,
embraced, but only by the wind.[7]

Former Vermont State Poet Laureate Galway Kinnell, one of the five judges for the 2002 Academy of American Poets award, describes Stone's poems this way: "They startle us over and over with their shapelessness, their humor, their youthfulness, their wild aptness, their strangeness, their sudden familiarity, the authority of their insights, the moral gulps they prompt, their fierce exactness of language and memory. Her poems are experiences, not the record of experiences. They are events, interactions between the poet and the world. They happen—there on the page before us and within us—surprising and inevitable."

Stone says the trick is being able to shut some of the world's sadness and the incongruity of life out, to take tragedy in manageable doses—and to balance it with more pleasant memories of the calmer, sweeter moments of life. "Otherwise we die. The suffering that goes on in this world is too terrible. Some man lost his entire family yesterday. I heard it on the news. A car accident and five people killed. That man had his whole life wiped out. I wept last night for him. It's absolutely beyond comprehension. You have to take comfort where you can—in the nuthatches coming to the feeder, in the warmth of the woodstove, in the voices of your lovely grandchildren. You have to allow yourself to take joy. Otherwise, you are no good to anyone."

A striking woman with long, henna-dyed hair swept into a careless topknot, expressive mouth, high cheekbones, and those electrifying brown eyes of hers, Stone maintains a humorous philosophy about her recent successes. "It's good to get it while I'm still around, but what took them so long?" she asks, then chuckles, adding, "Well, better late than never."

Photo by Chuck Clarino

## ABIGAIL STONE, STORYTELLER

Abigail Stone is proud of her existence on the fringe. She lives in a white house next to the stump dump on the outskirts of Middlebury. Her books and her songs reflect a certain self-derision that's allowed her to cope with her own challenges as she's raised three children by herself, often struggling simply to keep the house warm and enough food in the larder. To a certain degree, it's been a lonely life as she, like her mother, has cobbled out a living, supplementing writing income with occasional teaching gigs and selling antiques on eBay. Yet, Abigail Stone remains positive, her work humorous, deep and philosophical, politically relevant, and entirely accessible.

She says she's defended herself against pessimism by keeping play in her life—whether it's the childish pleasure of playing house and word games, collecting dolls, old books, antiques and whimsy or allowing herself to write the kind of novels she wants to write rather than submit to requests for mainstream pulp fiction. She learned that humor keeps a sad story from becoming maudlin and self-irony is good defense against despair. Her stories, while fictional, are grounded in the realities of a young single mother coping with poverty and cold in rural Vermont, and with many other real-life themes: terrorism and war as seen through the eyes of the Vietnam veteran; the young artist whose NEA grant is cut while millions are spent on defense; the single woman looking for Mr. Perfect in a bar frequented by three-time losers; the paranoia inherent in a society where phones and e-mail can be tapped or where your personal data is up for grabs at the grocery store checkout counter. You'll recognize the people in Abigail Stone's stories; you might even see yourself. That's because she's so adroit at capturing people and creating believable scenes that feel taken from everyday life in Vermont.

One reason her work is so successful is because she's so good at capturing dialogue. Abigail Stone says she's been paying close attention to oral language all her life. Skipping from one school to another, she often missed essential bits of information, both culturally and academically. She needed to pay attention to language to learn the idioms of her ever-changing school chums. She let her environment and the people in it, particularly writers and artists and musicians, be her teachers. And, early on, she began to capture conversation on the page in both stories and songs.

### Tips and Techniques

Dialogue does many things: it can provide background information, show the interaction of characters, tell us about events to come, and otherwise further the development of a book's plot. It is also a tool for creating character. Each character in a work, whether fictional or real, should have his or her own unique way of talking—not just favorite words and expressions but also tone and speed, rhythm and syntax. Many stories fail because there is not enough differentiation among the characters' individual voices.

Dialogue should sound as normal as possible but that only happens through careful construction. In normal conversation, we take shortcuts and use personal idioms. We talk quickly, mispronouncing or dropping words and sometimes speaking with regional accents that might be lost on the written page. So much of communication lies in the nuances of word selection, pronunciation, emphasis, and the accompanying body language; meaning is often conveyed through mannerisms as much as through the actual words. The writer's job in re-creating conversation, therefore, is quite complex. She needs to find ways to capture the particular mannerisms and choice of words that allow the reader to distinguish one character from another while also ensuring that the dialogue sounds natural. Too many uses of colloquialisms, arcane language, regionalisms, and dialect serve only to irritate the reader. Yet, we want to read language of a place and time, so some idioms and other quirks of speech and regionalisms are essential. A Valley Girl from the 1980s would use entirely different language than a rapper from the 2000s. A Vermont farmer in his seventies would speak differently than a burnt-out hippie in her fifties. But how many idioms and regionalisms and other conversational oddities are too many? The only way to know if your language is both individual enough to belong to the real or imaginary character who is speaking while also understandable and nongrating to the reader is to read it aloud and to have others read your composed conversations both to themselves and out loud. You'll hear places where the language clunks, where it sounds false or unnatural, where it's clichéd, gimmicky, or overdone.

Perhaps more than the other women in her family, Abigail Stone is interested in communication as a social tool, a tool for change. She's the most outspoken politically in the family and her work reflects her concerns about the environment, about war and poverty and environmental degradation much more directly than either her mother's or sister Phoebe's work. Her commitment arises in part from her place in the family: the youngest child, she grew up in the hotbed of the 1960s counter-culture. Also, as a song-writer, she's learned the power of repetition to underscore meaning. The songwriter also deals with contemporary themes more often than arcane philosophical ones. While no one would accuse Abigail Stone of being prac-tical—she'd spend her last penny on a prized volume or a collector's item rather than pay the phone bill—she's very aware of contemporary issues. She's also gutsy and frank. And so are her characters.

She describes her second novel, *Recipes From the Dump*,[8] as "a mock cookbook of our culture. Spoken in the first person, the main character is a single mother of three, trying to cope in a world that appears to be falling apart."[9] Her main character, Gabby Fulbriten, reads the personals and takes evening walks with her wise neighbor, Hester, all the while assembling recipes to make sense of life. Her neighbor Hester represents the world that was—older Vermont—while the condominiums the two women watch being built near their homes represent a changing Vermont, a new world. Gabby doesn't belong in either world. Somewhat romantic and old-fashioned (she listens to Shakespeare on cassette) she is sad about the state of love between men and women. Yet her dates with the men in town or, at least the ones she meets—garbage collectors and religious fanatics among them—are far from satisfying. The world is changing around her. Her chil-dren are growing and moving on. New people are moving into town. Yet Gabby's future remains unclear. She does the right things—diets and recy-cles the cat food cans—but love and contentment elude her.

Dialogue is essential to Abigail Stone's novels. The plot of *Recipes from the Dump* is told primarily through dialogue. At times, the narrator Gabby talks directly to the reader. Elliot Gilbert of the *California Quarterly* calls her method "weaving," meaning that, rather than write a narrative thread of chapters that follow a tight plot development, she presents events as they occur in real life—randomly and out of order.[10] Together, like a collage or a woven shawl, the scenes and Gabby's ruminations on them weave to-gether to create an unsettling mood, one that provides commentary on con-temporary life rather than contributing to a story told in the traditional sense of a novel.

"Life doesn't always happen in the neat, tied-up versions that are presented in most novels," Abigail Stone says. "What I write is lifelike fiction, leaping in to the story without long introductions, and ending it without marriage or death, in the way real life behaves." She observes that real life happens with few explanations. People act, they talk, they respond, but there's very little analysis. It all just happens, sometimes with fore-thought, often without. "I'm trying to create that same experience in my novels, to show the chaos of life, along with its surprising points of perfect comprehension."

Photo by Chuck Clarino

## PHOEBE STONE, ARTIST AND FICTION WRITER

Phoebe Stone says of her childhood, "Mother believed in the beauty of words, in the healing power of art. I believe I was made of poetry, because I heard so much of it growing up." You can hear the poetry—and also children's lullabies and the sounds of animals and nature itself—in Phoebe's writing. Even in childhood and youth, she filled her room with paintings. She painted on long canvas window shades she found in the attic when she couldn't get to the art store to buy canvases. Her room was full of books and notebooks of her own writing that she composed on "my crummy old typewriter that always seemed to need a new ribbon. I was always working on more than one thing at a time . . . writing a short story . . . making a painting. There were sewing projects strewn around the room, too, dolls I made and fabric I was block-printing. One year I designed and sewed my entire wardrobe for the year. I made my own patterns and every outfit included a hat. I worked hard on these things, my painting and my writing, my reading and my sewing, all through my childhood. I worked very hard."

Working hard, being productive, and having fun are still important to Ruth Stone's middle daughter. Phoebe Stone began her professional life as an artist. Her artwork, often giant canvases painted with pastel crayons, is flamboyant and fantastic. With her flying people, her wild animals and flowers, and the bright colors on her canvases, her work reminds one of Chagall or Gauguin. Yet it is entirely hers, populated by icons and memories from her own personal history. She began drawing so early in life that she can't remember a time when she didn't, but it was her father's death (when she was eleven) that ended what she considers an idyllic childhood and propelled her into storytelling in her drawings. Her paintings create a world, part fairy tale, part real life. It's as if real life isn't manageable without the enchanted past.

That need for a fairy-tale world is tangible as one strolls through her studio in Middlebury: peach-colored, surrounded by flowers outside, and decorated with homemade art inside. Tables and cabinets are painted with

Baltimore orioles, dancers, and elephants. Her collections of antique dolls, teddy bears, and furniture perfectly supplement the brightly painted walls and furniture. She's made some of her dishes, upholstered her chairs and couches in old-fashioned flowered chintz, and splashed color everywhere: "I like to create my own world. My editor says walking into my house is like walking into one of my books. I like that—the lack of separation between the world in which I live and the world that I create in my paintings and books. I need to be surrounded by beautiful things."

The editor of Jewish Lights Publishing, headquartered in Woodstock, Vermont, gave Phoebe Stone her start in illustrating children's books. In 1994, Stuart Matlins, of Jewish Lights, saw Phoebe's artwork at a gallery in Woodstock and asked her to illustrate a children's book called *In God's Name*. The book celebrates the underlying commonality among religions and, with more than eighty-five thousand books sold, remains one of Jewish Lights' most successful publications.[11]

Phoebe Stone compares the creation of her original thirty-two-page books, such as *When the Wind Bears Go Dancing*[12] and *Go Away, Shelley Boo!*,[13] to creating a symphony with many instruments or an opera with many singers. Not only does the text have to tell an engaging story with all the elements of affective narration—character, action, plot, situation, and resolution—but the illustrations need to tell a story on their own. (And, if you look carefully at a Phoebe Stone book, you'll see minor plots among minor characters.) Coordinating word story with picture story requires careful orchestration. Each illustration goes through several executions, each created with the detail of a fine-art painting.

Likewise, the stories in her young readers' books go through many revisions. Her stories, whether it's the young readers' books like *When the Wind Bears Go Dancing* and *Go Away Shelley Boo!* or the novels for older children such as *All the Blue Moons at the Wallace Hotel*[14] and *Sonata #1 For Riley Red,*[15] address common childhood fears—of storms, strangers, change, being different—although the characters in these books also operate from an inner strength that allows them to embrace their fears, quirks, and individuality. Phoebe Stone explains how she used real events and her imagination to construct *All the Blue Moons at the Wallace Hotel*, her first novel for readers aged ten: "I set the story near Poughkeepsie, New York, on the Hudson River where we lived when I was a child before my father died. The town I created was a fictional mishmash of Poughkeepsie memories and my memories of growing up in Goshen. For instance, I transformed the rambling old farmhouse on the mountain in Goshen into the dilapidated mansion where the family in *All the Blue Moons at the Wallace Hotel* lived. I used true details and fact to give feeling and validity to the dreamed-up world that I created. I worked in a kind of parallel dimension alongside of the truth, weaving in and out of it. Kip (a fictional friend in the novel) was a mishmash of boys Abby and I played with and loved as children."

In the novel, Fiona and Wallace Hopper live with their artist mother in a neglected mansion littered with half-finished sculptures. The children are ashamed of the condition of their home. They try to keep secret its disrepair and the tragedy that has immobilized their mother. Like her name, Wallace is unusual; she cares very little about what others might think of her. She wears two party dresses at once, dislikes wearing socks, and counts among her friends an elderly woman with an atrium full of exotic birds. Unlike Wallace, Fiona longs to be accepted by her peers; more than anything, she wants to perform in an upcoming ballet recital. Fiona practices tirelessly, knowing that she is meant to be a dancer. She can still remember when the house was filled with laughter, music, and parties, and she hopes that her family will emerge from the shadows of tragedy. Fiona's family loyalty is tested when Wallace disappears and Fiona must forgo a dance audition to search for her sister. Life takes unexpected turns and a disaster at the dance studio creates an opportunity for Fiona and her family, who not only learn to take risks and trust others but also learn how to be a family again.

Phoebe Stone's other young adult novel, *Sonata #1 For Riley Red,* explores similar themes of hope and fear. It features thirteen-year-old Rachel Townsend, the daughter of a jazz musician who now works as superintendent of the apartment building where the family lives. Rachel also lives with a painful secret that has made her a loner at school until she is rescued by two other eccentrics: the wealthy brother and sister team of drama queen Desmona and her cool, older brother Riley. Riley—named for his red hair—dresses like Bob Dylan and drives a little red sports car. Desmona collects the outcasts at school, including a boy named Woolsey who lives in the same apartment building as Rachel. The group, driven by Desmona's desire to do one "extraordinary great deed," drives around Harvard Square and environs rescuing cats and dogs from the pound and planning other animal rescues. This leads them to the zoo in a nearby city where they plot to rescue a neglected circus elephant. Then the plot really thickens.

Desmona and Riley's mother committed suicide by drowning while clutching pages of her poems. The children's stepmother is a former Miss West Germany, who doesn't understand Desmona as the girl stages a protest at the school cafeteria for serving veal or takes it upon herself to find homes for all the cats and dogs in the Somerville pound. And, Woolsey's life is no easier, with social service workers poking around and asking questions of his father, a man who spends his time watching the Red Sox from a wheelchair and reliving one fateful day in Normandy. The children have choices to make as the book unfolds, choices that many children face, although perhaps with less drama. Here, again, Phoebe Stone uses elements of her own childhood: trying to figure out how to fit in, what to do about the pain and anger she felt over the loss of a parent, an early sense of protectiveness toward wild and tame animals, and each person's need to establish her own values. She cautions would-be writers of children's literature not to assume that the writing is any easier simply because it's for a younger audience. Indeed, it may be harder. "You are not free to use the entire language but must tell your story from a part of yourself that you have grown beyond linguistically and emotionally," she explains. "The story must speak to both children and adults and must be told simply and powerfully with enormous economy of words. So you can see how having lived all my life with poetry comes in handy."

---

**◆§** FROM *In the Dark*

### "Am I"
by Ruth Stone

I am outside the Boston Psychopathic.
I ascend to the third floor and look in a window.
Dennis Leigh, Neuro-surgeon and Freudian analyst
is sitting at his desk. He has my case.
Later in a suburb of London he will say over the phone,
when I tell him my husband has hung himself,
"Well, what do you want me to do about that?"
His wife explains that it is his arthritis
that makes him so irritable.
The suicide had nothing to do with international crisis.
His death came between wars.
He may have identified with Keats (owls, nightingales,
Hampstead Heath), but it was only a rooming house.
The problem with all this is, first I saw the psychiatrist,
then the events. Did he die before or afterward?
However, the Doctor played tennis.
The window overlooks the Atlantic. The porthole
is open. The mineral air, so good for you.
Or in the ship's bar, queasy, listening, with the swell,
you smell the spar varnish.
How inadequate; right out of the avenues
of Indianapolis, running in from the outskirts,
you seem to have brought Mr Vogule along with you.
He was the gradeschool janitor from Switzerland
who had a tobacco-yellowed mustache
and danced and sang and slept by the furnace
and shoveled the path through the snow
to the girl's outdoor toilet. See, you say,
that was easy. The doctor knows you are there.
He is making his English effort to be severe with
your attractive body. You are sitting across from him
in the patient's chair. By now he will be seventy or dead.
He gave you bad advice. The usual educated ignorant

British male practice. If you looked quickly you could
see his slight smile go slack. All the time his wife
was secretly calling him from overseas. Someone
wanted him for hand ball. "Am I crazy," you asked an intern
late the first night in the sterilized room;
your personality like moth wings, shredding itself
on the hospital furniture. "I don't know," he said.
It was a hard fact.[16]

### "Another Feeling"

Once you saw a drove of young pigs
crossing the highway. One of them
pulling his body by the front feet,
the hind legs dragging flat.
Without thinking,
you called the Humane Society.
They came with a net and went for him.
They were matter of fact, uniformed;
there were two of them,
their truck, ominous, with a cage.
He was hiding in the weeds. It was then
you saw his eyes. He understood.
He was trembling.
After they took him, you began to suffer regret.
Years later, you remember his misfit body,
scrambling to reach the others.
Even at this moment, your heart
is going too fast; your hands sweat.[17]

---

◄§ FROM *In the Next Galaxy*

### "Mantra"
by Ruth Stone

When I am sad
I sing, remembering
the redwing blackbird's clack.
Then I want no thing
except to turn time back
to what I had
before love made me sad.

When I forget to weep,
I hear the peeping tree toads
creeping up the bark.

Love lies asleep
and dreams that everything
is in its golden net;
and I am caught there, too,
when I forget.[18]

---

**◄§ FROM *Recipes From the Dump***

by Abigail Stone

I fear for Mr. Boots's life. Earlier today he drove on through the gate and headed up to the back pastures to look after his herd. Frankly, I think the baby cow with hoof disease might die. He limped around for two days and the mother seemed to have given up on him entirely. After all that mooing and then Mr. Boots coming with the Clorox, maybe she felt there was nothing else she could do. In any case, she didn't nudge him to nurse or even wait for him when the herd moved on to the lower pasture.

Well, now, Mr. Boots has been out there for close to all day, I'd say, and the way he climbs over the fence and gets right in with them, I'm afraid they've knocked him down in this muddy season and have trampled him by accident. They wouldn't do it on purpose, would they? I think they love him, although when he was here with the Clorox they all clustered around me and the kids and wouldn't give him the time of day. He even remarked on it.

"They like you better'n they do me," he said.

And I said, "Maybe that's because they know what you have in store for them."

"Maybe," he agreed.

But now he has disappeared and I wonder . . . should I call the police? The game warden? Dorothy Stella? Today is Sunday and I'm sure Dorothy Stella is back from church. She's a churchgoing woman, I know.

This worry I have about Mr. Boots fits in with my walk yesterday with Hester. We went down the grassy road toward the back pasture, and when we got to the lower gate the cows saw us. They had been munching quietly, but they mooed wildly and moved in a great rush toward the fence.

"Let's go!" I shrieked, and we both hurried back the way we come.

"They can't get out," Hester said, running nevertheless.

"That big one looks like he could knock the gate over," I said.

"I don't care if he's been doctored or not," Hester said, slowing up a bit. "I won't walk in a pasture with a bull. Once a bull, always a bull, doctored or not."

It relates to all species, I think. It made me think, Well, maybe men will come around again. Once a man, always a man. I find a lot of wisdom in my neighbor.

"One of my boys was down today," Hester said on our evening walk. " He said he had a pair of bluebirds in his yard. . . . Why, I haven't seen bluebirds for . . . years."

I shook my head. "I know, I know!" I said, closing my umbrella and letting the rain fall on me. "I never see bluebirds."

"They say they are . . . well, scarce," Hester explained. She carried her little black umbrella over her head and walked beside me in striped shorts and a white T-shirt. I had been away for a few days and she had told me she missed me. "No one to walk with," she'd said.

"The hummingbirds aren't around anymore either," I said. "That's because the rain forests are being ruined. You know, they don't have anywhere to live. And the songbirds are all dying out from the pesticides. . ."

"Hey-yup," she said. "My boy brought up a mother duck with a stick to shove in the ground, you know . . . and a little baby duck that's white and one that's black, same as she is. They're all wooden and they go in the yard."

We stopped as she said this in front of the gate that led to the river. The river roared through the electric plant and followed the wide bed on through the Vermont countryside, way beyond Leadbelly.

When Hester and I walked home again, we noticed the rain had brought puddles to the road and in the puddles was an oily yellow substance.

"Is it paint?" I asked her. "Maybe it's raining pollution," I said.

"Maybe," she answered. "You finished yer sampler quilt?"

I said I hadn't. I had made a house square and a square of appliquéd flowers. The flowers were in a pink field with green leaves everywhere.

When I was little we used to run barefoot through fields full of Indian paintbrush and daisies. I worry that the wild flowers are disappearing too. I guess I worry too much, but I notice the fields are only full of McDonald's wrappers and tough grass, that even the cows seem unsatisfied with the colorless foliage.

I want to tell Hester something funny before we part for the evening, but I can't think of anything. My teenage daughter walks toward us, glaring and holding a purple umbrella. She is full of the empty hours of being thirteen . . . she would like to be recognized but her mother and her brother and sister don't see her for what she really is. Maybe we will, later on . . . or maybe she will tell us to help clarify. Anyway, I only say, "Well, I'll see you tomorrow, Hester. Bye," and I turn to go.

"I put on a little weight while you were gone," she calls to me, "so let's walk every morning, and evening too."

I say okay, I will, but I know I am confused with all the things I have to do. There is so much to do in this culture. We are required to do so many things. I don't know what they are exactly, but there's a lot of pressure out there to be perfect.

Perfectly Lovely Glacé

1. 1 home, so tidy, so clean, so gingham and cheerful, with pots on the walls that you never use, and dishes in cupboards that never fall off
2. A friendly husband who works at a wonderful job and wears checkered warm shirts and builds porches in the evenings. He laughs a lot and hugs you while you prepare dinner.
3. Children who never glare
4. A beautiful body, thanks to aerobics classes at the local health club. You work out with all the other good-looking married women in town. They laugh with you while you shower and dress in your clean, crisp, size 8 clothes.
5. A dog that doesn't smell or pee on the floor; a fluffy cat that doesn't urinate on your quilt pieces
6. An appetite that doesn't border on the psychotically voracious
7. A cheerful, rewarding job that lets you vacation a few times a year with your hubby in warm climates

Cookbooks always relax me because I can walk through them with my longing eyes and devour all the recipes and calming instructions and descriptions without ever dirtying a dish.[19]

---

◄§ FROM *All the Blue Moons at the Wallace Hotel*

by Phoebe Stone

We have finally made it home, but we ended up having to walk in the dark up the last part of the hill. Even with the chains on the tires, the cruiser couldn't get through the snow. Officer Wolf Mc-Kane carried Wallace, because she fell asleep in the car. My mother held the big police flashlight, and I had to carry the new teddy bear. It kind of felt good to hug something. It wasn't a long walk, and Alto got to run around ahead of us sniffing everything.

When we got up to the front door, we had to push the snow aside to get in. Officer Wolf McKane said, "Gee, I haven't been here in a long time. What's it been, four years?" He put Wallace down in the hallway and stomped the snow off his boots. Wallace didn't know where she was when she opened her eyes.

"You fell asleep, Wallace," I said.

"I did not," she said. "I was faking."

Officer Wolf McKane stands now in the hallway and looks around. He glances into the empty rooms behind me. I feel like covering the doorway with my body. *Stop. Don't look at our house*, I want to say. *Go away.* Then he slaps his gloved hands together and says, "Well, I guess if everything's all right now, I'll round up Alto and be on my way."

It's not that I don't like Officer Wolfe McKane. He has a nice face, but it reminds me of things. When I look at his face, it's the way I feel when I'm late for school, or the way I feel when I look out the window at the lonely orchard in the night. Nell thinks Officer Wolf McKane is handsome. Whenever she mentions his name, I always change the subject.

"Don't look so glum, Fiona," Officer Wolf McKane says to me. "We got your little sister home safe." He pats me on the back. I can feel the wool of his uniform brushing against my arm, and I remember the itchy, rough texture. I have this feeling he's going to say more, and I don't want him to. I want him to not say anything. I wish I could put my hands over my ears. I want to shout out, *NO, NO. Don't say anything else.*

My mother is looking at him, nodding her head up and down, but her eyebrows are pointed up as if she is pleading with Officer McKane. Her head goes up and down, up and down.

Suddenly I can't hear what he's saying anymore. I'm just remembering that I was outside in the garden with Wallace. I was standing near the window of the dining room and I could hear my father and a man I didn't know talking loudly. The man's voice grew louder and louder. He was shouting about money. Then my father started to shout, too. I was right near the window, trying to get a ball that had fallen into a bed of flowers. I was leaning over when I heard the terrible sound, the loudest sound I've ever heard, a terrifying explosion.

Then I heard my mother screaming. It filled the whole valley below. It filled the orchard and the trees along the road. It filled the whole world.

Then the man was running. He was knocking things over. He bumped into me and I fell in the flowers. Wallace was three and a half, and started to cry. I knew something was wrong, but I didn't want to go into the house.

"Daddy, Daddy," I called out, "Daddy, Daddy, Daddy."

Then I just lay there on my back, with Wallace lost in the tall sunflowers nearby. I just lay there on my back with bees flying all around me and the sky a dreadful, bright blue.

My father was an art dealer. The man was an art collector. He was crazy. He shouted and shouted. Then he shot and killed my Daddy while Wallace and I were in the garden. Officer Wolf McKane came to help. He wouldn't let me see my father, and he held me down. I was screaming, "Daddy, Daddy, Daddy."[20]

## Questions and Exercises for Reflection and Inspiration

When the Stone family was growing up, they didn't have television or video games. They used to play the Poetry Game.

> **Exercise 1:** You can play the game in a class, a writing group, with family members or friends, or at a party. Here's how to play: Everyone writes down a word (almost any word will do) on a scrap of paper. Your word doesn't have to be a big word or a "poetic word" but the game works best if you pick a noun, a verb, an adjective, or an adverb, rather than prepositions and articles. Try to pick a word that your game companions won't necessarily associate with you; the game is more fun if people don't know whose word is whose. One person collects all the words and puts them in an envelope or box, then reads them off in random fashion while the other players write them down. Each player writes a poem using all the words. The poem can be in any format: rhymed or not, stylized or free verse. When you're done, gather around and read the poems aloud. See how different your poems are, even though they share so many words.

> **Exercise 2:** Here's another poetry game for three or more people to play. Take a piece of blank typing or printer paper. Turn it sideways and fold it in half so your paper is roughly 5½ inches wide by 8 inches long. If you are writing with a large group of people, divide yourselves into groups of three or four players; give each group a piece of paper. The first writer in each group writes a line of verse (a sentence or phrase of six or more words will do) on the paper without the others seeing the words. Write fast; the game isn't any fun if the players think too much or too long. When the first player has finished his line, he reads the last two words only out loud, then folds the paper over so the words can't be seen. The next player writes a line of words on what is now the top of the paper, again silently, reading only the last two words aloud, then folds the paper over and hands it to the next player who writes his line of verse and so on. When you've gone through your group one time, the first player gets to write a line again. Try to write small enough so that everyone has three turns.

> When you are through, unfold the paper from its accordion-like shape and have one player from each group read the poem aloud. You'll be amazed by what you've written; invariably, a poem written this way has several threads running through it. Two things happen

at once in an exercise like this: there's the natural tendency to respond to your partners' words juxtaposed with the equally natural tendency to express yourself in your own words and voice. The combination of the two often creates a quite magical composition, a group poem with a found message. This is a fun activity for a party or special occasion, and it works equally well with good friends and people who are simply acquaintances. It's particularly fun if you have enough people for two groups.

Ruth Stone's poetry combines everyday elements—tissues, car keys, moth wings, pigs crossing the road—with more personal words that are specific to the impetus for writing a particular poem, such as the Boston Psychopathic clinic and Mr. Vogule. The reader embraces the unknown details because he or she has been supplied with universal images and metaphors around which to build an understanding of the poet's emotions.

**Exercise 3:** Write a list of generic nouns that represent a particular mood, such as anger, disappointment, fear, or hope. For anger, for example, you might use words like fire, scars, explosion, or poison. Take each word and play with using it metaphorically, making a list of metaphors that express the mood you're after. Extend the metaphor and combine it with something specific in your own life. For example, I might want to write a poem that compares a lost love with a forest fire, something many people can relate to. At the same time, however, I might want to make the poem particular to a real experience in my own life, something that haunts me years later. The end result might be something like:

> Our love was the kindling in a forest fire,
> Waiting to unleash its destructive power, scarring
> All that stood in its way when it finally exploded
> Full force, there on the unsuspecting Hogback Mountain.
> My body made it down the slope before the flames
> But I was like the conifers that stood, long years later,
> Blackened, heart-dead, sentinels against an uncaring sky.

All the images in this poem except Hogback Mountain are universal. The words "Hogback Mountain" carry both personal and universal meaning. A reader can picture a mountain that might be called Hogback, while the words relate to a very specific mountain. It is from the combination of universal and personal imagery that poems are made.

Try writing your own poem by combining universal images, metaphors. and details specific to an event in your own life. Remember that metaphors are bridges; they connect words that are not alike to create something new, an amalgamation of meaning that brings with it the strength of both words. In the poem above, "love," of course, has a whole host of meanings, as does "kindling." By connecting the two words, the poem's opening line suggests warmth and comfort at the same time that it implies danger. In your own poem, choose words that bring multiple meanings with them so that the reader experiences the pleasure of understanding the subtle undertones of meaning that you want to express without doing so directly.

Abigail Stone's work relies heavily on dialogue. In her stories, the narrator often speaks directly to the reader. It's as if we are in the reader's head, hearing her internal dialogue; or sometimes, as if we are reading her diary. This technique gives the work an intimacy that is both engaging and effective. Abigail weaves these internal dialogues with conversation between the narrator and other characters in the book in a way that makes the reader feel present while the conversation is going on. Dialogue must sound natural but also be accessible: the reader doesn't want to hear "um," "you know," and other sounds that normally occur in conversations. One way to get better at writing dialogue is to pay close attention to conversations going on all around you, particularly ones that you overhear randomly in coffeehouses, grocery stores, and other public settings—strangers' conversations,

**Exercise 4:** Try this technique for improving dialogue in your short story, novel, essay, or other creative work: Go to a public place, bringing your journal with you. Eavesdrop on the conversations around you and write down snippets of conversation as they present themselves. You'll notice that your notes will contain intimations of concern, fear, desire, happiness and/or unhappiness. That's because people often have intimate conversations over a cup of coffee or in a cozy setting like a bookstore café. That's why many of these conversations begin with statements like, "I'm so angry I could spit," or, "You'll never imagine what happened to me," or "So, what's happening between you and Peter?" You may also find it useful to record some particular details about the surroundings, the environment, and the people whose conversation you're overhearing. Later, try to construct a story around these characters, filling in an imaginary "backstory" for the conversation. Remember to give each speaker an individual voice and language so that the reader can easily distinguish between the speakers. Use the conversation both to create character and to further a simple plot. Remember that most stories are about people wanting something—material or immaterial—and either getting the object of their desire or being prevented from obtaining it.

Phoebe Stone realized as a young child that in-group members tend to bond together along lines of similarity—fashion sense, the right neighborhood, economic status—while a group of misfits tend to bond together along lines of their differences. In this way, unpopularity frees them to be different and to feel comfortable expressing their differences as members of a group of oddballs. That was the theme, for example, of the popular teenage movie of the 1980s *The Breakfast Club*, and it's the theme of her book, *Sonata #1 For Riley Red*. One could argue that there is greater freedom to appreciate the differences among friends in a group of misfits than in an in-group. In terms of fiction, it's certainly more fun to create oddball characters than ordinary ones or ones who follow the herd. Much of great literature has followed the theme of celebrating the oddballs in our midst and such is particularly true of Vermont literature.

> **Exercise 5:** Create your own cast of oddball characters, giving each a singular nickname, a curious hobby, an unusual favorite food, a distinctive way of dressing, and a commitment to some belief or ideal. Give them something to do together, such as setting off on a cross-country trip or shopping for Thanksgiving dinner. What happens to them in Idaho or South Dakota or in a Burlington grocery store? How do others respond to their oddness and how do they respond to the responses of strangers?

Photo by Rutland Studios of Rutland, Vermont

# 17  Tom Smith

## *Finding Oneself*

Born 19 March 1933, Schenectady, New York

Education: B.A., State University of New York; graduate studies, Rutgers
University

Lives in Castleton

First publication: poem, "A Game of Snow," in a small literary magazine,
in 1959

Books of Poetry: *Some Traffic* (1976); *Singing the Middle Ages* (1982); *Traffic*
(1985); *The Broken Iris* (1991); *Cow'sleap: A Nightbook* (1999); *Waiting
on Pentecost* (1999); *Trash: The Dahmer Sonnets* (2000); *Spending the
Light* (2004)

Novel: *A Well-Behaved Little Boy* (1995)

Awards: *Spending the Light* was nominated for a Pulitzer Prize

L IKE MANY VERMONT WRITERS, Tom Smith found himself living in the Green Mountain State first by happenstance and later by desire. In the years prior to his 1964 move to Castleton to teach at the small
state college located there (for what he thought would be just a year or two,
three at most) Smith had led a ribald life. He loved to throw a good party,
loved theater and acting, loved song and dance, and loved writing. But in
New York and New Jersey, where he had been acting and teaching college
courses before being hired to teach literature at Castleton State College, the
partying had too often taken precedence over the writing.

Here in Vermont, with an abundance of leisure time on his hands and a
reprieve from the heady social life, Smith's poetic voice grew to maturity.

He'd already been publishing poems and giving readings prior to moving to Vermont, but some time in those first years in Vermont, his inquiries about the nature of the human soul, his questions of gender and loyalty, his interest in human nature and his love of all sorts of games, myths, mysteries, oddities, and language coalesced into a very singular and individualistic writing style: "The thing I didn't know about the country was that you have to resort to your own resources to survive. It was exactly what I needed—and wanted—although I didn't know it at the time. It forced me to write. Vermont was a blessing. It's a place where you have peace of mind. Isn't that an interesting phrase? It could as easily be piece of mind. The lack of distraction here allows you to get work done, to focus your mind and whatever other faculties you use to make your craft. And, also, it's a lot easier to make a living here, especially if you land a teaching job, as I did. It's fairly hard to write when you're simply struggling to get by. I know I have been blessed."

Now in his seventies, Smith is a handsome man with thick, white hair, devilish blue eyes and an impishness that brightens the most melancholic conversation. He feels his life could have taken a short downward slide and acknowledges that landing in Vermont was a lucky break that put him on a path he'd always wanted, even if he didn't know it: a path of teaching and writing, being a father and husband, and belonging to a community that accepted him, despite his differences. Along with countless publications in literary magazines and the commercial press, he has published one novel and eight volumes of poetry, much of it coming into print in the last twenty years.

His work, like Smith himself, is a delightful amalgam of the old-fashioned and modern, of the classic with the experimental. He writes haikus, anagram poems, rhymed couplets, villanelles, sonnets, rhyming epigrams, and free verse. His subjects are equally diverse, simultaneously reverent and sacrilegious. He writes of the Virgin Mary and Jeffrey Dahmer, the mass murderer who ate his victims. He embraces the Greek myths and Elvis Presley, Alice in Wonderland, and tabloid journalism. The lover of word games enjoys Smith's poetry as much as the reader who enjoys analyzing symbols and metaphor.

While Smith is a serious scholar, he also likes to have a lot of fun with his writing. His poem "Woman Finds Dead Leprechaun in a Jar" is a good example of his use of wordplay. Like the other poems in his latest collection, *An Embarrassment of Riches*, this poem is based on an actual headline that Smith discovered in a newspaper.[1] Over the years, he's culled dozens of headlines from stories that have appeared in the media, from the *New York Times* to tabloid newspapers, and used these as inspiration for poems that, often humorously, explore human foibles.

### "Woman Finds Dead Leprechaun in a Jar"

Bridey Macabee faded slowly to her knees through the
    breathtaking
attic heat, folded into a seated position on the silverfish slivered
floor beside an heirloom trunk in the act
of claiming her inheritance. Her grandfather's old house whispered
behind her, around her, beneath. She harkened unable
to shape any word.
She lifted
the lid
to discover (among costumes and paraphernalia, relics
from the traveling sideshow of which her grandfather, still
in Ireland, had been the ringmaster)
the old man's journal and a mason
jar.
The quart-sized jar contained a wee man glowing green and no
bigger than a pickled pepper, grinning beneath the brim of a green
trilby, a rhinestone buckle on the band, and
matching buckles on the little dolly shoes, a grand
frock coat and breeches, also green, and candy
striped stockings.
The ancestor's journal claimed this was a leprechaun unearthed
from a peat bog in nineteen aught four, already long
drowned and preserved in those mystical
Irish waters.
Bridey Macabee observed that a leprechaun dead could not lead
her to buried treasure. Neither could he disappear if she simply
looked away. The fairy,
she thought, would make a curious display on the parlor mantel
flanked by candles and framed snaps, a family
shrine.

At any midnight now, in the sleeping house, the wee
man in the wee hours lifts the lid of his left eye
and the dull
orb sweeps the room in a counter-clockwise arc. In his glass
coffin, bored but not unhappy, he contemplates good or ill fortune,
a gas leak, a four-alarm fire, a fatal
collision, a winning
ticket.

—*Weekly World News*, 18 March 2003[2]

Here, Smith uses the language of the tabloid newspaper, albeit tongue in cheek, while also revisiting his Irish roots and mythologies. Irish luck, he knows as well as any Irishman, is often a mix of the good and bad. While the beneficiary of Irish luck might discover the silver lining in the direst occurrence, he would probably choose to avoid both the silver lining and the dark cloud, if he had his druthers. Like Pandora who opens the box containing chaos or Eve contemplating the apple, the woman in Smith's poetry is unaware of the potential good and harm that can come from her curiosity. The reader of this poem shares the knowledge that luck and opportunity are fickle companions, unpredictable and mysterious; the poem, inspired by a silly story in a tabloid magazine, reveals the uncertainty of existence. In its simplicity, like much of Smith's work, the poem suggests how little we really know of the life going on around and within us. And, all the while, he makes us smile. Smith has been doing that for nearly fifty years—since 1959, when his first poem was published.

Smith was born in March 1933 in Schenectady, New York. It was the Depression era; his father—a sometimes truck driver, sometimes bartender — was often out of work, which made life at home difficult. At the beginning of World War II, his father got a job at General Electric; conditions improved at home but life remained challenging for Smith who describes himself at age four as "a pretty boy, effeminate. . . . The only person in the world who ever walked quite naturally like Marilyn Monroe was me. I had to learn not to walk like that."

One can only imagine what life was like for a sensitive, feminine boy growing up in a straitened working-class neighborhood. "I suffered a lot in school because I was different," Smith recalls. "Later on, those differences become blessings but it was a struggle reaching that point. I was constantly called names; even the teachers ridiculed me."

Smith's younger brother was good in sports, "more normal," but, even though he enjoyed outdoor sports, from his earliest recollection, Smith much preferred spending his time going to the library, church, and the movies, reading poetry and writing. He liked the Catholic Church because it was pretty, "a great release from the ugliness of the neighborhood." The pomp and circumstance of the old Latin Mass appealed to his love of pageantry and his spiritual needs as well. It also appealed to his love of language, to the sound of words and to wordplay. The movies showed him the possibility of life beyond his working-class neighborhood. "What an escape they were," he recalls of his early love of cinema. "They took me not just out of Schenectady, but out of myself. Thank God for them. I'm still totally devoted to the movies."

Smith was writing by fifth grade. His first experimentations were stories based on the Nancy Drew mystery series (not the Hardy Boys). "The problem with my murder mysteries was I couldn't finish them; they just went on and on. I could never solve the crimes," he says, laughing. He discovered verse in ninth grade, and immediately began imitating his favorites

(Carl Sandburg and Emily Dickinson, in particular) without much understanding of how to write a poem or how to express his complex feelings in verse. In his imagination, he pictured himself growing up to escape Schenectady and becoming a famous actor who also sang and danced, someone like Fred Astaire or Gene Kelly, or a famous writer like Carl Sandburg. He was prone to developing personas and speaking in what he thought was a poetic and artistic manner. Others probably found him affected.

Smith thinks all this made his father a little afraid of him—not just afraid of his son's femininity (in that era, at least in Schenedtady, no one ever talked about boys who were effeminate) but also afraid of his son's differences, as if he were a stranger, an alien. Smith's mother was kind and loving, sweet and unprejudiced, but she too had had little education; other than to accompany her son to an occasional movie, she didn't have time for poetry and pageantry. As a result, Smith spent a lot of time alone; he later found that he liked time alone and that alone time was essential to his writing life.

He thinks he might have been the first in his family to make it beyond junior high school, let alone college. It's not that there weren't stories in the family and storytellers. He comes from an Irish and Native American heritage. Smith's favorite tale was about his father's grandfather, a Native American from the Hudson River Valley who went on to become mayor of the town of Red Hook, located in the Taconic Mountains. Still, he was the only one he knew in his neighborhood and school who loved books passionately and the only one he knew who fancied himself a writer. He kept most of the dreams about acting to himself, which was probably just as well. By fourth grade, his teachers were so concerned about his feminine behavior that they suggested to his parents, who agreed, that he be circumcised. The operation, they thought, might make Smith act more like a male. He recalls the event in the poem, "The Circumcision":

> Grade four was a battle
> of the sexes: he—unreachable
> sleeping beauty waiting
> for a kiss to wake him woman:
> Mrs. Buchanon, crown of thorns, determined
> he should be a boy. Though daily
> she'd point him out among his peers
> wagging her stout
> finger behind his wiggle: *is that*
> *a walk?* And nod
> heavily as the class
> shrilled over him fallen
> on the playground: *Maryjane!*
> Still he would show up Hallowe'en
> in lipstick and his mother's dress.

Mrs. Buchanon and the principal at last
called his mother to the office:
*something will have to be done*
*about Tommy.* The school
physician shrugged and suggested
circumcision. Tommy dreamed
for seven nights of the kiss
of the princely knife. Another seven
nights he dreamed of milkweed
pods exploding in shadow. The platinum
silk took flight.

I can remember very little
concerning the event: the bath
my mother gave me standing
me naked on a chair beside the zinc
blue kitchen sink. The blushing
Lifeboy lathering between my legs:
*this little piggy went to market.*
Also the redhead nurse whose laughter
teased me out of weeping as I came
from the anesthetic dark where time
and space caved in on dreams
and nothing was.

Tommy could remember only Tommy's eyes
that watched the milkweed mouth float
down to meet his gradual
dissolving
husk.[3]

The poem captures in heartbreaking understatement the confusion and helplessness of the child whose gender orientation didn't quite fit the mold. The poem "Circumcision" and the others collected in *Spending the Light,* (published in 2004) span work created over nearly fifty-five years. A line in the last poem in the book reflects upon the collection's title. It says of the aging poet, "He expects soon to be blind altogether." And so, Smith tells us, while light remains, the poet must use it to show how he has used the light all through his life. The book is a poetic roadmap through the events and places Smith has experienced, the people he has loved, the changes he has experienced.

When Smith talks of the experiences and differences that gave him pain as a child, but later became blessings, tops on his list would be his love for books and poetry. He may have been ridiculed in school for his effeminate behavior and love of learning, but he felt safe and nurtured in the library. His first job was shelving books in the library. There, the local librarian,

Dorothea Brown, paid attention to his interests, suggesting books he might enjoy and critiquing his work. It was his first clue that there was a life in letters and writing and that writing could be a career. "The public library had more to do with me finding my mind than the schools," he observes.

While still in high school, Smith met a male poet, a stern mentor of rigorous standards. The man was the late Luke Zilles, the author of a collection of poems entitled *A Conch of Bees*.[4] While at the State University of New York at Albany, Zilles published poetry regularly in the *New Yorker* and *Saturday Review*; later, he was a member of the Cedar Key Writers Workshop in Florida. Zilles was precisely what the young Smith needed. He gave "severe criticism. My stuff was never good enough for him. I think that was the greatest thing. He made me work, and then work some more," Smith recalls.

As high school was coming to an end, however, Smith was a bit lost. It was his teachers who knew that college was "the only place for me in the world." But his parents were no help with applications and the family had little money. Finally, several teachers urged him to apply for scholarships and Smith won a four-year scholarship to any of New York's state universities. The problem was that his grades in some subjects were so bad that he couldn't get accepted to any of them. The answer was a fifth year in high school, during which he buckled down and really applied himself to his studies—and enjoyed it. Smith went on to SUNY–Albany. Even though he had to live at home, commute by bus, and work for book and bus money, he loved university life. It provided him with his first taste of independence; even more important, for the first time he felt that he could be himself without constant ridicule.

At SUNY–Albany, he quickly made his way into not only literary circles but also dramatic ones, acting in *The Trojan Women, Macbeth, Mourning Becomes Electra, Desire Under the Elms,* and many other classics. And he was good; everyone said so. All his life, he had really wanted to be a movie star, performing in musical comedies, singing and dancing, doing all the things boys weren't supposed to do, Now, he was actually doing them. He pictured himself moving into a career that blended academia, writing, and acting; toward that end, he decided to go to graduate school.

At Rutgers University in New Jersey, he finally got to live on his own, without the scrutiny of his family. Here, too, he had a new mentor, Paul Fussell, author of more than a dozen books on culture, literature, and history. (Fussell's most famous book, *The Great War and Modern Memory*, won the National Book Award in 1976.)[5] Smith and Fussell became fast friends. Fussell's interests in writing, eighteenth-century literature, and twentieth-century social and cultural history, resonated with Smith, whose own interests ranged from classic literature, ancient myths, and biblical symbolism to American icons and movie stars. For someone whose interests and desires had been considered odd all his life, college and then graduate school were confirmations that others enjoyed the same kind of word games, heady conversations, and artistic pursuits as he did.

After college, Smith poured himself into his various interests: into writing, acting—and embracing the fact that he was gay. In his teens and early twenties, he was almost out of the closet. Later, he did tell his parents he was homosexual. Still, he desired normalcy and convinced himself that he would be happy if he just settled down. Thus, near the end of his senior year of college, he got married to a young woman he knew, hoping marriage would make him happy. It didn't: "We looked like a perfect couple but I was marrying her because she was conventional and she was marrying me because I was unconventional. We broke up after a couple of years. I was impossible, an alcoholic, promiscuous, gay male, leaving her on her own all the time. Just all around miserable."

After that marriage ended, he went to a therapist for a while and began to accept himself and put the marriage behind him. For a while, he devoted himself to the gay life. But he maintained one close female friend, Virginia DeAngelis, a talented soprano and actress who shared his passion for music, drama, and the arts. Over the months and then years, his friendship with Virginia turned into something else, something quite surprising. "We fell in love," he says. "She was a marvelous singer; she loved art and was such fun to be around, so accepting of who I was. Somehow it evolved into something else and that something else became marriage. Somehow that worked and it's worked ever since. We were married in 1965."

After graduate school and before finishing his thesis, he got the job teaching literature at Castleton. He and Virginia married after his first semester there; he planned to finish his thesis and earn his doctorate, but never did. Instead, he put his attentions into his teaching, writing, and family life. In the next three years, two sons were born. Virginia performed and gave vocal lessons. Tom taught and published in little magazines and literary periodicals. Life was good.

At first, Castleton had seemed like another planet from New York City or even New Jersey. Smith had accepted the job, thinking Castleton "wasn't that far from The City, that I could go anywhere from here." That was before he learned about three-foot snowdrifts and no public transportation. And before he learned about fatherhood. "I thought the country was shocking," Smith says, laughing now at his own terror about his move to Vermont. "I was scared to death of these people with guns in the back of their trucks. I didn't know how to drive. Virginia taught me how to drive. At first there was almost nothing here at Castleton [State College]. Many of the buildings you see now were built after I got here." When Virginia and I got married, it made a big difference. I found that married life and fatherhood were exactly what I wanted."

Eventually the two made many friends among people in the college community and surrounding towns. They threw spectacular parties. But the entertaining—and the drinking—stopped in 1973 when Smith turned forty. "It just had gotten out of hand and I realized how much I had, how lucky I was, how I, as my new book says, had an embarrassment of riches. I just didn't know how much I wanted to be part of a family and have children until I was a parent." Along with devoting himself to the family and his career, Smith and his wife have long acted in local and regional theater. Smith has now retired from Castleton State College, but still teaches an occasional workshop; the couple travel and take in Broadway shows and art exhibits. They have taken tango lessons and, at seventy, Smith began studying ballet.

And, every day, he writes. "I developed the habit of writing first thing in the morning after I do the crossword puzzle, when I'm at my freshest. The more you write every day, the more you don't have to get over that inertia from not writing and the more ideas come to you," he explains. "Everything about writing works better if you do it every day. It's hard to start over if you let time go by without writing."

Smith believes there are no taboo subjects for poems. He's written a whole series of poems about Elvis Presley, casting the singer in various mythological persona and scenes. He's written about colonoscopies (and their reminder that all of us are mortal) and flatulence. On the other side of the spectrum, his collection of poetry *Waiting on Pentecost* brings together eighty-one poems inspired by the Old Testament, beginning with Genesis and ending with Acts.[6] The opening poem, "The Word," establishes the book's theme of questioning, of looking for reason, and longing for the simple magic of belief:

### The Word

Adam strode across the field
and the field adored Adam.
He attracted every beast
and, tempted to give them names,
plucked some off green boughs of air.

In that moment all the air
trembled with spirit. The field
drank the word, whispered more names
in the ripe ear of Adam.
Adam fell, naming each beast.

Elephant and gnat, each beast,
whale and peacock, of the air,
or earth or water, Adam
knew as the taste of the field,
of words, of animal names.

He spoke and tasted the names
and he fell and every beast
knew him in its ears. The field
was a rainbow and the air
an orchard singing Adam.

In the beginning Adam
divided the word. Bright names
like a rain danced on the air
and in Eden every beast
danced to the tune of the field.[7]

*Singing the Middle Ages*, published in 1982, brought together poems he'd been writing over a period of twenty-six years. In an author's note, Smith wrote that he had long taken inspiration from the Middle Ages, but that inspiration had been more or less unconscious. The poems collectively, he says, "evoke a world in which lyricism and whimsy strangely combine, prettily, playfully, but always ready to open a perspective upon hell or heaven."[8]

One of the earliest poems in the collection, "A Game of Snow," was written in 1958, while Smith was still in college. Here's an excerpt from that poem that shows his early promise:

The window of the seminar
reveals the snowfall like a star
that gathers earth and air together.
The window opens on the weather,
The new snow falling, with the old
mingling, beneath the trees in the field.
Freshmen, bright and red in woolen
sweaters, rough the drifts they've stolen
from each other; tumbling, they
rough each other through each play,
their football game, in heaped formation,
without a ball. Revelation
is a game of snow.[9]

### Tips and Techniques

The haiku is one of the most important forms of traditional Japanese poetry. Haiku poems are known for their compression and suggestiveness. The form relies heavily on a combination of imagery and observation. It emerged during the sixteenth century and was developed by the poet Basho (1644–1694) into a refined medium of Buddhist and Taoist symbolism.

Traditionally, the haiku consists of three lines totaling seventeen syllables, measuring five–seven–five. Also, the haiku conventionally presents a pair of contrasting images: one suggestive of time and place, the other a vivid but fleeting observation on the broader issues of life and death. Working together, these images evoke mood and emotion. The poet does not comment on the connection but leaves the synthesis of the two images for the reader to ponder.

A haiku by Basho, considered to have written the most perfect examples of the form, illustrates this duality:

> Now the swinging bridge
> Is quieted with creepers
> Like our tendrilled life

The first two lines contain details taken perhaps from a walk in a Japanese garden; the third represents the thought of the poet. Elements of silence and respite are combined with an awareness of life's temporality. Count out the syllables to see that the first line has five syllables; the second, seven; and the third, five.

Often, the structure of the poem consists of an opening line that ends with a colon or ellipsis, suggesting a relationship between the ideas in the opening lines and the following ones, as in this poem, also by Basho:

> Sick on a journey:
> Over parched fields
> Dreams wander on.

When you write your own haiku poems, remember that the form is dependent less on what is said than on what is left unsaid. Because the form is so sparse, writers must carefully meditate on the choice of words and images. In the example above, Basho suggests that the journey taker may be lost or found. We do not know the outcome or the substance of his dreams. We may not be able to express the sentiment that the poem invokes in so many words but we understand its meaning at a deeper level. It is that understanding that makes a haiku so enjoyable.

Vermont figures only occasionally in Tom Smith's poetry. You see it most in his "seasonal album" of haiku and senryu poems collected together in *The Broken Iris*.[10] He has been experimenting with the haiku form since 1979 and publishing in magazines that specialize in this very demanding format. In her foreword to *The Broken Iris*, Joyce Thomas, herself a published poet and a professor of literature at Castleton State College, calls the haiku "verbal miniatures," in recognition of the fact that they are traditionally just three lines of verse. They are, she says, "economical in word and space; pared to the very core of experience; haiku glimmer on the page, clean as dew. Yet they evoke the world; their simple chords reverberate with cosmic mysteries." Thomas writes that Smith is a conjurer, creating "still shots, frozen moments in which the little subject shimmers with large presences. From shadows of the water spider and the mushroom's silence, to a fender-crawling ladybug and orange peelings in the snow, here are the bits of matter which litter, color and define the landscape of one's life, bits we all too often fail to see or weave together."[11]

## Questions and Exercises for Reflection and Inspiration

In his introduction to *Some Traffic*, Tom Smith writes of the poet: "All techniques of versification and diction that have been used, misused, or neglected in the past and any new ones he can discover for his need are, likewise, his to employ. He is not modern because he writes free verse or old hat because he dons or doffs a couplet. His need is determined by the demands of the poem at hand. He needs to be resourceful."[12] Some people feel that poetry should rhyme while others strongly dislike the old-fashioned rhyming poetry, especially verse written in the singsong, patter forms so often used in limericks. Do you like to experiment with writing (and reading) all sorts of structured poems or do you prefer free verse? Can a song be a poem? Can you think of any?

Along the same lines, Tom Smith says any subject is appropriate for poetry, even the stories of a cannibalistic mass murderer, as he tried to show in *Trash*.[13] Do you think some subjects are off-limits for poetry?

In the same introduction, Smith says, "The poem, rather than poetry or the poet, is important. We do not write to be poetic or to fit definitions of poetry. Indeed we must always redefine poetry to include the poems that are being made. Personally, I do not write poems to express myself; I write poems that demand to be written and they, usually, reveal me to myself. I find I depend on poems more than they depend on me."

All these subjects offer fruitful debate, especially the concept that the poem is more important than poetry or the poet him- or herself. What do you think this means? Does a poem have a life of its own once created, quite outside the control of the poet? Certainly, great poetry lives on long after its writer has died. But what does Smith mean when he says he writes poems that demand to be written? We already know that he gives himself assignments—anagram poems, poems around certain themes—as a way of challenging himself. How do these preordained structures allow poems to demand to be written? Have you ever had an experience where a poem came to you without your giving it much conscious thought?

> **Exercise 1:** Make a list of subjects that you believe are not poetic. Now, write a poem about one of them.

Tom Smith is interested in the music of words, in the sounds of words. He urges students to find words that do things in the mouth, that entertain us sensually as we say them and that both feel and sound like their meanings. He collects words and plays with unusual combinations, sometimes creating two-word lines. One of his favorites, a gift from a student, is *"Love mushrooms."* Which is the verb and which is the noun? It all depends on how you say it. Smith will sometimes begin his morning writing session by simply playing with the combination of two unlikely words. Sometimes a poem evolves; sometimes not. In *"love mushrooms,"* the word "love" sounds longer than four letters. The word "love" is fun to say. It begins with the tongue curled against the upper palate and ends with biting the lower lip; there's a lot going on there. Same thing with the word "mushrooms." That double *oo* followed by the letter *m* causes us to form our lips into a temporary kiss. The letters and the sounds these two words make apart and then together are as much a part of the line's meaning (and its fun) as the words themselves. And because both words can be nouns or verbs, there's an inherent playfulness in the line.

> **Exercise 2:** Try your hand at playing with the sound of letters and word combinations. First read aloud the poem from his collection *An Embarrassment of Riches* below. Pay close attention to the words *ruin* and *ridicule.*

### "Liberace Ruined My Life"

He's forty-one, drug-free, living
with a girlfriend in Connecticut. What

were the rocks? What was the siren song?
The sex? Drugs? Diets? Celebrity?
Money? Jewelry? A gold Rolls Royce? The plastic
surgery? The "hefty out-of-court settlement"? *Ruin*

is not a word that blooms much in the mouth.
The cheeks suck in on it. Lips pout.
Meanwhile, even as we listen to the boy

we are distracted remembering Liberace: his flesh
like gold leaf, his smile
like a grand piano keyboard, his extra-virgin pompadour
like the first pressings from a hillside grove in Tuscany, his hands
like birds of paradise or Zeigfeld girls
descending an ivory stair. He flashes

ermine and rhinestones and pearls, white velvet
tie and tails inside the studded cape that unfolds around him
like a night sky full of stars, an albino bat. How ridiculous

is the sublime! And how sublime
the ridiculous! What

a delicious word is *ridicule!*
Especially if pronounced with a little French accent, it froths
upon the tongue, strokes itself along soft and hard palates
like a cat against one's shins, fills the sensitive cavity
like a dog's tail wagging: *ridicule!* Every
thing
is so much more shadow than substance.

—*Globe*, 3 September 2002[14]

Notice how Smith has drawn our attention to the way these words sound: "*Ruin* is not a word that blossoms much in the mouth." He makes you think about what the word does in your mouth. The word doesn't give our mouth much action, especially compared to *ridicule*, a word that requires a little aerobic oral exercise. In drawing attention to the words, he's mocking the suit of the forty-one-year-old, plastic surgery–enhanced man now living with a girlfriend in Connecticut who brought a lawsuit against Liberace. He does it with sound as much as meaning.

Now, make your own list of words that have interesting sounds. You can do this by randomly leafing through a dictionary or by picking up a book or newspaper and writing down words whose sounds express some aspect of the word's meaning or do interesting things in your mouth. Or, you can simply collect words in your journal as you go through your day, over-hearing conversations, reading, listening to the radio, and talking with coworkers and friends. Once you have about twenty words, make combinations of two words that seem to have nothing in common. Be inspired by the "*love mushrooms*" example, looking for words that have double meaning or could be used as either a noun or a verb. Do any of the combinations inspire you to write a poem, or do you see a use for one of the combinations in a poem you've been working on?

Joyce Thomas considers haiku poems "clear lenses through which we view life's ephemeral strands come together in one momentary vision of connection."[15] A haiku is a moment in time that stands for many moments in time, an experience at once singular and informative. The rhythm in a haiku is often internal; it's subtle, almost innate. Its subject matter often involves observations of nature and the oneness among living things.

> **Exercise 3:** Take a walk in the woods or the garden, writing down sensory details as you go: white anemone, spider web, fern pollen, dew upon the grass, fireflies in the branches. Think about the emotion that these gifts of nature inspire in you. Then, try to write a haiku of three lines of seventeen syllables or fewer that captures the essence of your experience. If you like this format, this exercise can be incorporated into your daily routine: not only will it help you develop your powers of observation, it will provide you with a delightful way to record your thoughts and reactions along with details of the world you encounter in your travels.

Try Tom Smith's method for giving your brain (or psyche or creative juices or muse, call it what you will) time to work on a poem or story by reading the end of what you've written right before you go to bed. In the morning, go directly to your studio, office, or wherever you usually write and, without thinking too much, return to what you wrote last. Don't reread it and start editing; rather, pick up where you left off and just start writing. Try to think as little as possible and simply let the words and ideas come. If you don't come up with whole sentences or lines of verse, simply write down words that occur to you and then play with them. This may prove to be a great way to jump-start your writing each day and provide you with material from the subconscious (or whatever you want to call the place where inspiration and fresh ideas reside). If this doesn't work the first day, don't give up. It may take you a week or so to get attuned to calling on those below-consciousness voices, images, and ideas. They are there; just give them time to percolate up. If you find yourself getting frustrated or stressed that nothing is occurring to you, get up right away and give it another try another night.

In the following poem, Tom Smith uses a headline from a tabloid newspaper to explore the loneliness of the nighttime janitor at a museum, a loneliness that simultaneously embraces our fascination with Egypt and mummies while also exploring the cult of the dead. The poem is a little creepy, but so was the "story" that inspired it. Here's the poem:

**3000-YEAR-OLD MUMMY PREGNANT**
Janitor Admits: "'I'm the Father"

Night watchman Dobi Sitar swings his light
to the left and to the right, forward and back. Its beam
carves brilliant, transitory tunnels through the darkness
of high galleries, wide passages, lofty alcoves, discovering
a shank of Sphinx, a thigh of striding god
or pharaoh, a golden arm extended, ankh
in hand, a golden solar disk, winged pectoral, falcon's
sharp beak of Horus, of Osiris or Anubis
the jackal's ears, alert, cat's eyes of Bast, kohl
enshadowed eyes of Isis staring
down the faltering shaft of Dobi
Sitar's torch, following down
the light to the night
watchman's fist that trembles with fear or anticipation.
The echo of his workman's boots on marble soars
into the darkness beyond his light, the high, wide,
haunted darkness of the National
Academy of Archaeology in Cairo,
Egypt.

Night watchman Dobi Sitar knows where he is going,
knows the way. He is going
to make love to death,
to enter dead flesh and bone,
to spill into the dark and timeless womb his light

and laboring echoes of his passion,
to cast a little slime of life like pearls
to feed the dead, to feed upon
the dead.

Night watches night. Toward dawn
Dobi Sitar wakes to climb a graying darkness
through the gradual, emerging splendor of antiquity. Bewildered
quickenings reach after him, well after him and, then,
sink back, as Dobi Sitar thinks himself
back to the nursery of his desire.

—*Weekly World News*, 8 October 2002[16]


**Exercise 4:** Start making your own file of weird and wonderful stories from the daily news and try writing a poem or story inspired by something you read in the paper or on the Internet. You'll notice that this poem by Tom Smith uses the name of the janitor named in the article and relies upon some knowledge of Egyptian history and burial traditions. Much of the imagery, in fact, resonates with a knowledge of and appreciation of the items that were important in Egyptian ceremonies and procedures for preparing the dead for the afterlife. The headline of the story (and probably the story itself) is somewhat mocking and certainly unbelievable—not the act of coupling, but the purported result: a pregnant mummy. Smith doesn't analyze these aspects or spend much time on them; he's interested in something deeper and older: the power of the afterlife, the quest for immortality, and the cycle of life. In your own poems, search for ways to get beyond the trivialities and the particulars of the news article you've chosen.

Photo by Richard Coutant

# 18　Verandah Porche

*Telling Other People's Stories.*

Born 11 November 1945, Englewood, New Jersey

Educated at Boston University

Lives in Guilford

First publication: camp and school publications, followed by poems, such as "Undertow," in the *Boston University News*

Collections of Poetry: *The Body's Symmetry* (1975); *Glancing Off* (1989).

Anthology: *Home Comfort* (1973).

Anthologies created through residencies: *Right to Dream: Told Poems by Adult New Readers* (1995); *Self Portraits in Newport* (1998); *The Right to Dream, Told Poems by Adult New Readers* (1999); *They Know the Promise: the Art of Care in a Community Hospital* (2000); *SPIN in the Millennium* (2000); *Listening Out Loud: A Hundred Days in Parkville* (2003)

IN 1968, A STONE'S THROW from the White House, Ray Mungo, Marshall Bloom, and a host of young writer-activists at the *Liberation News Service* collected, wrote, edited, collated, stapled, rammed, addressed, and sent across America their weekly version of all the news they believed had been omitted from the public print. In their cluttered office, a massive telex machine churned out instant messages from enclaves of resistance and campus uprisings around the world. All the name-brand issues—the Vietnam War, civil rights, draft resistance, the nascent women's movement—consumed them. Verandah Porche, poetry editor of *LNS*, edited very little poetry but wrote a great deal of it between stints of editing on the Selectric and banging out addressograph labels. She worked cheek by jowl with Mungo, her old college chum, and Bloom. Often they would burst into song. Bloom could imitate Ethel Merman and Mungo did Bing Crosby. Porche could knock off Appalachian murder ballads or Cole Porter. The revolution was supposed to make a joyful noise.

Following the assassination of Martin Luther King on 3 April 1968, Washington, D.C. erupted in riots. Porche prowled around the city with her press pass as an invisible shield. The National Guard set up machine-gun nests aimed outward from the Capitol Building. On many corners, young white men in army camouflage looked away as looters, singing and crying, wheeled racks of suits from department stores or stacks of steaks from the grocery, or set fire to their own blocks. The city was a war zone. Thirteen people died and thousands were injured during three days of riots. Porche wandered spellbound, helpless, too naive to be afraid.

At the same time, differences about strategy and credibility in desperate times created hairline fractures on the Left that opened into bitter dispute. Porche began to long for peace, a chance to start over. On Easter morning, 1968, Porche woke Mungo and said, "Raymond, I want to go home." Mungo opened his eyes and said, "I know the place," and returned to sleep. The place turned out to be a rundown old farm in Guilford, Vermont.

Verandah Porche wasn't her given name; she'd been blessed with the much more prosaic Linda Ruth Jacobs, inspired by the popular post–World War II song with the memorable line, "I count all the charms about Linda." The name Verandah Porche came out of the wonderful inventiveness of the mid-1960s on American campuses and elsewhere where young people were anxious to shed their middle-class pasts and reinvent themselves, much as their parents and grandparents had changed their names and reinvented themselves when they immigrated to the United States. It wasn't so much respectability and acceptance that these young people were seeking, but rather names (and identities) that lifted them out of conformity. Indeed, when Porche was a student at Boston University, " I was always changing my name. Every time I read a book, I would try out the names of the characters. I needed a new personality, something more victorious and unforgettable. Also, I didn't want my parents to read my poetry. At the time, I was living in Somerville [Massachusetts], which has all these triple-decker houses with wonderful verandahs. My friends and I were always joking around, playing with names. One day, I was sitting on my front porch and just came up with the idea of Verandah Porch. The 'e' was an afterthought. When I moved to Vermont, Ray Mungo would always introduce me to everyone as "V.P.: The Queen of Poesy.'"

Queen of Poesy she has been for an ever-increasing cadre of recipients of her poems as well as her wise instruction in crafting poetry. Since moving to Vermont in 1968, Porche has published two collections of her own poetry. Her work has been featured on National Public Radio's *Artbeat*, on New Hampshire Public Radio's *Front Porch*, and in the Vermont State

House. But that's hardly the limit of her creative output. From her earliest days as a poet, Porche has pursued an alternative literary career. Some might call it a subversive literary career: she's as apt to give a poem away as try to publish it for money. She has written literally hundreds of poems, many of which she gives for birthdays or when a friend is sick. She also runs "Muse for Hire," writing poems on commission for organizations like Planned Parenthood, the Vermont Arts Council, and the Old Tavern at Grafton, and for ordinary people. And, she's brought poetry into dozens of schools around New England as a visiting writer who turns poetry into play and play into poetry.

Porche has also devoted herself to bringing poetry into nontraditional settings such as literacy and crisis centers, hospitals, factories, nursing homes, senior centers, a two-hundred-year-old Vermont tavern, and an urban working-class neighborhood. In these settings, she practices "shared narrative," allowing hundreds of ordinary people—those with a story to tell but who feel ill equipped to do so, and those who feel they have no story—to create, preserve, and share their personal literature. "It's my way of harvesting eloquence in unsuspecting places and trying to give people the power of their own voices," she says of her process. Those words, "harvesting eloquence," are typical Porche. She mines these situations for gems of communication and insight, carefully helping people to explore and articulate the stories within them, being ever watchful for those moments when poetry makes itself.

### Tips and Techniques

In her role as writing partner, Porche meets with and gets to know people living in institutions—jails, hospitals, nursing homes, schools—and in communities as disparate as a Vermont hamlet and an industrialized southern New England city. After some initial discussion with the person she's partnered with, she begins asking questions, eventually prodding him to tell some story from his life. The questions are usually fairly spontaneous, inspired by the situation. Using her laptop, Porche begins to write down the responses, looking for true and original turns of phrases and the point at which her writing partner forgets that Porche is writing down the words. She may prompt more discussion by open-ended questions: Well, what happened then? Or, What did you end up deciding? When the story feels over, she sits with her writing partner and goes over the words she has captured in the computer; often people are quite amazed and pleased to see their words written down. This sometimes encourages them to tell more, to correct or elaborate, to tell a new story. As she sits with her writing partner, Porche starts to give the piece a shape, and carefully edits superfluous words. How about this, she might ask as she moves a segment of the work that seems to logically follow another. Together, reading aloud, playing with the

words already on the computer screen and new words that come to
the writing partner, the two edit and trim, add and clarify. Porche
brings her understanding of language to the work but doesn't im-
pose her own language onto it. Eventually, the poem begins to take
shape. People are often exhilarated by the process; it's oddly freeing
to see one's story take the shape of something that seemed outside
their experience—like poetry.

She worked with a boy who could not see for about a year, during which
he wrote dozens of poems in which he recorded, for the first time, the richness of his perceptions and the dreams he harbored in his heart. Through
crafting poems, the boy was able to articulate his hopes and fears. Other
writing partners have been elderly people, portraying their families and
times before their stories become lost to death; factory workers, discovering their creative strengths despite the deadening work at the mill; and ter-
minally ill people expressing their sense of gratitude with a life well lived,
despite its brevity.

Several anthologies have come out of these exercises. A residency in
Newport, New Hampshire, during which she collected the stories of town
residents, resulted in *SPIN in the Millennium*, which was included in Newport's town report for 2000, and her residency at Gifford Medical Center
resulted in an anthology of patients' and caregivers' work, entitled *They
Know the Promise: The Art of Care in a Community Hospital*, also published
in 2000. The books provide a snapshot of a place and its people, juxtaposed
with Porche's signature observations and reactions. For the reader, these
collections provide a vehicle to step into a place for a moment in time, to
suffer and celebrate the small and large disappointments and victories of
strangers who become momentarily intimately known. More important,
people who never expected to be poets or the subject of a poem have the
opportunity to validate their lives and articulate feelings they've long kept
to themselves.

It's a delight just to listen to Porche speak. Her facility with language and
the quirky, insightful sentences that come out of her mouth, combined with
her naturally playful spirit, translate into sentences that sound like spontaneous poems. There's nothing highfalutin about Porche, despite the name.
She's very down-to-earth and accessible. Teachers often call her a "teacher's
teacher" because she so adeptly models good teaching techniques while
leading even the most recalcitrant students into constructing pantoums and
villanelles.

It's a role that she was raised for. The youngest of four children, she was
born in Englewood, New Jersey, in 1945, the first year of the Baby Boom.
She spent her early days in Palisades Park, home of the giant amusement
park. Her father had grown up in Hoboken where his father, a Trotskyist,
had started a small garment business in his own kitchen, eventually
expanding the operation into a factory. Her mother had grown up in

Brooklyn with a politically active father. Both sets of grandparents were Jewish immigrants, who had come from nothing, fleeing a threatening homeland. They had a sense of being self-made and a respect for knowledge that carried down to her generation. Porche's own parents were much older than those of her peers. Her father was forty-eight when she was born; her mother, forty-two. Her mother had wanted to be a teacher and, having had to give up her own formal education, valued education second only to family; her father loved to invent things and loved to write. So it was only natural that Porche was writing at an early age. When she was eight the family moved to Teaneck, New Jersey, a more cosmopolitan and integrated town, inspiring her to write the poem: "What will the neighbors say? Shhh!!! says the suburbs."

Music was the key influence in her house. "Everyone in the family sang those popular love ballads. My two sisters harmonized; my brother sang Spanish Civil War songs." Porche recalls. Her job was to entertain them all with words. From the first moments she could speak, she loved sounds and made up songs and poems. Although she now considers much of what she produced "babbling verse and doggerel," her siblings were amused by her precociousness. "I had a fair amount of encouragement. They egged me on. I began writing in verse before I was even in school. I wrote book reports in rhyme in third grade. It was all just an extension of talking to myself, making my mind decouple from the room and the social situation so I could have a conversation inside my head or pretend I was someone else or somewhere else. My hands would be going through the motions but my mind would be a thousand miles away."

When Porche was in ninth grade, her older sister went to Brandeis University and brought home paperback books that enchanted Porche: Thomas Hardy novels, Greek plays, poems by T. S. Eliot. Porche carried the books around, devoured them. "I could be a fake intellectual," she says of her young self. "I was excited about things I didn't understand." In eleventh grade, she had "a terribly important teacher, Marian Shelby, a mentor who had never trained as a teacher. I corresponded with her until she died. She introduced me to American literature. She threw a tremendous amount of poetry at us, treated us like grown-ups. She had parties, sunrise picnics at the Palisades, gatherings where we discussed literature for hours. I was always on my tiptoes trying to understand what she was saying, what she was having us read. She made us stretch. Even as an adult writing her letters, I always had such trepidation because she had such high standards. She was exacting and peculiar and that's what I'd like to be, to be authentic with my particular passions. I wrote a lot for her, winning little prizes that, for example, enabled me to take a poetry class at Columbia while still in high school." Nonetheless, Porche didn't ever consider poetry as a career. "My writing was always my private passion. I would share it with people but it wasn't really an academic pursuit or career goal. It was simply what I did."

After two years at Boston University, she left, came back again, left again, never completing her degree. There were more important issues for her: the antiwar and civil rights movements and the business of living. At Boston University, she worked on the college newspaper and met Mungo and other antiwar activists who would launch the Liberation News Service in 1967.

"The times were inspiring and terrible," she recalls, referring to the assassinations, police beatings of demonstrators, and rifts in the peace and civil rights movements. Burned out, a bit disillusioned, she and Mungo went to visit friends who had a "not-hunting camp" on Packers Corner Road in Guilford and learned that a neighboring farm was for sale. The commune they created there, jokingly named Total Loss Farm, exists today as a land trust; several of the original commune dwellers live around the neighborhood. Most of the time, Porche is the sole resident from those initial days, although old friends and former commune dwellers are always welcome.

The Total Loss Farm crew flung themselves into Vermont living with a passion, learning from their neighbors how to grow and preserve vegetables, cut wood, forage for wild foods, dip candles, raise pigs, make cheese, and navigate icy roads. They made do and did without. They spent the first two years writing and publishing. Mungo published a book called *Total Loss Farm*, which told their story of disenchantment with the political systems and their enchantment with living close to the earth in Vermont. Together, the residents of the Packers Corner commune published an anthology of their work called *Home Comfort* in honor of the wood-burning stove in their kitchen.[1] After the brutality of assassinations and arrests, the cycle of the farm and the seasons seemed like a dream. Porche found among the people living in her small community a wisdom she thought lacking in academic settings. She liked her neighbors' way of speaking, its deceptive simplicity and directness. After years of rhetoric, "I needed to learn a new vocabulary and a new cadence," she says. She wanted her "poetry to have a private use and a public use."

And so she began "marking the events of a very small community" by writing poetry for a small audience. Initially, that audience was the writers and artists and others who lived at Total Loss Farm and their friends. Porche lived the belief that "creating a poem was as valuable as hauling water or chopping wood." For someone who had grown up in a family that "had a deep distrust of the earth," Vermont was a revelation. "Life presented an overwhelming number of possibilities. I had time to read like a cannibal. I felt that living on the ground, the world's great literature made sense. My experience was one of just gratitude whether writing about a parsnip or a party."

After just a few months in Guilford, the nucleus of the community widened out as the Packers Corner crowd sought out the help and instruction of their neighbors. Porche savored the pace of her neighbor's language, their way of saying things. "Ultimately, I just tried to write them down," she recalls. "I wrote poems for people who had been generous to us, like an acrostic sonnet for Harvey L. Cutting, the retiring road commissioner, that was published in the *Christian Science Monitor*, poems for our postman, a dairy farmer. He taught us how to make sap beer; he was a tremendously eloquent and supportive person whose son had suffered during the Vietnam War. He was receptive to the hippies; he wanted to hear what we had to say as much as we wanted to hear what he had to say."

Porche says her first collection of poetry, *The Body's Symmetry*, was "published with really no rollout to my career."[2] By this, she means that—as so often happens with poetry—she was sent out on book tour, traveling with her first husband and first child, Oona, "going from one poetry reading to another. It was very frightening. No one knew who I was and I didn't know who they were. It was very alienating. My father died while I was on the West Coast flogging my book. I decided to go back to Iowa and do the last few readings that I'd committed to do and then to return to Guilford. I felt as if my work was concerned with the life work, not the hermetic life of people in academia." The experience confirmed her commitment to write for people she knew or would like to know and "to work in public places, to give readings in schools and find ways to share my voice with people to whom it might connect and, later, they could explore their own words with me. I wanted my life to be a poem and I wanted other people's to be poems, too."

Although Porche has always collected other people's stories, her formal efforts in this regard began in 1989 when she was invited to work at the Gill Old Fellows Home in Ludlow, Vermont, a rural nursing home with a vibrant arts program. The job showed her the possibilities inherent in shared narrative. Porche loved the work and the people: "the unheard eccentricity and their age, their wild age. The pairing of their need to transmit wisdom with my need to hear it and hold it and help shape it." She later received a grant to work room to room with the elderly residents of the home. Not only was she recording their insights, but she also "got deeply involved with their life worlds. Some of them took me under their wings. I honored their power, they befriended me."

Subsequently, in 1995, she worked on a statewide literacy project in Vermont with emerging adult readers. She was one of a team of teachers and writers who worked together to collect a body of work in a statewide anthology, entitled *Right to Dream*, in which ordinary people recorded their memories and insights, sharing knowledge about things they knew well.[3] She worked on a similar project in New Hampshire,[4] then went on to bring her process of shared narrative into prisons, hospitals, the industrial town of Newport, New Hampshire, a depressed neighborhood in Hartford, Connecticut, and a women's chorus in Brattleboro. In recognition of this work and her contributions to the state's cultural life, the Vermont Arts Council awarded Porche its Citation of Merit in 1998. She says her process, although it works well in many settings, is ideal for a place like Vermont where so many stories await telling. Vermont "was a lucky place to land because it hadn't been industrialized like New Hampshire. It had agrarian roots with ingenuity, traditions of neighborliness and a language and history of tolerance." These values help foster an environment in which a poet like Porche can use poetry as a tool to give voice to people who have been disenfranchised or whose stories might otherwise be lost.

Vermont and the Vermont experience is at the center of it all, Porche says. The state provided her with an opportunity to connect with people and share their lives in a way that might not have happened elsewhere. At the same time, she says, the cycle of the seasons and the richness of the natural life surrounding her small farm in Guilford provide daily lessons in humility and joy, a respect for forces much larger than human endeavor and a constant reminder that there's life going on all around us that has little to do with us but that humans can destroy with very little effort. "For a city girl who didn't know one tree from another when I arrived, to me [Vermont] was a total revelation," she says. "It still is."

The following is an example of one of Porche's "gifted poems," one written not necessarily for publication but for a friend.

### "To Hell in a Handbasket"
*for Andy Kopkind*

Andy, cancer tears you away
from the neighborhood where your
summer chickens strut and feed
among potted orchids and the whole

hill is coming out from under
April. *Like a patient etherised
upon the cruelest month*, you quip.
You need someone to go to your root

cellar for the tender show bulbs
to spread among good friends' gardens:
canna, calla, dahlia, glads.
*Reach into the crypt,* you laugh.

Below your kitchen, down steep stairs
I feel among heat ducts' hollow
curves. Things hang and seep, close
and moist: Is this what dark is like

within the body?—Remember unwrapping
*The Sex Life of Flowers*? Hummingbirds giving
head to bearded irises and monarchs
sucking milkweed. Andy, when the body

backfires blossoms stand in for all the
shapes a lover makes with us. —I load

my wicker basket with your brown trousseau.
Look how each bulb or tuber fits
like a hand grenade about to blow.[5]

The following is a poem Porche wrote as part of her collaborative residency with staff, patients, family, and community members at Gifford Medical Center in Randolph, Vermont, which was funded by the Susan G. Komen Breast Cancer Foundation and the Vermont Arts Council. The project produced the previously mentioned *They Know the Promise* and a traveling exhibition featured at the Vermont State House.

### "Poem Written with Howard William Menig"

The roots of plants
are *cussling* up now.
It's a springy thought.

The light of the garden
in the evening.

It's hard to tell
which way the plants
squiggle around.

No favorite flower yet . . .
I'll work in the garden soon.
The cool spring air—
O, I love it.[6]

Porche wrote this explanation of how the poem took form:

Howard Menig hums to himself without speaking as I write with others. After a long afternoon of creating poems with residents about their local lives, Howard and I sit quietly in front of the open French doors. At dusk in the May heat wave, we sing a few songs, *Bye Bye, Blackbird, O, How Lovely Is the Evening*.

Howard's poem comes in cadences whispered over the course of half an hour. Our dialogue:

*What about the garden? "Cussling" what a perfect word. How do the plants grow? Which ones have you liked? Do you plan to work in the garden?*

We joke about the weather: blizzard and swelter a few weeks away. His line about May perfects this sense.

He's fiddling with his buttons. I ask about night time. He says the line about buttons. I ask, *"buttons on what?"* There are daffodils all over. I am laughing. We're relaxed, and he has a whole sentence: *How many laughing daffodils are enough . . .*

I joke: for me? and he adds *for anybody.*

By now, I've repeated the whole poem several times. We enjoy the repetition. He's tired and says the part about *sink myself in bed. Broad moonlight* was a gift from the cosmos. I don't know where he got it.

I ask him to repeat it to make sure it's right.

Of course, I want to know what he'll dream of. We can hear bird songs. He looks pleased as I read it from the screen.

Later, when I say goodnight and read the poem a final time, he smiles and says, "It's a pretty thing," and, "Did you write it?"

## Questions and Exercises for Reflection and Inspiration

Porche has used the process of shared narrative with her own mother, capturing bits of family history and understanding that otherwise might have gone unknown. It's somewhat like interviewing a person for a journalistic article, except that there are no expectations. The questioner or collaborator allows the conversation to evolve the way it wants to go. And the end process is often quite free-form.

> **Exercise 1:** Pick a person whose story you've always longed to hear and ask that person to help you experiment with shared narrative. Or, pick someone in your class or group that you would like to get to know better. Begin interviewing the person about her life; when something intrigues you or seems important to your subject, ask a question, such as, "And how did you do that?" or simply ask the person to tell you more. Write key words down as you go along, gently prompting your partner to tell you more or explain something confusing. But don't try to push the conversation too far; let it simply unfold. You may write the responses on paper or on a computer. When the conversation comes to a natural end, review what you've written down with your partner. Break the lines up, letting the internal meaning of the poem lead you as you divide the poem into lines and stanzas. Allow the natural cadence of the poem to dictate its rhythm but allow room for surprises by carrying a thought from one line to another or allowing a word to stand alone on a line. Experiment with how it looks; look for places where the poem wants to tell a story, contradict itself, or make a subtle point. Eliminate superfluous words: "that," "the," "a," and overused adjectives. Don't, however, try to impose your language on the person's poem. Respect your partner's voice. As you edit and give shape to the poem, keep reading it aloud to hear the natural cadence and internal rhymes as well as places where the words sound false or vague. When you and your partner feel it's ready, type up a clean copy and read it aloud once more. You may find a few more opportunities to fine-tune it again.

When Porche teaches poetry in schools, she often uses a word box as a tool to help students write poetry. Her word box is composed of words taken from favorite poems rather than random words. She sometimes has the students make their own word boxes by combing through literature, looking for poems that resonate with them and then cutting the poems up into individual words. Her word boxes have literally hundreds of poems in them and, therefore, several thousand wonderful words. One way to play with the word-box offerings is to simply grab a pinch of words, spread them out on the desk, and look for words that seem to have special meaning, go together, or contrast with one another. Because words (and their meanings) are often elusive and because poetry is the most elusive form of writing, the act of selecting words and then moving them around to see how they sound in various combinations provides students with a tactile experience. It makes the elusive real. Sometimes, Porche pairs students up, each with his own pinch of words from the word box, and asks the students to combine their words, moving them around until a kind of intuitive (and often quite quirky) poem begins to evolve. She might have the students read their verses aloud or she might write them on the board, then ask questions about the students' choices, the ordering of their words, and the way they sound together. As she writes their words on the board, she might break up the lines to give them fresh meaning or ask the students to consider how the poem might sound with a slight alteration. There's no effort to formulate the poem here or place her sensibility upon it; rather she shows the student some possibilities and lets them decide on both the structure and the meaning

> **Exercise 2:** Create your own word box by typing out or copying your favorite poems and then cutting them up into individual words. You don't need words like "and," "but," "the," and "a." You may ask friends and members of your writing group to contribute their words as well. The more words, of course, the better. You may make up the rules for playing the game, deciding for example, that each person on a team gets to construct one line, or that each person randomly selects a word and the whole team gets to decide where it goes.

Pantoums come from Malaysia where people read them aloud, probably as a kind of game. Porche says people of all ages have made up great pantoums about foxes, friends, and money, even heartbreak. Here's one she wrote for a friend. See if you can follow the line structure.

### For Bill at 6 A.M.

When push comes to shove on the night shift,
you punch out,
dream of toast and dozing
through dank April drizzle home.

You punch out.
Light cuts in with clouds
through dank April drizzle. Home:
the kitchen fire's dead. No kindling. No bread.

Light cuts in with clouds.
Each dawn you wonder what sun was.
The kitchen fire's dead. No kindling, no bread.
The only paper left to burn you want to read.

Each dawn you wonder. What sun was
the stove remembers as you feed it
the only paper left to burn. You want to read
Spring between the lines of flame.

The stove remembers. As you feed it,
dreams of toast and dozing
spring between the lines of flame,
when push comes to shove on the night shift.

Here's the structure of the poem. The asterisk means the line will be repeated again in the poem

A * 1
  * 2
  * 3
  * 4

B   2
  * 5
    4
  * 6

C   5
  * 7
    6
  * 8

D   7
  * 9
  * 8
  *10

E   9
    3
   10
    1

**Exercise 3:** Try your hand at writing a pantoum. If you're short on ideas, grab a pinch of words from the word box or inspire yourself by looking at some photographs. Once you get going, you'll see how the playfulness of word repetition helps you think of fresh lines and word combinations.

# 19   Joan Connor

*Chronicling the Lives of the Forgotten, the Lost,*
*and the Downright Weird*

Born: 12 January 1954, Holyoke, Massachusetts

Education: B.A., Mount Holyoke; M.A., Middlebury College; M.F.A.,
    Vermont College

Lives in Belmont

First publications: elementary-school poetry in the local newspaper
    in Springvale, Maine; first short story, "This One Fact," in *RE:AL*
    (literary magazine) in 1980

Novels: *Here on Old Route 7* (1997); *We Who Live Apart* (2000); *History
    Lessons* (2003)

Awards: Best American citation (1986, 2003); Pushcart Prize, Philip Roth
    Fellowship, Jack Kerouac Fellowship, John Gilgun Award, Ohio Writer
    Awards in Fiction and Nonfiction; Associated Writing Programs
    Award in Short Fiction

R EADING A JOAN CONNOR STORY is like stepping into a weird
and wonderful world, a smart world, a troubled world, a world so
much like the one we all live in but looked at through Alice's looking glass
and then some. It's a pleasure, a challenge, mind aerobics, a front-row seat
at a comedy riff, and a meditation at the mirror—all rolled into one. Her
stories are dark and funny, insightful and mysterious, character-driven and
compelled by a plotline that may sometimes leave you breathless. Her mas-
tery of prose rhythms and dialogue, along with the variety of narrative tech-

niques at her employ, is brilliant. No wonder the Associated Writing Programs, the prestigious national organization dedicated to "serving American letters, writers, and programs of writing," awarded her book *History Lessons* its 2002 Award in Short Fiction.[1]

Connor is a professor of English at Ohio University and a member of the faculty at the University of Southern Maine's low residency M.F.A. program. But she does all her writing in Vermont, spending vacations from school, her sabbatical years, and any other moment she can garner to be in Vermont "where my heart is." Like many writers who have to balance several jobs along with their writing to make a living, Connor jealously guards her Vermont days and months, turning them into essays on everything from cheese making and the grange picnic to the war in Iraq and poverty at home. Her short stories explore subjects dear to Vermont and Vermonters (the disappearance of the family farm, the uncertain future of businesses located off the main drag, the ravages of winter) as well as those larger issues that so much of fiction has been concerned with from time immemorial (the struggle for personal power, isolation and ignorance, loneliness, hope, and despair).

These themes aren't ones a writer can step in and out of easily. They require concentrated energy, the light from a very tightly focused lens, and uninterrupted moments to explore fully in fiction. Connor says of her work as a college professor, "I love my students. I feel I'm changing the world one student at a time, exporting clarity of vision and sense of personal integrity and responsibility to be a good citizen in the world. I love my work as a professor and mentor. Unfortunately, I also love to write and I'm giving my life to my students and, too often, shortchanging my life as a writer. I can't write in increments. I really need uncluttered blocks of time. Everything goes out the window until I'm done. With a novel, I can only do it in the summer, when I have the time off. While I was writing the most recent one, I would not allow myself to leave my studio until I had four pages done. Some good days I wrote four pages, some only one, despite my most diligent efforts. When you are writing, the smallest interruption can mean you simply can't get back into the story, that a scene is ruined or the momentum gone."

It's a dilemma many writers face. That's why her time in Vermont is so precious. Connor has created a comfortable enclave in a converted barn on her parents' property in Belmont. Here, she not only finds the quiet and inspiration she needs for her writing; she also dips into a remarkable family resource, the generational history of life in Vermont. Her maternal grandmother's home was in Belmont and several aunts and cousins have long lived here. Connor was born in Holyoke, Massachusetts, but her family moved every two years or so as her father pursued his university education and then teaching jobs. (Her father, Walker Connor, is a well-respected scholar in ethnonationalism, and he has taught widely in the United States and abroad.) Before her parents retired to Belmont, the family considered her mother's family's place home. Connor says of her childhood, "Vermont was the only constant in my life."

Connor also traces her intellectual and moral education more to Vermont than to any of the public or private schools she attended over the years. She says, "My parents taught us values and instilled a strong sense of moral and social responsibility. It comes from their New England roots. In Vermont, you can't overlook your neighbor who doesn't have health insurance. You're compelled to help the people you see every day. Here, books and education matter, along with this sense of work ethic and social responsibility. It's part of what drives me to write and what I write about."

Each Christmas and June, the family would pile into the car, drive along Route 7 through Rutland, then take the shortcut at North Clarendon across Old Route 7 to Route 103, up to home for an extended stay. They might stop at the vegetable stand near the intersection, where her father would buy big bundles of gladiola. From her window, Connor would stare back down the road at the old cabins of a tourist court, long since bypassed with the building of the "new" highway, Vermont Route 7. Over the years of her childhood, she watched the cabins' slow deterioration in to long-term rentals. In summer, the cabins looked pretty enough, even if the grass sometimes needed to be mowed or the buildings painted; in fall, purple asters stole the eye from sagging roofs and rusting cars. But at Christmas, as the family drove by on their way to Belmont where there would be lights in all the windows of her relatives' homes and a superabundance of food, Connor would look at the icicles hanging from the cabins' roofs and find herself, year after year, thinking about the people who rented the cabins, people cooped up inside, living at the end of the road, as bypassed as Old Route 7.

She never knew anyone who actually lived along this stretch of the old highway; yet she thought she knew something of their hopes and fears, their love and desperation, their trials and errors, their small successes and large dreams. These imaginings, along with real events—Grange suppers and Guild Hall socials; conversations with the road commissioner, the car mechanic, the postmistress—were the inspiration for her first collection of short stories, *Here on Old Route 7*:[2] "The book predates my birth by about ten years. It tells the story of that American dream that climaxed a few years after the end of World War II, our myth of equal opportunity, that even the little guy can make it. Since then, we've learned differently. But the people who believed it then and failed thought it was they who were the failures." A Vermonter will easily recognize them: Paulie Bonay, a veteran and believer in the American dream, who builds the Sunset Motor Cabins Court and pins his future on its success; his wife Anna, raised in poverty by a French Canadian father who runs the local dump and gathers bits of wisdom along with the throw-always; Seige, another dreamer whose efforts to re-create his version of the American dream take the form of a Quonset hut that evolves from ballroom to roadhouse to country music dive; Red, the handsome accordion player who takes no responsibility for his actions until fate catches up with him in losses too big to ever recover from; Dave, who meets the American dream more than halfway with his drive-in theater, only to be bypassed as surely as Paulie's motor court; and Maria, a single mother from Puerto Rico, who hatches a new version of the American dream complete with a red Trans-Am and an adios to Old Route 7 each night as her four boys fall asleep on their cabin floor.

Long after you read this collection, you'll find yourself wondering about these characters. What happened to the end of the road folks? Did any of them find contentment? Did Maria or her boys ever make it out of poverty? Connor's wit and her attention to language elevate this book from accounts of sad sacks and roadside curiosities to meaningful explorations of life among New England's working poor and the losses that occur in the name of "progress."

At the time of its publication, Connor said this of Vermont and her stories: "What worries me—I don't want to be xenophobic—but we've become so trend-obsessed, so addicted to change and progress, that we fail to see what we are losing: those drive-in theaters, those motor courts, our diners, those signs and, more important, room for those people whose dignity depends on independence and a bit of irreverence. When you're not paying attention to what you're losing, you become vulnerable to becoming a parody of yourself or to be defined from the outside. What I want the reader to do is to think how might tragedy be averted. How do we help the working poor so life isn't so grim for them? We all know of people who work four jobs, none with benefits, people who are raising the kids, just scraping by while so many of their neighbors make more than they need to be comfortable. These are the issues I wanted to explore in these stories."

All that said, the reader will find himself laughing out loud as he turns the pages of a Connor story. In the story *A Hard Place*, we meet typical Vermont characters, cobbling a life from a mishmash of accidents. These lives unfold in a typical Vermont setting: The Rustic Roost, situated somewhere near Bethel and described as "a converted chicken coop with a concrete floor, chrome and red vinyl chairs and fifties' Formica tables. Natives insisted on wet days they could still whiff the chicken droppings. But I smelled only the chicory-bitter, warm brown of coffee steam, the bacon grease of the grill, the bubbly oil slick of the deep fryer." The narrator of this story moved to Vermont to be near her former boyfriend, a yarn-dyed, buffalo plaid-clad woodchuck (a Vermont term for a local yokel), and finds community at the Rustic Roost. Her college friend, Sabra, works temporarily as an archaeologist's assistant and hangs out in the Rustic Roost. Emmy, their waitress, is a native Vermonter who loves moose and might wonder what these two women, who had other options, are doing in her neighborhood. Emmy has had a hard life but she hasn't taken it lying down—when her husband hit her, she decked him and then threw him out. The story is about each person's concept of what is possible and what is not, about the power of imagination, and the gifts we can give one another.

Early in the story, there's this scene:

> One day during a busy lunch hour, Sabra sat at the counter, toy-
> ing with the tassels of her plum-colored scarf. "Do you have a heart
> place?"
>
> "A heart place?" I echoed, glancing at the coveralled coffee-
> drinker to Sabra's right who squinted at her, head cocked as he
> fished a cigarette from his pack.
>
> "You know," Sabra said, "some foreign landscape, never vis-
> ited, that mysteriously, mystically summons you. I am certain
> Tibet is calling me." The coffee-drinker lit his cigarette, and Sabra
> waved off his smoke with a flourish of her scarf.
>
> "Heart place," I said. "I don't know; I've always wanted to
> visit the Yucatan."
>
> "Visit?" Sabra asked, her dark eyes narrowing. "I'm talking
> about finding your spiritual home, your soul's nest, the heart
> place."
>
> The coffee-drinker spun a quarter-turn on his stool.
>
> I averted my eyes from his and watched Emmy scrape the
> grill. "Soul's nest? I don't know. The Yucatan has always in-
> trigued me."
>
> Sabra emptied a sugar packet into her mug and asked. "Is the
> Yucatan your heart place?"
>
> I looked up as Emmy, buttering an English muffin, inter-
> rupted, "I've been some hard places, I can tell you," she said.
> "And I don't feel the need to go to any more of them."[3]

This scene could have been presented as something pitiful. Two women sitting in a cement-floor diner that smells of either old chicken coop or bacon
grease, depending on your perspective, talking about some elusive "heart
place." But the simple, clear brilliance of the waitress cuts through the New
Age–ness of the "heart place." At the same time, the reader immediately
thinks of his or her own heart place and goes there while still keeping
in mind that very convincingly described diner, Emmy and the coveralled
coffee-drinker.

If you wanted to write a formula for effective writing, you could construct one from this scene: convincing character development through description, dialogue, thought, and action combined with realistic
scene-setting, combined with an element of conflict, desire, or interest. In
this case, of course, the reader wants to know where Emmy's heart place
might be. We feel that she deserves one more than anyone else in the story.
And it is on that desire—not just its fulfillment or lack of fulfillment, but
also its significance—that the story turns.

## Tips and Techniques

For the fiction writer, snippets of conversation, photos in an album, a fleeting glimpse of intimacy on a porch swing, or a ramshackle building seen in the rearview mirror are pieces of a puzzle. It matters not if most of the pieces are missing or if pieces of one puzzle get mixed with those of another. The writer supplies the order, creating a reality that explores essential questions: What's going on here? What does it mean? Who gets hurt and who gets healed? Who is saved and who is dammed?

Writers and teachers of writing view the short story as the most demanding genre: a life caught in an hourglass, a puzzle of intricate depth and complexity created with a minimum of pieces. To succeed, the short story must simultaneously lead toward a point of illumination while also leaving much to the readers' imagination. It only works when there is something at stake—something worth wanting—and when the writer provides just enough information to hook us and no more. Like poetry, what is missing is as important as what is told, so that some sentiment or question tugs at us after the last word is read, so that the interior significance of a piece is both immediately and continuously revealed, sometimes over hours, days, even weeks.

Connor returns to the dark New England of her first collection in her second book, *We Who Live Apart*, exploring divorce, childlessness, alcoholism, and other contemporary themes. The stories rise above the maudlin and the routine through the wonderful familiarity of the details; the rich, playful fabric of the language; and the ability of many of the characters to transmute their miseries into learning experiences and to, thereby, triumph over sorrow (or simply accept it). As many of us know, adversity is more interesting than ease; scary events, obstacles, moral dilemmas, conflict, and disappointment provide the best story material. Because experience has taught most people that the human condition guarantees heartache, we view over-rosy stories as unrealistic, unchallenging, and, often, boring. If Romeo and Juliet had met, fallen in love, married, and had a passel of children, if there had been no obstacle to their love, we wouldn't be reading their story all these decades later. And yet we can't read all gloom and doom. It's not only disheartening and depressing; it can become tedious. Connor doesn't avoid the dark avenues and bitter endings, but her fictions are so full of tenderness toward misfits and ne'er-do-wells and her language so playful that the melancholy goes down a bit easier.

In the short story "October," for example, we are introduced to Sherry and Dona, whose lives appear to have devolved over twenty years into the most basic of desires. Sherry and Dona live together in a trailer home, attend AA meetings and dream of finding Mr. Right. Dona cuts hair at Shear Delights, and Sherry waits on customers at Give Pizza A Chance. As the story progresses, we learn that both women are college dropouts, more from bad breaks than bad grades. Connor doesn't sneer at the women, even if they sleep around and used to be drunks. Life has straightened them out the hard way. By story's end, we care for these women and wish them the best—or, at least, peace of mind.[4]

The story is fueled by wonderful writing that brings Vermont to the written page. Connor writes, "October strips itself down to an essential solitude." She describes night biking in this line: "Sherry bumps onto Cold Creek Road where it turns to dirt, and the streetlamps queue up with lengthening expanses of darkness between them. . . . Ground fog's curling up like the earth's talking with warm, soft breath on a cold day."[5] There are, of course, people everywhere who have lost parts of their life to alcohol or drugs or bad decisions, but Connor's descriptions of these people's lives evoke a particularly Vermont take on these casualties of life, especially those who have gotten sober and are trying as best as possible to reconstruct their lives. "Entire episodes of her life have disappeared, leaving spaces like those between streetlights, like the papery spaces between book chapters or the cut-to scenes in TV serials when your imagination's supposed to supply instinctively the missing scenes, the continuity. Fill in the blanks," Connor writes. And then she poses the question that every survivor of lost time fears most. "But what if the missing filler between her memories was where she had truly, fully lived her life?"[6]

In her third collection of short stories, *History Lessons*, Connor finally got to publish her more original and experimental fiction. The collection won the Associated Writing Programs award for best short fiction in 2002. In choosing Connor's book, the judge of the award, Frederick Busch, the author of twenty-one books including six story collections and twelve novels, wrote, "[T]his collection demonstrates an enormous linguistic gift, and a passion for the possibilities of language . . . Sometimes the characters are presented realistically, sometimes as aspects of American prose, often as expressions of historical events and even linguistic behavior; but the people on these pages are never mere reflections of the writer's cleverness or [remarkable] knowledge. Every story is different, every story is a voice. While the voices range in tone from stormy to reconciled, most are tinged with genuine humor."[7]

The history lessons of the book are both personal and human. The collection begins with the first humans, Adam and Eve, and imagines them hanging out at the Automat, that icon of New York efficiency where food is dispensed in individual servings through glass doors. What would Adam and Eve think of this invention and what does it have to say about the state of the human at the end of the millennium (when the story was written) that we have chosen to dispense perfect red but tasteless apples on shelves that revolve behind little glass doors. The story is funny and pathetic, feminist and insightful, empathic and revealing; an excerpt appears below.

The next story in the collection is culled from regional history. "The Day the World Declined to End" fictionalizes the real life of William Miller, a resident of Low Hampton, New York, just over the Vermont border, who predicted the world would end in 1843 and, when it didn't, said he'd miscalculated and meant the next year. The beginning of the book is told from the point of view of a cow. Why a cow? Because the Millerites, the people who believed William Miller's predictions, were so intent on being comfortable in heaven that they dressed their cows in white ascension robes to await the end of the earth along with their owners. When the true believers rose to heaven, so too would the cows. The cows know nothing of assumption. They go about their huddling and chewing on their cud while Miller takes precautions, just in case he is wrong. "They do not know, they would not care to know that, four days before the end of the world, 1843, William Miller is stacking peach preserves in his pantry," Connor writes. Her story is a fabrication; no one but Miller really knows whether he believed his own predictions or not. But the story is constructed of things historians have recorded: the Millerites did dress their cows in assumption gowns; they did believe that they would rise to heaven at the end of the world.[8]

That's quirky enough, but what Connor does with these gems of history is magic. To imagine this behavior through the point of view of the cow, to experience the cow's cowness while all these preparations go on, tells us much about human nature in a thoroughly entertaining and singular manner. This original exploration of the absurdity and wonderfulness of modern culture is central to the stories in *History Lessons*. In another story, "Riding with Ray," Ray Charles calls a fan who had been convicted of stalking him and asks the woman to take him riding in her car. Ray actually wants to drive and the two proceed to get into an accident. The story is based on one factual report: that Ray Charles once took a car for a drive and had a small smashup. Connor invented the stalking fan to give her story a point of view from which to tell the tale. Other facts are peppered through this fiction, delighting us with the rightness of the details. Of course, the stalker will have a closet full of tight little black sheath dresses exactly like the ones that Ray Charles's backup singers, the Raelettes, wore. Of course, when the stalker meets Ray, he's wearing Ray-ban sunglasses and it's night. Of course, she's named Georgia. The story is not so much about Ray Charles, however, as it is about Ray Charles as an American icon, about the American's quest for identity, about icon love, about the blindness of those who can see but choose not to look.

In another of her history lessons, Connor writes about another, more unlikely, pop icon, the singer Tiny Tim who figures prominently in her short story, "The Butterfly Effect." Tiny Tim was a large man with rather wild, long hair, sometimes dyed red or black, who sang old-fashioned songs falsetto and played a tiny ukulele. He was best known for two things: singing "Tiptoe through the Tulips" on the *Rowan & Martin's Laugh-In*; and marrying a woman named Miss Vicky, live on the *Tonight Show*, in 1977.

Thirty-five million people (87 percent of TV viewers) watched the forty-six-year-old Tiny Tim (born Herbert Buckingham Khaury) marry his seventeen-year-old bride on a television set strewn with 10,000 tulips. By the time Tiny Tim died in 1996, his career had come and gone, although he kept hoping for a comeback. Connor finished the story the night before the pop singer died. In her story, as in real life, Tiny Tim lives in a hotel room, eating odd things—raw potatoes and salsa—and practicing hip-hop songs for his comeback. She writes that Tiny Tim "doesn't know that America is a novelty act." Like all of Connor's work, there's empathy for the Tiny Tims of the world, the people living in the shadow of their greatest moment.

Although Connor had been writing all her life, she didn't tackle the hard work of honing her craft and publishing stories until 1993 when, as a newly divorced single mother who hadn't worked professionally for several years, she enrolled in Vermont College's low residency M.F.A. program and began working closely with several mentors in the program, notably François Camoin and Tony Ardizzone. In 1995, when she graduated, "I was staking everything on writing. And, it's worked out pretty well," she observes, noting that she published three collections of short stories in six years and more than two hundred short stories and essays in literary magazines, and simultaneously won several prestigious awards, including both the Philip Roth and Jack Kerouac fellowships in writing.

Connor's subject matter comes from phrases or information she discovers that resonate with her. She has to be intrigued—to want to know more—before she can commit to a subject. She needs to have questions to ponder: what did William Miller think when his predictions didn't come true? What would a stalker do if the object of her desire called and asked for a favor? What was life like for Tiny Tim in that tiny hotel room in Des Moines? What would Adam and Even think of the Automat?

Because these odd and wonderful questions often occur to us at the most inopportune times—when we're driving in the car or falling asleep—they have a tendency to disappear from our brains in about two seconds flat. It's important, therefore, to write them down. Connor keeps a journal in which she merely records words, sentences, images, snippets of conversation, observations, quirky facts, questions, and other material that might someday be useful to the story. When she first began writing short stories, she would plot out the stories. Before she began writing, she would know her characters and what they were going to do. Over the years, however, she's learned to let go. "Now, I follow them; I have no idea what the characters are going to do. I let them loose and let them do what they want to do," she says.

Often, as Connor composes a story, she will open her journal of collected sentences and observations and randomly select some fact or snippet of dialogue and try to work it into the story. Almost always, she says, this exercise makes the story more interesting and takes it in a completely unexpected path, making the writing a process of discovery for her as well as the reader. That happened in "Parrot Man," a story in *History Lessons,* that tells the story of Matt, who's waiting for his life to begin while he works in the photo lab and waits on people at the lunch counter at Norman's, one of those dying soda-shop and pharmacy and photo service places somewhere in America. Every day, Matt waits on Parrot Man, who says everything twice, and Hummingbird, whose sentences have become such a jumble of broken syntax that he hums to himself a lot, and Ice Tea, a rich woman who orders iced tea but doesn't drink it while she waits to pick up one roll after another of film showing beautiful people doing beautiful things. Parrot Man and Hummingbird and Ice Tea were culled from different notations in different notebooks, fictionalized pieces of real life whose happenstance unite with other fictionalized scraps of reality and combine to make a delightful portrait of life in a place that is at once familiar and strange. "When I choose something arbitrary to include in a story," Connor explains, "I have to figure out how to fit it in. I find it's a really good way to destabilize the rational side of the brain a little bit and open it up intuitively. That's the surprise that communicates to the reader. It forces me to make connections I otherwise wouldn't."

Connor advises aspiring writers to turn their brains and imaginations on by collecting and reading as much as possible, not merely traditional history and culture, but information about odd and interesting people, places and events: "I love going to used book stores and patrolling their reference sections. I collect dictionaries. I have dictionaries of histories, of superstitions, of dreams. Then when I'm working on a story, I have a reference point to inform the story and give it texture. If there's a rooster in my story, for example, I can look up *rooster* in my book of superstitions and weave that into my story. I have a name dictionary and I read it sometimes when I'm naming my characters. While I don't expect my reader to know all of these references, they give the story texture. I'm always interested in fiction that's about something, that informs me about something I don't know. And, so, I envision a reader who is also an interested person, someone who wants to learn something, and I try to give them something."

Connor also advises developing writers to "learn from the poets—about rhyme, about repetition, about working with metaphors and motifs" and to practice writing about subjects that matter, not only about ourselves. "We start writing out of a kind of selfishness and we write ourselves. But that's only interesting for so long, at least for me, and often for the reader, too. Yes, writing is about self-discovery; you do have to come to terms with your own ugliness, but the stories that interest me the most don't indulge the narcissism of the author. Even though there are autobiographical elements in my stories, in the end they're not about me. I'm not that interesting." She also advises writers to read out loud. "I read my story out loud when it's getting to the finished state and then I hear what's missing. The eye misses things, the ear doesn't. The best editing technique occurs when I hear the story. It tunes you into what's going on with the language. You can hear when it doesn't work."

All these techniques that Connor uses (and recommends for other writers) are ones that help her grow and not get stale. She concedes, "One of the scariest things about being a writer is that you're losing it, that you've written your best work, that it's all downhill. After the Miller story, I was afraid I wouldn't write anything that good again. You want not to keep repeating what you've already done so you have to find ways to let your work evolve in new directions. Any writer has to constantly stop doing what she does well and try something else, something she doesn't do well. A writer will not get better otherwise."

Although she writes a good deal about what has changed in Vermont, Connor remains happy with what has not. "What hasn't changed, when so much has, is a joy in Yankee oddness. There's still an appreciation for peccadillo, for personal eccentricity. . . . There's something nonjudgmental going on. It's true no place can ostracize you like a small town can, but it's also true how quickly people respond when there's a tragedy in their midst. If you go off the road in Vermont, five people will come to your aid, whereas if you were someplace else, like New Jersey, you'd still be waiting," she says.

For writers, this translates into other benefits. Connor observes that many writers love nature and the environment so they're happiest living in a place where there is respect for environment. Writing requires long stretches of isolation and meditation, so writers are attracted to places where there's a respect for solitude. Writers require camaraderie and social intercourse to fuel their poems and stories; they are interested in what makes people tick. Therefore, she observes, writers choose to live in a place where there is respect for community. All that, she points out, defines Vermont. Beyond that, she says, as the world gets uglier and more homogenized, as it becomes less safe and more divisive, "You still have Vermont. And, for me, Vermont will always be home."

---

### ◀§ Adam and Eve at the Automat

Adam peered through the glass doors at the fish of the sea, and the fowl of the air, and all the cattle and herb of the earth, but he could not make up his mind. The bounty overwhelmed him. The diversity of the good earth's profusion, the miracle of the appearance, entire, of a pastrami on rye, of molded salad, of an open-face turkey roll sandwich, and reconstituted mashed potato in the cubicles of the automat awed him

Finally, he settled on a wedge of apple pie. He placed the pie on his stainless steel tray, paid the cashier, and bore the pie back to the table to have dominion over it and eat of it. And Adam joined Eve at the Formica table. And the hands behind the scene replenished the cubicle of the automat with another slice of pie.

"Are you sure you don't want anything to eat?" Adam asked. "Not even a bite?"

Eve shook her head. "Just my cup of Joe," she said.

And Adam watched the light ricochet off Eve's glossy coif, electroplated with Breck hair spray. He noticed how the light reflected the synthetic purples of her industrial-strength platinum dye.

"How beautiful you look by economical fluorescent light," he said.

Eve smiled. So this is how two great, Western mythic figures of failure speak to each other in an automat. She lit a Lucky Strike.

"The crust isn't Betty Crocker," Adam commented. "It's a little dry on top. Soggy bottom." He mashed an apple chunk with his fork.

Eve flicked her ash into the aluminum foil ashtray. She thought of the hands behind the scenes—furious, hyperkinetic, digits flicking, wrists flexing, muscles firing the impulses to keep the automat automatic, to keep the grid filled—coconut cream, banana cream, Boston cream, lemon meringue. . . . How tired He must be, she thought, patting a yellow wire back into her beehive 'do.' He could use another seventh day. "Every pie can't be perfect," she said. "He's doing the best He can."

"I guess it isn't as easy as apple pie," Adam said, snickering.

Eve winced. Another apple joke.

Adam crinkled the snakeskin off his straw, then elbowed the pie across the aqua boomerang pattern of the Formica. "Are you certain you won't have just a bite?"

Again, Eve shook her head. Arrows of artificial light pinged off the taut strings of her hair.

A man in a porkpie hat, seated at a neighboring table, leaned confidentially toward them. He glanced at Adam's apple pie. "The lemon custard isn't bad," he said. "It's wholesome and nutritious, fortified with eight essential vitamins, artificial colors and stabilizers, and has a remarkable shelf life for a perishable."

"Thank You," Eve said, and shot Adam a reproving glance for muttering something about 'Mr. Butt-in-ski.'

He was such a child, really, she thought, this flesh of her flesh, this handful of inspired dust. She plucked a pre-folded paper napkin from the E-Z Kleen dispenser and dabbed at a bit of apple on Adam's cheek. He caught her hand in his and held it a moment against his face.

"Are you happy, Eve?" he asked. "Am I the apple of your eye?"

And she nodded although the nod was a lie. And she suppressed the sigh arising from her knowledge of the imperfectability of Adam.

And Adam siphoned a dose of cherry Coke up his straw. And he tapped the top of the straw, suspending the drop above the pleated paper sheath. "Want to see me charm a snake?" he teased.

"No." She shook her head.

"Oops. Too late." Adam's index finger lifted. The paper writhed beneath the caramel drop. He grinned at her, waiting for a reaction.

The drop damped, blotted. The tissue puddle and dissolved. Novelty acts. She sighed and glanced at her Timex. She imagined again the hands behind the scenes racing against themselves, the hands of a clock, spinning around and around, refilling the ever-emptying shelves of the automat. And Eve sensed the futility of the endeavor—like trying to hide from God. She remembered and smiled at her past foolishness.

"Are you really happy, Eve?" Adam pressed her.

Eve squashed the Lucky butt under her heel. She hesitated at Adam's emphasis on "really." She could feel his eagerness, the atavistic urgency to align them, to replay a cosmic harmony, to tuck her like a notekey back into the xylophone of his ribcage where they could make beautiful music together to the conga beat of his heart.

And she felt again the ancient rebellion in her, the curious impulse against conscience that sent the world spinning.

"No," she said. "I am not really happy. I am tired of your jokes. I long for apple-pie disorder. I miss Abel, and I'm tired of raising Cain. In sorrow I brought forth my children, and in sorrow they went forth. All of them." And she stood up, her platinum cone of hair rising like the nose of a rocket, her arms sweeping expansively, inclusively over the towers of porcelain plates, hot from the dishwasher, the various labor-saving devices, the gleaming coffee urns, the steaming imitation hot chocolate machines, the black-and-white checkered linoleum, the man in the porkpie hat, and every creeping thing that creepeth in the automat.

But the gesture grew too large for her, and she fell back into her chair, exhausted.

"Are you okay?" Adam asked. "You don't seem yourself today."

His palm checking the heat of her forehead impressed her irritably with his claim on her, its legitimacy. She grew quiet beneath his palm and lit another Lucky. She inhaled slowly.

Really, she thought, the problem was Adam's restlessness. He needed a hobby. Retirement was tough on men, and there wasn't much shelf space in the job market for tillers of the soil anymore . . . grain surpluses . . . agri-biz . . .

And the kids flown from the nest, Cain, East of Eden, and Seth, God knew where, multiplying after their own images and in their own likenesses, each to the end of his days. All that begetting and begetting.

And Eve pressed her fingertips against her eyelids until she saw lights burst like sparks in the darkness, and she opened her eyes, and she looked at Adam and at the walls of shining steel and polished chrome and the checkerboard of black-and-white lino, and the kidney shapes of the Formica pattern, and the towers of porcelain plates and mugs, and the walls of glinting glass doors behind which nestled a host of eye-pleasing comestibles from all four of the major food groups selected for the modern consumer's delectation.

And she knew it was not good, but it was, at least, efficient. And she knew that she knew the difference between the two.

And she knew that, if she had the chance again to pluck the fruit of her desire, nearly two millennia old, she would. Dying to die, she would risk the flaming sword which turned every way. But there was no turning back. Her desire was a revolving door.

Eve understood desire. And fatigue.

She stubbed out her Lucky. She kissed Adam affectionately and dismissively. And Eve rose to the sound of dishes crashing to the floor behind the scenes. She tied on her apron of fig leaves.

"Where are going?" Adam cried as Eve walked toward the swinging door marked NO ADMITTANCE.

She faltered. She looked at Adam. "I'm so tired, dear," she said, "so tired. But we must keep up appearances."

And she went to meet her maker.[9]

## Questions and Exercises for Reflection and Inspiration

In the story, "Adam and Eve at the Automat," Connor liberally uses biblical languages and references as she tells her story. The many references to apples, to Cain and Abel and Seth, to begetting and begetting, to snakeskin and to the seventh day all come from the story of Genesis. It's what makes the story so downright enjoyable. But Connor doesn't merely borrow from Genesis and other biblical tales as she contemplates what Adam and Eve might think and do and say if they showed up in an automat. She plays with the possibilities, using metaphoric language to add layers of meaning that readers find delightful. The line about Adam wanting "to tuck her [Eve] like a notekey back into the xylophone of his ribcage where they could make beautiful music together to the conga beat of his heart," evokes a traditional guy who would prefer a nice quiet life, with no unexpected curve balls. Eve, on the other hand, is tired; she's still got a rebellious streak. The story reflects a feminist perspective—but just so far. Eve smokes her Lucky Strikes and contemplates a life away from Adam, away from the prescribed role of obedience. "The curious impulse against conscience that sent the world spinning" is still knocking around in her heart or soul; it's what allows her to open that door marked NO ADMITTANCE—but Eve only goes so far;

she's going out back to help the big guy with the broken dishes and the constant effort perfection requires.

**Exercise 1:** Take some other emblematic story or character from the past that is known by most people, one of deep resonance, and imagine the characters in the twenty-first century: at the mall, for example, or trying to figure out how to get a virus out of the computer. What would Joan of Arc think if she came back to France and learned about the European Union? Or put two historic figures together in heaven (or hell) and see what they have to say to one another: Einstein and Elvis, for example, or Eleanor Roosevelt and Marie Curie. Have fun and let the story take you where it wants to go.

**Exercise 2:** Write a story about a real experience that you have told to people before but, using Connor's writing tip, interject some fact, observation, quote, or event that is not part of the real story into your written account. Pay close attention to what happens when you introduce something fictitious into the original story. Have fun with this exercise and let the narrative take you in unexpected directions. Is Connor right that the introduction of odd information into a preordained tale allows you as writer to create something fresh and exciting? You may also do this exercise with a story that you are writing, introducing some random information or character into the piece and then seeing what happens. If you've been diligent about keeping your writer's journal, you should have some interesting sentences, characters, pieces of conversation, odd facts, or observations that you can throw in. But don't just interject the new information as a one- or two-liner. Follow the thread, letting the random, newly introduced material give new meaning and direction to your piece. If you haven't been keeping a journal, simply pick up the paper or turn on talk radio for a minute, jotting down some sentences that you hear. It may seem silly to you at first or irrational, but it's exactly the irrational that you're after. The irrational is often the unpredictable and we as readers (and writers) find the unpredictable interesting and intriguing.

Connor—like several other writers in this book, especially poet Tom Smith—is interested in iconic figures, people like Marilyn Monroe, or Elvis, or Henry the VIII, or Napoleon, or Nixon, people whose impact on society has been large or whose significance grows after their death. Sometimes, these figures have special significance for the writer (such as Ray Charles, whom Connor always enjoyed listening to and learning about). Other times, there is something about their lives (or deaths) that speaks quite clearly to what it is to be human—or, better, what it is to be human and have both gifts and vulnerabilities. When many people admire someone or follow his or her life, even after that person has shamed himself or fallen into disgrace, it signifies that there is something about the famous person that many people can relate to or envy or despise.

> **Exercise 3:** Take some figure whose story has significance beyond their accomplishments, someone, dead or alive, who elicits strong responses from the general public—Martha Stewart, for example, or John F. Kennedy—and write a fictional story imaging an ordinary event in his or her life: the day Martha Stewart had to call a plumber to unclog her drains, which were filled with potato peels from her experiment with potato pudding; the day the pope wanted his tarot cards read; the time Donald Trump got a flat tire and his chauffeur's cell phone was dead; the day Lorena Bobbitt bought her first tabloid newspaper; the day Clint Eastwood sang "Happy Birthday" to you at his Hog's Breath Tavern. Just go with it. Have fun. Do a little research about your chosen subject so you can interweave real facts into your fictional account.

Connor suggests filling your bookshelves with resource material. Beyond the ones she's suggested, many writers also collect anthologies, encyclopedias, atlases, gardening books, travel books, cookbooks, plant, animal, and rock identification guides and other material that will prove useful later. What books are on your reference shelf?

> **Exercise 4:** Take a reference book down from the library or from your home bookcase and open it to any page. Look for something interesting: a picture of a lemur in a dictionary, a description of a Van Gogh painting from an art history book, a detailed account of metamorphic rock from a geology text. Now, invent a character who is obsessed with details such as the one you've chosen and write a story about her. Make up some texts that might be on your character's shelf. What might this character want more than anything else in life? To see a lemur? To own a Van Gogh painting? And what might she do to get what she wants? And what's stopping her from getting it? You're on your way to a new story.

# NOTES

*Preface* (pp. ix–xv)

1. Charles Edward Crane, *Let Me Show You Vermont* (New York: 1942), 266, a valuable text for anyone interested in the history of Vermont. Crane was born in Illinois of Vermont parents. He moved to Plymouth at age six and grew up in the same valley that produced Calvin Coolidge. A staff reporter for the Associated Press in New York and elsewhere for fifteen years, he returned to Vermont in 1917 to own and manage a small paper and reacquaint himself with the state he had learned to love as a boy. The book is informative on a wide variety of subjects that include Vermont history, geology, art, character, weather, animals, linguistics and a wonderful hodgepodge of other facts and observations.

2. Bernard DeVoto, "Wayfarer's Daybook," *Harper's Magazine* (December 1951), 44–47. Many important writers like DeVoto had their first experience with Vermont as students and/or staff members at Middlebury College's Bread Loaf Writers Conference. Middlebury founded the Bread Loaf Writers Conference in 1926 upon the urging of Robert Frost and others. Since then, it has served as one of the nation's leading educational facilities for young and developing writers. Based near the Ripton home of Frost, the annual conference features daily classes and readings, some of which are open to the public.

3. Marguerite Hurrey Wolf, Leon W. Dean, eds., "Journey from Burlington to Hanover in 1801," *Vermont History* (Montpelier: Green Mountain Folklore Society), 24, no. 4 (October 1956).

4. Burgess Johnson, "Vermont the Nonconformed," *Saturday Review* (24 October 1953).

5. Arthur W. Biddle and Paul A. Eschholz, eds., *The Literature of Vermont: A Sampler* (Hanover, N.H.: University Press of New England, 1973), 3.

6. Tony Magistrale, ed., *Literature: Vermont as a Setting*, Vermont Academy of Arts & Science, Occasional Paper No. 22 (Middletown Springs, Vt., 1989).

*Introduction* (pp. 1–22)

1. Arthur W. Biddle and Paul A. Eschholz, eds., *The Literature of Vermont: A Sampler* (Hanover, N.H.: University Press of New England, 1973), 2–3. Hemenway is an important figure in early Vermont history and literature. According to Charles Edward Crane, in his *Let Me Show You Vermont* (New York: Knopf, 1946), 269, Hemenway "organized the town histories of the entire state through publication of a Vermont Quarterly Gazetteer," which ran to about six

thousand pages. For further exploration, see Abby Maria Hemenway, *Hemenway's Vermont* (Brattleboro, Vt.: Stephen Greene Press, 1972).

2. Michael Caduto is a singer, storyteller, songwriter, and ecologist. The author of twelve books for children and adults that include *Earth Tales from Around the World* (Golden, Colo.: Fulcrum, 1997), he is the founder of PEACE (Programs for Environmental Awareness and Cultural Exchange) an organization that brings environmental presentations into classrooms. Caduto, who is of Italian heritage, works closely with Abenaki writers such as Joseph Bruchak of New York, to bring Native American stories to life. Caduto and Bruchak's *Keepers of the Earth: Native American Stories and Environmental Activities for Children* (Golden, Colo.: Fulcrum, 1997) is an environmental classic for teaching children to respect the Earth. While continuing to work with Native Americans, in recent years Caduto has broadened his writing, performing and conducting workshops to include themes of Earth stewardship and cultural diversity, as explored through indigenous stories and wisdom traditions from around the world.

3. Crane, *Let Me Show You Vermont*, 267.

4. Ibid.

5. Biddle and Eschholz, *Literature of Vermont*, 5. A contemporary edition of *Danvis Folks* was produced by David Budbill and published by the University Press of New England in 1995.

6. Biddle and Eschholz, *Literature of Vermont*, 26.

7. Ibid.

8. Crane, *Let Me Show You Vermont*, 272.

9. Rowland E. Robinson, *Out of Bondage and Other Stories* (Rutland, Vt.: Charles E. Tuttle, 1936). "Out of Bondage" also appeared in the *Atlantic Monthly* in 1897. You can learn more about Robinson's life and work, as well as his home in Ferrisburgh, by requesting *Vermont History; Proceedings of the Vermont Historical Society*, 69 (Winter 2001). The document is available online at *www.vermonthistory.org/journal/69*.

10. Crane, *Let Me Show You Vermont*, 169.

11. Biddle and Eschholz, *Literature of Vermont*, 14.

12. Ibid., 14.

13. Ibid., 23.

14. Crane, *Let Me Show You Vermont*, 270.

15. Biddle and Eschholz, *Literature of Vermont*, 8.

16. Crane, *Let Me Show You Vermont*, 270–271.

17. Michael Sherman, "Daniel Pierce Thompson," *Online: Vermont Historical Society Website*, available at *http://www.vermonthistory.org/sherman/thompson.htm*. According to the website, "the Vermont Historical Society recently acquired a collection of letters, plot outlines, and other literary papers by Daniel Pierce Thompson. These include plot summaries, sketches, and sections of some of Thompson's incomplete and unpublished works. They supplement the Society's already large collection of Thompson's letters and papers."

18. Ibid.

19. George Perkins Marsh, *Man and Nature* (Cambridge, Mass.: Belknap Press of Harvard University, 1864).

20. John H. Lienhard, "Engines of Our Ingenuity," KUHF-FM Houston, episode 595. "Engines of Our Ingenuity" is a radio program, produced by Lienhard and heard on Public Radio, that tells the story of how our culture is formed by human creativity. You can hear the episode about Marsh at *http://www.uh.edu/engines/epi595.htm*.

21. You can read more about Marsh by visiting Clark University's website. Clark University is home to the George Perkins Marsh Institute, which promotes itself as "dedicated to research on one of the most fundamental questions confronting humankind: what is and ought to be our relationship with nature?" You can visit the website at *http://www.clarku.edu/departments/marsh/georgemarsh.shtml*.

22. "20 in 20: Vermont's Greatest Moments of the Twentieth Century," *Vermont Today*, a website created by the *Rutland Herald* and the *Barre-Montpelier Times Argus*. You can visit the site to read more about Walter Hard and other important Vermonters at *http://www.vermonttoday.com/century/mostinflu/whardsr.html*.

23. Walter R. Hard, *Some Vermonters* (Boston: Gorham, 1928), 5.

24. "20 in 20: Vermont's Greatest Moments of the Twentieth Century."

25. Biddle and Eschholz, *Literature of Vermont*, 341.

26. Ibid., 29.

27. Dorothy Canfield Fisher, "Vermont: Our Rich Little Poor State," *The Nation* (31 May 1922). For more on Fisher's views on Vermont, see also Mark J Madigan, *Keeping Fires Night and Day: Selected Letters of Dorothy Canfield Fisher* (Columbia, Mo.: University of Missouri Press, 1993).

28. Dorothy Canfield Fisher, *Vermont Tradition: The Biography of An Outlook on Life* (Boston: Little, Brown, 1953).

29. Ibid., 87.

30. Ibid., 153.

31. Walter John Coates and Frederick Tupper, eds. *Vermont Verse: An Anthology* (Brattleboro, Vt.: Stephen Daye Press, 1931), 229.

32. Ibid., 179. The golf course mentioned here is not in Manchester, Vermont, as many people have assumed, but rather a course located in Macon, Georgia, home of the PGA tournament.

33. Stuart Murray, *Rudyard Kipling in Vermont: Birthplace of The Jungle Books* (Bennington, Vt.: Images From the Past, 1997).

34. Buck had adopted the male pseudonym as a response to the rebukes she received from the male-dominated literary world when she received the Nobel Prize.

35. Helen and Scott Nearing, *Living the Good Life: How to Live Sanely and Simply in a Troubled World* (Harborside, Maine: Social Science Institute, 1954).

36. Scott Nearing, *The Great Madness: A Victory for the American Plutocracy* (New York: Rand School of Social Science, 1917). Nearing had been formally charged under the Espionage Act with impeding the United States' intervention in World War I. You can read Nearing's closing argument, delivered in U.S. District Court for the Southern District of New York on 19 February 1919, at *http://www.afn.org/~vetpeace/ nearing.html*.

37. Scott Nearing, *Oil and the Germs of War* (Ridgewood, N.J.: Nellie Seeds Nearing, 1923).

38. Helen and Scott Nearing, *The Maple Sugar Book* (New York: Schocken Books, 1950), xii. The Thoreau Institute at Walden Woods in Lincoln, Massachusetts, has a rich collection of documents spanning eight decades in the lives of Scott and Helen Nearing.

39. Sinclair Lewis's speech to the Rutland Rotary Club on 23 September 1929.

40. Peter Kurth, *American Cassandra* (Boston: Little Brown, 1990), 139.

41. Ibid., 270.

42. Sinclair Lewis, *It Can't Happen Here* (New York: AMS Press, 1935). The novel was scheduled to be made into a movie in 1936, but it was censored by Will Hays. Hays, the former chairman of the Republican National Committee, was president of the Motion Picture Producers and Distributors of America. As such, he had the last word on movie content. Even though the fictional politician in Lewis's novel, Buzz Windrip, ran for president as a Democrat, Hays like many others read the book as a criticism of the Republican Party. In 1935, any attack on Hitler's Germany was viewed as Democratic Party propaganda as many powerful members of the Republican Party were opposed to war with Germany.

43. Kurth, *American Cassandra*, 269.

44. In *The Collected Poems of Robert Penn Warren*, ed. John Burt (Baton Rouge: Louisiana State University Press, 1998), 65.

45. The position of Vermont State Poet was established by the Vermont legislature in 1961. Robert Frost, then eighty-seven, received the first honor. The position was dormant for many years after his death, and reestablished in 1990 with Galway Kinnell serving the first four-year term, followed by Louise Gluck, Ellen Bryant Voigt, and Grace Paley.

46. Among Vermont writers, David Budbill is probably the most active Vermont writer in using the Internet to make his written material available to the general public. Along with an e-zine (that is, an online magazine), Budbill maintains a website with numerous links to his works. Here, for example, is where you can find a synopsis of the play *Judevine*, along with a production history and reviews. The summary quoted above comes from this site, which you can view at *http://www.davidbudbill.com/jude2pl .html*.

47. David Howard Bain, *Whose Woods These Are: A History of the Bread Loaf Writers' Conference, 1926–1992* (Hopewell, N.J.: Ecco, 1993).

48. Fisher's work on eugenics and her exploration into sterilization of people with

mental retardation and those of Abenaki heritage certainly distance her ideologically from Paley whose lifework has included support for the enfranchisement of people with disabilities and an eradication of stereotypes and racism.

### Howard Frank Mosher (pp. 25–46)

1. You can learn more about Chichester by visiting the community's website at *http://www.chichesterville.net/articles.htm*.

2. Howard Frank Mosher, *North Country: A Personal Journey Through the Borderland* (Boston: Houghton Mifflin, 1997).

3. Katie Bacon, "A Disappearing Eden," *The Atlantic Online*, 2 October 1997, *http://www.theatlantic.com/atlantic/unbound/book auth/hfmint.htm*.

4. Howard Frank Mosher, *Where the Rivers Flow North* (New York: Penguin, 1978).

5. Howard Frank Mosher, *Disappearances* (New York: Viking Penguin, 1977), 8-9.

6. Howard Frank Mosher, *The True Account: A Novel of the Lewis & Clark & Kinneson Expeditions* (Boston: Houghton Mifflin, 2003).

7. Howard Frank Mosher, *A Stranger in the Kingdom* (New York: Dell, 1989).

8. Howard Frank Mosher, *Waiting for Teddy Williams* (Boston: Houghton Mifflin, 2004).

### David Budbill (pp. 47–62)

1. David Budbill, *Hardwick Gazette* (Hardwick, Vt.), 9 July 1997. Budbill's commentary originally aired on the National Public Radio show *All Things Considered* on 8 July 1997.

2. David Budbill, *Seven Days* (Burlington, Vt.), 15 December 1999.

3. Ibid.

4. David Budbill, *The Chain Saw Dance* (Woodstock, Vt.: Countryman Press, 1983). This book was first published by Crow's Mark Press (Johnson, Vt.) in 1977.

5. David Budbill, *Judevine* (White River Junction, Vt.: Chelsea Green, 1989). A revised, expanded, and updated version was published in 1999.

6. David Budbill, *From Down to the Village* (Cambridge, Mass.: The Ark, 1981).

7. David Budbill, *The Pulp Cutters Nativity* (Woodstock, Vt.: Countryman Press, 1981).

8. Alice Mary Kimball was born in Woodbury in 1886 and published her first piece in the *Hardwick Gazette* at age ten. Kimball became a well-known journalist, working for the *Kansas City Star*, the *Saturday Evening Post*, *Reader's Digest*, and other national publications. Her book of poetry, *The Devil Is a Woman*, won her national acclaim. She used both her poetry and her journalism to campaign against the Ku Klux Klan, for workers' rights, and for peace and civil rights at home and abroad. She and her two brothers founded the Adamant Music School in 1942 as a place where students from New York could practice piano in pleasant, quiet surroundings. The school also served as a refuge for Jewish musicians suffering anti-Semitism at home and abroad. Still in existence, the beautiful 200-acre campus in Adamant offers traditional and master classes each summer. You can learn more about the school at *http://www.adamant.org/index.html*.

9. David Budbill's play, *Part of It*, was first performed at the Lost Nation Theater in Montpelier in the summer of 1993, with ten performances from 23 June through 4 July. Tammy Fletcher, a Vermont blues singer, played the role of the blues singer in the play. In 1995, a revised version of the play, titled *Little Acts of Kindness*, was produced by Center Stage Company, which toured Vermont and New Hampshire with the play, putting on fourteen performances from September through November 1995. Tammy Fletcher and the Disciples played the blues band.

10. David Budbill, "Vision of the Spirit or Potted Plant," delivered as the keynote address to the annual meeting of the Vermont Council on the Arts at the Chandler Music Hall in Randolph, Vermont, on 21 November 1987.

11. Sebastian Matthews , "Back There: A Conversation with David Budbill," *Rivendell: Literary Arts Journal* 1, no. 2 (Summer 2003): 10–30. You can read part of the interview at *http://www.greenmanwalking.com/North_of_Boston/budbill.shtml*.

12. David Budbill, *Moment to Moment: Poems of a Mountain Recluse* (Port Townsend, Wash.: Copper Canyon Press, 1999).

13. David Budbill, *Moment to Moment*, 50.

14. Matthews, "Back There," 13.

15. David Budbill and William Parker,

*Zen Mountains/Zen Streets* (New York: Box-holder Records, 1999).

16. You can peruse Budbill's website at *http://www.davidbudbill.com*.

17. David Budbill, *Moment to Moment*, 118.

18. Ibid., 6.

19. David Budbill, *While We've Still Got Feet* (Port Townsend, Wash.: Copper Canyon Press, 2005).

20. Ibid.

21. This poem is an amalgam of other poems that Budbill has published and appears in much altered form in *While We've Still Got Feet*. You can read more about this piece at *http://www.davidbudbill.com/emperorlive.html*.

## Chris Bohjalian (pp. 63–78)

1. Chris Bohjalian, *Idyll Banter* (New York: Harmony Books, 2003), 12.

2. Rebecca Bain, "The Fine Print," *Nashville Public Radio*, 26 September 1998. You can hear the interview on Nashville Public Radio's website at *http://www.wpln.org/fineprint/fineprint98.html*.

3. Chris Bohjalian, *A Killing in the Real World* (New York: Horizon Books, 1994).

4. Chris Bohjalian, *Before You Know Kindness* (New York: Shaye Areheart Books, 2004).

5. Chris Bohjalian, *Midwives* (New York: Harmony Books, 1997).

6. Chris Bohjalian, *Trans-Sister Radio* (New York: Crown, 2000).

7. Chris Bohjalian, *The Law of Similars* (New York: Harmony Books, 1999).

8. Chris Bohjalian, *Water Witches* (Hanover, N.H.: University Press of New England, 1995).

9. Chris Bohjalian, *Buffalo Soldier* (New York: Shaye Areheart Books, 2002).

10. Chris Bohjalian, *Before You Know Kindness* (New York: Shaye Areheart Books, 2004).

11. Bohjalian, *Idyll Banter*, 4.

## Joseph A. Citro (pp. 79–92)

1. Joseph Citro, *Green Mountain Ghosts, Ghouls and Unsolved Mysteries* (Shelburne, Vt.: Chapters Publishing, 1994).

2. Joseph Citro, *Shadow Child*. (Hanover, N.H.: University Press of New England, 1987).

3. Matt G. Paradise, "Purging Talon," *Not Like Most*, a website of the occult. The interview with Citro can be read at *http://www.purgingtalon.com/nlm/citro.htm*.

4. Robert E. Weinberg, *Lovecraft's Legacy* (New York: Tor Books, 1990).

5. Joseph Citro, *Deux-X: The Reality Conspiracy* (Sparta, N.J.: Twilight Publishing, 1984).

6. Joseph Citro, *The Gore* (Hanover, N.H.: University Press of New England, 2000). First published in 1990.

7. Joseph Citro. *Lake Monsters* (Hanover, N.H.: University Press of New England, 2001). First published in 1991.

8. Joseph Citro, *Green Mountain Ghosts, Ghouls and Unsolved Mysteries* (Shelburne, Vt.: Chapters Publishing Ltd., 1994), 23–32.

## Jeffrey Lent (pp. 93–105)

1. Jeffrey Lent, *In the Fall* (New York: Atlantic Monthly, 2000).

2. Ibid., 23–24.

3. Jeffrey Lent, *Lost Nation* (New York: Atlantic Monthly, 2002).

4. Ibid., 1.

## David Moats (pp. 109–120)

1. David Moats, "A Conscientious Start," *Rutland Herald*, 11 February 2000. Moats's editorials are at *http://www.rutlandherald.com*.

2. David Moats, "A Charitable View," *Rutland Herald*, 9 February 2000.

3. David Moats, *Civil Wars* (New York: Harcourt, 2004).

## Sydney Lea (pp. 121–136)

1. Sydney Lea, *Hunting the Whole Way Home* (Hanover, N.H.: University Press of New England, 1994).

2. Ibid., 104.

3. Ibid.

4. Ibid.

5. Ibid., 20–21.

6. Sydney Lea, *To the Bone: New and Selected Poems* (Champaign: University of Illinois Press, 1996).

7. Ibid., 14.

8. New York Writers Institute website. *http://www.albany.edu/writers-inst/halllea.html*.

9. Marie Jordan Giordano, "An Interview with Sydney Lea," *The Writer's Chronicle* (September 2004), *http://www.mariejordan.com/publishedreviewsA/*.

10. Ibid.

11. Ibid.

12. Ibid.

### Grace Paley (pp. 137–152)

1. Grace Paley, *Just as I Thought* (New York: Farrar, Straus and Giroux, 1998).

2. Alexis Jetter, "State of Grace," *Vanity Fair* (March 1998).

3. Grace Paley, *Begin Again: Collected Poems* (New York: Farrar, Straus and Giroux, 2000), 147.

4. Grace Paley, *Grace Paley: The Collected Stories* (New York: Farrar, Straus and Giroux, 1994), 50–65.

5. Grace Paley, *Just As I Thought* (New York: Farrar, Strauss and Giroux, 1998), 299–300.

6. Ibid., 300.

7. The story "Goodbye and Good Luck" is Paley's first story. It was published in *The Little Disturbances of Man: Stories of Women and Men at Love* (New York: Doubleday, 1959).

8. Grace Paley, "Two Ears, three Lucks," *Grace Paley: The Collected Stories*, 3.

9. Grace Paley, "Like All the Other Nations," *Just As I Thought*, 44–45.

10. Grace Paley, *Just As I Thought*, 31–35.

### Ellen Bryant Voigt (pp. 153–168)

1. Ellen Bryant Voigt, *The Flexible Lyric* (New York: Norton, 1999).

2. Ellen Bryant Voigt, *Two Trees* (New York: Norton, 1992), 61–63.

3 Ibid.

4. Procne is a tragic Greek figure who kills her own son to bring revenge on her husband, Tereus, after he defiled her sister, Philomena, and cut out Philomena's tongue so she couldn't tell of her assault; Philomena embroiders the story in graphic detail on a shawl so others will know. When Procne learns the story, she and her sister revenge Tereus by killing his son. When he finds out what they have done, Tereus chases after them but the two women pray to the gods to save them. Procne is turned into a nightingale who constantly cries out her sorrow, singing her son's name, "Itu, Itu." Philomena is turned into a swallow.

5. *Book Magazine* (July/August 2000). You can view the article at *http://www.book magazine.com/archieve/issue11/poetics.shtml.*

6. *Atlantic Monthly*, 24 November 1999.

You can view the article at *http://www.the atlantic.com/unbound/poetry.voigt.htm.*

7. Ellen Bryant Voigt, *Kyrie* (New York: Norton, 1995).

8. Ibid., 11.

9. Ibid.,15.

10 . Ibid., 16.

11. Ibid., 17.

12. Ibid., 19.

13. Ibid., 22.

14. Ellen Bryant Voigt, *Shadow of Heaven* (New York: Norton, 2002).

15. Ibid., 21.

16. Ibid.

17. Ibid., 19.

18. Ibid., 86.

19. Voigt, *Kyrie*, 18.

### David Huddle (pp. 169–180)

1. David Huddle, *Paper Boy* (Pittsburgh: University of Pittsburgh Press, 1979).

2. Huddle, *La Tour Dreams of the Wolf Girl* (Boston: Houghton Mifflin, 2002).

3. Huddle, *Tenorman* (San Francisco, Calif.: Chronicle Books, 1995).

4. Huddle, *The Writing Habit* (Salt Lake City, Utah: Peregrine Smith, 1991).

5. Huddle, *Summer Lake* (Baton Rouge: Louisiana State University Press, 1999), 56–57.

6. Huddle, *Only the Little Bone* (Boston: David R. Godine,1986), 45.

7. Huddle, "In the Mean Mud Season," in *High Spirits: Stories of Men and Women* (Boston: David R. Godine, 1989), 209–210.

8. Dan Wicket, *Emerging Writers Forum*, 20 March 2002. The interview is online at *http://www.breaktech.net/EmergingWriters Forum/View_Interview.aspx?id=17.*

9. Huddle, *The Writing Habit*, 9.

10. Ibid., 43.

11. Huddle, *The Story of a Million Years* (Boston: Houghton Mifflin, 1999).

12. Huddle, The Writing Habit, 43.

13. Ibid.

14. Huddle, *Tenorman*, 1–4.

15. Huddle, *The Writing Life*, 25.

16. Ibid., 25–26.

17. Ibid., 27.

### Galway Kinnell (pp. 181–192)

1. Galway Kinnell, *A New Selected Poems* (Boston: Houghton, Mifflin, 2000), 39.

2. Galway Kinnell, *What a Kingdom It*

*Was* (Boston: Houghton Mifflin, 1960).

3. Kinnell, *A New Selected Poems*, xii.

4. Cary Nelson, ed., *Modern American Poetry*, an online journal and multimedia companion to *Anthology of Modern American Poetry* (London: Oxford University Press, 2000), *http://www.english.uiuc.edu/maps/poets/g_l/kinnell/life.htm*.

5. Galway Kinnell, *Flower Herding on Mount Monadnock* (Boston: Houghton Mifflin Co., 1964).

6. Galway Kinnell, *Imperfect Thirst* (Boston: Houghton Mifflin, 1994), 76.

7. Kinnell, *A New Selected Poems*, 160.

8. Ibid., 95–96.

9. Ibid., 83–86.

## Jay Parini (pp. 193–210)

1. Jay Parini, *Some Necessary Angels* (New York: Columbia University Press, 1993), 3.

2. Ibid., 4.

3. Any serious student of literature or writing should be familiar with the work of Robert Graves, who was equally at home writing poetry, prose, reviews and other forms of nonfiction. His historical novels are considered among the best in the genre. Between World War I and World War II, he wrote politically astute novels that looked at the causes and results of war and evaluated the geopolitical significance of the Middle East at a time when the attentions of the world were turned elsewhere. His books include *Good-bye to All That* (1929), an outspoken treatise on his war experiences; *King Jesus* (1946). one of his many unorthodox historic novels; and *The White Goddess*, a study of the mythological and psychological sources of poetry and philosophical thought and one of the most influential books on contemporary writers. For more information, see *http://faculty.ed.umuc.edu/~rschumak/bio_rg.htm*.

4. Jay Parini, *Some Necessary Angels*, 5.

5. Ibid., 6.

6. Jay Parini, *Singing in Time* (St. Andrews, Scotland: Starglow, 1972).

7. Jay Parini, "Writers on Writing: Saluting All the King's Mentors," *New York Times*, 25 February 2002, Sec. E, 1.

8. Jay Parini, *Some Necessary Angels*, 15.

9. Ibid.

10. Ibid., 43.

11. Jay Parini, *Theodore Roethke: An American Romantic.* (Amherst: University of Massachusetts Press, 1979).

12 Jay Parini, *The Love Run* (Boston: Atlantic Little Brown, 1980).

13. Jay Parini, *Anthracite Country* (New York: Random House, 1982).

14. Ibid., 10.

15. Jay Parini, *The Apprentice Lover* (New York: HarperCollins, 2002).

16. Samuel Hazo, "Something there is that loves this new biography of Frost," *Pittsburgh Post Gazette*, 11 April 1999. The article is at *http://www.post-gazette.com/books/reviews/19990411review222.asp*.

17. Jay Parini, *House of Days* (New York: Henry Holt and Company, 1997), 17–18.

18. Ibid., 73.

19. Ibid., 48.

## Aleksandr Solzhenitsyn (pp. 213–223)

1. These three books have been collected in the three-volume *The Red Wheel* (New York: Farrar, Straus & Giroux, 1989).

2. Tore Frängsmyr and Sture Allén, eds., *Nobel Lectures, Literature, 1968–1980* (Singapore: World Scientific Publishing, 1993), *nobelprize.org/literature/Laureates/1970/solzhenitsyn-autobio.htm*.

3. Aleksandr Solzhenitsyn, *One Day in the Life of Ivan Denisovich* (New York: Everyman's Library, 1995).

4. Aleksandr Solzhenitsyn, *The First Circle* (New York: HarperCollins, 1968).

5. Aleksandr Solzhenitsyn, *Cancer Ward* (New York: Dial, 1968).

6. Frängsmyr and Allén, *Nobel Lectures, Literature, 1968–1980*, *nobelprize.org/literature/Laureates/1970/solzhenitsyn-autobio.htm*.

7. Aleksandr Solzhenitsyn, *The Gulag Archipelago* (New York: Harper & Row, 1974–1978).

8. Solzhenitsyn, *One Day in the Life of Ivan Denisovich*.

## Jamaica Kincaid (pp. 225–236)

1. Jamaica Kincaid, *Lucy* (New York: Farrar, Straus & Giroux, 1990).

2. Jamaica Kincaid, "Lucy," in *At the Bottom of the River* (New York: Farrar, Straus & Giroux, 1984).

3. Jamaica Kincaid, *Annie John* (New York: Farrar, Straus & Giroux, 1985).

4. Jamaica Kincaid, *Lucy* (New York: Farrar, Straus & Giroux, 1990).

5. Jamaica Kincaid, *The Autobiography of My Mother* (New York: Farrar, Straus & Giroux, 1996).

6. Jamaica Kincaid, *My Brother* (New York: Farrar, Straus & Giroux, 1997).

7. Ibid., 71.

8. Ibid., 176.

9. Jamaica Kincaid, *Mr. Potter* (New York: Farrar, Straus & Giroux, 2002).

10. Jamaica Kincaid, "Girl," *At the Bottom of the River* (New York: Farrar Straus Giroux, 1984), 3–5.

### Julia Alvarez (pp. 237–250)

1. Julia Alvarez, *¡Yo!* (Chapel Hill, N.C.: Algonquin Books, 1997), 1.

2. Julia Alvarez, *The Woman I Kept to Myself* (Chapel Hill, N.C.: Algonquin Books, 2004).

3. Julia Alvarez's website is *http://www.alvarezjulia.com*.

4. Julia Alvarez, *How the García Girls Lost Their Accents* (Chapel Hill, N.C.: Algonquin Books, 1991); Donna Rif Kind, "Speaking American," *New York Times Book Review*, 6 October 1991, BR14.

5. Julia Alvarez, *In the Time of the Butterflies* (Chapel Hill, N.C.: Algonquin Books, 1994).

6. Julia Alvarez, *How Tía Lola Came to Visit Stay* (New York: Knopf Books for Young Readers, 2001).

7. *http://www.alvarezjulia.com*.

8. Julia Alvarez, *The Secret Footprints* (New York: Knopf Books for Young Readers, 2000).

9. Julia Alvarez, *A Cafecito Story* (White River Junction, Vt.: Chelsea Green, 2001). The Alta Gracia website is *www.cafealtagracia.com*.

10. Hilary McClellen, "In the Name of the Homeland," *Atlantic Monthly* (19 July 2000), *http://www.theatlantic.com/unbound/interviews/ba2000-07-19.htm*.

11. Ibid.

12. Julia Alvarez, *Before We Were Free* (New York: Knopf Books for Young Readers, 2002.)

### Ruth, Phoebe, and Abigail Stone (pp. 251–274)

1. Abigail Stone, *Maybe It's My Heart* (Franklin Lakes, N.J.: Lincoln Springs, 1989); *Recipes from the Dump* (New York: Norton, 1996).

2. Ruth Stone, *In an Iridescent Time* (New York: Harcourt Brace, 1959).

3. Ruth Stone, *In the Next Galaxy* (Port Townsend, Wash.: Copper Canyon, 2002).

4. Ruth Stone. *In the Dark* (Port Townsend, Wash.: Copper Canyon, 2005).

5. Cathy N. Davidson et al., eds., *The Oxford Companion to Women's Writing in the United States* (Oxford: Oxford University Press, 1995), 854.

6. Aliki Barnstone and Willis Barnstone, eds., *A Book of Women Poets from Antiquity to Now* (New York: Shocken Books, 1987).

7. Ruth Stone, *In the Dark*, 44.

8. Abigail Stone, *Recipes from the Dump* (New York: Norton, 1996).

9. Abigail Stone, *Plowshares: the literary journal of Emerson College*, Spring 1991. *http://www.pshares.org/issues/article.cfm?prmArticleID=3061*

10. Ibid.

11. Sandy Eisenberg Sasso, *In God's Name* (Woodstock, Vt.: Jewish Lights, 1994). You can look inside the book online and see Phoebe Stone's illustrations at *http://www.jewishlights.com/books/265.html*.

12. Phoebe Stone, *When the Wind Bears Go Dancing* (New York: Little Brown, 1997).

13. Phoebe Stone, *Go Away, Shelley Boo!* (New York: Little Brown, 1999).

14. Phoebe Stone, *All the Blue Moons at the Wallace Hotel* (New York: Little Brown, 2000).

15. Phoebe Stone, *Sonata #1 for Riley Red* (New York: Little Brown, 2003).

16. Ruth Stone, *In the Dark*, 21.

17. Ibid., 5.

18. Ruth Stone, *In the Next Galaxy*, 26.

19. Abigail Stone, *Recipes from the Dump*, 91–100.

### Tom Smith (pp. 275–290)

1. Tom Smith, *An Embarrassment of Riches*, manuscript collection, 2004.

2. Ibid., 26.

3. Tom Smith, *Spending the Light* (McKinleyville, Calif.: Fithian, 2004), 27–28.

4. Luke Zilles, *A Conch of Bees* (New York: Dutton, 1956).

5. Paul Fussell, *The Great War And Memory* (Oxford: Oxford University Press, 1977).

6. Tom Smith, *Waiting on Pentecost* (Delhi, N.Y.: Birch Brook, 1999).

7. Ibid., 10.

8. Tom Smith, *Singing the Middle Ages* (Woodstock, Vt.: Countryman, 1982).

9. Ibid., 31.

10. Tom Smith, *The Broken Iris* (Whispering Pines, N.C.: Perspehone, 1990). (A senryu is a lighter, less stylized haiku-like poem.)

11. Joyce Thomas, introduction to ibid., 8.

12.Tom Smith, *Some Traffic* (Venice, Calif.: Beyond Baroque NewBooks, 1976), 5.

13. Tom Smith, *Trash: The Dahmer Sonnets* (Winchester, Va.: Soffietto, 2000).

14. Tom Smith, *An Embarassment of Riches*, 44.

15. Joyce Thomas, introduction to *The Broken Iris*, by Tom Smith, 7.

16. Tom Smith, *An Embarassment of Riches*, 21.

*Verandah Porche* (pp. 291–303)

1. Ray Mungo et al., *Home Comfort: Life on Total Loss Farm* (New York: Dutton/Plume, 1973).

2. Verandah Porche, *The Body's Symmetry* (New York: Harper Colophon, 1975).

3. Verandah Porche et al., *Right to Dream: Told Poems by Adult New Readers* (Montpelier, Vt.: Vermont Council on the Humanities, 1995).

4. Verandah Porche, *The Right to Dream: Told Poems by Adult New Readers* (Concord, N.H.: New Hampshire Council on Literacy, 1999).

5. Verandah Porche, *Poetz.com*, January 2004. The site is at *http://www.poetz.com/*.

6. Verandah Porche, *They Know the Promise: the Art of Care in a Community Hospital*, (Randolph, Vt.: Gifford Medical Center, 2000), 49.

*Joan Connor* (pp. 305–320)

1. Joan Connor, *History Lessons* (Amherst: University of Massachusetts Press, 2003).

2. Joan Connor, *Here Along Old Route 7* (Columbia: University of Missouri Press, 1997).

3. Ibid., 109–119.

4. Joan Connor, "October," in *We Who Live Apart* (Columbia: University of Missouri Press, 2000), 9–21.

5. Ibid., 14–15.

6. Ibid., 15.

7. For Busch's most recent work, see Frederick Busch, *A Memory of War: A Novel* (New York: Norton, 2003).

8. Joan Connor, "The Day the World Declined to End," in *History Lessons*, 6–16.

9. Joan Connor, "Adam and Eve at the Automat," in *History Lessons*, 1–5.